FC
97
.P37
M36
1987

A PASSION FOR IDENTITY

CANADIAN MENNONITE UNIVERSITY
LIBRARY
500 SHAFTESBURY BLVD
WINNIPEG, MANITOBA
CANADA R3P 2N2

A PASSION FOR IDENTITY

INTRODUCTION TO
CANADIAN STUDIES

Edited by
ELI MANDEL and DAVID TARAS

 METHUEN

Toronto New York London Sydney Auckland

Copyright © 1987 by Methuen Publications
(A Division of The Carswell Company Limited)

All rights reserved. No part of this publication may be reproduced, stored in a retrieval system or transmitted in any form or by any means, electronic, mechanical, photocopying, recording or otherwise, without the prior written permission of Methuen Publications, 2330 Midland Avenue, Agincourt, Ontario, Canada M1S 1P7.

Canadian Cataloguing in Publication Data

Main entry under title:

A Passion for identity : introduction to Canadian studies

Bibliography: p.
Includes index.
ISBN 0-458-80560-2

1. Canada — Civilization. 2. National characteristics, Canadian. 3. Regionalism — Canada. I. Mandel, Eli, 1922-
   II. Taras, David, 1950-

FC97.P38 1987   971   C86-094590-1
F1021.P38 1987

Publication has been made possible, in part, by a grant from the Endowment Fund of The University of Calgary.

Acknowledgments for poetry appear following the index.

Cover: "The Painted Flag," Charles Pachter,
       acrylic on canvas, 1981
       36" × 72"
       Private collection, Toronto
Cover design: Don Fernley

Printed and bound in Canada

1 2 3 4   87   92 91 90 89 88

CONTENTS

Preface   7

SECTION ONE: CANADIAN IDENTITY: THE NATION   9
   Introduction, David Taras   10
   At the tourist centre in Boston, Margaret Atwood   17

1. THE CONCEPT OF HISTORY   19
   Manor Life, Anne Hébert   20
   The Economy of the North, Donald Creighton   21
   Conclusion from *The Fur Trade in Canada*, Harold Innis   26
   The Relevance of Canadian History, W.L. Morton   37
   Frontierism, Metropolitanism, and Canadian History, J.M.S. Careless   51

2. THE DRAMA OF SOCIETY AND POLITICS   65
   The Only Tourist in Havana Turns His Thoughts Homeward, Leonard Cohen   66
   Revolution and Counterrevolution: The United States and Canada, S.M. Lipset   68
   Mosaic versus Melting Pot?: Immigration and Ethnicity in Canada and the United States, Howard Palmer   82
   Uneven Development: A Mature Branch-Plant Society, Wallace Clement   97
   The Governments and Societies of Canadian Federalism, Alan C. Cairns   114
   From Middle to Foremost Power: Defining a New Place for Canada in the Hierarchy of World Power, James Eayrs   131

3. THE DYNAMICS OF CULTURE   145
   Elegy 9, Dennis Lee   146
   The Problem of a Canadian Literature, E.K. Brown   149
   Survival, Margaret Atwood   162
   The Casual Incident of Death, Margaret Atwood   173
   In Defence of North America, George Grant   181
   Our Two Cultures, Patricia Smart   196
   Sharing the Continent, Northrop Frye   206

SECTION TWO: REGIONAL IDENTITIES 217
Introduction, Eli Mandel 218
Where the World Began, Margaret Laurence 222

1. SENSIBILITIES 227
   On the Concept of Region in Canadian History and 228
      Literature, William Westfall
   Canadian Regions and Regionalisms: National Enrichment 239
      or National Disintegration, William C. Wonders

2. QUEBEC 263
   Speak White, Michèle Lalonde 264
   The Development of Ideologies in Quebec, Marcel Rioux 267
   Has the Quiet Revolution Finally Ended? Ramsay Cook 289

3. THE MARITIMES 301
   Author's Note from *Each Man's Son*, Hugh MacLennan 302
   An Atlantic Region Political Culture: A Chimera, 305
      J. Murray Beck

4. ONTARIO 319
   To the Avon River Above Stratford, Canada, James Reaney 320
   Is There an Ontario Identity? Robert Drummond 322

5. THE WEST 337
   On Being an Alberta Writer, Robert Kroetsch 338
   Changing Images of the West, R. Douglas Francis 342
   The Pattern of Prairie Politics, Nelson Wiseman 360
   British Columbia: The Company Province, Martin Robin 377

6. THE NORTH 387
   Laurentian Shield, F.R. Scott 388
   Contemporary Native Life: Images and Realities, 389
      Michael Asch

Selected Readings in Canadian Studies 399
Index of Names 405
Index of Subjects 410
Poetry Acknowledgments 413

PREFACE

This book is based on a Canadian Studies perspective. As such, it is intended to be interdisciplinary and is an attempt to present interpretations from different fields of study and scholarly traditions as well as to integrate diverse materials. Almost all of the texts on Canada currently available are targeted for particular disciplines and more often for specific fields within disciplines. This may be valuable to specialists, but it can deprive students of the breadth, and the intellectual underpinnings, needed to grasp Canadian realities. The broad dynamics of history, politics, economics, society, and culture are the focuses of the Canadian Studies perspective. While specialization is critical to knowledge, it can be fatal to understanding.

Although this collection is designed to meet the needs of Canadian Studies students, it will also be useful in courses on Canadian history, the development of political institutions and ideologies, the cultural and literary landscape, and Canadian society.

To some degree, the book may be seen as a collection of classics: works that have withstood the test of time, are significant contributions by major scholars, or contain important frameworks for analysis. Part of the motivation for assembling this reader was the fear that some works were becoming increasingly inaccessible and could be lost to a new generation. We also felt strongly that there should be a single source wherein one could find critical and noteworthy statements about Canadian identity.

This book is divided into two sections: the Canadian identity and regional identities. The first section contains three subsections: the concept of history, the drama of society and politics, and the dynamics of culture. Canadian nationalism is therefore seen through a number of different windows. The section on regional identities has two general overviews; one is written from the perspective of literature and history and the other describes the geography of regionalism. These are followed by works on Quebec, the Maritimes, Ontario, the West, and the North. The vein of writings about Canada's regions is rich, and selecting representative articles was difficult, especially considering space constraints. Each of the sections and subsections begins with a poem or literary exerpt that captures the flavours, dilemmas, delights, or passions of the forces or regions under study.

Unfortunately, because of space constraints, cuts had to be made in a number of articles. These are indicated by ellipses. Every effort has been made to maintain the basic integrity of each article.

Throughout, we were conscious of the need to present a variety of disciplines. We also attempted to select from different time periods, so as to trace the evolution in thinking about Canadian identity. Most important, each work contains explanations and concepts that are significant. The essential criteria for inclusion in the collection were frameworks that allow for a better understanding of key problems and tools that can be used in research and teaching. Together they represent a kaleidoscope of interpretations. That is the strength of the book and of the country it portrays.*

We would like to thank Gurston Dacks, Douglas Francis, Susan Jackel, David Mills, Howard Palmer, Randy Pelletier, Beverly Rasporich and Patricia Smart for their suggestions and advice. Lorry Felske contributed wise counsel and unwavering support. We owe a debt to Peter Milroy of Methuen for his professionalism and vision. David Taras would like to thank Daphne Gottlieb Taras for her magnificent effort always and for helping with the introduction when our son, Matthew Ari, was only a few days old.

---

*Dr. Mandel's introduction to Section Two was written before an illness suffered in the late summer of 1986. As a result, his introduction does not include references to Michael Asch's article on contemporary native life in the North, which was added at a later date.

SECTION ONE

CANADIAN IDENTITY: THE NATION

INTRODUCTION

DAVID TARAS

Much of the writing on Canada has stressed the problem of bringing unity and common pattern to a country divided by language, ethnicity, and region. Canada, it is argued, has faced several challenges to its existence and has only recently begun to have a self-assured identity. Canadian nationhood has been slow to evolve and Canadians slow to find collective symbols, standards, and ideals. Many observers still regard Canadian identity as incomplete and fragile. In the debate currently being waged on the issue of freer trade with the United States, there is widespread concern that institutions and allegiances stretched thinly across an east-west axis cannot withstand the pull of a more powerful and integrated north-south economy. Fear remains about Canada's cohesiveness, integrity, and existence.

This section on Canadian nationhood offers a different interpretation. Our view is that while the factors causing disunity have been formidable, the country has been shaped by powerful unifying elements. Canada has not survived merely because of the whims of fortune or its distance from cataclysmic events. The roots of unity are deeply embedded. A conservative social system, sweeping economic patterns, the prominent role played by the state, and the habit of political compromise were all important foundations. Moreover, there has been throughout Canadian history a passion for identity. The desire to come to terms with oneself in place and time and in relation to others is itself a national instinct. The articles presented in this section provide ample evidence of this quest. Writing from the perspective of different disciplines, the authors have given distinct descriptions of the core values underlying Canadian identity. Each has made a statement that is in a sense part of a larger statement about Canadian identity.

The first subsection deals with the concept of history. The four articles represent several contending interpretations and schools of Canadian historiography. Donald Creighton's majestic description of the "Empire of the St. Lawrence" is contained in the first article. Creighton, long regarded as the country's leading conservative historian, was among the first to articulate a passionate vision of Canadian history. Writing with great drama, Creighton conveyed a feeling for the grand sweep of history, as well as for the lives of those propelled by these enormous forces. In this brief excerpt from the first chapter of his classic work on the subject, Creighton argues that the St. Lawrence River became the fulcrum for a vast economic system. Based largely on the fur trade and linked to Europe, the economic corridor was not only shaped by natural geography but also by bold ambitions. The "Empire of the

St. Lawrence" was to become the basis for Canada. The present country is the extension of this early economy and of the contours of geography that produced it.

The second selection is by Harold Innis, the leading economist of his day in Canada. Innis's contributions, however, extended well beyond the boundaries of economics as he formulated theories that have become important to the studies of history and communications. In the conclusion to perhaps his most important work, *The Fur Trade in Canada*, Innis delineated the staples theory of Canadian development. In Innis's view, an economy based on the exploitation of a series of staples — cod, fur, lumber, and wheat — determined Canada's growth and character. The emergence of each staple forced an expansion of settlement, the creation and then the strengthening of indigenous metropolitan centres and capital, and the building of supporting economic and political structures. The staples theory reinforces a point made by Creighton in the first article that Canada emerged not despite geography but because of it. The east-west corridor formed by the river systems was the basis for the trade in staples as it was for Creighton's "Empire of the St. Lawrence."

The next article in this subsection on the concept of history is by W. L. Morton, the premier historian of western Canada. Morton was intensely proud of his own British heritage and tended to see Canada's evolution and identity from that perspective. According to Morton, four factors have shaped Canada's development. First, it is self-consciously a northern nation, not only in terms of geography but also in culture, and the product of the extension of Europe's northern and maritime frontier. Second, Canada has had a long history of being dependent on Britain and then on the United States. The habit of dependency is deeply ingrained. That Canada has embraced the monarchy is perhaps the most critical factor to Morton. The monarchy was the anchor ensuring that Canada would not drift toward American political influences and a unifying symbol the existence of which allowed for the flourishing of different expressions. The fourth factor is that Canada is now allied in world affairs with a far more powerful country, the United States, and this close alliance presents a challenge to the preservation of Canada's integrity. Morton concludes by stressing that although Canada has deep roots as a country, its survival depends on "the relevance of Canadian history." The question is whether the values that determined Canadian identity will be preserved by Canadians themselves, and whether the United States will continue to recognize and respect this unique culture and tradition.

The final article is J. M. S. Careless's survey of the various schools of historical thought in Canada. Although he discusses the Britannic and Liberal perspectives on Canadian history, Careless concentrates on comparing the frontier thesis with the metropolitan theory. According to the frontier thesis, developed largely from the work of the American historian Frederick Jackson Turner, the frontier experience transformed society. In taming the frontier and in meeting its harsh challenges, European values were gradually replaced by North American ones. Custom and hierarchy receded as individual initiative and an egalitarian spirit took hold. Democracy was born and sustained at the frontier. The frontier was the cutting edge of change. The metropolitan school offers a contrasting view. According to this interpretation, metropolitan centres are where significant history occurs and decisions are made. The metropolis is the centre of the wheel, the hub of population, capital, and organizational power. The hinterland — the frontier — is powerless and dependent. Its purpose is only to supply resources, and it is there to be exploited. Careless contends that metropolitanism is the more valid interpretation of Canadian history. The enormous pull of urban culture throughout modern Canadian history and the power exerted by metropolitan centres in shaping confederation and the National Policy are offered as evidence that this perspective provides a more powerful explanation of Canadian development.

The subsection on the drama of society and politics contains five articles each of which explores a different aspect of Canadian development. It begins with an article by the American sociologist and political scientist Seymour Lipset. When this article first appeared over twenty-five years ago, it sparked considerable controversy and debate among scholars. Lipset's hypothesis was that while Canadians and Americans share many of the same values, Canadians are on the whole more conservative, law-abiding, collectively oriented, and less driven by a desire to achieve than are Americans. In Lipset's view, these differences can be traced to the outcome of the American Revolution. Canadian values emerged from the experience of the Loyalists, those who fled to Canada out of loyalty to the Crown and because of their opposition to American republicanism. Fueled by this counterrevolutionary ethos they built a society in which there was deference to law and authority, a large role for government, and close relations between established churches and the state. In contrast, the United States was formed in the cauldron of revolution, and its founding principles included a strong faith in individual rights and achievement, a profound suspicion of government, and the separation of church and state. These differences still persist despite the passage of time. They are the core values of two distinct societies.

A second article compares Canadian and American experiences and attitudes with respect to immigration and ethnicity. Howard Palmer argues that the terms "mosaic" and "melting pot" do not describe accurately the patterns that really existed. Canada, in particular, for much of its history was not the mosaic that it is currently depicted as in the popular imagination. In English Canada, the dominant framework was anglo-conformity, as the majority feared that its traditions would be lost amid an onslaught of strange languages and customs and the newcomer's inexperience with democracy. Forceful efforts were made to ensure that anglo traditions would continue to dominate. Resistance to immigration was particularly noteworthy during the inter-war years. In French Canada, immigration was feared and resisted even more strongly. It was felt that immigration would destroy the political balance within Canada and that the country had a special obligation to preserve the cultures of its two founding peoples. French Canadians could lose their status and be overwhelmed by the flood of immigrants. Against this background Palmer describes the development of the current immigration and multicultural policies. While Canadian identity has been transformed considerably as a result of these changes, many of the old fears and antagonisms remain.

Sociologist Wallace Clement's article criticizes Canadian society from a political economy perspective. The political economy school tends to see Canada as an underdeveloped and dependent society dominated by American power and capital. Canada's possibilities are therefore limited, and natural development and progress is impossible. Clement's article is among the best of this genre. The main argument is that the vast penetration by American capital and the resulting branch-plant structure of key industries has created an uneven economy and society. It has brought disparities between the industrial heartland in Ontario and the rest of the country, an unbalanced class structure, and a distorted and uncertain role for the state. While some sectors are allied to American capital and enjoy tangible benefits, others are excluded and are destined to remain marginal. Clement describes the changes that are now taking place in the structure of the work force, changes that are likely to perpetuate this uneven development. His vision is of a country dependent, vulnerable, and unable to fulfil its inherent capacities.

"The Governments and Societies of Canadian Federalism" is Alan Cairns's 1977 presidential address to the Canadian Political Science Association. Cairns's view differs substantially from Clement's. For Cairns, governments' power to shape society has been the major factor determining Canada's development. Building upon the authority given to them under the British North America Act of 1867, governments have had a natural bureaucratic tendency to expand their power and control. Since the Second World War, there has been a dramatic increase in the governmentalization of society with governments encroaching into virtually every sector of Canadian life. Elites and interests have been drawn into the orbit of those governments most concerned with their affairs. As a result, governments have been able to affect the values and allegiances of their citizens and create limited societal identities. According to Cairns, the clashes between federal and provincial governmental systems are the fault lines of Canadian society. These cleavages are reinforced continually by the existence of distinct elites, bureaucracies, and societies that are the result of the assertion of governmental authority in the first place. Therefore, federalism is the main axis of our political culture. The constitution has shaped society and not vice versa.

In the concluding article on the drama of society and politics, James Eayrs, one of Canada's leading diplomatic historians, argues that because of changes that occurred in the 1970s, Canada has gained new stature and enhanced power in world affairs. While many writers bemoan Canada's powerlessness, and dependency has become a popular notion in the academic community, these assumptions may not reflect contemporary reality. Eayrs contends that Canada has made the transition from being a middle to a foremost power. It has achieved a place of prominence and now has the ability to affect events and influence outcomes. While Eayrs admits that power is an elusive concept, he asserts that Canada's relative strength has increased during the 1970s because Canada was blessed with abundant energy and natural resources at a time when both were assuming critical importance. During this same period, the United States, while still a superpower, lost some of its self-confidence, was hamstrung by an inability to apply power directly, and was declining in influence. Eayrs suggests that Canada now enjoys enormous opportunities as a trading state and, "if we produce a foreign policy to match," can be a force in world affairs.

The last subsection is on the dynamics of culture and focuses on the evolution of a distinctly Canadian cultural perspective. The first of the five articles is by the writer Edward K. Brown. Writing over forty years ago, Brown described the inhibitions that prevented the full blossoming of a Canadian literature. Although much has changed and a number of Canadian authors have gained significant domestic and international followings and reputations, some of the obstacles portrayed by Brown persist today. Canada is divided into two linguistic communities, and its book-reading public remains small. Moreover, Canadian authors must compete directly with the best American and European writers whose works are promoted by major international publishing houses. Psychological barriers are also identified by Brown: a colonial mentality that sees more authentic events occurring elsewhere, a puritan spirit that is uncomfortable with emotions and sexuality in particular, an intense regionalism that limits the development of a national sensibility and imagination, and a frontier ethic that derides intellectual achievements in favour of activities that produce wealth. One can argue that the achievements of the present era are all the more remarkable because of the existence of the very conditions that Brown so aptly described.

Appropriately, Brown's lament over the state of writing in Canada is followed by selections from Margaret Atwood, the writer who has probably done the most to enhance the status of Canadian literature. By capturing aspects of the Canadian imagination in her work vividly and movingly and winning popular and critical acclaim, she has become a symbol to many. In these chapters from her book *Survival*, Atwood identifies the central themes that underlie much of Canadian literature. In the first selection, she argues that survival is the principal theme: survival amid a hostile climate and wilderness, cultural survival for both French and English Canada, and spiritual survival in a deadening world. The pervading image is that Canadians have been victims. Yet Atwood contends that defeat need not be inevitable. There are options. One can consciously choose not to be a victim and work at overcoming a disheartening and pessimistic reality. In "The Casual Incident of Death," the Canadian attitude toward heroes is described. While in other countries heroes are enshrined in history, ideals, and even mythology, in Canada heroes are not accorded much reverence. This is largely because nation-building was mainly the product of collective efforts, bureaucratic and organizational forces, and decisions by an established order. Although many appreciate the heroism of such people as Brebeuf, Riel, or William Lyon Mackenzie, efforts and sacrifice that prove to be futile and pointless are not respected. Individual heroism has rarely succeeded against impersonal collective forces. In Canada "it's the collective that's alive."

"In Defence of North America," by philosopher George Grant, is something of a classic. It is tempting to view Grant's critique of North American society as a loyalist counterattack. But his anger at and contempt for the values that surround him are rooted in a theological worldview that is all encompassing even as it is narrow and personal. Writing at the height of the American involvement in Vietnam, Grant condemns the extent to which a belief in technology has become the prime instinct in North American life. Grant, an archconservative who is wary of and seems emotionally geared to resist modernity, argues that North America has become detached from the resources of Greek and Christian thought, which are the foundations of Western civilization. What we see in North America is technology divorced from morality in a society driven increasingly by destructive energies. Grant wants us to return to the religious principles that were fundamental to the development of western Christianity in Europe. The Calvinist spirit, which is to blame for our present moral condition, is not a valid expression of these earlier principles.

The fourth article on the dynamics of culture is by Patricia Smart, a scholar specializing in the literature of French Canada. Smart examines the ways in which Canadian identity and the relationship between the two major linguistic communities are portrayed in the recent work of leading French- and English-Canadian authors. Her review reveals a number of vivid images: Aquin's description of two warriors drawn to each other by a fascination and the heat and emotion of battle; Godbout's and Atwood's image of the two cultures as Siamese twins; and Brossard's portrait of two women standing back to back. Smart delves beyond these powerful but agonizing images. She identifies the impulses and distinctive characteristics that shaped the perceptions of the two language groups. English-Canadian writers tend to believe in the power of reason and the necessity for compromise, and they accept the reality of time and space. In contrast, writers in French Canada tend to feel cramped by the present and imprisoned in unbearable situations. They desire escape, and their writing often has a dreamy yet explosive tone. Where English-Canadian writers accept boundaries and press those boundaries with their vision and imagination, French-Canadian authors refuse to be confined, breaking down barriers, real and imagined, with the violence and eloquence of their language.

The concluding article is by Northrop Frye, widely acknowledged as Canada's leading literary critic. To some extent, Frye's article may be seen as a companion to Lipset's. While both articles view Canadians and Americans as sharing many of the same values and characteristics, they both concentrate on the differences between the two countries. The evolution of a distinct Canadian cultural imagination and how it differs instinctively from the American one is the central focus of Frye's argument. The United States, he contends, has always been more clearly defined. Its geography, history, and political ideals are sharply formed. In contrast, Canadians have been slow to explore and come to terms with their country's vast spaces, indefinite landscape, political compromises, and diverse regional patterns. Despite these obstacles, a disciplined imagination has evolved over time, and two strong national cultures now share the continent. In Frye's view, Americans should be pleased that another cultural identity is thriving in North America. Also, it is of considerable importance that a country at the crossroads of international trade and communications should be repatriating its culture. By resisting the vast homogenizing forces of a global culture, Canada can by example make more than a modest contribution to the world.

Frye's article is a fitting way to end this section on Canada's national identity. Beginning with Creighton, we have presented a diverse series of portraits, each articulating an aspect of Canadian identity. Some visions are angry and despairing, and reflect a keen anxiety. Some have been bold in their certainty and in their forceful advocacy of a single explanation. All together they represent complexity. They also provide evidence for Frye's contention that a creative search for identity has led to the emergence of a national perspective.

At the tourist centre in Boston

MARGARET ATWOOD

There is my country under glass,
a white relief-
map with red dots for the cities,
reduced to the size of a wall

and beside it 10 blownup snapshots
one for each province,
in purple-browns and odd reds,
the green of the trees dulled;
all blues however
of an assertive purity.

Mountains and lakes and more lakes
(though Quebec is a restaurant and Ontario the empty
interior of the parliament buildings),
with nobody climbing the trails and hauling out
the fish and splashing in the water

but arrangements of grinning tourists —
look here, Saskatchewan
is a flat lake, some convenient rocks
where two children pose with a father
and the mother is cooking something
in immaculate slacks by a smokeless fire,
her teeth white as detergent.

Whose dream is this, I would like to know;
is this a manufactured
hallucination, a cynical fiction, a lure
for export only?

I seem to remember people,
at least in the cities, also slush,
machines and assorted garbage. Perhaps
that was my private mirage

18 / At the tourist centre in Boston

which will just evaporate
when I go back. Or the citizens will be gone,
run off to the peculiarly-
green forests
to wait among the brownish mountains
for the platoons of tourists
and plan their odd red massacres.

Unsuspecting
window lady, I ask you:

Do you see nothing
watching you from under the water?

Was the sky ever that blue?

Who really lives there?

1
THE CONCEPT OF HISTORY

Manor Life

From the French of Anne Hébert

Here is an ancestral manor
Without a table or fire
Or dust or carpets.

The perverse enchantment of these rooms
Lies wholly in their polished mirrors.

The only possible thing to do here
Is to look at oneself in the mirror day and night.

Cast your image into these brittle fountains
Your brittler image without shadow or colour.

See, these mirrors are deep
Like cupboards
There is always someone dead behind the quicksilver
Who soon covers your reflection
And clings to you like seaweed

Shapes himself to you, naked and thin,
And imitates love in a long bitter shiver.

The Economy of the North

DONALD CREIGHTON

When, in the course of a September day in 1759, the British made themselves the real masters of the rock of Quebec, an event of apparently unique importance occurred in the history of Canada. There followed rapidly the collapse of French power in North America and the transference of the sovereignty of Canada to Great Britain; and these acts in the history of the northern half of the continent may well appear decisive and definitive above all others. In fact, for France and England, the crisis of 1759 and 1760 was a climax of conclusive finality. But colonial America, as well as imperial Europe, had been deeply concerned in the long struggle in the new continent; and for colonial America the conquest of New France had another and a more uncertain meaning. For Europe the conquest was the conclusion of a drama; for America it was merely the curtain of an act. On the one hand, it meant the final retirement of France from the politics of northern North America; on the other, it meant the regrouping of Americans and the reorganization of American economies. . . .

. . . Two colonial societies, rooted in two different American landscapes, had come into existence on the continent; and while one was scattered sparingly along the giant system of the St. Lawrence and the lakes, the other, more compact and populous, had grown up on the Atlantic seaboard. These two societies differed from each other, and among the differences which distinguished them were some which had been imported from Europe. Fundamentally, the civilization of each society in North America is the civilization of Europe. An inward necessity, instinctive and compelling, had driven the immigrants to preserve the mysterious accumulations of their cultural heritage; and the price they were forced to pay for its preservation should not entirely obscure the extent of their success. Undoubtedly, these two societies, one almost exclusively French and the other predominantly English, were differentiated by race, language, laws and religion. The distinctions which had been inherited from the old world lived on in the new with an almost inextinguishable vitality; and undoubtedly they helped to foster and prolong the rivalries between the first Americans.

But the society of the St. Lawrence and the society of the Atlantic seaboard were divided by something else, which was perhaps more fundamental and

---

Abridged from Donald Creighton, "The Economy of the North," *The Empire of the St. Lawrence* (Toronto: Macmillan of Canada, 1956), pp. 1-8. Copyright © 1956 by Donald Creighton. Reprinted by permission of Macmillan of Canada, A Division of Canada Publishing Corporation.

which was purely American. It was, in fact, the continent of North America itself. Immediately these migrants had to come to terms with the new continent. From it they had to wrest a living; and since they were Europeans and not Indians, a living meant not merely the food to sustain life but the amenities of West-European civilization which alone could make it tolerable. They had to find means to produce their own necessities and to pay for their imports from Europe. They had to live in and by the new world; and they were driven, by this double compulsion, to understand the possibilities of the new continent and to exploit its resources. They could escape neither the brutal dictates nor the irresistible seductions of North American geography; and in an undeveloped world the pressure of these prime phenomena was enormous and insistent. Each society, after long trial and recurrent error, had read the meaning of its own environment, accepted its ineluctable compulsions and prepared to monopolize its promises. And each, in the process of this prolonged and painful adjustment, had acquired an American character, a purpose and a destiny in America.

Chance flung the first English colonists on the edges of the Atlantic seaboard and opened the single great eastern waterway of the interior to the French. In the history of the different economies, of the cultural patterns which were to dominate North American life, these were acts of first importance. For each cultural group, the English and the French, fell heir to one of America's geographic provinces, and both these regions had their laws, their promises and their portentous meanings. Of the two, the Atlantic seaboard conformed more nearly to the geographic conditions of western Europe, which had been for centuries a forcing-house of nations. It was, for North America, a fairly small and compact area, sharply defined by obvious natural frontiers. From the coastline the land stretched westward to rise at last in the ridges of the Appalachians, which were unbroken from the St. Lawrence valley to the Floridas, save where the Hudson-Mohawk system gave access to the west. It was a boundary; but during colonial times it was not a barrier in the sense that it confined a restless and ambitious people determined upon its assault. Because they shaped the courses of the rivers, the mountains helped to focus the attention of the English-Americans upon that other boundary of the Atlantic seaboard, the ocean. Their faces were turned east rather than west; and during the greater part of the colonial period, the commercial energies of the population were concentrated in the numerous short rivers, in the bays and sounds and harbours which fretted the coastline, and sought their objectives eastward on the sea. For New England especially, whose economy was based upon its fisheries, the pull of the coastline and the submerged continental shelf beyond it, was enormous. The prohibitions, the invitations and the varieties of this seaboard empire directed, in a kindly fashion, the energies of an adaptive people. While the land configuration concentrated their pursuits, the climate and soil gave them variety. The area meant stolidity, gradual settlement, the inescapable necessity to produce and the possibility of diversified production. Seaward, it meant a commercial empire which would cease to be imperial because it would inevitably become oceanic.

The river up which Cartier ventured gave entrance to the totally different dominion of the north. It was a landscape marked off from the other geographic provinces of the new continent by the almost monotonously massive character of its design. A huge triangle of rocky upland lay bounded by a river and a string of giant lakes. It was a solemn country, with that ungainly splendour evoked by great, crude, sweeping lines and immense and clumsy masses. The marks of age and of terrific experience lay heavy upon it. It was an elemental portion of the earth, harshly shaped by the brutal catastrophes of geological history. The enormous flat bulk of the Precambrian formation was not only the core of the whole Canadian system, but it was also the ancient nucleus of the entire continent. It lay, old and sombre and ravaged, nearly two million square miles in extent. The ice masses, during the glacial period, had passed over and beyond it, and they had scarred and wrenched and altered the entire landscape in their advance and their retreat. Scouring the surface of the Shield itself, pouring boulder clay into the valleys to the south, the ice sheets had hollowed the beds of new lakes and had diverted the courses of ancient rivers. There was left a drainage system, grand in its extent and in the volume of its waters, but youthful, wilful and turbulent. The wrinkled senility of the Precambrian formation was touched by a curious appearance of youth. The countless meaningless lakes and lakelets, the intricately meandering rivers and spillways, the abrupt falls and treacherous rapids, which covered the face of the Shield, seemed to express the renewal of its primitive strength. To the south, below the Shield, the ice masses had throttled the waters into new lakes and had dammed the St. Lawrence into a long southern loop, leaving Niagara, the Long Sault and Lachine as evidence of the novelty of its course.

The Canadian Shield and the river system which seamed and which encircled it, were overwhelmingly the most important physical features of the area. They were the bone and the bloodtide of the northern economy. Rock and water complemented each other, fought each other's battles and forced each other's victories. The Shield itself, a huge lop-sided triangle, whose northern points were Labrador and the Arctic east of the Mackenzie, occupied over one-half of the land area which was to become the Dominion of Canada. For the French and for their successors it was unescapable and domineering....

... From the beginning it exercised an imperious domination over the northerners, for though it was a harsh and an exacting country, it offered lavish prizes to the restless, the ambitious and the daring. It was an area of staples, creating simple trades and undiversified extractive industries; and its furs, its forests and its minerals were to attract three great assaulting waves of northerners. Fur was the first great staple of the north. And with the fur trade, the Precambrian formation began its long career in the Canadian economy as a primary, instead of as a subsidiary, economic region. It was upon these ancient rocks that the central emphasis of the Canadian system was placed at first, and the initial importance of the Shield is of deep significance in the history of the economy of the north.

To the south lay the lowlands of the St. Lawrence. Here the intense winters of the Precambrian formation were softened and the hot, bright summers flamed more slowly out of long springtimes and faded gradually into reluctant autumns. North of the lakes, the lowlands stretched from Quebec city to Georgian Bay — a narrow but slowly broadening band of fertility, crowded a little oppressively by the sombre masses of the Shield. South and west, beyond the river and the lakes, they lapsed easily into the central lowlands of the continent and the basin of the Mississippi. In the centre of this rich region lay that immense organization of waters which issued from the continent by the river of Canada; and this drainage system, driving seaward in a great, proud arc from Lake Superior to the city of Quebec, was the fact of all facts in the history of the northern half of the continent. It commanded an imperial domain. Westward, its acquisitive fingers groped into the territory of the plains. Aggressively it entrenched upon the dominion of the Mississippi. It grasped the Shield, reached southward into the valley of the Hudson and at last rolled massively seaward between sombre approaches which curved away southward into the Maritimes and rose north-eastward past Quebec and Labrador to Newfoundland.

It was the one great river which led from the eastern shore into the heart of the continent. It possessed a geographical monopoly; and it shouted its uniqueness to adventurers. The river meant mobility and distance; it invited journeyings; it promised immense expanses, unfolding, flowing away into remote and changing horizons. The whole west, with all its riches, was the dominion of the river. To the unfettered and ambitious, it offered a pathway to the central mysteries of the continent. The river meant movement, transport, a ceaseless passage west and east, the long procession of river-craft — canoes, *bateaux*, timber rafts and steamboats — which followed each other into history. It seemed the destined pathway of North American trade; and from the river there rose, like an exhalation, the dream of western commercial empire. The river was to be the basis of a great transportation system by which the manufactures of the old world could be exchanged for the staple products of the new. This was the faith of successive generations of northerners. The dream of the commercial empire of the St. Lawrence runs like an obsession through the whole of Canadian history; and men followed each other through life, planning and toiling to achieve it. The river was not only a great actuality: it was the central truth of a religion. Men lived by it, at once consoled and inspired by its promises, its whispered suggestions, and its shouted commands; and it was a force in history, not merely because of its accomplishments, but because of its shining, ever-receding possibilities....

Each of these two geographic provinces was a matrix in which a distinct American economy was crudely fashioned. The boundaries of these rival economies were coextensive with the limits of two conflicting political dominions and two antipathetic social groups. It was certain that man, with his political capacities and economic resources, would modify the crude stamp of the geographical matrix; and it was equally certain that the geographical matrix itself would alter slightly under the force of human ingenuity and effort. Yet, in the first simplicity of early settlement, the pressure of geography bore with continuous persistence upon an unprotected people; and a brutal necessity drove the first Americans to come to terms with the landscape they had inherited. To exist as men, to live as West Europeans, they must immediately read the meanings of their respective empires, capitalize their obvious resources, fulfil their manifest destinies. The riddle of all migratory peoples confronted them; they must tie together the cut threads of their material and spiritual history, they must weave a new pattern of existence out of the stuffs of their new homeland and of the old world of Europe. It was a gigantic task; and in their deep need and desperate hurry, they turned naturally to the most immediate and the most easily obtainable of their resources. What the continent flaunted, they took; they could not be made to seek what it seemingly withheld. Their economies grew naturally organically out of the very earth of the new world. It was not the sage wisdom of European statesmen which determined their development, but the brute facts of North American life. And the character and development of these two economies were to affect decisively not only their separate relations with the old world, but their mutual relations in the new.

Conclusion from
The Fur Trade in Canada

HAROLD INNIS

1. THE IMPORTANCE OF STAPLE PRODUCTS

Fundamentally the civilization of North America is the civilization of Europe and the interest of this volume is primarily in the effects of a vast new land area on European civilization. The opening of a new continent distant from Europe has been responsible for the stress placed by modern students on the dissimilar features of what has been regarded as two separate civilizations. On the other hand communication and transportation facilities have always persisted between the two continents since the settlement of North America by Europeans, and have been subject to constant improvement.

Peoples who have become accustomed to the cultural traits of their civilization — what Mr. Graham Wallas calls the social heritage — on which they subsist, find it difficult to work out new cultural traits suitable to a new environment. The high death rate of the population of the earliest European settlements is evidence to that effect. The survivors live through borrowing cultural traits of peoples who have already worked out a civilization suitable to the new environment as in the case of the Indians of North America, through adapting their own cultural traits to the new environment, and through heavy material borrowing from the peoples of the old land. The process of adaptation is extremely painful in any case but the maintenance of cultural traits to which they have been accustomed is of primary importance. A sudden change of cultural traits can be made only with great difficulty and with the disappearance of many of the peoples concerned. Depreciation of the social heritage is serious.

The methods by which the cultural traits of a civilization may persist with the least possible depreciation involve an appreciable dependence on the peoples of the homeland. The migrant is not in a position immediately to supply all his needs and to maintain the same standard of living as that to which he has been accustomed, even with the assistance of Indians, an extremely fertile imagination, and a benevolent Providence such as would serve Robinson Crusoe or the Swiss Family Robinson on a tropical island. If those

---

Abridged from Harold A. Innis, "Conclusion," from *The Fur Trade in Canada* (Toronto: University of Toronto Press, 1956), pp. 383-402. Footnotes have been omitted. Copyright © Canada 1956, University of Toronto Press. Reprinted by permission of the publisher.

needs are to be supplied he will be forced to rely on goods which are obtainable from the mother country.

These goods were obtained from the homeland by direct transportation as in the movement of settlers' effects and household goods, involving no direct transfer of ownership, or through gifts and missionary supplies, but the most important device was trade. Goods were produced as rapidly as possible to be sold at the most advantageous price in the home market in order to purchase other goods essential to the maintenance and improvement of the current standard of living. In other words these goods supplied by the home country enabled the migrant to maintain his standard of living and to make his adjustments to the new environment without serious loss.

The migrant was consequently in search of goods which could be carried over long distances by small and expensive sailboats and which were in such demand in the home country as to yield the largest profit. These goods were essentially those in demand for the manufacture of luxuries, or goods which were not produced, or produced to a slight extent, in the home country as in the case of gold and of furs and fish. The latter was in some sense a luxury under the primitive conditions of agriculture in Europe and the demands of Catholic peoples. The importance of metropolitan centres in which luxury goods were in most demand was crucial to the development of colonial North America. In these centres goods were manufactured for the consumption of colonials and in these centres goods produced in the colonies were sold at the highest price. The number of goods produced in a north temperate climate in an area dominated by Pre-Cambrian formations, to be obtained with little difficulty in sufficient quantity and disposed of satisfactorily in the home market under prevailing transport conditions, was limited.

The most promising source of early trade was found in the abundance of fish, especially cod, to be caught off the Grand Banks of Newfoundland and in the territory adjacent to the Gulf of St. Lawrence. The abundance of cod led the peoples concerned to direct all their available energy to the prosecution of the fishing industry which developed extensively. In the interior, trade with the Indians offered the largest returns in the commodity which was available on a large scale and which yielded substantial profits, namely furs and especially beaver. With the disappearance of beaver in more accessible territory, lumber became the product which brought the largest returns. In British Columbia gold became the product following the fur trade but eventually lumber and fish came into prominence. The lumber industry has been supplemented by the development of the pulp and paper industry with its chief reliance on spruce. Agricultural products — as in the case of wheat — and later minerals — gold, nickel, and other metals — have followed the inroads of machine industry.

The economic history of Canada has been dominated by the discrepancy between the centre and the margin of western civilization. Energy has been directed toward the exploitation of staple products and the tendency has been cumulative. The raw material supplied to the mother country stimulated manufactures of the finished product and also of the products which were in demand in the colony. Large-scale production of raw materials was encouraged by improvement of technique of production, of marketing, and of transport as well as by improvement in the manufacture of the finished product. As a consequence, energy in the colony was drawn into the production of the staple commodity both directly and indirectly. Population was involved directly in the production of the staple and indirectly in the production of facilities promoting production. Agriculture, industry, transportation, trade, finance, and governmental activities tend to become subordinate to the production of the staple for a more highly specialized manufacturing community. These general tendencies may be strengthened by governmental policy as in the mercantile system but the importance of these policies varies in particular industries. Canada remained British in spite of free trade and chiefly because she continued as an exporter of staples to a progressively industrialized mother country.

The general tendencies in the industrial areas of western civilization, especially in the United States and Great Britain, have had a pronounced effect on Canada's export of staples. In these areas machine industry spread with rapidity through the accessibility of the all-year-round ocean ports and the existence of ample supplies of coal and iron. In Great Britain the nineteenth century was characterized by increasing industrialization with greater dependence on the staple products of new countries for raw material and on the population of these countries for a market. Lumber, wheat, cotton, wool, and meat may be cited as examples of staple imports. In the United States the Civil War and railroad construction gave a direct stimulus to the iron and steel industry and hastened industrial and capitalistic growth. These two areas began to draw increasingly on outside areas for staples and even continental United States has found it necessary with the disappearance of free land, the decline of natural resources, and the demand for new industrial materials, notably rubber, to rely on outside areas as shown in her imperialistic policy of the twentieth century. Canada has participated in the industrial growth of the United States, becoming the gateway of that country to the markets of the British Empire. She has continued, however, chiefly as a producer of staples for the industrial centres of the United States even more than of Great Britain making her own contribution to the Industrial Revolution of North America and Europe and being in turn tremendously influenced thereby.

2. THE FUR TRADE

The history of the fur trade in North America has been shown as a retreat in the face of settlement. The strategic campaigns in that retreat include the Conquest of New France, the Quebec Act of 1774, the American Revolution, the Jay Treaty of 1794, the amalgamation of 1821, the Oregon Treaty of 1846, and the Rupert's Land Act of 1869. The struggle continues in the newly settled areas of the Dominion. The trade has been conducted by large organizations from the artificial and natural monopolies of New France to the Northwest Company and the Hudson's Bay Company which still occupies an important position. It has depended on the manufactures of Europe and the more efficient manufactures and cheaper transportation of England. Control of the fur trade was an index of world importance from the standpoint of efficient manufactures, control of markets, and consumption of luxuries. The shift from Paris to London of the fur trade was significant of the industrial growth of France and England — just as possession of Canada after the American Revolution was significant of the industrial limitations of the United States. The demands of the Indians for cheaper and greater quantities of goods were determining factors in the destiny of the northern half of North America. . . .

The early history of the fur trade is essentially a history of the trade in beaver fur. The beaver was found in large numbers throughout the northern half of North America. The better grades of fur came from the more northerly forested regions of North America and were obtained during the winter season when the fur was prime. A vast north temperate land area with a pronounced seasonal climate was a prerequisite to an extensive development of the trade. The animal was not highly reproductive and it was not a migrant. Its destruction in any locality necessitated the movement of hunters to new areas.

The existence of the animal in large numbers assumed a relatively scant population. It assumed an area in which population could not be increased by resort to agriculture. Limitations of geological formation, and climate and a cultural background dependent on these limitations precluded a dense population with consequent destruction of animal life. The culture was dependent on indigenous flora and fauna and the latter was of prime importance. Moose, caribou, beaver, rabbit or hare, and fish furnished the chief supplies of food and clothing. This culture assumed a thorough knowledge of animal habits and the ability of the peoples concerned to move over wide areas in pursuit of a supply of food. The devices which had been elaborated included the snowshoe and the toboggan for the winter and the birch-bark canoe for the summer. This wide area contained numerous lakes and difficult connecting waterways, to which the canoe was adapted for extensive travel. Movement over this area occasioned an extended knowledge of geography and a widespread similarity of cultural traits such as language.

The area which was crucial to the development of the fur trade was the Pre-Cambrian shield of the northern half of the North American continent. It extended northwesterly across the continent to the mouth of the Mackenzie River and was bounded on the north by the northwesterly isothermal lines which determined the limits of the northern forests and especially of the canoe birch (*B. papyrifera*). The fur trade followed the waterways along the southern edge of this formation from the St. Lawrence to the Mackenzie River. In its full bloom it spread beyond this area to the Pacific drainage basin.

The history of the fur trade is the history of contact between two civilizations, the European and the North American, with especial reference to the northern portion of the continent. The limited cultural background of the North American hunting peoples provided an insatiable demand for the products of the more elaborate cultural development of Europeans. The supply of European goods, the product of a more advanced and specialized technology, enabled the Indians to gain a livelihood more easily — to obtain their supply of food, as in the case of moose, more quickly, and to hunt the beaver more effectively. Unfortunately the rapid destruction of the food supply and the revolution in the methods of living accompanied by the increasing attention to the fur trade by which these products were secured, disturbed the balance which had grown up previous to the coming of the European. The new technology with its radical innovations brought about such a rapid shift in the prevailing Indian culture as to lead to wholesale destruction of the peoples concerned by warfare and disease. The disappearance of the beaver and of the Indians necessitated the extension of European organization to the interior. New tribes demanded European goods in increasingly large amounts. The fur trade was the means by which this demand of the peoples of a more limited cultural development was met. Furs were the chief product suitable to European demands by which the North American peoples could secure European goods. . . .

The extension of the trade across the northern half of the continent and the transportation of furs and goods over great distances involved the elaboration of an extensive organization of transport, of personnel, and of food supply. The development of transportation was based primarily on Indian cultural growth. The birch-bark canoe was borrowed and modified to suit the demands of the trade. Again, without Indian agriculture, Indian corn, and dependence on Indian methods of capturing buffalo and making pemmican, no extended organization of transport to the interior would have been possible in the early period. . . .

The increasing distances over which the trade was carried on and the increasing capital investment and expense incidental to the elaborate organization of transport had a direct influence on its financial organization. Immediate trade with Europe from the St. Lawrence involved the export of large quantities of fur to meet the overhead costs of long ocean voyages and the imports of large quantities of heavy merchandise. Monopoly inevitably followed, and it was supported by the European institutional arrangements which involved the organization of monopolies for the conduct of foreign trade. On the other hand, internal trade, following its extension in the interior and the demand for larger numbers of *voyageurs* and canoes to undertake the difficult task of transportation and the increasing dependence on the initiative of the trader in carrying on trade with remote tribes, was, within certain limits, competitive. Trade from Quebec and Montreal with canoes up the Ottawa to Michilimackinac, La Baye, and Lake Superior could be financed with relatively small quantities of capital and was consequently competitive. Further extension of trade through Lake Superior by Grand Portage (later Kaministiquia) to Lake Winnipeg, the Saskatchewan, Athabasca, the Mackenzie River, and New Caledonia and the Pacific coast involved heavy overhead costs and an extensive organization of transportation. But the organization was of a type peculiar to the demands of the fur trade. Individual initiative was stressed in the partnership agreements which characterized the Northwest Company. The trade carried on over extended areas under conditions of limited transportation made close control of individual partners by a central organization impossible. The Northwest Company which extended its organization from the Atlantic to the Pacific developed along lines which were fundamentally linked to the technique of the fur trade. This organization was strengthened in the amalgamation of 1821 by control of a charter guaranteeing monopoly and by the advantages incidental to lower costs of transportation by Hudson Bay.

The effects of these large centralized organizations characteristic of the fur trade as shown in the monopolies of New France, in the Hudson's Bay Company, and in the Northwest Company were shown in the institutional development of Canada. In New France constant expansion of the trade to the interior had increased costs of transportation and extended the possibilities of competition from New England. The population of New France during the open season of navigation was increasingly engaged in carrying on the trade over longer distances to the neglect of agriculture and other phases of economic development. To offset the effects of competition from the English colonies in the south and the Hudson's Bay Company in the north, a military policy, involving Indian alliances, expenditure on strategic posts, expensive campaigns, and constant direct and indirect drains on the economic life of New France and old France, was essential. As a result of these developments control of political activities in New France was centralized and the paternalism of old France was strengthened by the fur trade. Centralized control as shown in the activities of the government, the church, the seigniorial system, and other institutions was in part a result of the overwhelming importance of the fur trade.

The institutional development of New France was an indication of the relation between the fur trade and the mercantile policy. The fur trade provided an ample supply of raw material for the manufacture of highly profitable luxury goods. A colony engaged in the fur trade was not in a position to develop industries to compete with manufactures of the mother country. Its weakness necessitated reliance upon the military support of the mother country. Finally the insatiable demands of the Indians for goods stimulated European manufactures.

The importance of manufactures in the fur trade gave England, with her more efficient industrial development, a decided advantage. The competition of cheaper goods contributed in a definite fashion to the downfall of New

France and enabled Great Britain to prevail in the face of its pronounced militaristic development. Moreover, the importance of manufactured goods to the fur trade made inevitable the continuation of control by Great Britain in the northern half of North America. The participation of American and English merchants in the fur trade immediately following the Conquest led to the rapid growth of a new organization which was instrumental in securing the Quebec Act and which contributed to the failure of the American Revolution so far as it affected Quebec and the St. Lawrence. These merchants were active in the negotiations prior to the Constitutional Act of 1791 and the Jay Treaty of 1794. As prominent members of the government formed under the Quebec Act and the Constitutional Act, they did much to direct the general trend of legislation. The later growth of the Northwest Company assured a permanent attachment to Great Britain because of its dependence on English manufactures.

The northern half of North America remained British because of the importance of fur as a staple product. The continent of North America became divided into three areas: (1) to the north in what is now the Dominion of Canada, producing furs, (2) to the south in what were during the Civil War the secession states, producing cotton, and (3) in the centre the widely diversified economic territory including the New England states and the coal and iron areas of the middle west demanding raw materials and a market. The staple-producing areas were closely dependent on industrial Europe, especially Great Britain. The fur-producing area was destined to remain British. The cotton-producing area was forced after the Civil War to become subordinate to the central territory just as the northern fur-producing area, at present producing the staples, wheat, pulp and paper, minerals, and lumber, tends to be brought under its influence.

The Northwest Company and its successor the Hudson's Bay Company established a centralized organization which covered the northern half of North America from the Atlantic to the Pacific. The importance of this organization was recognized in boundary disputes, and it played a large role in the numerous negotiations responsible for the location of the present boundaries. It is no mere accident that the present Dominion coincides roughly with the fur-trading areas of northern North America. The bases of supplies for the trade in Quebec, in western Ontario, and in British Columbia represent the agricultural areas of the present Dominion. The Northwest Company was the forerunner of the present confederation.

There are other interesting by-products of the study which may be indicated briefly. Canada has had no serious problems with her native peoples since the fur trade depended primarily on these races. In the United States no point of contact of such magnitude was at hand and troubles with the Indians were a result. The existence of small and isolated sections of French half-breeds throughout Canada is another interesting survival of this contact. The half-breed has never assumed such importance in the United States.

"The lords of the lakes and forest have passed away" but their work will endure in the boundaries of the Dominion of Canada and in Canadian institutional life. The place of the beaver in Canadian life has been fittingly noted in the coat of arms. We have given to the maple a prominence which was due to the birch. We have not yet realized that the Indian and his culture were fundamental to the growth of Canadian institutions. We are only beginning to realize the central position of the Canadian Shield.

3. THE FOREST INDUSTRIES

Canada emerged as a political entity with boundaries largely determined by the fur trade. These boundaries included a vast north temperate land area extending from the Atlantic to the Pacific and dominated by the Canadian Shield. The present Dominion emerged not in spite of geography but because of it. The significance of the fur trade consisted in its determination of the geographic framework. Later economic developments in Canada were profoundly influenced by this background.

The decline of the fur trade in eastern Canada which followed the export of furs from the Northwest through Hudson Bay after 1821 necessitated increased dependence on other staple exports. Wheat and potash had become increasingly important but they were overshadowed by the rise of the lumber trade. The transport organization and personnel of the fur trade and its capitalistic beginnings were shifted to the development of new lines of trade. An extended financial organization under the fur trade was attested by the plans for the first establishment of a bank in Canada with the strong support of Phyn and Ellice and the establishment of the Bank of Montreal in 1817 with John Gray, an old fur trader, as president and John Richardson of Forsyth, Richardson & Company, as a strong supporter. McGill University persisted as a memorial to the wealth acquired by James McGill. Edward Ellice became an important figure in London with strong colonial interests and Simon McGillivray retained an interest in colonial activities. On this basis, with the advantages of preference in England and abundant and cheap shipping after the war, the lumber exports to Great Britain increased rapidly in the face of Baltic competition. . . .

The lumber industry created an important problem of overhead costs. Ships sailing from Quebec with lumber were in search of a return cargo which emigration provided. "Coffin ships" suitable for the lumber trade were employed to take out emigrants. Immigration and settlement brought an increase in imports of manufactured products and in exports of potash, wheat, lumber, and other products. . . .

With increase in exports and imports to Upper Canada the demand for improved communication on the upper St. Lawrence became more insistent. Rafts of timber could be floated down the rapids but loads of grain and merchandise both up- and downstream became more difficult to handle. The demand of settlers for cheaper transport was an important factor in the struggle over the control of revenue to finance the construction of canals. The Act of Union of 1840 offered a solution and was followed by rapid construction of canals in the decade to 1850. Improvements of waterways were rendered obsolete through the disadvantage of water transportation, especially on the St. Lawrence with its northerly direction and its long closed season, and the construction of railroads to the seaboard in the United States. Railway lines were built after 1850 to shorten the water routes as in the road from Toronto to Collingwood. The Grand Trunk was extended from Sarnia to Montreal and Portland on the open seaboard. These railways not only joined the important settlements along the waterways but provided for the settlement of territory distant from the lakes and rivers. They provided an all-year-round outlet for lumber and agricultural produce from Canada and the United States, and for the import of merchandise.

The improvement of transportation in canals and railways had important effects on the lumber trade in providing for an extension of the supply of raw material and of the market for the finished product. The increasing demand for lumber in the United States following the rapid development of settlement in the Middle West and the growth of towns, as Chicago, stimulated the production of planks and boards. Decline in the size of trees and an increase in the number of saw logs and of smaller logs facilitated the introduction of modern sawmill technique with gang saws and band saws adapted to mass production. More recently the decline in supplies of American lumber and the rise in price of lumber hastened production on a large scale. . . .

The increasing demand for paper in the United States and the exhaustion of more available supplies of pulpwood were factors responsible for the development of the pulp and paper industry especially after 1900. Machine industry in lumber production provided a basis for the pulp and paper industry with its demands for large quantities of capital. . . .

4. CAPITALISM AND THE STAPLES

The lumber industry of eastern Canada was largely responsible directly and indirectly for the improvement of waterways and for the construction of railways prior to Confederation. Canal and railway construction was synonymous with heavy capital investment. Capital was obtained through private enterprise and substantial guarantees and aid from the imperial and colonial governments. Heavy expenditures involved the development of a strong centralized government in Canada. Canada's financial organization had been greatly strengthened through the strains incidental to the lumber industry. The crises in Great Britain and the United States in 1825-26, 1837, 1847, and 1857 had serious effects on construction industries and on the trade of a country interested in the export of lumber. The collapse of weaker banks in these periods contributed to the centralization of banking structure which became conspicuous in the period after Confederation. The fur trade and the lumber industry contributed the basic features essential to expansion after Confederation.

Capital investment in the transport improvement of eastern Canada brought serious problems. Immigration, settlement, and agriculture were hastened by the railroads but these were not adequate to support the overhead costs incidental to the heavy initial outlay in railroad construction and early railroad finance.

Grand Trunk interests in 1863 acquired control of the Hudson's Bay Company in London. This step was followed by Confederation in 1867, the sale of Rupert's Land to Canada in 1869, and finally the construction of the Canadian Pacific Railway. At one stroke Imperial interests and Grand Trunk interests favourable to the new technique replaced Hudson's Bay Company interests favourable to the fur trade. The large central organization in the fur trade facilitated the transfer and the organization of the new technique over a wide area. The fur trade and its personnel continued to be fundamentally important. The fur trade had not only produced a centralized organization but it had produced a succession of fur traders who were typically self-reliant, energetic, and possessed of keen bargaining ability and high organizing capacity. D. A. Smith, later Lord Strathcona, was not only an important official in the Hudson's Bay Company, trained in the school of the fur trade, but he was an influential force in the construction and management of the Canadian Pacific Railway which heralded the new industry. The relationship which existed with the opening of western Canada, in which important officials of the Hudson's Bay Company were prominent in the activities of the Bank of Montreal, of the Canadian Pacific Railway Company, and of the Dominion government, was not accidental....

The construction of the Canadian Pacific Railway to the Pacific implied a marked advance in technology such as characterized the construction of transcontinental roads in the United States, notably cheap production of iron and steel and high explosives and standardized methods of railroad construction. The westward movement in the United States which had been speeded up with the steamboat and the railroad, eventually reached the northern part of the plains area. The stretch of level and agricultural territory in western Canada was settled during the period at which industrialism had gained momentum on the North American continent. The construction of a railway across the Canadian Shield added to the overhead costs incidental to earlier construction in eastern Canada. Rapid settlement of the prairies, rapid increase in the export of wheat and in imports of manufactured products, were encouraged as a means of increasing traffic. Wheat became a new staple export demanded to an increasing extent by the industrially deficient countries and produced, transported, and manufactured on a large scale only through the efficiency of modern industrialism. With the addition of other transcontinental lines the main framework of the railway system was completed and Canada came under the full swing of modern capitalism with its primary problems of reducing overhead costs....

The relation of the government of Canada to general economic growth has been unique. The heavy expenditures on transport improvements, including railways and canals, have involved government grants, subsidies, and guarantees to an exceptional degree. The budget debates on the heavy debt of the Canadian National Railways are an annual reminder of the relation between transport and government. The Canadian government has been an important contributor to the prosperity of the Canadian Pacific Railway and to the maintenance of the Canadian National Railways. The unique character of this development has been largely a result of the sudden transfer of large areas tributary to the fur trade to the new industrialism. The British North America Act, like the Act of Union, has provided for a strong central government. The prairie provinces as producers of wheat were controlled from Montreal and Ottawa as they were controlled in the earlier period as producers of fur under the Northwest Company. With the United States, residuary powers were left with the states whereas in Canada they remain with the federal government or rather with eastern Canada. Canada came under the sweep of the Industrial Revolution at one stroke whereas the westward movement of the United States was a gradual development. There are no transcontinental railroads controlled by one organization in the United States. In Canada transcontinental roads are distinct entities controlled in eastern Canada. Similarly in financial institutions the branch bank system with headquarters in the east has been typical of Canada but not of the United States. No such tendency toward unity of structure in institutions and toward centralized control as found in Canada can be observed in the United States. The Canadian government has a closer relation to economic activities than most governments. The trade in staples, which characterizes an economically weak country, to the highly industrialized areas of Europe and latterly the United States, and especially the fur trade, has been responsible for various peculiar tendencies in Canadian development. The maintenance of connections with Europe, at first with France and later with Great Britain, has been a result. The diversity of institutions which has attended this relationship has made for greater elasticity in organization and for greater tolerance among her peoples. This elasticity of institutions facilitated the development of the compromise which evolved in responsible government and the British Empire. Having failed in her own colonial policy England was able to build up an empire in Canada on the remarkable success of French colonial policy. The fur trade permitted the extension of the combination of authority and independence across the northern half of the continent. Moreover, the business structure shifted from the elastic organization characteristic of the Northwest Company along the St. Lawrence from the Atlantic to the Pacific, to the more permanent organization from Hudson Bay. The diversity of institutions has made possible the combination of government ownership and private enterprise which has been a further characteristic of Canadian development. Canada has remained fundamentally a product of Europe....

The Relevance of Canadian History

W.L. Morton

Relevance, for the purposes of this paper, may be understood to mean the relations between the history of Canada and the histories of other communities. It also means the orientation given to Canadian history by the interaction of those relations with the environment and historical development of Canada. How those relations and that orientation are defined will in turn suggest the interpretation of Canadian history embodied in a work approaching completion. Relevance, finally, means what universal or philosophic significance belongs to the Canadian historical experience.

By Canadian history also is to be understood one history, not one French and one British, but the entire history of all Canada. There are not two histories, but one history, as there are not two Canadas, or any greater number, but one only. Nor are there two ways of life, but one common response to land and history expressed in many strong variants of the one, it is true, but still one in central substance. The reason for this is that the history of Canada after 1760 is only a continuation and extension of the history of Canada before 1760. There is but one narrative line in Canadian history.

The argument of this paper is equally simple. It is that the relevance of Canadian history takes its rise in the relations and orientations which result from four permanent factors in that history. These are a northern character, a historical dependence, a monarchical government and a committed national destiny — committed, that is, to special relations with other states.

The northern character springs not only from geographical location, but from ancient origins in the northern and maritime frontier of Europe. That frontier extends from Norway by Scotland and the North Atlantic islands to Greenland and Canada. Within that area from medieval to modern times there is discernible a frontier of European culture developing across the northern latitudes in which the forward movement was largely by sea. It was not a Turnerian frontier, but it was a frontier in every sense, and it was this frontier which began the exploitation and settlement of Canada. Many of its characteristics survive in Canada to this day, and presumably will continue to do so indefinitely.

Abridged from W.L. Morton, "The Relevance of Canadian History," from Canadian Historical Association *Annual Report*, 1960, pp. 1-21. Reprinted by permission of The Canadian Historical Association and the author's estate.

The historical characteristics of this northern maritime frontier are clear and definite. The most evident was that of coastal and riverine settlement. The largely Precambrian geology of the region afforded few extensive or fertile plains. The shelves in the fjords, the estuaries of seasonal rivers, the terraces around bays, these were the foothold and the baseland the northern frontier afforded to settlement. Even the Laurentian trench in America simply raised the foothold to continental proportions but did not change its character. Moreover, the maritime character of the frontier tended to settlement by the sea, even when extension of the economy inland was possible. . . .

The northern and maritime frontier had its own northern economy with characteristics equally explicit. It was an extensive and a gathering economy, dependent on new lands, new seaways, and the transport the seas and rivers afforded. It required a base of arable soil and habitable climate for the farmstead settlements. The farmstead was a highly self-subsistent unit, but it was the base of an economy which as a whole was an exchange economy to a high degree. The surplus staples of fish, fur, and timber, with exotics like arctic ivory and oil, falcons, and polar bears, earned the funds with which to buy the metals, the cereals, the church goods, and the luxuries the northern settlements needed or desired. Some of the traffic was inter-regional; it was, for example, its timber that made Vinland of primary interest to the Greenlanders.

That the Canadian economy historically has been an economy of this kind requires no demonstration. The great staple trades have been extensive, in-gathering trades. The population which carried them on lived in and worked from relatively narrow bases of good land in the sea inlets and river valleys; most of Canada is simply a hinterland extensively exploited from the soil base of the St. Lawrence and Saskatchewan valleys, and from the delta of the Fraser. The Canadian economy has also largely bought its external supplies by the sale of surplus staples.

The first discovery and early exploration of the lands which were finally to be united in Canada were the outcome of the advance westward of the northern and maritime frontier of Europe and the extension of the northern economy to America. These discoveries and the first occupation of Canadian shores were made by way of the northern approach. Somehow, by methods yet only guessed at, the Viking frontiersmen, Bristol traders, and Norman fishermen made their way across the North Atlantic. Their sea skill and navigational science was so far developed that they could use the brief and uncertain easterlies of late spring and early summer, which blow as the belt of the westerlies shifts north with summer, to make their way across by a northern route. They did not, like the Spaniards and the Elizabethan English, use the long but certain southern route of the trade winds. The discovery and occupation of Canada was separate and distinct from the discovery and occupation of the Americas.

Nor was it the result of high-pitched, scientific exploration aimed at the trade of Asia. It was the outcome of the piecemeal ventures of Norse seamen/

farmers probing the northern seas for new harbours and fisheries, new hay meadows and timber stands. The process is scantily documented. Government archives record it scarcely at all; it can now be understood and comprehended only by an understanding of the character of the northern frontier and economy, an understanding which is as bold an extension of the hints of the sagas as were the original voyages themselves.

The evidence, however, is slowly accumulating to suggest that between the last connections with Greenland and the voyages of the Bristol seamen there was no break in sea knowledge or experience. The Bristol men, with the knowledge of the Azoreans and, presumably, of the Normans and Bretons, were taking over the western half of the old Norse sea empire, and were being caught in the westward tug of the northern frontier. It is scarcely to be doubted that their own efforts would have discovered the Newfoundland fisheries if John Cabot and Henry VII had not imposed on their limited and practical efforts the scientific concepts of the Italian navigators and the first imperial impulse of Tudor England. In any event, the outcome was the same. Asia was not discovered, nor was the English empire founded in the fifteenth century, but the Newfoundland fishery of the English west country, and of Normandy and Brittany, was in being by the opening of the sixteenth.

This, then, is the first orientation of Canadian historiography. Canadian history is not a parody of American, as Canada is not a second-rate United States, still less a United States that failed. Canadian history is rather an important chapter in distinct and even a unique human endeavour, the civilization of the northern and arctic lands. From its deepest origins and remotest beginnings, Canadian history has been separate and distinct in America. The existence of large areas of common experience and territorial overlap no one would deny. History is neither neat nor categorical; it defines by what is central, not by what is peripheral. And because of this separate origin in the northern frontier, economy, and approach, Canadian life to this day is marked by a northern quality, the strong seasonal rhythm which still governs even academic sessions; the wilderness venture now sublimated for most of us to the summer holdiay or the autumn shoot; the greatest joys, the return from the lonely savagery of the wilderness to the peace of the home; the puritanical restraint which masks the psychological tensions set up by the contrast of wilderness roughness and home discipline. The line which marks off the frontier from the farmstead, the wilderness from the baseland, the hinterland from the metropolis, runs through every Canadian psyche.

We come now to the second factor, that of dependence, of the external ties and background of Canadian history. Canada throughout its history has in varying degrees been dependent economically, strategically, and politically. The northern economy, for example, was self-subsistent only at the base. Even there it was not necessarily so, as the extinction of the Greenland colonies grimly demonstrated, and as the plight of the prairie provinces in the 1930s re-emphasized. As a whole, however, the northern economy was a highly dependent one. It was a hinterland economy dependent on the sale of a few basic staples and a few exotics in a metropolitan market.

That is, the whole culture of the northern and maritime frontier, to suceed as well as survive, required from outside a high religion, a great literature and the best available science and technology to overcome its inherent limitations. Those very limitations of climate and of material and human resources made the frontier dependent on a metropolitan culture for those essentials. The alternatives were extinction or complete adaptation to the lowest level of survival in northern conditions. Was not the basic difference between the north European and the Eskimo that the former had a central and metropolitan economy and culture on which to draw, while the latter had none until very recent times and lived in a wholly and wonderfully self-subsistent culture?

The northern economy, then, was a dependent one, both for the markets which absorbed its staples and exotics, and for the supply of the needs of mind and body which raised life on the northern frontier above the level of subsistence and enabled it to produce in Iceland the literature of the sagas and in modern Canada the political fabric which unites the technology of a highly civilized and industrialized baseland with the exploitation of the resources of a harsh and enormous hinterland....

The factors of economic and strategic dependence were until the end of the nineteenth century also expressed in terms of political dependence. The French exploitation of the fisheries and the fur trade, with the zeal of French missionaries and an intermittent interest in a trade route to the Far East, had led to the development of the French empire in America. On the private commerce of the fishery and the fur trade, with their need of defence and regulation, the French Crown imposed its own interests in the conversion of the native people and the colonization of Acadia and Canada. Underlying these interests was the strategic purpose of establishing in New France a base for commerce with the new lands and, if possible, with the Far East.

This partnership of royal power with the northern economy was often an uneasy and a fretful one, as when the *coureurs de bois* after 1672 defied the royal policy of limiting the fur trade and carried their enterprise westward. Yet in the end the two were reconciled in the imperial purpose after 1700, when France began to use its northern base and its continental spread to confine the English colonies to the seaboard. The primitive northern economy had penetrated the continent by the great river systems, as the Swedish Vikings had Russia, and the rivers, the canoes, the fur traders, and the Indians were the means used to check the advance of the English settlers. The union of the primitive and the sophisticated, of war and trade, of small means and ranging enterprise, which characterized the northern culture, was never better exemplified than in Canadian captains, such as Iberville, or in the French empire in America in the eighteenth century.

The first British empire had developed similar characteristics in the north. The Hudson's Bay Company was the outcome, and a continuation of, the search for the North West Passage. It, too, needed metropolitan protection, and only escaped absorption into the French empire by Marlborough's victories in Europe. On the New York frontier in the days of William Johnson the English developed the same alliance with the Indian and the northern economy of the fur trade that the French had done. And in Nova Scotia the same factors of colonial dependence and imperial purpose produced Halifax. When the British empire in America broke up in the War of Independence, it was in part because the differences between the old northern empire of France and the old colonies of England had not been reconciled. And when the disruption was complete, the union of northern dependence with imperial strategy ensured that Nova Scotia and Canada, the northern elements of the fishery and the fur trade should remain within the British Empire.

British America had the same northern character as French America, a base for the fisheries, and the fur trade, for trade by the St. Lawrence with the continental interior and for naval power and Northwest exploration. How true this was is apparent if a glance is taken at what imperial policy actually did in British North America between 1783 and 1871. It paid a considerable part of the costs of government of the colonies from that date until well into the nineteenth century. It regulated its external commerce, to the benefit of both empire and colonies until 1846. It ensured, and largely paid for its defence down to 1871, fighting one considerable war on its behalf and preparing to fight two others. To the naval base of Halifax on the east coast it added that of Esquimalt on the west. From 1818 to 1854 it employed Franklin and his fellow explorers in the same scientific exploration that under Cook's genius had led to the opening of the Pacific and the colonization of Australia and New Zealand. At the same time it halted Russia in Alaska by diplomacy, and forestalled it in the arctic archipelago by the great feats of naval exploration of Parry, McClintock, and Rae. By so doing, it laid the groundwork for the Canadian occupation and development of the Arctic. Finally, imperial policy was a major element in Confederation, not only in ensuring its achievement, but also in delivering to it, as to a new metropolitan base, the whole of the northwestern and arctic hinterland. By this stroke, the northern and maritime frontier of the empire of the North Atlantic became a northern and a continental one in the Dominion of Canada. The new Dominion was meant to be a new nation. Yet its northern character, the limitation imposed by its situation and climate, meant that in fact the new nation was to remain still dependent on other states, the United Kingdom and the United States, for capital, technology, and defence. The continued support of the United Kingdom was needed to discourage the intermittent continental stirrings of the United States. American engineers were needed to build Canadian railways, and British capital was needed to finance them. Anything like instant and full-blown independence was neither possible nor desirable. The two factors of national aspiration and external support were slowly reconciled by the gradual transformation of continued dependence in a free association which ensured the needed support while affording the desired independence. The character of Canada's association with both the Commonwealth and the United States is thus the outcome of its historical development as a northern frontier.

That association derives also from another aspect of the northern frontier, the form of its political dependence. Although its remoteness and the separation of communities created a spirit of local independence, the limitations of its economy made for political dependence. That dependence found the most ready historical and the most satisfying psychological expression in allegiance to a monarchy. Until the rise of modern communication it was difficult to maintain unity in states based on popular sovereignty. Moreover, in Canada two historic factors combined to make monarchical allegiance a particularly satisfying political tie.

One was the French monarchical tradition of the old regime. The royal government of France, and particularly in New France, was largely military in organization and combined much personal independence in its subjects with a regular hierarchy of rank and subordination. It was also paternalistic in that all ranks looked to the higher for the defence of rights and the grant of help. The exercise of the power conferred on the king and his officers by the system was extraordinarily humane, and the bureaucracy remained a surprisingly serviceable one, partly because the personal royal will might always be invoked to correct hardship or bestow favour, partly because it was suffused with the religious principle that royal authority was a trust to be exercised for the doing of justice and the granting of mercy. The failure of the early British regime to capture and perpetuate some of this spirit is to be explained not so much by the fact of conquest as by the pressure of the "old subjects" and Loyalists for government favours and by the fears aroused by the French Revolution. None the less, much of the old attitude to government and public service survived in French Canada.

The second factor was the great strengthening in the bond of allegiance in British America caused by the American Revolution. The decisive act of the Revolution was, of course, the throwing off of allegiance by the Declaration of Independence. Equally decisive was the resolution of the Loyalists to maintain their allegiance. How clearly the matter was understood is shown by the declaration required of settlers in British America after 1783, in which they were required to acknowledge "the Authority of the King in his Parliament as the Supreme Legislature of this Province." Not only allegiance was required, that is, but an acknowledgement of that theoretically unqualified supremacy of the Crown in Parliament against which the thirteen colonies had revolted. The second British Empire was founded explicitly on allegiance and the legislative supremacy of the king in Parliament.

Nor was a theory of government wanting to support the constitutional position. It was ready to hand in the stock view of the nature of constitutional monarchy at the time, the theory of the mixed government of monarchy, aristocracy, and democracy, which had not only the fact of British usage but the authority of antiquity to sanction it. In such a mixed government monarchy operated to check that "excess of democracy" which, it was held, had led the American colonies to revolt.

Monarchy by that theory had itself to be checked by other elements, and in the colonies these had been weak or absent, namely, aristocracy and an established church. Accordingly, efforts were made to correct these defects in the surviving colonies by strengthening the governor's council in its legislative capacity and by aiding an establishment of religion. If monarchical authority was to be strengthened, however, no one intended to bring about any diminution of freedom. All the safeguards of civil liberty were maintained, *habeas corpus* and trial by jury and the procedure of the Common Law. All the political liberty compatible with imperial subordination was freely granted and exercised: the election of an assembly on a broad franchise, the control of taxation by vote and appropriation except for the routine expenses of government, and the exercise of local taxation under the royal veto. Empire, that is, was held to be compatible with liberty, and liberty was guaranteed by the obligation of monarchical government to maintain the inherited rights of its subjects.

This ancient British ideal was, of course, challenged by one also British in origin, but now largely of American development and formulation. From 1783 to 1848 it was to dispute with the older British concept how the political evolution of British North America should proceed. That was the ideal of government founded not on allegiance but on the social compact. Strongly advocated by the extremer Puritans in the Great Rebellion, it had been driven underground with the Restoration, but was restored to respectability by Locke and the Revolution of 1688, and found an especially congenial climate in the American colonies. As the doctrine of the covenanting people, it underlaid the colonial institutions of New England, and in particular made for the increase of the power of the assembly over that of the executive. . . .

While responsible government was a Canadian concept amplified by Joseph Howe and sanctioned by Durham, there can be little doubt that in Canada the compromise its adoption embodied was made possible in large and perhaps decisive measure by the great British migration that began after Waterloo and was at flood tide when responsible government finally became a basic convention of Canadian government at mid-century. English Canada had until 1812 become largely American in population and in the functioning of its institutions. After 1815 the old American stock, both Loyalist refugee and mere immigrant, was swamped by the new British immigrants. Political power in English Canada was taken from the native-born by the British-born by the 1850s, a process which happened, to a lesser degree and much more slowly, in the Atlantic provinces. The names tell the story, Baldwin, Hincks, Gowan, Draper, Harrison, Macdonald, Brown — all were British-born. Only the French remained to represent the native-born in the first exercise of the new powers of self-government. . . .

Certain it is that by Confederation in Canada and Nova Scotia, the politicians who achieved Cabinet rank from time to time had learned and were at home in the mixture of traditional form and business-like dispatch with which the prerogatives of monarchy were exercised in the service of democracy. It was this familiar and valued working system that British American politicians thought infinitely preferable to the democratic presidency and the government of separated powers of the United States. The belief was not a mere provincial prejudice, but the sober judgment of mature and experienced men who had learned their art in one of the most difficult of all schools, a democracy of diverse ethnic groups. For it is to be remembered that there were not only French and English in British America; there were Highland Scots, Catholic Irish, and Lunenburg and Loyalist Germans, all of whom had had small experience of parliamentary government, though they were as quick as the French to learn all the tricks of the game. In such a society responsible government had been made to work so that local communities and special interests could get done what they wanted done, if it were not blatantly contrary to the public interest.

Extraordinarily little republican sentiment, always to a degree endemic in Canada as in the United Kingdom, seems moreover to have survived in the last years of the generation after the rebellions. There was therefore a great consensus of opinion in both French and English British America that in any future union the basic institution of responsible Cabinet government in the Queen's name should be embodied in the new general government and continued in the continuing local ones. "The Executive Government and authority of and over Canada continues and is vested in the Queen," was to be the most significant, as it is the most simple and direct of all the sections of the British North America Act. On that basic principle there was neither hesitation nor complexity to blur the simple, positive affirmation. The language is lucid, the intent unquestionable. Canada was to continue a constitutional monarchy.

So insistent is the emphasis on monarchy in the Confederation debates and in the speeches made throughout the provinces that it is necessary to ask just what was meant by it. No one spelled it out. By inference from the whole of what was said and from the historical context in which it was said, it is legitimate to suppose that it meant on the one hand the retention of personal allegiance to the Crown with responsible and parliamentary government, and on the other the avoidance of popular sovereignty (or democracy) and a federal union.

The desire to continue personal allegiance to the Crown, after liberal principles had triumphed in British America with the grant of responsible government, and at a time when British America was, by uniting, about to take a great and conscious step towards nationhood, calls for explanation. Responsible government, of course, had been a compromise in which parliamentary democracy had been combined with constitutional monarchy on the British model. The monarchical element was in fact central to the compromise. By it a number of things were accomplished, over and above the essential matter of maintaining the personal bond of allegiance between the Queen and her subjects in British America. One was the maintenance of the imperial connection. The material bonds of empire, it is true, had ended with the commerical revolution of 1846-49. There was, moreover, no good reason, commercial or financial, still less military, why the connection between the United Kingdom and the colonies should be kept up. And there were those who looked to a speedy end of the connection. But there were other reasons, important to British America, for maintaining the tie. The main and central one was that the imperial connection sustained the whole constitutional heritage of the colonies. Without the connection, the allegiance to the Crown would have ended and the monarchical principle would have been lost. With it would have gone the compromise of responsible government and all the gains made since 1837. The ending of the connection would have thrown the control of events into the hands of the extremists, *les rouges*, the Clear Grits and, so do extremes meet, the old Compact Tories, none of whom valued responsible government, and all of whom would have plumped for republican institutions and annexation.

With parliamentary and cabinet government would have gone other matters of value to the moderates and conservatives of that day, a few of which are still of value to most Canadians. One was the limited franchise and the idea that the franchise was a trust. Another was the British system of justice, challenged at the time, of course, by the principle of election applied to the selection of judges by the Jacksonian democrats across the border. Yet another was the sense of public rank and personal honour, then still strong in British as in French Canada. Finally, there was the instinctive feeling, an articulate perception in French Canada, that monarchical allegiance allowed a diversity of customs and rights under law in a way that the rational scheme and abstract principles of republican democracy did not. The monarchy, in short, subsumed a heterogeneous and conservative society governed in freedom under law, law upheld by monarchy, where the republic would have levelled the diversities and made uniform the various groups by breaking them down into individuals, free indeed, but bound by social conformity and regimented by an inherent social intolerance....

Finally, the emphasis on monarchy by the Fathers of Confederation arose from their conviction that monarchical institutions had enabled them to avoid the necessity of resorting to a federal union in their scheme of union for

British America. It was true that they had left the provincial governments in being. It was true that the scheme could be described and defended as a federal one. But they were persuaded that they had not recognized the principle of coordinate sovereignty, as they were convinced they had avoided those weaknesses of federal union which had plunged the United States into Civil War. They thought in fact that, under the supremacy of the imperial Crown in Parliament they had created a Canadian Crown in Parliament which would be actively supreme in the union as the imperial power was supreme, if with a supremacy mostly latent in the empire. The union, to their minds, was a legislative union, not a federal or a quasi-federal one, and the anomalies of the special rights of French Canada, or provincial legislatures which possessed all the potent apparatus of responsible government, were no more striking than the many which the empire in the amplitude of its consitutional variety had nourished from the covenant of Plymouth Colony to the latest experiment in Western Australia.

The monarchical emphasis of the Confederation debates was unusual in Canadian politics, a response both to the profounder than usual reflections of the nature of Canadian government prompted by the work of constitution making, and also to the collapse of the American scheme of government in the Civil War. But as a consequence, the monarchy continued in its central place in the Canadian political tradition to become after 1931 the symbol of association with the Commonwealth, and that association is one part of the commitment of Canada. The second part is the new and unfamiliar alliance with the United States. The association with the Commonwealth expresses exactly the Canadian desire for an association compatible with independence. The alliance with the United States, however, raises the question of whether an alliance of states so unequal in power and so intimately linked by economy, language, and culture can in fact be compatible with independence. The question will not be explored here. That the American alliance is a major and a growing commitment of Canada is evident. The point made here is that the preservation of Canadian integrity in that alliance will depend upon the relevance of Canadian history, on its cultural and moral significance in universal history, and on American recognition of that relevance.

The relevance of Canadian history lies, then, in the morally defensible character of Canadian purpose in maintaining a northern nation in independence and vigour in the circumstances of the second half of the twentieth century. The first element of that purpose is to be found in the realization of the northern economy. For that Canada possesses the necessary land bases in the great river valleys of the south. It possesses also in ever-increasing measure the industrial power by which to bring to bear on the Canadian shield and the Arctic the technological skill and power to conquer the North. It possesses in its scientists and its universities the knowledge and the capabilities in research to fathom the deep secrets of the North and to measure the hair's breadth difference between disaster and success in northern development.

In this, there need be no thought of turning the Canadian back on the south. The northern economy has never been self-sufficient, nor can it ever be. But it is manifest from Canadian history that every time that Canada has sought a destiny in the south, disaster has threatened. Every time that impulse came from outside, from the imperial aims of the House of Bourbon in 1701, from the European strategy of la Galissonière in 1749, from the desire of Great Britain to tap the commerce of the Mississippi Valley between 1783 and 1846. The effort was beyond the resources of a northern economy and a northern people, and every time Canada was thrown back upon the shield and the Northwest.

That is not to say that ordinary, or even special, ties to southward need be harmful; on the contrary. Reciprocity, on Canadian terms, as in 1854 and 1935, strengthened the northern economy. The great areas of overlap in the Atlantic provinces, the Eastern Townships, the Ontario peninsula, in Michigan, Wisconsin, Minnesota, and the prairies, and on the Gulf of Georgia, reveal how rough the division between the northern and the continental economies has been. But the division was made and remains, and the areas of overlap have been areas of exchange in which the two economies mingle and strengthen each other by a traffic in raw materials, goods, and skills, which, however, is the exchange that arises from difference, not from uniformity.

The northern economy is a clear and evident thing, explicit in history. Not so definite, but still discernible, is what may be called the northern outlook of Canadian arts and letters. The mere reflection in art of northern scenery, or northern life, important though that is, is not what is meant. What is meant is the existence in Canadian art and literature of distinctive qualities engendered by the experience of northern life. These are a tendency to the heroic and the epic, to the art which deals with violence, a tendency not only realized in the work of E. J. Pratt, but also indicated in that of Louis Frechette, and in the much less successful writings of Charles Heavysege and William Wilfred Campbell. The later canvasses of Lawren Harris and those of Emily Carr have this same heroic quality stylized.

That is the art of the hinterland. The art of the baseland is the lyric of Archibald Lampman, of Octave Cremazie, and the landscape of Cornelius Krieghoff and W. J. Phillips. The great cities of the baselands have their sophisticated art, of course, and that eludes the generalization attempted here, as it should. The reference is only to what is characteristically Canadian, not to what is universal as well as Canadian.

To the heroic and the lyric, the satiric is to be added. For northern life is moral or puritanical, being so harsh that life can allow little laxity in convention. But the moral affords the substance and creates the disposition for satire. Canadian literature has been comparatively rich in satire, from the parody of Sam Slick's Yankee sharpness by a Tory Loyalist to the extravaganzas on small-town life of Stephen Leacock, or prairie rural life of Paul Hiebert. For satire feeds upon the gap between profession and performance, and the puritan both displays the gap more and sees it in other men's performance more readily than those of less rigid standards. The excellence of Canadian political and social caricature stands on the same satiric footing. In all these qualities, Canadian literature has, of course, affinities with both Scottish and Icelandic literature. They give promise of a literature, and an art, as idiomatic as it is significant universally.

Finally, the northern quality of Canadian life is maintained by a factor of deliberate choice and natural selection. As the American frontier has always been open, absolutely or comparatively, to Canadians, Canadians have always been free to live as Canadians or to become Americans. Many who make the latter choice do it with reluctance, but the choice is nearly always made on the grounds of greater reward or wider opportunity. That is, they have rejected the harder life and smaller material rewards of Canada. The result is that Canadians to an extraordinary degree are Canadians by choice. In consequence, Canadians become generation by generation more and more a northern people, either because northern origins have fitted them for northern life, or because they have become adapted to it.

One element in that choice has often, perhaps usually, been the desire to maintain the Canadian allegiance. Canada has never been a country royalist in sentiment any more than Canadian society has remained formally hierarchical in structure. Canadian manners have always tended to be simple, and Canadian society has steadily become a society of social equals. But for many reasons it has been a monarchical country, and not a country of the social compact like its great neighbour. The reasons for this have been historic rather than sentimental. Allegiance means that the law and the state have an objective reality embodied in the succession of persons designated by Parliament and hereditary right. They do not rest on contemporary assent, although the policies and acts of government do. In Canada, therefore, government possesses an objective life of its own. It moves in all its parts at popular impulse, but if there were no impulse, it would still move. In the United States government is subjective. It is designed to move on popular impulse, and if there is no impulse, the movement soon flags and falters. The republican government, massive as are its institutions, historic as is its momentum, in a very real sense rests upon assent periodically renewed. Such a government requires as basis a society of great intrinsic unity and conformity in which a consensus works to a common end. In Canada, a country of economic hazard, external dependence, and plural culture, only the objective reality of a monarchy and the permanent force of monarchical institutions could form the centre and pivot of unity. Allegiance was a social and political necessity of national existence and prevailed over the manifest and insistent attraction of republican institutions and republican liberty.

Not life, liberty, and the pursuit of happiness but peace, order, and good government are what the national government of Canada guarantees. Under these, it is assumed, life, liberty, and happiness may be achieved, but by each according to his taste. For the society of allegiance admits of a diversity the society of compact does not, and one of the blessings of Canadian life is that there is no Canadian way of life, much less two, but a unity under the Crown admitting of a thousand diversities.

For this reason it is not a matter of political concern that Canada has two major cultures and many smaller ones. It would be foolish to deny that the dual culture is one of history's many harsh gifts to Canada, that the duality arose from the ordeal of conquest and suppression and that it has given rise to friction and to weakness. But it is manifest that it is a gift which admits of transmutation into something rich and strange, into a political order as liberal as those which Lord Acton, by way of example, thought approached nearest the ideal. The transmutation can be wrought when the two cultures are seen as variations on a common experience of the land and history of Canada, and of the common allegiance in law and spirit to the traditions and the Crown of that land.

That common experience has created a common psychology, the psychology of endurance and survival. Canadian experience teaches two clear lessons. One is that the only real victories are the victories over defeat. We have been beaten many times, defeat has been our national portion in America, but we survive and we go on in strength. And our experience teaches also that what is important is not to have triumphed, but to have endured. The pride of victory passes, but a people may survive and have its way if it abides by the traditions which have fostered its growth and clarified its purpose.

The common experience extends also to the Canadian achievement of the secret of Commonwealth, that free association in self-government is a bond of union which may yet outlast the controls and authority of empires, however strong. That achievement was the work of Canadians of both the major stocks, it is the outward expression of our domestic institutions, and its spirit informs Canadians of all other origins with an equal pride in free institutions elaborated by the Canadian political genius. We must bring to the working out of the American alliance the same persistence in freedom and the same stubborn ingenuity, recognizing always that this special relationship with the United States is different in kind from the historic association of Canada and can in no sense take its place.

In the end, that common experience extends to a common affirmation of moral purpose, the purpose which makes Canadian history relevant to universal history. Canadians, if one may judge by their history, believe that society cannot live by the state alone. Society has its own autonomous life, which is sustained by sources which may enrich the life of the state, but over which the state has neither authority nor control. Those sources are religious or moral, and flow into society only through persons. The personality of the individual citizen, then, is the object of the justice the state exists to provide and of the welfare society exists to ensure. The individual thus possesses the ultimate autonomy, since he is the end to which both state and society are means. But that autonomy carries with it a sovereign obligation to respect and safeguard the autonomy of his fellows, primarily by manners, which are the dealings of man with man, and secondarily through the social and political order. So reciprocal and delicate a complex of justice, welfare, and good manners may function only in an organic unity of state, society, and individual. It was such a unity of king, church, and people Canadians, both French and English, inherited from their remoter past and have elaborated in their history as a monarchical and democratic nation.

The preservation of such a national society is not the unique mission of Canada, but it is the central fact of Canadian history that it has been preserved and elaborated by Canadians in one of the largest, harshest and most intimidating countries on earth. Canada, that is, has preserved and confirmed the essentials of the greatest of civilizations in the grimmest of environments. It is an accomplishment worthy of a better end than absorption in another and an alien society, however friendly and however strong in its own ideals. In that accomplishment and its continuance lies the relevance of Canadian history.

Frontierism, Metropolitanism, and Canadian History

J.M.S. CARELESS

Like any other history, that of Canada has been written within the framework of intellectual concepts, some of which have been consciously applied by historians, while others have shaped their work more or less indirectly through the influence of the surrounding climate of opinion. It would obviously be impossible to draw and catalogue all the concepts that have affected the writing of Canadian history, even in the most general way. Yet it does seem possible to discern certain underlying ideas or patterns of thought that have given character to various phases of Canadian historiography. And in more recent times, in particular, one can note the powerful influence of what might be called (for want of a more precise term) "frontierism" in the history of Canada.

The idea of the dynamic frontier as a great and distinctive force moulding North American development has left an enduring mark on the writing of history in Canada, just as it has in the United States. No doubt this frontier idea is no longer as fresh and vital in its application to this country as it was in the period before the Second World War: indeed, it is largely because its original influence has declined, and the concept has thus become a historical phenomenon in itself, that we are entitled to discuss and assess its influence. Nor was the frontier thesis proper, as propounded by Frederick Jackson Turner and elaborated by his disciples, ever adopted as fully or dogmatically in Canada as it was in the United States — and there, of course, it has long been the subject of qualification and criticism. Nevertheless, the frontier interpretation broadly affected the thinking of a number of distinguished Canadian historians who in the main began their work about a quarter-century ago. Today we can hardly examine the current state of Canadian historiography, and perhaps project its lines of growth, without giving heavy weight to the North American-environmentalist view of our history which stemmed originally from Turner's frontier thesis and which still leaves a rich heritage on both sides of the Canadian-American boundary.

There were other approaches to Canadian history before the rise of frontierism, and at present there are still others, which may involve the modification, complication, or even the virtual reversal of the frontier concept.

Abridged from J.M.S. Careless, "Frontierism, Metropolitanism and Canadian History," *Canadian Historical Review* 35 (March 1954), pp. 1-21. Footnotes have been omitted. Reprinted by permission of the author and University of Toronto Press.

Accordingly, in order to put frontierism in its proper context, it is first necessary to generalize — rather alarmingly, perhaps — on several "schools" of Canadian history. Each of these had some sort of interpretative approach, or at least some underlying assumptions, which gave a broadly similar character to the works its members produced.

These schools, however, are being set forth merely for convenience in tracing the general patterns of Canadian historiography and not as an all-inclusive filing system; for when individual historians are considered they do not always fit neatly into one particular classification. Some may change their school allegiance with the passage of time, while others, so to speak, may fall between schools. Furthermore, since the writing of history in French- and English-speaking Canada has largely been carried on as two separate enterprises, it would be of small consequence to try to link French-language schools with the English ones to be established below. And yet, despite these limitations, it can still be asserted that at various stages in Canadian historiography certain general approaches have been followed by important groups of historians, so that the designating of "schools" to illuminate that fact is by no means an unprofitable exercise.

I

The first school to be so designated might be termed the Britannic, or Blood is Thicker than Water School. The writers of this group were often convinced imperialists of the later nineteenth or early twentieth centuries and were closely attached in sentiment and background to Great Britain. They tended, as William Kingsford, that dull dean of Canadian historians, said he did, to make their theme the emergence of a new Britannic community within the empire, a part of one imperial organism, whose people enjoyed the British institutions of their forefathers and were worthy members of that indefinable company, the "British race." This Britannic School was inclined to ignore North American forces except when they were concentrated in the threatening power of the United States. The defeat of American pressure from without in 1776, 1812, and 1867 had "kept Canada British." So much for North America: a foe to be resisted.

Yet this group contributed something of lasting significance to the thought of Canadian history: the idea that Canada represented a declaration of independence from the United States, an attempt to build a second community in North America outside the American republic, and one marked off from it, indeed, by the longer persistence of the imperial tie. For some time this Canadian community would look to the bond with Britain to offset American dangers. But in the young twentieth century, when the days of actual threat had passed, that bond seemed to change increasingly in its implication — from protection to subordination. It was now that another school of Canadian historians began to arise, who viewed the imperial tie more critically in the light of the growing spirit of nationalism. And their main theme now became the march of Canada to political nationhood, through many a parliamentary manoeuvre and struggle of words as colonial limitations were progressively overcome.

This new School of Political Nationhood chiefly concentrated on the paper-strewn path to national status, directing Canadian history to Colonial Office dispatches, the records of imperial conferences, and tense questions of treaty-making powers. Two phases, however, may be discerned in the writings of this school, though both were concerned with the peaceful and piecemeal evolution of Canada to nationhood. The first of these mainly treated the achievement of responsible government and confederation, and on the whole was favourably disposed to things British, since leading historians like Chester Martin and R. G. Trotter saw these national advances as being considerably aided by British advocacy and still as taking shape within the general framework of British institutions. As this indicates, there was really no sharp break here between the Britannic and Nationhood schools, and contemporary opinion in Canada largely tended to think in terms both of national development and of maintaining some degree of connection with Britain. Yet gradually a watershed was being crossed, as more and more stress was laid on the winning of national rights. Thus came the second phase, which dealt primarily with the achievement of autonomy in external affairs, and the motto of most of its authors might well have been, A Canadian Citizen I will Die.

Sometimes, it is true, these historians might welcome the emergence of the new British Commonwealth as the concomitant of Canada's advance to nationhood. But generally they were less friendly to British influences, and the nationalist note was clear, as in the writings of J. W. Dafoe or O. D. Skelton. British influences, in short, were largely equated with imperial leading strings, and the more nationalistic writers were ever on guard against imperialist designs to enmesh pure young Canada in a web of power politics — though one might wonder why gentlemen so keenly perceptive of the harsh realities of power in the European world could not recognize, in fixing their watchful eye on the British menace, that, after 1918, at least, the fearsome British lion had become rather a straw-stuffed beast. Still, this preoccupation with straw men or straw lions may perhaps be explained by the fact that much of their writing was done amidst the somewhat unreal atmosphere of Mackenzie King's bold crusade of the 1920's for Canada's right to have no foreign policy. And these authors were often strongly Liberal in sympathies. At times they seemed to write as if Canadian history was in essence a steady Liberal broadening-down of freedom to the ultimate end of national status — after which absolutely memorable History would come to a dead stop.

Nevertheless the Political Nationhood group, first phase or second, did solid service in uncovering the process whereby Canada obtained the various attributes of self-government. Moreover, in stressing the theme of nationhood they were themselves expressing the basic truth that a society distinct from that of Britain had taken shape in Canada and was demanding recognition and the full right to manage its own affairs. As these historians, however, generally talked in political and constitutional terms, they did not effectively analyze the social, economic, and intellectual forces within North America which were creating a Canadian community increasingly conscious that it was far from being an overseas projection of Britain.

To fill this gap, a new school of historians began to take shape in the later 1920's, although it is important to note that its members were often closely related to the nationalist authors of the day. Indeed, this was nationalism in another sphere, seeking to demonstrate that Canadian desires for nationhood were rooted in the native North American environment: that Canadian institutions and viewpoints were not simply British, but were in their own way as American as those of the United States. The environment had done it. This, then, was the Environmentalist School, or North Americans All.

It was this group that built particularly on the concept of the frontier in North American history derived from Turner and his followers in the United States. The frontier, where man came most immediately into contact with the North American physical environment, was the great seed-bed for the growth of a truly North American society. From the start, as the United States and Canada had spread across the continent, environmental influences that first began on the frontier had worked to shape a native American character different from that of the Old World, left far behind. Here was the key principle to be applied by Canadian environmentalist historians: that thanks to the continuous process of adaptation to the environment, an American content had steadily grown in Canada within external forms of government, society, or culture inherited from Britain or France.

It followed that Canadian history could be most fruitfully compared to that of the United States in its essentially North American nature and course of development. In pursuing this promising theme, however, these writers took over the general approach and mood of Turner and company — the frontier and its agrarian population as emblematic of native democratic, progressive, perhaps even of "Good" forces in the history of the continent — rather than the precise frontier thesis, which received little direct application in Canada. Yet because that original thesis was so powerful in its impact and so pervasive in its influence, it requires examination here; although, admittedly, the subject is hardly a new one.

II

Turner had held in his frontier thesis that "the greatest formative influence" in American history had been the long existence of "the open frontier, the hither edge of free land," continually moving westwards. The conditions of frontier society had determined the character of western institutions, and these in turn had reacted on the East. Out of the frontier, in fact, had come American individualism, democracy, inventiveness, coarseness, and idealism.

Turner wrote that the seeds of American democracy were not carried to the New World in the *Mayflower* but sprang up out of the native forest. The effect of the frontier was to make Americans out of Europeans. In brief, the West was the true America, that ever taught the populous but effete East the American way of life.

This was environmental determinism at its most forthright. The wilderness and the men it produced had made America. Defenders of Turner might claim that he had not proposed a frontier hypothesis as the only key to American history, but it was widely seized upon as the true explanation, especially as its nationalist and romantic implications gripped the American imagination. Its effects may still be found today, on different cultural levels in the United States. Indeed, it may not be irrelevant to note that Hollywood, that lowest common denominator of the American mind where myths are mass-produced, still pours forth a flood of highly techni-coloured Westerns each purporting to touch the very soul of America, as some pioneer rugged individualist with iron hands and blazing guns "carves out an empire" for the nation at various points west, while Indians in their thousands from Central Casting Office go down before the onward march of democracy....

How does all this relate to Canadian history? To some extent there have been similar stages in the use of the frontier interpretation, though these, indeed, might overlap. In the first stage, there were stimulating applications of frontierist themes and concepts to the Canadian half of the North American environment, seen most clearly perhaps in W. N. Sage's paper of 1928, "Some Aspects of the Frontier in Canadian History." This treated Canadian expansion across the continent as an integral part of a total North American frontier movement that ignored the international boundary. Then there were the valuable investigations of F. H. Underhill into the nature of Canadian political parties, and especially the Clear Grit Liberal movement directed by George Brown and the Toronto *Globe*. With regard to Canadian parties, Professor Underhill traced their development according to conflicts between western agrarian areas and eastern business interests, in sound Turnerian fashion (1935). With regard to the Clear Grits, he saw them as "an expression of the 'frontier' in Canadian politics" (1927). E. H. Oliver applied frontierism to Canadian religious development, and in his *Winning the Frontier* (1930) depicted the Canadian churches as being moulded by a frontier environment. Somewhat later A. S. Morton emphasized the dominant power of the environment in the extension of settlement into the Prairie West (1938). And A. L. Burt effectively used a frontier interpretation to show how the people of New France were shaped by North American forces to become truly an indigenous people, not just a seeming copy of Old World "feudal" France (1940).

In the second stage, there came criticisms and modifications of the frontier interpretation, although the environmentalist emphasis was still much in evidence. A. R. M. Lower noted in a paper of 1930, "The Origins of Democracy in Canada," that "There can be little question but that American democracy had a forest birth." Yet he went on to assert that frontier equality might not result in political democracy unless "theoretical positions as to its nature" had already been projected into the frontier environment. In Canada's case, the egalitarian conditions of pioneer life had interacted with traditions brought from across the Atlantic; and Canadian democracy had developed more slowly than American because of Canada's briefer, more limited frontier experience, its stronger attachments to the Old World, and the long-enduring, overriding power of the imperial authority in government. Nevertheless, despite this recognition of non-environmental, transferred influences, Professor Lower, in his *Colony to Nation* (1946) continued to stress the power of the New World "to change old institutions and give them new form and spirit." North American democracy, he reiterated, was "forest-born." In short, though this was modification, environmentalism sprung from the frontier concept still remained strong.

In the third stage, as in the United States, new emphasis was given to the role of eastern rather than western forces in Canada, to urban interests and to the dominating power of the organizing, controlling metropolis. Thus Professor Underhill, for example, noted in 1946 that the original frontier agrarianism of the Clear Grits had subsequently been qualified by urban and business leadership introduced to the party by George Brown and other Toronto worthies. And Professor Lower in his same *Colony to Nation* paid marked attention to the economic power wielded by metropolitan centres like Montreal and London, which, he made clear, did much to affect the course of events in raw Canadian settlements. On another tack, Professor Fred Landon, in describing the frontier era in western Ontario, gave chief place to the transmitted influence of American democratic ideas and practices rather than to actual frontier conditions in forming the outlook of the pioneer community. But this only pushed the influence of the environment one stage back, to patterns of life worked out in the former frontier states below the Great Lakes. In any case it was evident that, despite qualifications and shifts of emphasis, environmentalism was still flourishing in Canadian history.

Still, it should be plain from this discussion that Canadian environmentalists did not generally follow any rigid frontier dogma and did show regard for other than native or western forces in analysing Canadian developments. After all, in a country which had obviously maintained many transatlantic ties and long continued as a colony there could not be as strong an assertion as in the United States of a separate North American growth in isolation from the world. And yet there was an inclination for environmentalists to see as much as possible of the history of Canada in terms of common North American experience in driving back the wilds — to suggest that the really important features in Canadian development had in truth been "forest-born"; in other words, that the various Wests had been the principal source of transforming energy and of national progress, in which they had pulled along and supported the conservative, exploitative East.

There was, moreover, a certain tendency to fix values. Thus pioneer society, the West, and simple farmers became virtuous and forward-looking to the beholder, while town society, the East, and un-simple business men became selfish and reactionary. There might be an element of truth here, but moral overtones somewhat coloured the picture, so that western farmers who wanted free trade established in their interests were Good, while eastern business men who wanted a protective tariff enacted in theirs were Evil. Similarly, the West appeared as the true home of Canadianism, while the East, which worked out a distinctive Canadian economic nationalism in railway and tariff policy, was hardly Canada at all. No doubt powerful eastern business interests fattened themselves considerably through these arrangements. But could environmentalists properly become moral about business elements adjusting themselves to problems of the environment in their own way?

In sum, Canadian environmentalists frequently displayed the compelling mood of the frontier school, with its moral implications of a struggle between sound native democratic forces and elements that clung to privilege, exploitation, and empty Old-World forms. In so doing they often oversimplified a conflict between West and East, or better, between pioneer agrarian interests and exploitative urban centres. As a result, major Canadian movements for political change might be viewed too narrowly in the light of frontierism. For example, Upper Canadian radicalism of the 1830's, Clear Grit Liberalism of the mid-century, and Progressivism of the 1920's might all be explained in terms of the upsurge of the then newest West, as western forces of pioneer individualism launched crusades against privilege and urban business domination. Yet it could also be shown that Mackenzie radicalism was probably more influenced by the working model of American political democracy and the ideas of British radicalism; that Clear Grittism was closely organized about the rising urban centre of Toronto; and that Western Progressivism was not based on self-sufficient pioneer farmers but on organized grain specialists engaged in a highly complex kind of agricultural business, whose goals involved not the triumph of individualism but the replacement of a set of unfavourable government controls centred in the tariff with another represented by Wheat Boards and government provision of major services.

Furthermore, it might well be a result of frontierism, sprung as it was from the mid-western heart of the continent, that a viewpoint characteristic of mid-western isolationism often appeared among environmentalist writers in Canada. Their view of the environment, like Turner's, was primarily continental. Thus it tended to neglect the influence of the seas beyond, the "maritime environment" that had always tied the continent to Europe. Canada might be treated as a northern extension of certain continental physiographic provinces, without due consideration of geographic and historic forces that had from the beginning of white penetration made this country an east-to-west projection from Europe. And logically it would follow that geography — in the continental sense only — had shaped Canada as a number of disparate American regions, held out of the American republic by mainly emotional forces and by the chance of history: in short, a loose grouping of less well-favoured, somewhat backward, American states. A rather paradoxical basis, this, for the nationalism environmentalists usually professed.

However, it is worth repeating that leading contemporary historians who have been referred to here in connection with the vigorous environmentalist phase of Canadian history have themselves, in more recent writings, not only shown awareness of the shortcomings of interpretations stemming from frontierism but have also done much to reconsider and to correct them. Nor, certainly, have their ideas ceased to develop beyond this one approach. None the less it may be hazarded that the effects of frontierist teachings remain strong today in suggesting for Canadian history, and doubtless for its readers, certain stereotypes about the dynamic West and the torpid East, and about the nature of Canada as a more restricted, backward version of the American model to the south. And frontierism may still leave a tendency to overvalue the influence of native North American forces and the material environment, and a tendency to undervalue forces transferred from Europe and the non-material environment: that of ideas, traditions and institutions. Yet these latter factors were particularly important in a portion of North America that did not undergo a revolutionary upheaval, emotional as well as political, to break ties with Europe, and which continued to place a special premium on the word "British" as applied to institutions and ideas. In fact, it is these very things which chiefly mark off the development of Canada from that of the United States. They give validity to the study of a separate Canadian history, one which is not just a counterpart of United States history in having a similar North American content.

Accordingly, while in no way underrating the very great contributions which frontierism and environmentalism have made to the understanding of Canada as a part of North America, it does seem necessary to look for a wider framework for Canadian history. But this, indeed, was already taking shape while the frontier interpretation was being usefully applied, and to a certain extent grew out of it, as an examination will show.

III

This next framework was in some ways a qualified version of environmentalism and in others the frontier concept reversed. It has appeared in most explicit form in the writings of D. G. Creighton, particularly in his *Commercial Empire of the St. Lawrence* (1938) and *Dominion of the North* (1944), but its foundations were laid in earlier works by H. A. Innis which broke rich new ground in Canadian economic history, notably *A History of the Canadian*

Pacific Railway (1923) and *The Fur Trade in Canada* (1930). These studies of major Canadian economic enterprises, which were essentially great systems of continent-wide communications, pointed the way to a new general interpretation of Canadian history that would be forcefully developed by Professor Creighton.

His approach, in fact, has been said to establish a "Laurentian School" of Canadian historiography, since it largely rests on the idea that the long St. Lawrence water route and its connections across the continent became the basis of an extensive communications system around which Canada itself took shape. The commercial empire of the St. Lawrence, the broad domain of Montreal, first flung a Canadian fur trade across the continent, then competed vigorously with New York and the American seaboard through canal and railway enterprises for control of the trade of the mid-western heartlands of America, and finally built a new economic dominion across the northwestern plains to the Pacific that was, in fact, the Dominion of Canada. It followed that the existence of a separate Canada was not just a fortuitous result of the American Revolution, of French determination to survive, nor of Loyalist emotional resolves to "stay British" — despite the hard facts of the environment — nor again of the mere continuance of the imperial tie. It was also rooted in powerful factors of geography and commerce that underlay the whole Canadian development.

This, in a sense, was environmentalism, since the St. Lawrence was as real a feature of the North American environment as the North American forest, and a good deal more permanent. Environmentalists had stressed before that the main natural lines of North American geography ran north and south, linking the regions of Canada more effectively with their United States counterparts below the border than with their Canadian neighbours to east and west. But the St. Lawrence, the Great Lakes, the Saskatchewan, and the Fraser traced lines across the continent that were quite as natural; and, as the writings of Professors Innis and Creighton indicated, they made possible the east-to-west linking of Canadian regions from the earliest days of the fur trade, as communications spread by the lakes and river valleys from sea to sea. Perhaps we could even call this the Waterways School, especially since it made clear that the environment did not stop short at the Atlantic edge of North America. For the St. Lawrence system that funnelled traffic from the continental interior out to the sea was closely connected with British finance and markets across the waters in an east-west trading network that thus reached halfway around the world.

Yet the Laurentian interpretation did not mean just a new emphasis on material environmentalism, since it also revealed that this huge communications and transport system could transfer immigrants, ideas, and impulses in one direct channel from Britain deep into the heart of the continent. As a result, the Ontario frontier of the earlier nineteenth century might actually be in closer contact with the sea and the mind of Europe than were the midwestern regions of the United States, more isolated behind the Appalachian barrier in a Mississippi Valley world of their own.

The Laurentian School, however, tended to go even further, and to reverse the earlier environmentalist position in this respect: it looked not from the forest-born frontiers for its perspective of Canadian history but from developing eastern centres of commerce and industry. Indeed, it primarily studied the effects of the East on the West, and largely regarded business men and conservative urban political elements as agents of national expansion who might well be more far-sighted in their outlook than were their agrarian opponents. Here then was a metropolitan rather than a frontier viewpoint. Moreover, this Laurentian view could be effectively linked with the monumental studies of H. A. Innis on the organization of the staple products trade of broad North American areas through costly and complex transport systems controlled in large urban centres. The result was virtually to establish "metropolitanism" in Canadian historiography, the study of the role of metropolitan forces in this country, a vitalizing approach that may yet undergo considerable development.

Metropolitanism is at root a socio-economic concept that has already seen some application in Canadian history. As mentioned earlier, Professor Lower has made use of it in *Colony to Nation*, and elsewhere as well, but it has been most closely applied in D. C. Masters' work, *The Rise of Toronto*, 1850-1890 (1947). In this he traced the rise of the city to a position of metropolitan dominance over Ontario, while at the same time it entered into vigorous competition with Montreal business interests for control of a broader Canadian hinterland. Toronto's climb to metropolitan stature is an instructive particular theme in Canadian history, but the rise of the metropolis in general is one of the most striking features of modern Western society. Briefly this implies the emergence of a city of outstanding size to dominate not only its surrounding countryside but other cities and their countrysides, the whole area being organized by the metropolis, through control of communications, trade, and finance, into one economic and social unit that is focussed on the metropolitan "centre of dominance" and through it trades with the world. Political activity, too, may often become centred on the metropolis.

London and New York are of course the classic examples of modern metropolitanism. But the metropolitan relationship is a chain, almost a feudal chain of vassalage, wherein one city may stand tributary to a bigger centre and yet be the metropolis of a sizable region of its own. Thus, for example, Winnipeg is Montreal's subsidiary but is the metropolis of a large area of the prairie West. The Toronto metropolis is a subsidiary of both New York and Montreal, while Canada's main metropolitan centre, Montreal, has traditionally been bound to London. These facts are not new in themselves; but when it is remembered that the metropolitan pattern includes not only economic ties but social and cultural associations also, then many effective lines of inquiry may present themselves. For example, one might suggest that the survival of British customs sometimes noted in the English-speaking ruling class of Montreal, or Toronto's split personality, whereby it strives both to be a minor New York and to maintain its "British" character, may be comprehended through the weighing of various metropolitan connections and influences in these cities' history.

At present, however, the chief point to observe is that the rise of metropolitanism is the other side of the coin to frontier expansion. One may speak of the constant expansion of the frontier, or of the constant extension of the metropolitan power that is pushing out the frontier. What Webb called the "Age of the Great Frontier," might just as well be called the "Age of the Great Metropolis," when western Europe in general, by spreading out its system of communications and commerce, organized the world about itself. The age of this great European metropolis has passed away. Its predominant focus, London, has yielded in primacy of economic power to New York — though now there is no one main world metropolitan region, since, despite the rise of North America, Europe still maintains a vast overseas economic network, while a far-flung separate trading system is emerging in the Communist-dominated world.

Returning to the frontier itself, one might say that it is developed by a metropolitan centre of dominance which supplies its capital, organizes its communications and transport, and markets its products. The frontier's culture, too, originally stems from a metropolitan community; at root, learning and ideas radiate from there — and thus is Turner answered. True, there may be frontier religious movements, but these begin with preachers going out to the frontier and end in the focusing of the sect on the city. The economic and cultural metropolitan processes go hand in hand, as newspapers, books, and men of education spread from the centre. Frontiers may often supply grievances for political movements. Urban centres as often supply the intellectual leadership; so that frontier demands take form at the hands of urban journalists and professional men.

It may be seen when this analysis is carried through that the frontier, far from being essentially independent and self-reliant, is in the largest sense a dependent. It constantly requires metropolitan aid and control, though by the same token it may come to resent and resist it. Frontier protest movements are a natural accompaniment of the extension of metropolitan power into new areas. The dynamic, organizing, hard-pressing forces of metropolitanism bring reaction on themselves. This may occur either at moments when the frontier as such is rapidly expanding, and full of problems of adjustment, or when it is actually declining; that is, becoming organized into a more mature and integrated region with a new metropolitan centre of its own, which hopes to wrest control of the local economy away from the older centre, and therefore gives voice and leadership to a regional protest movement.

How does this pattern fit Canadian history? No good historian would try to make it fit too exactly: if we reject a frontier determinism we should hardly replace it with a metropolitan determinism. Still, there may be an approach here as instructive for Canadian historiography as the frontier interpretation was in its day. For example, one might examine the unrest in Upper Canada in the 1830's, when this frontier area was rapidly expanding with the tide of British immigration, as a result of the vigorous extension of powerful business interests into a broad new domain, and of the spread of educated men and stimulating ideas from older communities, displayed notably in the rising power of the press and the journalist on the Upper Canada scene. On the other hand, the Clear Grit movement of the 1850's would appear as the organizing of the maturing western community around Toronto, the rising young metropolis, in a common campaign against the domination of the region by Montreal, the older centre. In this campaign Toronto supplied both intellectual leadership, in the form of the *Globe*, and strong party direction, in the form of George Brown and other wealthy and prominent business or professional men: the urban element was critically important. And as for Western Progressivism in the 1920's, was it not bound up with the rise of Winnipeg as a prairie metropolitan centre, was not a good deal of intellectual leadership centred in that city, and is there not evidence that here was a maturing western community now ready to contest outside metropolitan domination on a large scale?

Metropolitanism can be seen operating even more clearly in Canadian history where there are no frontiers of actual settlement to block the view, so to speak, and by their undoubted colour and liveliness rather steal the centre of the stage. In the Canadian fur trade, from earliest French times on, the role of the dominant organizing metropolis is plain: Montreal and Quebec the metropolitan centres for the posts of the whole fur-trading West, Paris and later London the metropolis for these Canadian towns. On the Canadian lumbering and mining frontiers, in our present northern expansion, the directing, extending, organizing, and exploiting functions of metropolitan interests are evident once more. In fact, metropolitanism has shown itself even more clearly in Canadian development than in American, precisely because we have had far less fertile acreage for agricultural settlement than has the United States. Hence the agrarian frontier of the sort that Turner described has played proportionately less part in our history. This, then, is a distinctive attribute of Canada's own version of the North American story.

Furthermore, in Canada, with its small population heavily concentrated in certain areas, metropolitan influences have had a particularly free sweep. The United States, of course, has much bigger metropolitan cities like Chicago, Philadelphia, and New York. But it also has many more large centres, each organizing its own region, though all ultimately subordinate to New York. Canada, however, has only three first-ranking metropolitan centres today: Montreal, the greatest, Vancouver, which by organizing effective communications has extended its hinterland eastward into the prairies, and Toronto, which controls wealthy southern Ontario and is steadily advancing its empire in the mining North. In Canada, therefore, metropolitan power is in comparison to the United States more directly centralized and more immediately apparent.

Historically speaking, the functioning of metropolitanism may do more to explain the course of Canadian history than concepts of frontierism borrowed from the United States and set forth before the significance of the modern metropolis was clear. For example, the greater conservatism of Canada as compared to the United States may be read as a mark of the much stronger influence exercised in this country by conservative-minded eastern urban centres — which were certainly far removed from any impulses of forest democracy. Moreover, the stronger influence of British ideas and institutions — and even of colonialism — must have been fostered in Canada by its long and close focusing on the British metropolis itself. Finally, the fact that Canada has pioneered not so much in democracy as in the large-scale combination of public and private interests to overcome the problems raised by a difficult environment, again suggests the greater power throughout Canadian history of the forces seeking to organize communication systems and extend commerce. One might well say that the building of the C.P.R. so far ahead of settlement, and Macdonald's policies of economic nationalism in general, were plain manifestations of the power of metropolitan influences in Canadian politics. And many other instances might also be brought to mind.

It could be objected with regard to some of the foregoing examples that applying a metropolitan interpretation only restates old problems in somewhat different terms. It may be so: but what is particularly needed is a restatement, a new perspective that may disclose new vistas and produce new patterns for Canadian history. At any rate, frontierism, along with earlier schools and approaches, has had its use and its day. Environmentalism needs recasting, and is being recast. The metropolitan approach largely recognizes what is already going on in Canadian historiography and provides a new framework — one which pays heed both to the distinctive features of the history of this country and to a notable modern phenomenon, the rise of metropolitanism all around the world.

2
THE DRAMA OF SOCIETY AND POLITICS

The Only Tourist in Havana Turns His Thoughts Homeward

Leonard Cohen

Come, my brothers,
let us govern Canada,
let us find our serious heads,
let us dump asbestos on the White House,
let us make the French talk English,
   not only here but everywhere,
let us torture the Senate individually
   until they confess,
let us purge the New Party,
let us encourage the dark races
   so they'll be lenient
   when they take over,
let us make the CBC talk English,
let us all lean in one direction
   and float down
   to the coast of Florida,
let us have tourism,
let us flirt with the enemy,
let us smelt pig-iron in our back yards,
let us sell snow
   to under-developed nations,
(Is it true one of our national leaders
   was a Roman Catholic?)
let us terrorize Alaska,
let us unite
   Church and State,
let us not take it lying down,
let us have two Governor Generals
   at the same time,
let us have another official language,
let us determine what it will be,
let us give a Canada Council Fellowship
   to the most original suggestion,
let us teach sex in the home
   to parents,
let us threaten to join the U.S.A.
   and pull out at the last moment,

my brothers, come,
our serious heads are waiting for us somewhere
   like Gladstone bags abandoned
   after a *coup d'état*,
let us put them on very quickly,
let us maintain a stony silence
   on the St. Lawrence Seaway.

Havana
April 1961

Revolution and Counterrevolution: The United States and Canada

S.M. Lipset

The strong cultural similarity between English-speaking Canada and the United States has often led citizens of the latter to wonder why the two remain in separate politics. Yet, although these two peoples probably resemble each other more than any other two nations on earth, there are consistent patterns of difference between them. To discover and analyze the factors which perpetuate such differences among nations is one of the more intriguing and difficult tasks in comparative study....

... Both nations are largely urbanized, heavily industrialized, and politically stable. They share many of the same ecological and demographic conditions, approximately the same level of economic development, and similar rates of upward and downward social mobility. To a very great extent Canada and the United States share the same values, but, as Kaspar Naegele has pointed out, in Canada these values are held much more tentatively. Both are new peoples and new states, but Canada's relationship to Britain has helped perpetuate in a North American nation elements of a set of values having Old World origins and a more conservative character. Thus, while equality and achievement are values emphasized in both North American societies, in Canada the emphasis is somewhat less, and therefore the contrast between the nations remains one of degree....

Status distinctions, which exist in all nations, have less legitimacy in the United States than they do in Canada.... Naegele concluded that the evidence on the subject indicates there is "less emphasis in Canada on equality than there is in the United States" and "a greater acceptance of *limitation*, of hierarchical patterns." For example, the greater strength of elitist and ascriptive value emphases in Canada would seem to be reflected in a paternalistic organization of the family, in the reverence paid to the clergy by the laity, in the diffuse deference granted the old by the young, men by women, teachers by students, and politicians by electorate. From James Bryce to S.D. Clark, sociologically oriented observers have stressed the greater respect for political leaders in Canada than in the United States, symbolized in part by Canadian loyalty to monarchical institutions. W.L. Morton has pointed out that

---

Abridged from S.M. Lipset, "Revolution and Counterrevolution: The United States and Canada," in Thomas Ford (ed.), *The Revolutionary Theme in Contemporary America* (Lexington: The University Press of Kentucky, 1965), pp. 21-64. Reprinted by permission of the author and the publisher.

among the institutions and norms linked to monarchy and cabinet government has been

> the limited franchise and the idea that the franchise was a trust. Another was the British system of justice, challenged at the time by the principle of election applied to the selection of judges by the Jacksonian Democrats across the border. Yet another was the sense of public rank and personal honor.... The monarchy, in short, subsumed a heterogeneous and conservative society governed in freedom under law, law upheld by monarchy, where the republic would have levelled the diversities and made uniform the various groups by breaking them down into individuals, free indeed, but bound by social conformity and regimented by an inherent social intolerance.

It is significant that Canadian political debates concerning the suffrage in the late nineteenth century still involved discussions of how much property a man should have to qualify to vote. Manhood suffrage was not enacted federally until 1898. In the United States, the egalitarian emphasis facilitated the extension of male suffrage among whites almost everywhere by 1845.

The American populist and egalitarian ethos also "leads to certain impatience with legal process and, occasionally, to outright disrespect for law." There are several indicators of the differences in Canadian and American respect for public authority. Where diffuse respect for public authority exists, we should expect to find greater reliance on informal social controls based on traditional obligations. One indicator of the relative strength of the informal normative mechanisms of social control as compared with the restrictive emphases of legal sanctions may be the extent to which a nation requires police protection or lawyers. The data indicate that the United States ratio of police to population is more than one-third greater than that of Canada, a difference that holds for communities of the same size. The proportionately fewer lawyers in probate practice in Canada (one for 1,630 people) as compared to the United States (one for 868) points to the much lower propensity of Canadians to rely on the law, even for civil matters.

The greater obedience to the law by Canadians may be reflected also in varying crime rates in the two countries. Though data on crime rates are far from amenable to accurate cross-national comparisons, both countries offer the same definition and report statistics for several major criminal offenses. Perhaps the most dramatic of such differences is that only one police officer in Canada was killed by criminal action while on duty, compared to 37 killed in the United States in 1961. By 1963, the United States figure had risen to 55 police officers killed in a single year, while the figure in Canada remained at one. (The United states has about ten times the population of Canada.) The data indicate that United States crime rates for various offences are substantially higher than Canadian rates for the same offences.

It is therefore not at all surprising, as one writer has remarked, that "Canadians are today perhaps more aware of the differences in their attitudes toward the law than anything else distinguishing them from Americans." Half a century ago, James Bryce suggested that this habit of obedience to the law among Canadians "was formed under governments that were in those days monarchical in fact as well as in name, and it has persisted.... The sentiment of deference to legal authority, planted deep in days when that authority was regarded with awe as having an almost sacred sanction, has lived on into a time when the awe and sacredness has departed...."

Many have argued that the more widespread deferential respect for the elite in Canada as compared with the United States, rather than a more libertarian popular opinion, underlies the freedom of political dissent and guaranteed civil liberties so characteristic of English-speaking Canada. The emphasis on diffuseness and elitism in the Canadian system is reflected in the ability of the more unified and influential elites to control the system so as to inhibit the emergence of populist movements, such as McCarthyism, which express political intolerance. However, as S.D. Clark warns, McCarthyism (like Coughlinism and the Ku Klux Klan) does not indicate greater intolerance in the United States as compared to Canada so much as it reflects the strength of populist, anti-elitist values:

> The attack of Joseph McCarthy upon Communist influences in the government of the United States is a clear and genuine expression of the American frontier, isolationist spirit. In Canada it would be hard to conceive of a state of political freedom great enough to permit the kind of attacks upon responsible leaders of the government which have been carried out in the United States. More careful examination of the American community in general, and perhaps of the academic community in particular, would probably reveal that, in spite of the witch hunts in that country, the people of the United States enjoy in fact a much greater degree of freedom than do the people of Canada.

In Canada legal officers tend to have life tenure, and are not directly involved in politics. Judges in Canada at every level are appointed for life by the federal authorities. Crown attorneys are designated by the provincial governments for indefinite terms, and are rarely terminated before retirement. They are not fired when a new party comes to power, and since prohibited from political activity, they are never under pressure to handle cases in a way that might facilitate their re-election or attainment of higher electoral office.

In the United States not only are more legal offices open to election, but elections are more frequent than in any other modern society. In a discussion of American urban politics, Edward Banfield and James Wilson point out that

> our government (in the United States) is permeated with politics. This is because our constitutional structure and our traditions afford individuals manifold opportunities not only to bring their special interests to the attention of public officials but also — and this is the important thing — to compel officials to

bargain and to make compromises ... there is virtually no sphere of "administration" apart from politics.

Such a comment underlies the populist sentiments and structures that pervade the American polity. The strong egalitarian emphasis in the United States which presses for expression in the *vox populi* makes Americans more derisive and critical of their politicians and government bureaucrats.

The same differentiating factors seemingly are reflected in varying administrative practices at the national government level. Alexander Brady, a prominent Canadian student of comparative political institutions has strongly emphasized these differences:

> In Ottawa, no less than in London, the dividing line between the politician craving publicity and the permanent official cherishing anonymity is drawn higher in the administrative hierarchy than in Washington. A political party replacing another in power does not, as in the United States, introduce to public office a new and large retinue of top advisors and administrators. It assumes that in the civil service it will find a reliable and competent corps of officials to supplement its thinking and implement its decisions. The deputy-minister as the permanent chief of a department is a non-political figure who normally brings to the aid of his minister the resources of seasoned experience and knowledge.

The lesser respect for the law, for the "rules of the game" in the United States, may be viewed as inherent in a system in which egalitarianism is strongly valued and in which diffuse elitism is lacking. Generalized deference is not accorded to those at the top; therefore, in the United States there is a greater propensity to redefine the rules or to ignore them. The legitimacy and decisions of the leadership are constantly being questioned. While Canadians incline toward the use of "lawful" and traditionally institutionalized means for altering regulations which they believe are unjust. Americans seem more disposed to employ informal and often extralegal means to correct what they perceive as wrong.

The greater lawlessness and corruption in the United States may be attributed in part to the greater strength of the achievement and self-orientation values in the more populous nation. As Robert Merton has pointed out, a strong emphasis on achievement means that "the moral mandate to achieve success thus exerts pressure to succeed, by fair means if possible and by foul means if necessary." Merton accounts for the greater adherence to approved means of behavior in much of Europe compared to the United States as derivative from variations in the emphasis on achievement for all. And the same logic implies that since Americans are more likely than their Canadian neighbors to be concerned with the achievement of ends — particularly pecuniary success — they will be less concerned with the use of the socially appropriate *means*; hence we should expect a higher incidence of deviations from conventional norms in politics and other aspects of life south of the forty-ninth parallel....

The greater diffidence of Canadians with respect to their adherence to achievement and self-orientation values may also be reflected in their reluctance to be over-optimistic, assertive, or experimentally inclined in economic affairs. This Canadian caution manifests itself in several ways: one is

> that Canadians take out more insurance *per capita* than any other race in the world. Another is that they buy considerably less on hire-purchase (installment plan) than the Americans. The average Canadian is also cautious about his savings, favouring Government bonds and savings banks. Whereas over the years the American big investor has tended to take a risk on the future of Canada and invest heavily in more speculative Canadian enterprises, the wealthy Canadian cautiously puts his money into Standard Oil of New Jersey.

The earliest empirical efforts to determine Canadian self-perceptions, made in the thirties, indicate that Canadians of that period thought of themselves as "quieter, slower in tempo, and saner in quality" than Americans, saw Americans as loud, shrewd, less honest, and more anxious to get rich quickly. Clearly, as Canadian sociologists Kaspar Naegele and Dennis Wrong have argued, the Horatio Alger success story has never taken hold in Canadian society, perhaps because of Canadian resistance to economic aggressiveness, social informality, and unabashed materialism. Canadian historian Arthur Lower has even argued that

> Henry Ford was a figure who could hardly have been other than American. Canada did not provide a stage for such as he. Yet this was not on account of lack of opportunities here (in Canada) for accumulating wealth, but rather because that process called for more betting on the sure thing than was necessary across the border.

The variation in the strength of the achievement and self-orientation values in the United States and Canada may account for another political difference — the fact that "free enterprise" ideology, though accepted in Canada, has never been the source of as violent political conflicts there as in the United States. The greater respect for government and political leaders, derived in part from elitism and in part from the need dictated by special historic circumstances requiring that the central government intervene repeatedly in economic and local political matters to assure national survival, has inhibited the development of strong economic individualism as a dominant political virtue. As James Bryce remarked some decades ago,

> The policy of *laissez-faire* has few adherents in a country which finds in governmental action or financial support to private enterprise the quickest means of carrying out every promising project. So when party conflicts arise over these matters, it is not the principle that is contested . . . but the plan advocated by the Government or the Opposition as the case may be.

Canada has clearly been much more collectivity oriented than the United States. In recent years, proposals for medicare, grants for large families, government intervention in the economy, and public ownership of major enterprises have encountered much less opposition north of the border than south of it. "The extreme economic individualism expressed by such slogans as 'the best government is the one that governs least' does not have such deep roots in Canada as it has in the United States." As one English writer notes:

> One of the strange contradictions of Canada is that although it has never had anything resembling a Socialist Government in Ottawa, the list of its "nationalized" industries is almost as imposing as Britain's: more than half the railways; the principal airline; most of radio and television; the Atomic Energy Corporation and one of the biggest uranium producers; a big plastic industry; many of the power utilities (and telephone and telegraph); and the entire liquor retailing business.

And as a Canadian points out, "it is interesting to note that at a time when the *laissez-faire* philosophy was prevailing in the rest of the Western World, there was no protest in Canada against government intervention and interference, not even from business circles...."

The emphases on achievement and self-orientation in the United States are strongly linked to universalism. In the United States there is a proclaimed need to treat everyone according to the same standard. This universalistic objective underlies the concept of the "melting pot" which holds that no one should be disqualified from full participation on the grounds of ethnic origin or other social distinctions. The melting-pot concept is the achievement orientation applied to entire ethnic groups. In contradistinction to the melting pot of the United States, Canadians speak of their society as a "mosaic," a concept which enunciates in theory the "right to sustained collective individuality." As Canadian sociologist John Porter points out, the difference between the ideas of the *melting pot* and the *mosaic* is one of the principal distinguishing features of United States and Canadian society at the level of social psychology as well as that of social structure. Vincent Massey, former governor general, has expressed the Canadian stress on the preservation of particularistic values:

> We have been successful in our manner of adjusting the relations of the varied communities making Canada their home. About one out of three speaks French as his mother tongue. He is no minority assimilated within a common Canadianism, but rather a partner sharing equally in the joint project of Confederation. Then there are the "new Canadians" of whom two million from Great Britain and from Europe have reached our shores since 1945. We try to fit in the newcomers much as they are, as pieces in the Canadian mosaic.

Canadians emphasize the contribution which diverse ethnic and linguistic groups bring to Canadian life in the form of cultural heritage. "New Canadians have been encouraged to maintain many of their distinctive folk traditions, and their songs, dress, and folklore," and they "are often publicized as indication of the richness and diversity of Canadian life — an approach to ethnic differences that is much less common in the United States...."

... Many writers seeking to account for value differences between the United States and Canada suggest that they stem in large part from the revolutionary origins of the United States and the counterrevolutionary history of Canada, from two disparate founding ethos. The Loyalist emigrés from the American Revolution and Canada's subsequent repeatedly aroused fears of United States encroachment fostered the institutionalization of a counterrevolutionary or conservative ethos. By contrast the core values of the United States, linked to the utopian ideology which emerged during the revolution, were codified in the Declaration of Independence and elaborated in the principles successfully pressed by the Jeffersonian Democrats in the formative post-Revolutionary decades.

In these counterrevolutionary beginnings of Canada, we find the clue to the continuance of British ascriptive and elitist value patterns. The Canadian historian Arthur Lower has pointed out that "in its new wilderness home and its new aspect of British North Americanism, colonial Toryism made its second attempt to erect on American soil a copy of the English social edifice. From one point of view this is the most significant thing about the Loyalist movement; it withdrew a class concept of life from the south, moved it up north and gave it a second chance."

During the American Revolution, Nova Scotia had a population of 17,000; almost double the number of Loyalists entered it afterward, "swallowing the older 'neutral Yankee' elements in an ardently Loyalist mass." New Brunswick was set up as a separate province in 1784, largely because of the great Loyalist influx. The Loyalist settlers in Upper Canada (now Ontario)

> would form the backbone of western resistance in a second war with the United States, the War of 1812. They were the original founders of the present province of Ontario, and did much to mould its character. On one hand, they brought to Canada a conservative outlook, a quick distrust of any new idea that might be called republican, and a readiness to make loyalty the test for almost everything. On the other, they themselves represented a declaration of independence against the United States, a determination to live apart from that country in North America.

Thus Tory conservatism and anti-Americanism affected "not only the St. John Valley where the Loyalists were a majority, but other regions where they were a minority." These "interlocked neatly with the prevalent conceptions of oligarchy and privilege."

After the Revolution, undisguised efforts were made to check American influences. Simcoe and Carleton, the first governors of what is now Ontario and Quebec, were men who had played a leading role in fighting the Revolution. To them republican principles were an anathema. The antirevolutionary and anti-American character of Canada's political and social development helped strengthen ethnic particularism and ecclesiasticism. The English Protestant rulers of French Canada opposed assimilation and weakening of the semi-Establishment status of the Catholic church in Quebec as a means of resisting Americanization. Sir Robert Falconer says that "as late as 1822 Lord Dalhousie favored the French Canadians of the lower province as a means of make-weight against Americanizing tendencies which he discerned in Upper Canada." Support for the hierarchically organized churches, Anglican and Roman, served to reinforce hierarchical, anti-democratic tendencies. As the famed Canadian historian Harold Innis noted, a "counterrevolutionary tradition implies an emphasis on ecclesiasticism."

Continued Canadian allegiance to the British Monarchy undoubtedly has also contributed to the greater sense of legitimacy for hierarchical distinctions characteristic of the northern nation. In the early history of Canada, the public authorities tried consciously to foster such values as a barrier to American influences....

The unification of the British North American colonies into a federal union was procured by Empire-oriented Canadian Conservatives who feared United States expansion across the border, and the growth in influence within Canada of reform-minded "pro-American" frontier settlers who favored local autonomy. The decision to provide Canada with a strong central government, which unlike that of the United States would be able to veto or "disallow" provincial laws, was designed to resist the democratic threat within and across the border. According to W.L. Morton,

> With the Reformers committed to local democracy, and the Conservatives to continental expansionism, it is not surprising that Confederation was, by and large, a Conservative party measure, and also a measure conservative in tone and substance. A striking venture in federalism, it neither, except in establishing representation by population, widened the basis of self-government nor altered the depository of sovereignty.

In contrast to Canada, the United States is the result of successful revolution and prolonged war of independence organized around the ideology embodied in the Declaration of Independence, which proclaimed the validity of egalitarian and universalistic social relations. Out of a sort of Utopian conception of men's egalitarian and universalistic relations with one another a national consciousness arose which infused men with a new awareness and new confidence in what they were and in their own kind. The new value consensus and normative prescriptions of the American people were sustained by at least two major conditions: territorial expansion and nonalignment with European nations.

In newly independent societies there has often been a transition from a system dominated by traditionalist, usually aristocratic, values to one characterized by egalitarian concepts. Consequently, most struggles for independence have employed leftist ideologies — socialism today, and equality in revolutionary America — in which man's status is to depend not upon inherited but achieved qualities. Thus the system in America was geared to abolish all forms of privilege and primogeniture and to reward achievement.

Despite the conviction of many revolutionary leaders that the struggle for independence was primarily an issue of political and national independence, large segments of the American people organized against the emergence of any ruling oligarchical forces. Many insisted that the franchise be extended to everyone, that the people be regarded as the source of power and authority. The very early arguments for the extension of the suffrage to all were "based on the rights of man given special impetus by the Declaration of Independence and the terms of conflict of the American Revolution." ...

The significance of the "leftist" egalitarian populist character of core values in the American political tradition may best be perceived from the vantage point of comparative North American history. For although American historians and political philosophers may debate the extent of radicalism, liberalism, leftism, or even conservatism, in Revolutionary and postcolonial American politics, there is little doubt in the mind of most Canadian historians. Looking at the divergent political history north and south of the border, they see the continued politics of their nation as reflecting the fact that it is a descendant of a counterrevolution, while the United States is a product of a successful revolution. Once these events had formed the structure of the two nations, their institutional characters were set. Subsequent events tended to enforce "leftist" values in the south and "rightist" ones in the north. The success of the Revolutionary ideology, the defeat of the Tories, and the emigration of many of them north to Canada or across the ocean to Britain — all served to enhance the strength of the forces favoring egalitarian democratic principles in the new nation and to weaken conservative tendencies. On the other hand, the failure of Canada to have a revolution of its own, the immigration of conservative elements, and the emigration of radical ones — all contributed in making Canada a more conservative and more rigidly stratified society. This does not mean, as S.D. Clark has pointed out, "that revolutionary forces developed no strength in Canada. We have had our revolutions but they have been largely unsuccessful, and being unsuccessful we try to forget them. Thus we have tended to dismiss our rebels of the past as misguided individuals out of accord with their fellow Canadians." ...

... The differences between American and Canadian religion have been of considerable significance in producing the admittedly small differences between the values of the two countries, as well as affecting national differences in political and economic development. Denominational religion, often evangelistic, secular, and voluntary in character, has contributed to the American emphasis on self-orientation, egalitarianism, universalism, and achievement. Conversely, religion in Canada retained its ecclesiastic character and its strong relationship to the state with the consequence that religious organization in Canada, emphasizing elitism and particularism, acted as a counterforce inhibiting excessive individualism (self-orientation) and egalitarianism.

In the first half century of the American Republic, the champions of religious traditionalism were seriously weakened, as the various state churches — Anglican in the South and Congregationalist in New England — were gradually disestablished. From the beginning, the United States was heir to a Calvinistic Puritanism which was stronger in the colonies than in the mother country, and it was congenial to modernity in a sense that the Anglican Church in English Canada and the Gallican Church in Quebec were not. The two denominations, Methodist and Baptist, which became dominant in the early nineteenth century, stressed religious doctrines that supported "anti-aristocratic tendencies." ...

The abolition of established religion in the United States fostered a strong commitment to voluntarism. This commitment, together with the considerable strength of the dissenting and anti-statist Methodist and Baptist denominations, meant that religion not only contributed to the economic orientations of the people, but also reinforced the egalitarian and democratic social ethos. Tocqueville pointed out that all American denominations were minorities and hence had an interest in liberty and a weak state. As he put it in discussing Catholics: "They constitute a minority, and all rights must be respected in order to assure to them the free exercise of their own privileges. These ... causes induce them, even unconsciously, to adopt political doctrines which they would perhaps support with less zeal if they were preponderant." Denominational voluntaristic religion not only reinforced the support for minority rights in the religious sphere, but also found deeply religious men in government arguing strongly that the rights of the irreligious and of Jews must be the same of those of Christians.

In Canada state-related religion has provided that country with a hierarchical and traditionally rooted control mechanism that is largely lacking in United States history. Because of the strong tie between church and state in Canada, religious development there, in contrast to religious movements in the United States, has been less prone to both fundamentalism and experimentalism.

Both the Church of England and the Roman Catholic Church, which were hierarchically organized and received overt governmental support, gave strong support to the established political and social order. Hence one found mutually reinforcing conservative forces at the summits of the class, church and political structures.

The interlocking character of political and religious conservatism may be seen in the extent to which patterns of marriage and divorce have been affected by religious practices. As recently as World War II, the law of most provinces, including Ontario, did not provide for civil marriage. The extent to which Canadian religion has been more successful than American in maintaining traditional and conservative principles may be seen in the much lower divorce rate in Canada as compared with the United States. The greater moral conservatism of English Canada is also revealed in the fact that many "blue laws" and Sunday observance regulations remained in force much longer in the north than the south, and, in fact, a number of such restrictions on behaviour still exist in many Canadian cities.

The ecclesiastical character of the predominant Canadian religions has also greatly inhibited the development of egalitarian and achievement emphases comparable to those fostered by anti-elitist sects and denominations in the United States. American Protestantism, with its emphasis on the personal attainment of grace, reinforced the stress on personal achievement dominant in the secular value system. Both sets of values stressed individual responsibility, both rejected hereditary status. The Methodists and Baptists, who together contained the great majority of American Protestants, stressed religious doctrines that reinforced "anti-aristocratic tendencies." In English Canada, the Anglican Church "set a standard of dignity for all the leading denominations which was absent in the United States." . . .

Religious sects have, of course, developed in Canada, facilitated by much the same social conditions inherent in rapid social change as in the United States, i.e., the heavy shift of population to the frontier or the growing cities and the related social mobility, which have torn individuals from their traditional ties and made them available for recruitment to new loyalties. However, the fact that religion is less explicitly separated from the "national community" in Canada has meant that sects have been less able to survive there than in the United States. . . .

. . . Once the historic sects allied themselves with the established institutions in the community, their differences became less important and they found it easier to forget about sectarian beliefs and unite. As a result the union of the major "nonconformist" Protestant denominations proceeded much more rapidly in Canada than in the United States. The United Church of Canada was formed in 1925 out of a merger of Methodist, Presbyterian, and Congregationalist denominations. In many parts of English Canada, it now shares an unofficial but real "establishment" status with the Anglican church. . . .

. . . Some of the flavor of the social distinctions in Canada and the United States which reflect the greater strength of traditionalist and conservative values in the former may be traced also to a Canadian frontier fashioned in a spirit of cautious defensiveness against American absorptionist tendencies. For this reason, "It was the established tradition of British North America that the power of the civil authority should operate well in advance of the spread of settlement."

> This famous force (Mounted Police) was organized in 1874. To the 300 men who composed it was given the task of seeing that the law was obeyed from

Manitoba to the Rockies and from the forty-ninth parallel to the Arctic Circle. Organized whiskey traffic with the Indians was broken up within a year. Horse stealing was made so precarious that there was seldom need for the drastic community action which was the normal procedure in many parts of the American West. Perhaps most important of all, Canada was enabled to avoid the series of desperate conflicts with the Indians which was necessary to clear the way for the final advance of settlement in the United States.

The Canadians, being more prone to identify liberty and democracy with legal traditions and procedures than with populism, the right of the people to rule, or with the freedom of business and enterprise, have given equal juridical rights to minority and ethnic groups, while in the United States debates over the position of minority groups have been at the root of Indian wars and of the Civil War. On the American frontier the quality of law enforcement was often dependent on local police authority which reflected the values of the frontiersmen, including their prejudices against Indians and their lack of understanding for legal procedures incorporating the guarantee of due process. In Canada, Indian chiefs "were impressed by the fact that, if Indians were punished for crimes against the whites, the whites were equally punished for outrages against the Indians. Their previous experience (with American whites) had taught them to appreciate such impartial justice." The Queen's peace was maintained even in the mining camps, which were characteristically undisciplined in the United States. Conditions during the gold rush in British Columbia differed greatly from those in the American Western mining frontier. There were no vigilantes or massacres of Indians.

The presence of national governmental controls weakened the development of excessive individualism which expressed itself south of the border in a greater faith in the future and a greater willingness to risk capital, personal security, or reputation. The Canadian frontier experience did not undermine the traditional bases of authority; Canadians even on the frontier retained a more deeply internalized sense of obligation, of the need to conform to the rules even when there was no visible threat of coercion. As the Canadian historian Arthur Lower has put it:

> We have always carried authority and a code along with us, no matter how far from "the law" we have happened momentarily to be.... The result has been less non-conformity in Canadian life than in America, less experimentation, more acceptance of standards built up in the long history of the English-speaking race.

The frontier settlers in both North American nations spawned important reformist movements. They tended to see themselves as exploited by the dominant economic and political power centered in the Eastern cities. To a considerable extent, those located at the farther reaches of the nation sought to free themselves from this control. "It was this insistence upon local autonomy, this separatist spirit, which was the dominant characteristic of those revolutionary or reform movements which grew up in the interior parts of the continent." For Canada, frontier separatism was always a threat to the integrity of the nation, and often constituted a pro-American liberal response. The Canadian government consequently engaged in systematic actions to reduce frontier autonomy, to guarantee that national institutions and values would dominate on the frontier. The American government, however, had no reason to fear that frontier movements would be a source of secessionism, or would lead to demands for incorporation by a foreign neighbor.

In the United States, frontier agricultural, ranching, and mining areas, uncontrolled for long periods by any central government or policing system, provided unlimited opportunities, and disposed settlers to use their own resources as they saw fit. And these rugged individualists, the cowboy, the frontiersman, and even the vigilante, not the uniformed disciplined Mountie, are the heroes of American Western settlement. The frontiersman, on the other hand, has never been a figure for special glorification in Canadian literature as he has been in American. "Canadian writers and critics drew back in well-bred horror from the distasteful crudities of the frontier, and looked, more resolutely than ever, eastward across the Atlantic to the source of all good things."

Geography also served to reinforce social factors in reducing the influence of the more democratic and egalitarian practices of the frontier on the rest of the country. The Canadian prairies, the provinces of Manitoba, Saskatchewan, and Alberta, were separated from the populous East by the Great Lakes and a one-thousand-mile, almost uninhabitable, rock shield which ran north of the lakes. These "provided an effective barrier to close and constant intercourse." And these same geographic factors reinforced the need for systematic government intervention to assure communications, since private enterprise could not afford the great cost of bridging the gap between East and West.

> The colonization of the West, in Canada, was to a large extent a government enterprise and not a purely private venture as in the United States. The central government owned the land, brought the people, mainly immigrants, provided directly or indirectly the transport system and made sure that wheat would move within Canada at low rates.

The considerable involvement of the Canadian government in fostering economic development enhanced the emphasis on collectivity as distinct from self-orientation values discussed earlier. Whether Conservative or Liberal, leftist or rightist, Canadian political leaders have recognized that a sparsely settled country bordering on a wealthy, powerful, and attractive neighbor must supply many services through governmental agencies which could be furnished by private enterprise in nations with more densely settled populations....

Canadian national identity is clearly not bound up with the ideology of a successful revolution or a dramatic political movement. Rather, as we have seen, Canadian identity is the product of a victorious counterrevolution, and in a sense must justify its *raison d'être* by emphasizing the virtues of being separate from the United States. Frank Underhill has pointed out that Canadians are the world's oldest and continuing anti-Americans. The Canadian sense of nationality has always felt itself threatened by the United States, physically in earlier days, and culturally and economically in more recent years. As S.D. Clark has put it: "Canadian national life can almost be said to take its rise in the negative will to resist absorption in the American Republic. It is largely about the United States as an object that the consciousness of Canadian national unity has grown up.". . .

There is at present extensive United States capital investment in Canada, high consumption of American goods, and wide circulation of American communication media. Many have rebelled against this penetration into Canadian life. The Canadian nationalist points to such facts as proof of "domination" by the United States.

Nationalism in English Canada has undergone some curious changes from the time when it represented a left-wing, often pro-United States protest against the Imperial connection, and the closed economic-political-ecclesiastical system sustained by this connection. Today it is often the left-winger who is most anti-American and pro-British. The more traditional form of Canadian nationalism would seem to continue in the French-Canadian protest movements with their anti-English and anti-establishment overtones directed at those within Canadian borders who represent English cultural, political, and economic domination. As English Canadians seek to isolate Canada from the United States, French Canadians look for means to assure the safety of their culture surrounded by 200 million English speakers. In a sense both English and French Canadians have similar objectives, to protect two tiny minority cultures from being absorbed by more powerful neighbors.

Mosaic versus Melting Pot?: Immigration and Ethnicity in Canada and the United States

HOWARD PALMER

Many Canadians believe that Canada's experience with ethnicity, at the level of both social attitudes and social reality, has been different from that of the United States. This difference is often envisioned as one between a Canadian mosaic, where ethnic groups have maintained their distinctiveness while functioning as part of the whole, and an American melting pot, where peoples of diverse origins have allegedly fused to make a new people. There is, of course, some truth to this distinction, but it oversimplifies both the American and the Canadian experiences. It ignores the fact that the mosaic approach has not always been the prevailing attitude toward immigrant adjustment in Canada. It obscures the fact that Canada and the United States have shared very similar immigration policies (particularly on the question of which ethnic, national, and racial groups were the most desirable), and it neglects the fact that, at least with regard to immigrant groups, the history of racism, nativism, and discrimination has been very similar in the two countries.

In comparing the American and Canadian experiences with immigration and ethnicity, the focus of this paper is on immigration policy, nativist (or anti-foreign) sentiment, and public attitudes toward immigrant adjustment, rather than on the degree to which immigrant ethnic groups have survived as distinct cultural entities within the two societies. An examination of public attitudes toward ethnic minorities reveals basic assumptions about ethnicity which can be traced over time. Some attempt is also made to look at the consequences of attitudes toward immigration and ethnicity by examining the influence of public opinion on immigration policy and by analysing patterns of discrimination. The actual rates of assimilation of different immigrant groups are more difficult to determine — because of the combined difficulty of defining what one means by the term assimilation and of ascertaining rates of assimilation from available historical records, and also because of the dearth of studies which compare the experiences of one particular minority group on both sides of the border. In discussing ethnicity in Canada and the United States, I have limited my attention to "immigrant" groups in the post-1867 period, thus excluding any discussion of the maintenance of

---

Abridged from Howard Palmer, "Mosaic versus Melting Pot?: Immigration and Ethnicity in Canada and the United States," *International Journal* (Summer 1976), pp. 488–528. Reprinted by permission of the author and the publisher.

ethnicity among Canada's French and British colonists or American blacks (who were forcibly brought to America) or the native peoples.

In Canada, as in the United States, three theories of assimilation have dominated discussion of immigrant adjustment in the past century: first, Anglo-conformity (and, in Canada, its French-Canadian counterpart, Franco-conformity) demanded the renunciation of the immigrants' ancestral culture and traditions in favour of the behaviour and values of the "Anglo-Saxon" group; secondly, the "melting pot" envisaged a biological merging of settled communities with new immigrant groups and a blending of their cultures into a new Canadian type; and thirdly, "cultural pluralism" (also referred to in Canada as the "mosaic" or "multiculturalism") postulated the preservation of some aspects of immigrant culture and communal life within the context of Canadian citizenship and political and economic integration into Canadian society. These three approaches have had varying degrees of acceptance in the two countries and there have of course been shifts in public opinion. In English-speaking Canada, because of the economic, social, and political predominance of the British group and because of Canada's colonial ties to Britain, Anglo-conformity was the main approach to assimilation until the Second World War (although there were some advocates of the melting pot and of cultural pluralism during the 1920s and 1930s).

In the United States, where a "new nation" was being consciously formed, Anglo-conformity was not as powerful and the melting pot approach prevailed throughout the late nineteenth and twentieth centuries and into the 1960s. As numerous historians and sociologists have pointed out, the melting pot did not always melt, and many of those who advocated the melting pot drew lines as to who should be included in the pot (non-whites were usually excluded, at both the level of social attitudes and social reality). Nonetheless, the melting pot idea (as envisaged by the Franco-American farmer Crèvecoeur in *Letters From an American Farmer* and by the Jewish-American playwright Israel Zangwill in his epic drama, *The Melting Pot*) served as the most pervasive ideal toward which Americans should be striving. However, a variety of factors has helped to make cultural pluralism more acceptable in both Canada and the United States during the last fifteen years. New quasi-social movements have developed in each country advocating pluralism — in Canada under the rubric of multiculturalism, and in the United States under the rubric of the "new ethnicity." These movements are remarkably similar, and an attempt is made later in the paper to compare them, as well as the debate which each has provoked.

THE IMMIGRATION BOOM AND ANGLO-CONFORMITY 1867-1920

The central element in Canada's history and cultural development has been the existence of two cultures, British and French. The two peoples had been made co-inhabitants of British North America by the British conquest of 1759.

It has been argued that the American revolutionary movement helped to guarantee the survival of French society in North America by forcing the British government to give full recognition to existing French institutions in the Quebec Act of 1774, thus ensuring the loyalty of the French to Britain at a time when the other colonies in North America were moving toward rebellion. Consequently, the fate of French culture in British North America was to be substantially different from its fate in Louisiana, where its persistence was limited largely to isolated rural parishes. Among the several objectives of the architects of the Canadian confederation in 1867, none was more important than the effort to accommodate the needs of these two cultural communities; the political arrangement of federalism was seen as the best way of doing this. There was virtually no recognition of ethnic diversity aside from the British-French duality. This is, of course, somewhat understandable since at the time of Confederation, only 8 per cent of the population of three and one-half million were of non-British or non-French ethnic origin.

Immigration to Canada remained slight until nearly the turn of the century because the United States proved more attractive for most European emigrants. In fact, the United States was attractive for many Canadians as well, and the dominion barely maintained its net population. But with the closing of the American frontier around 1890 which coincided with improving economic conditions in Canada and an active immigration promotion campaign by Wilfrid Laurier's Liberal government, many immigrants began to come to the newly opened land of western Canada in the late 1890s.

The early years of this century were the boom years for immigration to both countries. Between 1900 and 1920, three million immigrants came to Canada, while nearly fifteen million went to the United States. Between 1901 and 1911, Canada's population jumped by 43 per cent and immigrants came to constitute more than 22 per cent of the population. Between 1900 and 1910, the American population increased by 21 per cent with immigrants representing 15 per cent of the population. A comparison of the composition of the two flows shows that the United States drew much more heavily on the "new" immigration from central, southern, and eastern Europe. Between 1900 and 1910, one-third of the immigrants coming to Canada were from central, southern, and eastern Europe while 71 per cent of those going to the United States were from these areas. Thus, by 1920 there was a much larger proportion of Jews, Italians, Greeks, South Slavs, and Poles in the United States than in Canada because these groups were more urban bound, and Canada was seeking immigrants who would farm. There was, however, a selective migration from eastern Europe to Canada of those groups most devoted to agriculture — Mennonites, Doukhobors, and Ukrainians. British immigrants formed a much larger proportion of the immigrants coming to Canada, in part because Canadian policy actively encouraged British immigrants, and also because many Britons preferred to remain in the empire. Indeed the British formed the largest group coming to Canada at this time, followed in numbers by the over half a million Americans who came to the prairie provinces to continue farming.

The destination of non-British immigrants was different in the two countries. Non-British immigrants in the United States concentrated in the large urban centres, while those in Canada were found for the most part in rural areas of western Canada since Canadian immigration policy was geared to securing farmers. Some non-British immigrants who came to Canada did find jobs working in mines, on the railways, or doing the menial and difficult labour jobs in cities like Vancouver, Winnipeg, and Toronto. But Canada wanted farmers to settle the west, and the United States sought an industrial working class for its expanding industries. It was these needs that helped determine where the immigrants went.

Throughout the entire period of this large-scale immigration, indeed until World War II, Anglo-conformity was the predominant ideology of assimilation in English-speaking Canada. For better or for worse, there were few proponents of either the melting pot or cultural pluralism, contrary to the flood of recent political speeches and scholarly articles on ethnicity in Canada which assume that the "mosaic" approach has always been predominant. Supporters of Anglo-conformity argued that it was the obligation of new arrivals to conform to the institutions of Canadian society — which were already fixed. If the immigrant could not conform, he should be excluded. These English Canadians shared the American view of which groups could be assimilated most readily and which nationalities were cause for concern. British immigrants may have been considered more desirable in Canada than in the United States, but generally northern Europeans were welcomed in both countries since they were regarded as the most culturally similar and, hence, the most easily assimilable immigrants.

As in the United States, considerable opposition developed in Canada to Asians and to those from central, southern, and eastern Europe. There were widespread fears that these immigrants could not be assimilated. While concern about an alleged connection between immigration and slums, radicalism, intemperance, and criminality served as a powerful support for nativism, the most pervasive fear of opinion leaders was that southern and eastern Europeans would wash away Anglo-Saxon traditions of self-government in a sea of illiteracy and inexperience with "free" institutions. Many American and English-Canadian intellectuals thought that North America's greatness was ensured so long as its Anglo-Saxon character was preserved. Writers emphasized an Anglo-Saxon tradition of political freedom and self-government and the "white man's" mission to spread Anglo-Saxon blessings. Many intellectuals viewed Asians and central, southern, and eastern Europeans as a threat to this tradition and concluded that since they could not be assimilated, they would have to be excluded. Thus, the introduction in Canada of a head tax on Chinese immigrants, a "gentlemen's agreement" with Japan which restricted the number of immigrants from that country, the passing of orders in council which restricted immigration from India, the gradual introduction of restrictive immigration laws in 1906, 1910, and 1919, and the tightening of naturalization laws were based in considerable part on the assumptions of Anglo-conformity — immigrants who were culturally or racially inferior (or at least different) and incapable of being assimilated should be excluded.

Patterns of discrimination in both Canada and the United States after 1870 paralleled preferences of immigrant sources with northern and western Europeans encountering relatively little discrimination, central and southern Europeans and Jews encountering more discrimination, and non-whites encountering an all-pervasive pattern of discrimination which extended to almost all aspects of their lives. Discrimination was one of the main factors which led to the transference (with only a few exceptions) of the same ethnic "pecking order" which existed in immigration policy to the place each group occupied in the social structure with the British at the highest levels, and so on down to the Chinese and blacks who occupied the lowest levels. The effects of such discrimination were felt not only in the economy, but also in local and national politics. Restricted access to the labour market and to political participation severely limited the social power of central, southern, and eastern Europeans and non-whites in both countries right up to the Second World War.

Although the trend toward restrictionism in Canada during the early 1900s and the existing patterns of discrimination reveal the predominance of the assumptions of Anglo-conformity, for the most part there was no explicit federal government policy between 1867 and 1945 with regard to the role of non-British and non-French ethnic groups in Canadian society. It was generally assumed, however, that immigrants would eventually be assimilated into either English-Canadian or French-Canadian society. The federal government's main concern was tied to the economic consequences of immigration. It had encouraged Mennonites and Icelanders to settle in blocs in Manitoba during the 1870s and had given them special concessions (including local autonomy for both and military exemptions for the Mennonites) to entice them to stay in Canada rather than move to the United States. This was not because of any conscious desire to make Canada a cultural mosaic, or because of any belief in the value of cultural diversity (although politicians sometimes gave lip service to pluralism). Rather, as the American railway companies had earlier discovered in their immigration settlement operations, bloc settlements, by providing social and economic stability, were a way of getting immigrants to settle in the west and remain there. The government's policy was pragmatic and concerned primarily with economic growth and nation-building; there was little rhetoric in immigration propaganda picturing Canada as a home for the oppressed.

Provincial governments were faced with the problems of assimilation more directly than the federal government since the provinces maintained jurisdiction over the educational systems. The whole question of the varying attitudes of provincial authorities toward assimilation is much too complex to outline here; suffice it to say that with some notable exceptions (like the bilingual school system in Manitoba between 1896 and 1916 which included French-English, German-English, Polish-English, and Ukrainian-English schools and the school system which was established for Hutterites in Alberta), Anglo-conformity was the predominant aim of the public school system and was an underlying theme in the textbooks....

While Anglo-conformity prevailed in English-speaking Canada prior to World War II, Franco-conformity, or assimilation to a French-Canadian norm, was not widely promoted in Quebec. Most French Canadians did not espouse any ideology of assimilation with regard to "other ethnic groups" (as non-British, non-French, and non-native groups were later designated by the Royal Commission on Bilingualism and Biculturalism). They were generally more preoccupied with the defence of their own status. Also, relatively few non-British, non-French immigrants went to Quebec, and a large number of those in Quebec were Jews who did not want to be assimilated into French-Canadian society and whom French Canadians did not want to assimilate. Nationalist critics of Laurier's immigration policy like Henri Bourassa did not try to urge a policy of Franco-conformity as a French-Canadian counterpart to Anglo-conformity. Their argument held that immigrants were upsetting Canada's demographic balance (because of the small numbers of French immigrants) and therefore they should all be excluded. There has been little research on the attitudes of French Canadians in western Canada towards other ethnic groups, although we do know that their clergy made special attempts to secure Ukrainian and Polish priests to ensure that these immigrants would not be assimilated into the Protestant majority. Yet while some of the French-Canadian clergy were acting out their belief in pluralism, other French-Canadian nationalists were arguing that pluralism threatened French Canada, since it would ultimately generate demands by the English-speaking majority for the assimilation of French Canadians along with other minorities in order to avoid social and linguistic chaos. These French-Canadian nationalists feared, as some still do, that non-British, non-French immigration would undermine a bicultural perception of Canada.

The more one scratches the surface of the period up to 1920, the more difficult it becomes to differentiate between the immigration histories of Canada and the United States. In Canada, the existence of French Canada, the rural destination of the majority of immigrants, the size of the different groups, and the different political system did give a different face to the immigrant experience. But once one begins to examine the two basic questions of how the host society regarded the immigrants and what was the nature of immigrant life, one must come to the conclusion that these differences are relatively minor. If one looks at the experience of immigrant groups in terms of emigration area, causes of emigration, the traffic and business of immigration, the problems of adjustment, the process of chain migration and the natural ecology of immigrant neighbourhoods, the reasons for and the types of ethnic businesses and organizations, the reasons for and types of conflict both within individual ethnic groups and between groups, class position and areas of occupational specialization, and efforts at language and cultural maintenance, parallels keep emerging between the experiences of both groups on both sides of the border. This is not to say that the experiences were identical, but there were probably more variations between individual immigrant groups, and between different regions of the two countries, than there were between the two countries as a whole....

In analysing the development of immigration policy, the course of nativist sentiment, and attitudes toward assimilation, one is again confronted by basic similarities between Canada and the United States. Although they began in the late 1800s with basically open immigration policies, both countries gradually restricted immigration in response to nativist concern about the biological and social impact of southern, central, and eastern Europeans and Asians and in response to labour organizations worried about economic competition.

The three main strands of nativism which John Higham has delineated in his study of American nativism — Anglo-Saxon nativism, anti-Catholic nativism, and anti-radical nativism — also had considerable impact on Canada. Each nativist tradition had however a slightly different origin within the Canadian context. Fears about the decline of Anglo-Saxon "stock" were given added impetus by the colonial desire to preserve Canada as "British." Anti-Catholicism was complicated by the fact that the largest single group of Catholics in Canada was French-speaking. The existence of French Canada gave Catholics a greater sense of legitimacy in Canada; yet at the same time anti-French feelings could add additional fuel to Protestant anti-Catholicism. The American anti-radical nativist view that violent opposition to the status quo was "characteristically European and profoundly un-American" also had its Canadian counterpart. But Canadian hostility to radicalism did not stem from a "liberal" tradition as it did in the United States. Rather, it stemmed from the basic conservatism of Canadian values and politics which emphasized order rather than liberty. While in each country the timing of each of the expressions of nativism was different, nativist sentiments appealed to basically the same social and economic groups in each country and had a comparable impact on the formation of national policy, particularly during the First World War....

THE SECOND WORLD WAR AND POSTWAR IMMIGRATION 1940-1960

The war and early postwar years were a transitional time in both countries with respect to attitudes toward immigration and ethnicity. Although the outbreak of war brought renewed hostility toward enemy aliens, a number of developments during the war eventually worked to undermine ethnic prejudices. Many prewar prejudices lingered and ethnic minorities encountered considerable pressure for conformity during the new wave of immigration to Canada and the United States in the late 1940s and 1950s, but economic prosperity and changing intellectual and social assumptions diminished nativism and prejudice and helped pave the way for a growing acceptance of pluralism by the 1960s.

The war period itself hardly seemed conducive to ethnic tolerance or pluralism. Patriotic groups grew quickly and many turned their attention to the loyalty of "enemy aliens." Germans and Italians, since they were now well established, did not meet the same degree of hostility in either country that the Germans had faced in World War I. But the Japanese encountered intense enmity. The irrational build-up of hostility toward the Japanese on the west coasts of both countries and their forced relocation inland indicated that in both countries there was continuing racism, a complete ignorance of the history of a group which had been in North America for forty years, and a continued willingness on the part of both governments to respond to public bigotry and violate the civil rights of ethnic minorities who were regarded as second-class citizens. . . .

A new wave of emigration to both Canada and the United States commenced after the Second World War with the influx of refugees from wartorn Europe and the arrival of thousands of German, Dutch, and British immigrants seeking better economic opportunities. The 1950s and 1960s also brought to Canada a growing number of immigrants from Mediterranean countries — Portugal, Greece, and particularly Italy, thus serving to make the ethnic composition of Canada more like that of the United States, since the United States had previously had much larger communities from Mediterranean countries.

But the immigrants who were involved in this wave of immigration were still predominantly European. This reflected the continuing assimilationist and racist basis of postwar immigration policy in both countries which gave preference to northern Europeans and virtually excluded Asians and other non-whites. Prime Minister Mackenzie King probably spoke for the majority of Canadians in his 1947 speech outlining the federal government's postwar immigration policy when he stated that immigration should be limited to those groups that could be "absorbed." In the United States, the McCarran-Walter Act of 1952 preserved the quota system based on national origin instituted in 1924 and thus upheld the view that immigration laws should be based on assimilationist and racist assumptions. Both Canada and the United States did, however, make provisions for small numbers of Asian immigrants to allow for family reunifications.

In Canada, there was much less resistance to these postwar immigrants from Europe than there had been to earlier arrivals from eastern Europe. The two principal political forces of resistance to immigration — French

Canadians and organized labour — had modified their positions by the end of the war and were favourable to immigration. Opposition from these groups had dwindled as they became convinced of the connection between immigration and economic growth, as the government promised to take greater control over the whole immigration process, and as pressures for ethnic tolerance were brought increasingly to bear. The revulsion against Hitler and Nazism had also extended to a discrediting of ideas of a superior race. Most English-speaking Canadians were favourable to immigration: the allegiance in Canada to all things British was in retreat, earlier arrivals had accustomed English Canadians to diversity, the war had enabled some previously unaccepted groups to prove their loyalty, and the tie between immigration and economic growth was firmly cemented in the public mind. Although all of these factors played their part in increasing the acceptance of immigrants, probably the most important factor in both Canada and the United States was the large proportion of educated and skilled individuals among the postwar immigrants. In a break with prewar policy, during the 1950s both countries began to seek out skilled industrial and urban-oriented immigrants capable of assisting industrial expansion and of "integrating" more rapidly than rural immigrants. The settler in a sheepskin coat and the "huddled masses yearning to breathe free" were replaced by immigrants with a slide rule. Hence the greater acceptance of immigrants in the postwar period in both Canada and the United States stems only partly from increased levels of tolerance.

It was not until the early 1960s that international pressures for ethnic tolerance and a growing realization of the inequity of the existing immigration laws finally led to the introduction of regulations which eliminated the old ethnic and racial biases in both Canada and the United States. In Canada, changing immigration regulations in 1962 eliminated the old geographic preferences while in the United States the Immigration and Nationality Act of 1965 removed racial discrimination as embodied in the national origins quota system. In both countries, these changes have brought an increasing number of non-whites, sparking renewed controversy over the desirability of non-white immigration, particularly in Canada (which has admitted a proportionately larger number of non-whites).

Both countries now emphasize as basic cornerstones of their immigration policy family reunification, the need for skilled and professional immigrants, the need to make immigrants fit labour market requirements, and a willingness to make special provisions for refugees.

The crucial difference between the postwar immigration policies of Canada and the United States has not been so much in which types of immigration or which nationalities were allowed to enter (though there are some important differences), but in the numbers of immigrants which have entered. In the postwar period, roughly half as many immigrants have entered Canada as the United States, although Canada has only one-tenth the population of the United States. Given the importance of immigration to the maintenance of ethnicity, this difference is really the key fact in explaining differences in current developments in Canada and the United States. Ethnicity and immigrant life are now more visible in Canada than in the United States, particularly in the large metropolitan centres of Toronto, Montreal, and Vancouver (the destinations of the majority of postwar immigrants). There are simply no American cities which now compare with Toronto as an "immigrant city." In some respects, Toronto is the successor to cities like New York, Chicago, and Winnipeg which were the "immigrant cities" at the turn of the century.

Differing government policies toward ethnic minorities already in the country did not play an important role during the 1950s and 1960s in determining this greater visibility of ethnicity on the Canadian scene. As sociologist Jean Burnet has pointed out,

> Prior to 1971, the ideology concerning ethnic relations in Canada was summed up in the term mosaic, and its floral and gustatory analogues — bouquet, flower garden, salad, vegetable soup, stew. The mosaic was proudly contrasted with the American melting pot. However, less effort was expended by Canadian governments to maintain the mosaic than was spent by governments in the United States to keep the melting pot bubbling: in the public school systems and in broadcasting, to take only one example from provincial and one from federal jurisdiction, no tangible aid was given to ethnic groups in preserving their old-world heritages, and, on the contrary, considerable pressure was exerted in the direction of "integration" or "assimilation." The mosaic was lent support chiefly in speeches by governors general and by politicians.

How can we account for Canada's greater willingness to allow immigrants to enter in the postwar period? Was it primarily a result of a greater degree of tolerance and acceptance of immigrants in Canadian society? Or was it due basically to different levels of economic development in the two countries? Canada has not accepted immigrants for primarily humanitarian reasons. Throughout the postwar period, immigration has been closely linked to Canada's economic needs. Immigrants have filled skilled technical and professional jobs when the country's educational system was not producing enough people to keep pace with Canada's industrial growth. Immigrants have also filled many of the jobs which Canadians were unwilling to do — including work in resource industries in remote frontier areas as well as menial jobs and the backbreaking construction work in Canada's burgeoning metropolitan centres. The United States has also drawn on immigrants to do jobs which Americans do not want such as hand labour in agriculture, but its large urban centres have been able to draw on large numbers of migrants (both black and white) from the south to fill the jobs on the lower end of the economic scale. Public opinion in Canada has not been notably open in its attitudes toward immigration — indeed since 1952, over half of those surveyed in Gallup polls have said that Canada does not need more immigrants. Therefore it is difficult to say whether Canada's greater willingness to accept immigrants is a question of Canadians being more open to immigration, or simply a question of politicians in Canada being less responsive to negative opinion. There is no denying, however, that proportionate to its size, Canada has accepted a much greater number of immigrants than has the United States, including a significantly larger proportion of refugees and displaced persons.

It would seem that although immigration and immigrants are more a part of the national symbolism and national consciousness of the United States, postwar Canada has had a greater sense of openness and unfulfilled expectations and, hence, has been more open to immigration. For most Americans, the basic contours of their society had already been formed, while Canadians have had a greater sense of a nation in the making. This may be one of the reasons for Canada's greater willingness to accept immigrants.

MULTICULTURALISM AND THE "NEW ETHNICITY"
Some of the current similarities and differences between ethnicity in Canada and the United States become apparent when we compare the development of multiculturalism in Canada with what has been called the "new ethnicity" in the United States. Both developed during the 1960s in response to changing social and political conditions in each country, and both movements are also part of an international resurgence of ethnicity. They have the same types of leaders and they share many common aims. Both movements have provoked debates in each country with a striking similarity in the arguments advanced. However most of the literature on multiculturalism and the new ethnicity is polemical rather than analytical and must be treated with caution. Any generalizations about the two movements must therefore be tentative.

Multiculturalism as a movement developed in Canada during the 1960s for a variety of interrelated reasons. It emerged from a quest for identity and acceptance among upwardly mobile second- and third-generation central and eastern Europeans. It also developed in reaction to French-Canadian nationalism and to the work of the Royal Commission on Bilingualism and Biculturalism which was established by the Pearson government in 1963. In its hearings across the country the commission soon discovered an ethnic backlash against its terms of reference which seemed to place non-British and non-French groups into the category of second-class citizens. The term "multiculturalism" itself arose as a response to the attempt by the commission to define Canada as "bicultural." The public debate surrounding the work of the commission also necessarily raised the question: if it is valuable for French Canadians to maintain their distinctive culture and identity, why is it not so for other groups?

The feeling that biculturalism placed all other ethnic groups in a state of second-class citizenship helps explain the resistance some of these groups expressed to the policies and programmes introduced by the federal government in response to the recommendations of the Royal Commission to secure the status of the French language in Canada. The place of the "other ethnic groups" in a bicultural society became a vexing one for federal politicians, who had originally hoped that steps to ensure French-Canadian rights, including the recognition of French as an "official" government language, would go a long way toward improving inter-ethnic relations. The partial resolution of this dilemma was the Trudeau government's introduction, in October 1971, of a multicultural policy within a bilingual framework. The policy has attempted to give public recognition of Canada's ethnic diversity through programmes of Canada's national cultural agencies and has attempted to encourage the maintenance of Canada's diversity through financial assistance for some of the activities of ethnic groups. The federal opposition parties expressed basic agreement with the policy and four provinces with large numbers of the "other ethnic groups" — Ontario, Manitoba, Saskatchewan, and Alberta — have also initiated their own multicultural policies. The federal Liberal government went one step further after the 1972 election and to bolster its sagging fortunes among some ethnic groups (particularly those from eastern Europe disturbed by Canada's rapprochement with the Soviet Union) appointed Toronto member of parliament Stanley Haidasz to the cabinet with responsibility for multiculturalism....

In attempting to analyse the new ethnicity in the United States, one is faced with a difficult task, because of the largely polemical nature of the literature. Superficially at least many parallels with the Canadian experience emerge. Just as French-Canadian nationalism spurred on other groups in Canada, the civil rights movement and black power in the United States reawakened the ethnic consciousness of "white ethnics," particularly among those of southern and eastern European origin. The new ethnicity developed then partly as a response to a feeling of media and academic neglect or even hostility, and partly through the black example of how organization and political muscle could help a disadvantaged group. In the United States, the new ethnicity also drew on the sense of a need for security, identity, and rootedness in a society torn apart by war and political scandal, and a society which was questioning the value hitherto attached to upward mobility, individualism, and progress. To what extent an increased awareness of the way in which ethnicity could provide a basis for personal and cultural identity in an impersonal technological society also played some part in giving rise to multiculturalism in Canada is difficult to say; perhaps this was merely a rationalization for the idea. What is clear is that similar social forces were giving rise to similar movements at the same time....

The arguments which have been advanced both pro and con multiculturalism and the new ethnicity are remarkably similar. In Canada, academic critics of multiculturalism like sociologist John Porter argue that the policy will only serve to perpetuate the "vertical mosaic" in which class lines coincide with ethnic lines, by preserving conservative values which are detrimental to the social and economic mobility of individuals from minority ethnic groups and by diverting energy from economic advancement to group maintenance.

Pluralists in both countries argue, on the contrary, that successful pluralist policies will raise the self-concept of low status groups, break down discriminatory attitudes, and hence facilitate the mobility of individuals from minority ethnic groups.

Assimilationists are also concerned about the stress that some pluralists place on group maintenance and belonging as opposed to individual self-development, while the latter often argue that ethnicity can provide a liberating rather than a constricting context for identity. This question of reconciling ethnicity with individualism is a greater issue, however, in the United States than in Canada since individualism is a much more deeply rooted part of the American ethos. Perhaps the basic fear about multiculturalism and the new ethnicity is that they will further fragment their respective societies. Pluralists are also concerned about national identity and unity, but see pluralism as the essence of national identity and believe that pluralist policies will contribute to the equality of all citizens, and hence strengthen national unity.

Another major group of critics of multiculturalism in Canada have been those who have argued that multiculturalism threatens the status of French Canadians. These critics, who include some of the most influential intellectuals in French Canada, argue that multiculturalism is a distortion of the realities of Canadian life, because there are in Canada only two main cultures tied to the two main language groups. In their opinion, it is contradictory to have an official government policy of bilingualism along with multiculturalism because language and culture are inseparable. Multiculturalism is viewed as being not only sociologically mistaken but politically dangerous since it detracts from the status of French Canadians. It also is seen as inconsistent with the Quebec desire to assimilate the children of immigrants to Quebec into French-Canadian society. Similarly in the United States, some blacks see the new ethnicity as a threat to them and are leery about making alliances with the "white ethnics." Just as French Canadians see the most important ethnic question in Canada to be that of English-French relations and the need to establish official bilingualism as a permanent national policy, many blacks see white racism as the most important issue and worry that the new ethnicity might detract from the fight against racism.

From an analytical point of view, the new ethnicity and multiculturalism both fit into the new view of ethnicity as described by the distinguished American sociologists Nathan Glazer and Daniel P. Moynihan in a recent book, *Ethnicity: Theory and Experience*. Their view has been aptly summarized by Canadian sociologist Jean Burnet: "[it] stresses ethnic groups as forms of social life rather than survivals from the past, as mobilizers of interests rather than bearers of cultures or traditions, and as collectivities with which people choose to identify rather than as groups into which they are born and from which they sometimes struggle to escape." Superficially, it would seem that this view would apply more to the new ethnicity, with its emphasis on class issues, than to multiculturalism, but Burnet has shown that this view can also be applied to the recent Canadian experience.

If the new ethnicity and multiculturalism are similar in origins, aims, leadership, and sociological significance, what comparisons can be drawn about their impact? This is much more difficult to assess, because so little research has been done. It is certainly becoming more acceptable to be "ethnic" in both countries, if "ethnic" buttons, T-shirts, and bumper stickers, public folklore and handicraft festivals, and parades may be taken as evidence. There has also been a boom in travel to the "homelands" by oldsters and young people alike and a growing interest among students in the languages and history of their ancestors. It is really too early to say how successful these movements will be in achieving their goals — or indeed to what extent their various goals are mutually compatible....

CONCLUSION
In summary then, how much truth is there to the melting pot/mosaic distinction? At the level of ideology, it ignores the existence of the new ethnicity and its striking parallels with multiculturalism in Canada. The comparison also distorts the intentions of native Canadians, most of whom, until the 1940s, were almost as anxious to "Canadianize" immigrants as native Americans were to "Americanize" them, although Canadians were less able to define a norm of assimilation.

The distinction between the mosaic and melting pot also implies that Canadians have been notably more tolerant toward minority groups than Americans. This is doubtful....

The contrasts between the ethnic composition and the maintenance of ethnicity in the two countries are much too complex to be adequately summed up in the melting pot/mosaic distinction. At the level of social reality as opposed to social attitudes, the comparison between the melting pot and the mosaic underestimates the degree to which pluralism has been maintained in the United States and overestimates the degree to which pluralism has been maintained in Canada among the non-British and non-French groups. The assimilating forces of the public and separate schools, of the mass media, and of intermarriage have also been at work in Canada. There has been considerable "melting" of non-British, non-French ethnic groups into either English-Canadian or to a lesser extent French-Canadian society, although the rate of assimilation has varied considerably with different ethnic groups. That ethnicity has remained a more significant aspect of Canadian life than of American is due less to the fact that Canadians have not demanded as much conformity as Americans, than to two other factors: circumstances worked to maintain a regionally concentrated French-Canadian culture; and during the twentieth century, immigrants have continued to come to Canada in substantial numbers in proportion to the total population....

Thus, attempts to present Canada as a mosaic whose attitude toward assimilation has always been enlightened as compared to the United States, where crass "melting potism" has prevailed, are on shaky historical ground. Nevertheless, there have been some differences between Canadian and American experiences with regard to ethnicity. The existence of French Canada, the absence of a strongly developed Canadian ethos due to Canada's colonial past, and economic factors in Canada which have promoted continued large-scale immigration have been basic determinants of these differences.

Uneven Development: A Mature Branch-Plant Society

WALLACE CLEMENT

UNEVEN DEVELOPMENT IN THE HISTORICAL WORLD SYSTEM

Foreign domination has distorted the Canadian economy and hence its class structure. This distortion did not begin with U.S. branch plants, although they are in part a reflection of the initial distortion resulting from dominance by the United Kingdom and a focus on resource extraction. To come to an understanding of Canada's current position, it is necessary to provide a brief historical sketch of Canada's uneven development. It will be seen that the sphere of circulation and service has been overdeveloped within Canada by the indigenous capitalist class, while there has been an indigenous underdevelopment of the sphere of production and the vacuum has been filled by U.S. capitalists in the areas of manufacturing and resources. The manufacturing sector is truncated and the resource sector geared to external requirements; both are vulnerable to the whims of metropolitan capitalists. It will be argued that a fraction of the indigenous Canadian capitalist class has benefited by the penetration of foreign capital and has struck an *unequal* alliance with U.S. capital, while another fraction of Canadian capital has been "squeezed out" by these two dominant fractions. It will further be argued that the distortions of the capitalist class are also reflected in regionalism and Canada's international investments. Finally, some tentative observations concerning the implications of uneven development for the Canadian state and class formation will be offered.

Until the First World War, British capitalists used Canada as an outlet for their surplus capital and manufactured products and as a source for important resources. These resources were commercial staples, such as fish, fur, timber and grain. In order to extract these resources it was necessary to create an infrastructure of roads, ports, shipping, railways, brokerage houses and financial institutions. The vehicle by which the capitalists of the United Kingdom created this infrastructure was portfolio or loan capital. This was interest-bearing capital that Canadian capitalists borrowed to invest, in turn, in the necessary infrastructure, typically under the guarantee of the Canadian state.

Abridged from Wallace Clement, "Uneven Development: A Mature Branch-Plant Society," *Class, Power and Property: Essays on Canadian Society* (Toronto: Methuen Publications, 1983), pp. 55-84. Copyright © 1983 by Methuen Publications. Reprinted by permission of the author and the publisher.

Over time, this invested capital paid a return and the initial loans to British capital could be repaid, leaving Canadian capitalists in command of these institutions.

Thus, Canada developed as a trading nation dependent on resource extraction and the whims of the world market; in turn, it served as an outlet for the goods of Britain, retarding its own manufacturing capacity. Even when and where this capacity was developed locally, little was done to sustain it. Indeed, the dominant fraction of Canada's capitalist class bought out much of this early manufacturing capacity and extended its holdings because it controlled the critical transportation networks essential for access to the national market and the necessary capital for expansion. As will be expanded upon later, many areas of Canada, particularly the Atlantic provinces, experienced a de-industrialization around the turn of the century, while other areas experienced the imperialism of central Canada in the form of the railway and the development of a wheat economy with the products destined for Europe.

Within Britain important changes were taking place. The first was the decline of mercantile capitalists, the counterpart of the indigenous Canadian capitalist class in the sphere of circulation, and the rise of industrial capitalists. This was marked by a movement toward free trade, which undermined the protected position and secure markets Canadian capitalists had had within the British Empire. The second change was the decline of Britain as the imperial centre and the rapid rise of the United States to this central position.

Initially, Canada had simply been a dumping-ground for U.S. surplus production. Tariff walls were created in reaction and this stimulated the establishment of branch-plant operations within Canada to maintain these markets. After the First World War these branch plants became important outlets for Canadian capital, both as investments and as buyers of Canadian manufacturing plants. This was particularly the case in high-technology, secondary manufacturing. They were seen by dominant Canadian capitalists and the Canadian state as a surrogate for indigenous industrialization. They represented industrialization from without; local industrialists lacked the technology, financial resources and access to markets these branch plants could provide. Small-scale Canadian manufacturers continued to survive so long as there were local or regional markets they could serve. Once the economy became a national and then rapidly a continental one, they could no longer compete. Foreign-controlled branch plants soon came to dominate the sphere of production.

The shift in capital terms is illustrated with the following figures: in 1926, 66 per cent of the outside capital invested in Canada was in the form of portfolio investment, 30 per cent in direct investment and 6 per cent miscellaneous. By 1974 direct investment accounted for 60 per cent, portfolio for 34 per cent and miscellaneous for 6 per cent. Canada's external dependence had simultaneously shifted from Britain to the United States.

While the indigenous fraction of Canada's capitalist class was nurtured on British portfolio investment and found its niche in finance, transportation and utilities, U.S. investment had a very different impact. Direct investment, as expressed in the branch plants of multinational corporations, involves an entire "package" consisting of technology, access to markets, access to capital, and management. Unlike portfolio investment, over time direct investment expands and widens the scope of control for its owners. In Canada 80 per cent of the foreign direct investment is owned in the United States. In time this investment eventually expands at a rate faster than new investment, using both internally generated capital and capital borrowed within the investing country, and actually drains off more capital than is invested from without. This position was reached in Canada during the early 1960s. Branch plants do not require the development of an indigenous capitalist class for their operation, since they remain externally controlled. They serve, rather, to displace existing capitalists in the activities they engage in or prevent them from emerging. In Canada these firms found a welcome ally in the dominant indigenous capitalist class, anxious to invest in their secure operations and to benefit from the activity they generated.

U.S. corporations began to penetrate the Canadian economy with great intensity after the Second World War. This penetration was motivated by two forces. The first was the push for an expanded market for their manufacturing capacity; the second, a search for resources to feed industrialization at home. Both were designed to expand U.S. hegemony and maintain profitability. The first was simply an expansion of tendencies that had existed since the turn of the century but on a grander scale. The second was a conscious reaction to the experience of the Second World War and the Korean War, after which the U.S. government began to assess its future resource requirements....

In 1946, 35 per cent of Canada's manufacturing was foreign controlled, but this rose to 50 per cent by 1953, and 56 per cent by 1957; in mining and smelting, the increases during the same years rose from 38 per cent to 57 per cent to 70 per cent. Thus, in the course of a decade, the productive cornerstones of Canada's economy ceased to be Canadian and became foreign dominated.

This development was welcomed by many Canadian capitalists. They participated in foreign control in a variety of ways. For example, by 1970 Canadian capitalists had committed some $5.8 billion to U.S.-controlled companies in Canada, representing 21 per cent of the value of U.S. direct investment. They also benefited from the secure loans they made, guaranteed by the foreign parents, the transportation and utilities branch plants used, and the access to technology and foreign markets they produced....

What implications for Canada's class formation stem from this pattern of uneven development? This is a question that has seldom been asked except in regard to the capitalist class. It is evident that foreign ownership, because of its impact on capital formation and structure and on the uneven development of the Canadian economy, has a strong impact on class formation and class structure but has a much more indirect impact on class relations. . . .

Both foreign and private Canadian investment are predicated on capitalist ownership of the means of production, although the relative concentration and stage of development of each source of ownership tends to differ significantly. Foreign ownership dominates in most resource-based activities and in secondary manufacturing. Moreover, it is much more heavily concentrated in the largest firms within these industries. Since foreign ownership is most commonly in the form of a branch plant of a much larger multinational corporation, many of the functions and activities associated with the entire corporation, such as research and development or marketing, are often performed outside the country. An obvious consequence is the "exporting" of a large number of highly skilled jobs in these areas. Canadian capitalists, on the other hand, tend to be overdeveloped in finance, transportation, utilities and general services.

Closely corresponding to patterns in the economy is control of the labour movement. International unions, an anachronism for U.S.-headquartered unions, are concentrated in the same industries that U.S. corporations dominate, while in the areas where Canadian capital or the state dominate, national unions or no unions at all tend to be predominant. The specific implications for Canada's class formation, aside from the implications for the capitalist class, which will now be discussed, will be analysed in a later section. . . .

It must be made clear, however, that the nature of this relationship is a most unequal one. While part of the Canadian capitalist class does participate directly in the expansion of U.S. corporations and benefits from this expansion, the overall effect is to drain capital from Canada to the United States. In 1974 the net drain of capital was $1,481 million. The effect is to make Canada capital poor and more reliant on external capitalization. The circle of direct investment is a vicious one, leading only to greater and greater dependence.

It is important to note, however, the mediating role some Canadian capitalists have had in this structure of dependence. Much of their capital is invested in U.S. corporations, and these Canadian capitalists are also given positions on the branch plants of these companies in Canada. In fact, of the indigenous fraction of the dominant capitalist class in Canada, 31 per cent sit on the boards of U.S. branch plants in Canada. In addition, 7 per cent of the members of the Canadian economic elite hold positions directly on the boards of companies in the United States. Of the 113 dominant Canadian companies, 63 (or 56 per cent) are interlocked with U.S. dominants; of the 194 dominant U.S. companies, 73 (or 38 per cent) have interlocks with dominant Canadian companies. The direction of these ties is mainly from U.S. manufacturing to Canadian finance and back again, suggesting that at least part of Canada's capitalist class is able to operate within the continental economy.

UNEVEN DEVELOPMENT AS REGIONALISM
Uneven development has two main manifestations in Canada. These are expressed in its regional inequalities and in the sector-specific activities of fractions of the capitalist class, as discussed above. Regional uneven development is marked by the fact that the centre of Canadian manufacturing and finance is located in the "golden triangle" between Windsor, Toronto and Montreal. The rest of the country is heavily reliant upon key resources typically foreign-controlled and destined for external markets. For the North, it is mining and minerals, following traditional furs; in British Columbia, it is wood, pulp and paper, mining, fish, agriculture and some hydro; it is natural gas, petroleum and potash, along with grain, on the Prairies; it is mining and pulp and paper in the northern areas of Manitoba, Ontario and Quebec, along with hydro; in Atlantic Canada, it is pulp and paper, agriculture, fish, some coal, and hydro. These regions feed the golden triangle and U.S. markets with their resources and, in turn, consume the manufactured products from these centres. The economies of these different parts of the country, in turn, produce different types of class structures in these regions and have consequences for the nature of the Canadian state.

Both forms of uneven development result in large measure from the effects of foreign pressures that have penetrated and shaped Canada. Initially, France and then the United Kingdom colonized what is now Canada in search of staple commodities, and used it as an outlet for their surplus capital, which was invested in building the nation's infrastructure — its roads, canals, ports, railways and financial institutions — essential to moving these staples abroad from Canada. These colonizers provided a ready outlet for Canada's commercial staples — fish, fur, timber and wheat — while the colonies were a ready market for their manufactured products....

Because the primary form of capital used by the United Kingdom in Canada was portfolio or loan capital, this necessitated the development within Canada of an indigenous capitalist class and a stable state structure that could guarantee these loans and oversee their investment. This arrangement continued until, in 1846, marked by the abolition of the Corn Laws in Britain, there was a movement toward free trade and an end to Canada's privileged position within the empire. Canadian capitalists then floundered in search of another imperial centre to which Canada could become attached. Many signed the Annexation Manifesto of 1849 calling for commercial union with the United States; they settled for the Reciprocity Treaty of 1854. Soon followed Confederation, whereby central Canadian capitalists would become their own colonizers, turning east and west. The foundation of their economy remained that of mediators between Canada's resources and foreign markets, but alongside this, there was beginning to be developed small-scale manufacturing interests that had grown to serve the Canadian market. These were basically local in nature and tied to the local populations in Ontario, Quebec and the Atlantic provinces.

The position of small-scale manufacturers was, however, a precarious one. Dominant central Canadian capitalists controlled the transportation networks essential for getting goods to market and the pools of capital necessary for expansion. In addition, the United States by this time had become an important industrial nation, itself searching for outlets for its products and sources for raw materials. These two factors combined to cause the demise of indigenous Canadian industrialization, particularly in Atlantic Canada.

T.W. Acheson has summarized the position of Atlantic Canada within Confederation:

> Crisis occurred in the depression of 1874-79, when the British and American markets for Canadian wood products and grains experienced a sharp downturn. To further aggravate the situation many American businessmen, faced with contracting domestic markets, began dumping large quantities of manufactured products on the Canadian market at substantially reduced prices. The combination of failing markets and foreign competition drove hundreds of manufacturers into bankruptcy and seemed to threaten the very survival of the small and comparatively inefficient Canadian manufacturing sector.

In light of the fluctuating demand for Canadian staples and the dumping of surplus production by U.S. capitalists on the Canadian market, Sir John A. Macdonald devised the now famous National Policy of 1879. This policy was based on a program of tariffs to bring industry into Canada, railways to produce a national economy, immigration to fill the West, and production of wheat destined for the world commodity markets. It served to stimulate manufacturing within Canada but, as will be seen, did little to sustain it. As Acheson has illustrated:

> The National Policy increasingly fulfilled its promise of making the entire domestic market available to Canadian producers. Thus, in reaction to the problems of an international economy which was unable to consume Canadian staples, and in response to the demands of a variety of concerned business interests, the Canadian government moved to restore the traditional metropolis-hinterland economic relationships.... The effect of the reorganization was to create a new economic metropolis, centred in Montreal, replacing the traditional British and American centres.

All did not fare equally well under this new structure: "The Canadian metropolis was unable to perform most of the functions usually associated with a dominant centre.... The most critical metropolitan failure was the inability of the Central Canadian market to consume the output of these new regional industries." The result was the destruction of Atlantic industry, its takeover by central Canadian capitalists by the time of the First World War, and its replacement by branch-plant industries and central Canadian banking consortia....

In Atlantic Canada, a once thriving manufacturing base reverted to staples production, and with that, dependency. Whereas staples had accounted for

32 per cent of the Atlantic output in 1911, this grew to 38 per cent by 1951. Not only did the region return to staples production, it also turned to the U.S. market as its primary outlet. By 1966 two-thirds of Atlantic exports were sent to the United States, and forest, mining and fish products accounted for 85 per cent of its exports. The decline in manufacturing coincided with the mass exodus of many workers to other parts of Canada and the growth of the state and service sectors. More than anywhere else in Canada, Maritime workers were employed in these sectors and experienced the highest rates of unemployment. The consequence of such a pattern of development, James Sacouman argues, has been that "capitalist underdevelopment in Atlantic Canada has for many years capitalised two exportable commodities: raw materials and human labour."

The weight of the National Policy shifted many benefits to central Canada. By the time its effects were fully felt, central Canada housed the major financial centre of the nation and established a monopoly over manufacturing, extending its power over the East through branch operations and exports. By 1910 four-fifths of Canada's manufacturing capacity was located in Ontario and Quebec. Increasingly, this capacity was no longer controlled by small-scale Canadian capitalists. Some had shifted into the hands of Canadian finance capitalists in the steel, pulp and paper, and food and beverage industries as they expanded into corporate ventures by buying out many small operators and creating monopolies. Outside these areas of industry, U.S. capitalists led the way, particularly in the technology-intensive secondary manufacturing and resource sectors. This served to reinforce and aggravate the problems of regionalism in Canada....

By 1931 two-thirds of U.S.-controlled manufacturing plants were located in Ontario, with Quebec accounting for another 16 per cent. Today Ontario receives 62 per cent of the taxable income from U.S.-controlled manufacturing companies even though it has only 36 per cent of the population. All other regions are significantly underrepresented. Thus, the penetration of the Canadian market by U.S. branch plants in Ontario served to draw even more economic power into the centre, further distorting the economy and failing to build a truly national market, since Canada was immediately drawn into a continental market where the United States dominated.

Central Canadian capitalists, both indigenous and foreign controlled, extended their dominance to the West. Following a path blazed by the Hudson's Bay Company, the CPR was given control over most of the West's productive land. In the vision of central Canadian dominance, the West was turned into a resource hinterland so that central Canadian capitalists could continue their historic role as mediators of Canadian resources for the markets of the world and the West would be a market for central Canadian produced goods. This left western farmers vulnerable. As Paul Phillips has shown:

The farmer had to sell his output, mainly grain, on an unprotected (European) international market, but had to buy his finished goods on a highly protected domestic market increasingly dominated by American manufacturers. What is significant, of course, is that the western producer had no control over either his market or his supplier.... caught between the fluctuating world grain prices and more stable finished-goods prices, the western producer suffered wide variation in real income.

Added to their burden was the discriminatory freight rates imposed by the CPR whereby the wheat rate "was almost three times that for comparable distances in competitive eastern areas" and consuming "half of the farmer's gross income from his grain crop." At least until the Second World War, the agrarian petite bourgeoisie, as expressed in the Social Credit and Co-operative Commonwealth Federation parties, dominated the politics of the West in reaction to the domination of their markets, transportation systems, financial sources, and implement supplies by central Canadian capital. While unable to protect themselves totally against the exploitation of this system, they did manage to create important institutions to moderate its impact with, for example, the introduction of the Wheat Board and the cooperative movement.

Today freight rates continue as a major obstacle in industrial development in the West. As fewer and fewer farmers are needed to work the more mechanized farms, people are forced off the land and into the urban areas but find little employment in manufacturing industries. It has been difficult to attract manufacturers to the region because the freight rates make it more profitable to remain in central Canada and ship to regional markets.... Besides freight rates, however, the historical legacy of central Canadian manufacturing ensures that the entire country will be served from one location that monopolizes the markets, thus preventing the development of regional competitors.

Since 1947, however, the West has had petroleum as an important lever in its dealings with central Canada. This industry, as one of the key industrial staples, is dominated by foreign, largely U.S.-controlled oil companies. When western oil came on stream, a world oil monopoly had already been established. Western oil simply became another domain for the Seven Sisters already in command of the markets and technology necessary to develop these resources. While petroleum gave the West an important counterpoint against central Canada, it in fact drew the West into a greater structure of domination (albeit one that would produce tremendous wealth). As Larry Pratt has convincingly argued, "Canadians are not receiving fair value for the exploitation of their resources; that it is the handful of multinational companies holding almost exclusive leasing privileges in the tar sands, that are dictating the conditions for their development." The costs of dependence are important, as provincial governments remain dependent upon single resources for their survival. Multinational companies often shift the risk and costs to the state while at the same time ensuring their own profitability. "Thus government must shoulder the enormous financial burden of building the massive infrastructure required to service and supply these remote projects, providing equity and debt financing, royalty holidays, guaranteed returns and prices, ensure labour stability, train a work force, underwrite environmental studies and costs — all of which carried a price tag in the billions."

The fact that several important Alberta-based, resource-related firms have emerged during the past decade is certainly an important occurrence. It cannot be overlooked, however, that control over the vast majority of energy remains with a few large multinational energy companies. The provincial state clearly has expanded its revenues as a result of capturing more rent from its energy, but so have the international oil companies. The dividends from these corporations are the property of their foreign parents. Rents collected by the state may provide the potential for alternative strategies but, depending upon how these revenues are used, need not lead to greater control over the destiny of the province's economy. The minimum that such a strategy should achieve is the maximization of petroleum-related industries, such as equipment manufacture and an extensive petrochemical industry, using the petroleum to manufacture final products. The maximum could be investment of these rents in non-petroleum activities that would produce jobs, build a diversified industrial base and reduce external dependence. Neither strategy has been systematically implemented with these rents.

The main factor accounting for the prosperity of Alberta in the 1970s has been the effectiveness of the Organization of Petroleum Exporting Countries (OPEC) and thus the rapid rise in world oil prices. This, of course, is not the result of policies carried out by the Lougheed government, nor of the rise to power of a "new middle class" in Alberta, nor even of the demise of the multinationals. Whether an apparently "successful staple," such as energy in Alberta appears to be, will lead to an equalization of power with central Canada remains to be seen. Much will depend on how successfully the West pursues the strategy of capturing the advantages of forward and backward linkages and whether or not the exceptionally high cost of energy will bottom out. In either case the balance of economic power rests with the international oil companies, not likely candidates to seek a balanced Canadian economy.

A repeat of Canada's history of uneven development is again taking place in the North. The Berger Report calls the North "an area of production remote from the main markets of Canada and from the homes of those who own and invest in its resources.... The first great staple industries in the North were the fur trade and whaling; then followed by mining; now there is gas and oil." Each of these staples has left its stamp on the North, but the most recent developments in mining and minerals have been the most disruptive, serving exclusively outside interests. As Mel Watkins has shown, the fur trade involved the native people as gatherers of fur. They acted as independent commodity producers, selling their products to the fur-trading companies, thus giving them a measure of autonomy and control over their homeland. With mineral production, however, capitalists demand "both rights to the use of land and people who will work for a wage." The linkages generated by this search for industrial staples benefit industrialized parts of the country but have only disruptive effects on the traditional economy of the native people. Moreover, the benefits of this development accrue primarily to the United States, and not even to industrialized Canada. As Edgar Dosman has shown, "In most well-established countries, the development of a peripheral region would be a largely domestic issue. In Canada, however, the development of the North was inextricably linked to the issue of the Canadian relationship with a foreign power, the United States." This is because the United States is the major recipient of Canadian gas and oil exports and because the companies controlling these resources are U.S. controlled. As has been characteristic of the entire Canadian economy, the exploitation of natural resources for foreign markets has placed Canada in a vulnerable position in the world system. In the North this means the destruction of the native people's final homeland, their last refuge from a mode of production that destroys their traditional culture and livelihood.

Uneven development obviously has different consequences for the various regions of Canada. Southern Ontario's successful diversification from its initial reliance on wheat to a powerful industrial base has not been matched elsewhere. Indeed, the concentrated industrial power of this area, along with its far-reaching control over finance and transportation, has been a major reason why the rest of the country has become so reliant on resource extraction, has failed to develop a strong industrial base (as in the case of the West), and has had its industrial base destroyed (as in Atlantic Canada). The industrial capacity of southern Ontario has, however, been built upon the uncertain sands of foreign ownership. With the recession of the late 1970s, much of that industry has been shaken as foreign firms retrench, leaving behind shells of factories and laid-off industrial workers. The totally foreign-dominated automobile industry has been hardest hit. As of July 1980, 23,200 auto workers were on indefinite layoffs, and fifteen plants were closed in the previous half year alone.

While southern Ontario has — with justification — been the traditional locus of regional antagonism in Canada, in the post-OPEC period attention has shifted to oil-rich Alberta. Both areas, it needs to be stressed, have foreign-controlled corporations dominant in their major industrial and resource activities. While the fortunes of one currently appear to be on the rise and the other on the wane, neither is really a "master-of-its-own-house." Both are subordinate to the powers of the multinationals.

UNEVEN DEVELOPMENT IN THE CONTEMPORARY WORLD SYSTEM

A further expression of Canada's uneven development is evident in its relationship with the rest of the world. Investment from Canada falls into two types, closely corresponding to the relative strengths of Canadian and foreign capitalists within the Canadian economy. The first is real Canadian investment abroad, located primarily in finance, transportation and utilities. At the pinnacle of this are the five dominant Canadian banks. As the people from the Development Education Centre have argued:

> The Canadian banking trusts chose very early an international strategy, rather than bearing the risks of boom and bust in the Canadian "staples" economy or in underwriting a potential national manufacturing strategy. Profits were more stable and insured in cooperation with Wall Street or London, no matter whether the action was at home or abroad.

The fortunes of Canada's banks abroad followed those of first the British and then the U.S. empire. For example, "branches and sub-branches of Canadian banks in the Caribbean and Latin America peaked at 140 in 1926; that figure was not reached again until 1958." Today, riding on the crest of U.S. hegemony, Canadian banks have grown to be the third largest in international financial circles. The five dominant Canadian banks, which control over 90 per cent of Canada's banking, all earn a fifth or more of their total revenues from foreign operations, and this share has been increasing. The international operations expanded at a rate of 667 per cent between 1966 and 1976, considerably faster than the 394 per cent growth in their domestic operations for the same period.

Besides the indigenous Canadian investment abroad, there is a second rather unusual form of "Canadian" investment abroad. This is "go-between" investment whereby branches, typically of U.S. companies, are used to control other branches in the rest of the world. As early as 1929, companies like Union Carbide, Ford Motor Company, Standard Oil of New Jersey, and Aluminum Company of America used Canadian subsidiaries as a means to avoid U.S. laws and take advantage of preferential Canadian tariffs. Today this pattern remains and a good deal of Canadian foreign investment in the manufacturing and resource sectors is usually controlled outside of Canada, with the Canadian branch acting as a go-between. Thus, foreign investment distorts not only Canada's national economy but its international relations as well. ...

THE RELATIVE DEPENDENCE OF THE CANADIAN STATE

It has been argued to this point that Canada is characterized by uneven development both internally and internationally. Another important area where this unevenness expresses itself is in the Canadian state. The most obvious expression is in federal-provincial relations and in conflicts among the provinces themselves. Uneven development as regionalism, discussed earlier, means that conflicting economic interests which are translated into political struggles become dominant issues. This fragmentation becomes further complicated by the demands of various fractions of the capitalist class, outlined earlier as yet another expression of uneven development. The problem is thus not simply to provide an analysis of the state but to create an analysis of society. It is an illusion to think the state operates independent of society. It is both generated by society and influences that society; in other words, the state is wedded to the socio-economic make-up of society. In the case of Canada, unevenness is a dominant feature....

The major division within Canadian capital is between big- and medium-sized capitalists rather than between Canadian and foreign capitalists, and the overall weight of the Canadian state is such that it reinforces these dominant capitalists. Canadian capitalists, especially those in the giant banks, life insurance, trust and holding companies, back winners, whatever their nationality; their interests are inextricably bound to the international system of capital.

Basic to the Canadian state and its various branches is the need to balance contradictory requirements on the part of the U.S. and Canadian capital. The outcome has been that some Canadian capitalists who "fit" the demand of U.S. capitalists have benefited by Canada's distorted development and struck an unequal alliance, while others have been left by the wayside. While it is important for the state's legitimacy to project an appearance that this does not occur or that it is acting to prevent it, in the end state economic policies have followed the demands of the most powerful sectors of the society. This is not simply because the state is ideologically predisposed to do so but because the most powerful are those that can make things happen, get things done. They are the backbone of economic activity and thus crucial to the viability of any capitalist state....

It is quite apparent why the uneven development discussed earlier would lead to confusion on the part of the Canadian state in its performance of its accumulation function. Canada is an advanced industrial society whose mainstay is resources rather than manufactured products and whose industrial capacity is mainly foreign owned; it is a trading nation that sends over two-thirds of its exports to one country (the United States) and receives over two-thirds of its imports from that same country....

As both a recipient of and base for foreign investment, the Canadian state is forced to "play both sides of the fence." It must maintain the legitimacy of foreign investment, since it sanctions a good deal of it in the rest of the world under the guise of Canadian investment abroad, while at the same time it must contend at home with the massive problems foreign investment causes.

As a result, there is no clear focus for the Canadian state. It is a state of confusion, since it contains within it contradictory interests and forces. It consequently is weak in its ability to deal with basic economic problems: trade, inflation, unemployment, development strategies and so on. . . .

In its rush to meet the increasing demands on its resources, the various branches of the Canadian state have found themselves running to the New York money markets. The costs of building a resource infrastructure and maintaining the false economy of branch-plant industry are enormous. In 1976 government borrowing was $8 billion, of which $3.5 billion was raised outside Canada. Compare this with the $7.6 billion borrowed by private business, only $400 million of which was raised outside (see *Weekend Magazine*, 18 December 1976:4). Canada is being made capital poor because of the costs of foreign ownership and the demands being placed on its revenues. The Canadian state is now in a position where it must borrow to repay the interest on its loans. According to Garth Stevenson, "By 1973 interest charges on all provincial debts amounted to nearly $1.2 billion, substantially more than the total of *all* provincial expenditures in 1950." By 1977 all levels of government were making interest payments of $8.94 billion annually. Ottawa alone paid over $225 million in interest in 1977 on *foreign* loans. It is not possible for the state to continue indefinitely in its giveaways and concessions.

The closeness of the capitalist class in Canada to the state makes it all the more difficult for the state to be autonomous. This is especially so when fractions of the capitalist class, at times in concert and at times in conflict, have very close relations with different branches and levels of the state. Since corporate power is political power, these interests become translated directly into contradictory state policies and behaviour. As the scope of these demands enlarge and call for increasing state action, the contradictions must become manifest.

DISTORTION IN CANADA'S CLASS FORMATION

Most of the previous focus has been on the capitalist class and its various fractions, with only a few oblique references to the effect of uneven development on other classes. As with the state sector, it will only be possible here to sketch some ways uneven development has affected the class structure of Canada. The following should be regarded as a very preliminary outline, which subsequent papers begin to elaborate.

It was illustrated earlier that there is an unequal distribution of manufacturing capacity in Canada, with the industrial heartland residing in the golden triangle. Outside this area most productive workers are part of a "resource proletariat" whose jobs are in activities like mining, minerals, pulp and paper, lumber, fishing or hydro. They tend to live in single-industry towns far from major urban centres, and their costs of living are high. Most important, they tend to work with non-renewable (or poorly managed) resources, and their livelihood is constantly threatened by exhaustion of these resources or fluctuations in world markets. Boom-bust cycles for Canada's resource proletariat are legion; there are constant fluctuations between labour shortages and labour surpluses in these industries because their fate depends so heavily on external demands.

Traditionally, many people working in staple industries were independent commodity producers. In fact, up to the Second World War, the petite bourgeoisie was the most powerful class outside the capitalist class and accounted for much of the political resistance to the dominant class. Increasingly they have been drawn into wage labour. In 1957, 79 per cent of the labour force were paid workers, and by 1976 this increased to 89 per cent, while the proportion working for themselves decreased from 12 per cent to 5 per cent.... It is important to note, however, that the decline of the traditional petite bourgeoisie of fishermen, farmers and small shopkeepers has not meant a proportionate increase in the traditional industrial working class. What has occurred instead, as will be argued shortly, is a dramatic rise in the number of state workers, thus resulting in a situation where a major part of the working class is employed by various branches of the state....

It goes without saying that the state in Canada does not use class categories in its various information-gathering agencies. As a result, census and labour force surveys provide only approximations of classes, not classes themselves....

Distribution of the Labour Force by Sector, 1901-78
(percentages)

	Primary	Secondary	Tertiary
1901	44.3	27.8	27.9
1921	36.4	25.8	37.8
1946	29.4	30.8	39.8
1955	30.8	32.5	47.7
1964	12.5	32.5	56.3
1970	9.3	28.7	62.0
1973	7.9	28.7	63.4
1978[a]	7.6	26.8	65.6

[a] As of October 1978.
Sources: Statistics Canada, *Canada Year Book 1962 (Ottawa, 1962), p. 711*; Statistics Canada, *The Labour Force*, cat. #71-001, various issues.

The most basic kind of information about changes in the labour force concern broad sectoral shifts from primary to tertiary activities. The movements have been dramatic: the primary sector has declined from being the main location of the labour force at the turn of the century to now occupying a minor place. It has been replaced by the tertiary sector, while the secondary sector has not changed significantly throughout the twentieth century. The pattern of a declining primary sector and rising tertiary sector is not unusual; what is unusual is the absence of a period when the secondary sector, which is mainly composed of manufacturing, has the dominant position. It began the period equal to the tertiary sector but is now well under half the size of this sector. Canada's secondary sector is proportionately smaller than that of other advanced capitalist societies. The major disparity is in manufacturing. Moreover, 40 per cent of Canada's manufacturing labour force in 1971 "worked in industries chiefly engaged in the transformation of raw materials of the land, sea, forests and mines." ...

... The most dramatic decline has been in agriculture and to some extent other primary industries, while manufacturing has declined significantly in its relative position as an employer. It is clear that a declining proportion of workers in production are being required to support a rapidly growing sphere of circulation. The single greatest contributing factor to the overall pattern since the turn of the century is the decline of agriculture. In 1881 nearly half (48 per cent) of the labour force was engaged in agricultural pursuits; this declined to two-fifths in 1901 and again to a third by 1921 and a quarter by 1941. Now this sector accounts for only one-twentieth of the labour force. The twenty-percentage-point drop in agriculture between 1946 and 1978 presented is sufficient to account for almost the entire increase in the circulation sector over the period, while the production sectors stagnated. Why has the shift in employment occurred in this way? The data themselves cannot tell us because they only describe, they do not explain; explanation lies at least partially in the uneven development of Canadian society. ...

To some extent, the overall decline in the sphere of production and rise in the sphere of circulation is partially reflective of changes in the sexual composition of the labour force. Between 1931 and 1971 the proportion of women has risen by 346 per cent, while men only increased by 74 per cent. On the other hand, the proportion of men classified as industrial proletariat has remained fairly constant, while women have declined substantially. Women have dominated and continue to dominate the commercial proletariat, while they are virtually absent from the resource proletariat. ...

Hugh Armstrong has shown that the state sector has grown more rapidly than any other, accounting for more than a third of all new jobs since the Second World War. It has increased from 8.9 per cent in 1946 to at least 21.2 per cent of the labour force in 1974, with provincial employees increasing at a much faster rate than federal ones. Because of the increasing pressure for legitimation of the state with the myriad of contradictions it must face, the state has grown to meet these demands. ...

Alongside this is the general growth in the number of clerical workers. This is the result of two types of changes, those within factory offices and those through the growth of "clerical industries." The first process is reflected in the following figures for Canada: the proportion of administrative and office workers in Canadian manufacturing increased from 11 per cent in 1917 to 19 per cent in 1939 to 22 per cent in 1954 and 28 per cent in 1971. The second is the rise of "paper empires," such as companies in the commercial sector (banks, trust companies, life insurance, real estate, etc.), which are primarily clerical, and to some extent sales, in their work. Their main activity involves accounts, stocks, payrolls and so on....

Another factor of importance is the weakness of Canada in terms of research and development, with much of it taking place under the command of parent corporations outside of Canada. Of related concern is the exporting of resources and importing of processed goods, which means that labour and skill-intensive jobs are also exported. As the studies by Pierre Bourgault have shown, "When we examine the nature of our imports and exports, we find that we export mainly raw materials and resource-based products while importing most manufactured goods, particularly those which have a high knowledge content," that is, those jobs involving advanced technology and skilled labour. Little wonder Canada's employment rate runs at about 10 per cent *officially* — over a million people. Canada's uneven development affects not only the distribution of the labour force but also the number of jobs in the labour force itself. Even the rapid increase in state employment has not been able to meet the demand for jobs caused by the capital-intensive foreign control of Canada's productive sector and the decline of the traditional petite bourgeoisie....

CONCLUSION
Canada cannot be characterized as an independent capitalist society; nor can it be grouped with the various periphery nations often called the "Third World," although it shares some features with each. Rather, Canada is a politically independent nation state, enveloped by the economic spill-over of the most powerful capitalist society in the world. While Canada's economy is largely controlled and shaped by U.S. economic power centres, these external centres do not operate in a complete power vacuum in Canada. What has been forged over the past century is an unequal alliance between the leading elements of Canadian and U.S. capital, which mutually reinforces the power and advantage of each. The leading forces of capitalism in both Canada and the United States benefit by this alliance, while smaller Canadian capitalists and the Canadian populace experience its costs.

Not all Canadian capitalists are pleased with this continental power structure, particularly smaller capitalists in vulnerable manufacturing and trade activities, but the state in general and dominant capitalists in particular have been unable to see beyond their immediate economic gains arising from this method of "nation building" and surplus extraction. Over the past century, the two economies have become so intertwined because of these dominant continental interests that it becomes difficult for many capitalists and members of Canada's ruling class to visualize the two economies apart from one another. Thus, the resource and market demands by U.S. capitalists and the internal opportunism of Canada's ruling class have created a continental political economy wherein U.S. capitalists dominate but some Canadian capitalists also benefit. . . .

. . . Canadian workers are often engaged in resource extraction and subject to the booms and busts of this industry, while many others are employed in manufacturing branch plants where the employment priorities are U.S. oriented. Canadian workers are particularly vulnerable, a fact which is reflected in the million unemployed and 10 per cent official unemployment rate. Capital is more mobile than labour, particularly with active state controls on the migration of labour, thus leaving labour especially vulnerable to shifts of capital both within the nation or internationally. A fragmented labour movement adds to the weakness of the Canadian workers, all the more so since it is dominated by international unions, which are subject to pressures and interests emanating from the United States.

It is not only the Canadian working class that is vulnerable. The Canadian state is also within a relatively dependent position within the system of U.S. hegemony. This is reflected in its international political and military role as "mediator" between the interests of the United States and other nations. Internally, various branches and levels of the Canadian state struggle over foreign investment, further weakening and fragmenting resistance to domination. Self-determination for the people of Canada will necessarily mean resistance to foreign domination *and* the dominant fraction of the Canadian ruling class, which has mediated this dependence within the world system.

The Governments and Societies of Canadian Federalism

ALAN C. CAIRNS

> If you marry the Spirit of your generation you will be a widow in the next.
> — *Dean Inge*

The Canadian political system, now in its second century, can no longer be taken for granted. It is altogether possible, some would say probable, and some would say desirable, that major institutional change, not excluding the fragmentation of Canada, is on the immediate horizon. It is therefore an opportune time to reflect on the century-long interaction between government and society in Canada. I use the word "reflect" advisedly, for this is not the type of interaction about which hard statements can be confidently made.

The impact of society on government is a common theme in the study of democratic polities. Less common is an approach which stresses the impact of government on the functioning of society. I have chosen the latter for the guiding theme of my remarks, because I am convinced that our approach to the study of Canadian politics pays inadequate attention to the capacity of government to make society responsive to its demands.

With some exceptions, my remarks will be confined to senior governments operating in the institutional framework of federalism. Particular institutions, such as the electoral system, the Senate, and many others will be ignored or given only minor attention.

Since the depression of the thirties, the analysis, criticism, and defence of federalism have been the major stock-in-trade of political scientists attempting overall perspectives on the Canadian political system. Rising and changing political expectations in Quebec, culminating in the victory of the *Parti québécois* in November 1976, have set us on the path towards yet another brooding inquiry into our federal condition. Unfortunately, our capacity to make wise choices for the future is seriously curtailed by our limited understanding of the political system we are urged to leave behind. In the last half century students of Canadian federalism have been consistently taken aback by the unexpected transformation of the subject matter to which their expertise applied. There is no compelling reason to believe that our scholarly fate will be different....

I do not expect the remainder of this paper to provide an analysis of Canadian federalism that will not be belied by the future; nor do I intend to

---

Abridged from Alan C. Cairns, "The Governments and Societies of Canadian Federalism," *The Canadian Journal of Political Science* (December 1977), pp. 695–725. Reprinted by permission of the author and the publisher.

join the army of constitution writers who will bedazzle or bedevil us in the next few years with the fertile products of their imagination. My task is simply to try and identify the major shortcoming in the approaches we employ in the analysis of federalism, and to propose an alternative perspective.

The reaction against traditional political science, with its alleged overemphasis on the formal, legal aspects of the polity at the expense of the social forces which worked it, was given striking emphasis for students of federalism in W. S. Livingston's famous assertion in 1956 that "Federalism is a function not of constitutions but of societies." The dynamic of the system was to be sought not in government, or in features of the constitution, but in society. In the elaboration of this sociological perspective political systems are seen as superstructures devoid of autonomy, and lacking independent coercive and moulding power *vis-à-vis* their environment.

Two decades before the appearance of Livingston's seminal piece, the depression of the thirties produced a great outburst of federalist literature, or, more properly, anti-federalist literature, in English Canada, which presupposed "The Obsolescence of Federalism." This literature viewed the central government as the fortunate and necessary beneficiary and provincial governments as the hapless victims of overwhelmingly powerful socioeconomic forces. In essence, it was argued that technological interdependence and the evolution of a national market made centralized leadership necessary for planning purposes, and destroyed the sociological basis for the vitality and meaningful survival of the provinces. Provincial governments, considered out of tune with fundamental requirements and urgent imperatives rooted in society and economy, apparently had no resources adequate to stay the execution decreed for them by scholars with the future in their bones.

The centralization predicted in the thirties seemed firmly and securely in place in the forties, and for much of the fifties. It was explained in 1957 by Professor J. A. Corry as a product of technological necessity. Corry, responding to prevailing interpretations of the nature and direction of socioeconomic change, produced a polished epitaph for any significant future role for provincial governments. The growth of "giant corporations, national trade associations, and national trade unions" created a nationalizing of sentiment among elites who backed the central government and thus contributed to the centralization of authority in Ottawa. The most a province could hope for, he asserted, "is freedom for minor adventure, for embroidering its own particular patterns into harmony with the national design, for playing variant melodies within the general theme.... [I]t is everywhere limited in the distance it can go by having become part of a larger, although not necessarily a better, scheme of things."

To the distress of a later generation of liberal-left critics of federalism, Corry's prediction of a nationalization of politics and the continuing centralization of authority in federal hands proved premature. For John Porter, writing in the mid-sixties, when the centralizing impulse born of depression, war, and post-war reconstruction had faded, the federal system was little more than a pious fraud devoid of real meaning for the citizenry, and sustained by academics with a vested interest in their esoteric knowledge of the system's functioning, and by political and bureaucratic elites happy to place federal roadblocks in the way of class politics. To Porter, reiterating an argument widely employed in the thirties, the "conditions of modern industrial society and international relations... [made] it... almost essential that the central government acquire power at the expense of the provincial... governments." Canada, however, was relatively exempt from this necessary and beneficial trend. The cause of this regrettable backwardness was located in the political system with its exaggerated obsession with national unity, and its bias in favour of provincial rights. Reduced to essentials, Porter's position was simply that the class cleavage, based on the economic system, was the true, natural, and dynamic cleavage, while regional cleavages stimulated and fostered by the political system were fundamentally artificial, meaningless, and accordingly undeserving of respect. A well-functioning, modern political system, in marked contrast to the existing federal system, would serve, above all else, as an instrumentality for the expression of creative politics founded on the class struggle of advanced industrial society, with regional considerations shunted to the sidelines. This may be called the sociologist's ideal political system, for it awards primacy to his subject matter....

In a sense, Livingston's plea to search for the determinants of a changing federalism in society, not constitutions, was not needed in Canada. From the mid-thirties to the present we have not lacked sociological approaches to federalism. The weakness of our understanding lies elsewhere, in a failure to treat government with appropriate seriousness. The remainder of this paper is an attempt to redress the balance by arguing, contrary to Livingston, that federalism, at least in the Canadian case, is a function not of societies but of the constitution, and more importantly of the governments that work the constitution.

The great mystery for students of Canadian federalism has been the survival and growth of provincial governments, particularly those of English Canada. Sociologically-focussed inquiries, with Quebec as an implicit model, have looked for vital, inward-looking provincial societies on which governments could be based and, finding none, have been puzzled why these governmental superstructures, seemingly lacking a necessary foundation, have not faded away.

The sociological perspective pays inadequate attention to the possibility that the support for powerful, independent provincial governments is a product of the political system itself, that it is fostered and created by provincial government elites employing the policy-making apparatus of their jurisdictions, and that such support need not take the form of a distinct culture, society, or nation as these are conventionally understood. More specifically, the search for an underlying sociological base, whatever its nature and source, as the necessary sustenance for viable provincial political systems, deflects us from considering the prior question of how much support is necessary. Passivity, indifference, or the absence of strong opposition from their environment may be all that provincial governments need in order to thrive and grow. The significant question, after all, is the survival of provincial governments, not of provincial societies, and it is not self-evident that the existence and support of the latter is necessary to the functioning and aggrandisement of the former. Their sources of survival, renewal, and vitality may well lie within themselves and in their capacity to mould their environment in accordance with their own governmental purposes.

In the analysis of contemporary party systems much has been made of the extent to which today's parties represent the historic residue of the cleavages of yesteryear. In the Canadian case the freezing of party alternatives fades into insignificance compared with the freezing by the federal system of initially five and now eleven constitutionally distinct and separate governments. The enduring stability of these governments contrasts sharply with the fluctuating fortunes of all parties and the disappearance of many. Governments, as persisting constellations of interests, constitute the permanent elements of the Canadian polity which, thus far, have ridden out the storms of social, economic, and political change.

The decision to establish a federal system in 1867 was a first-order macro decision concerning the basic institutional features of the new polity. It created competitive political and bureaucratic elites at two levels of government endowed with an impressive array of jurisdictional, financial, administrative, and political resources to deploy in the pursuit of their objectives. The post-Confederation history of Canadian federalism is little more than the record of the efforts of governing elites to pyramid their resources, and of the uses to which they have put them. Possessed of tenacious instincts for their own preservation and growth, the governments of Canadian federalism have endowed the cleavages between provinces, and between provinces and nation which attended their birth, with an ever more comprehensive political meaning.

The crucial, minimum prerequisites for provincial survival and growth have been the preservation of jurisdictional competence, and of territorial integrity. In terms of the former, it is notable that explicit change in the constitutional responsibilities of the two levels of government has been minimal, in spite of strong centralizing pressure on occasion. The division of powers has been altered to federal advantage only three times, in each of which unanimous provincial consent was obtained, and in two of which provincial paramountcy was respected.... The paucity of amendments dealing with the division of power, and the long-standing opposition of provincial governments to any formally agreed amendment procedures which might diminish their lawmaking authority without their express consent, strikingly reveal an entrenched governmental conservatism where the constitutional base of provincial governing capacity is concerned.

Equally indicative of provincial tenacity in self-preservation is the integrity of provincial boundaries. No province has given up territory to which it had clear and undisputed possession. Where territorial "loss" has occurred, as in the 1872 case of the San Juan boundary settlement by the German Emperor which denied the claims of British Columbia, or in the case of Labrador decided by judicial determination in favour of Newfoundland in 1927, provincial frustrations have been pronounced, and in the latter case long-lived. Half a century later the claim of Quebec to Labrador remains a live issue to the Quebec government. Disputed cases, such as offshore mineral resources caught between the counterclaim of federal and provincial governments, illustrate the vigour with which provincial positions are defended, even in the face of adverse court decisions. Where the possibility of territorial expansion has existed, or still exists, with respect to contiguous territory outside provincial boundaries, the provinces have consistently manifested a revolution of rising expectations not yet dead. It has not only been the federal government assiduously extending the range of its jurisdiction from the limited Canada of 1867 to the ten-province Canada of 1949, and now extending its effective writ over Canada's Arctic frontiers, which displays a well-developed drive for territorial acquisition. The original boundaries of Quebec, Ontario, and Manitoba contained only a small portion of the land masses they now control....

The three Maritime provinces, doomed by location to be deprived of attainable territorial ambitions, have been tenacious in not giving up the political control over defined territories they individually possess. They resisted amalgamation in the 1860's, and in spite of the urgings of the Deutsch Report, they resist it today. "By any administrative logic," stated *The Economist*, "the three provinces should be bundled into one. But nobody will be crazy enough to try." The hostile stance of Newfoundland to any possible reopening of the Labrador case by an independent Quebec further attests to the territorial conservatism of the provinces, tightly holding on to what they have won in the historical lottery of land acquisition. The provincial protection of, and search for *Lebensraum* is a relatively unexamined aspect of federal-provincial history deserving as much scholarly investigation as their better-known safeguarding of their formal jurisdictional authority.

The protection of jurisdictional authority and the protection and expansion of provincial territory have been accompanied by an ever more vigorous employment of provincial legislative competence. Related to this as both cause and effect has been a concomitant increase in government personnel. A similar expansion of personnel, and a no less aggressive exploration of the limits of its constitutional responsibilities, have been displayed by the federal government.

It would be a serious mistake to view these governmental mountains as molehills. The several hundred political officeholders constitute only a trivial minority of those who wield government power, and/or derive their income directly from public positions. The growth of one federal and ten provincial governments has produced large and powerful complexes of institutions and personnel with their own professional and personal interests, and their own official purposes for the provincial and federal populations they govern.... Nearly one out of every nine members of the Canadian work force is employed by the two senior levels of government, while municipal government employs a further 256,000. They are not indifferent to the fate of the governments they serve.

The astute observation of Alexander Hamilton in Federalist Paper No. 1, two centuries ago, has not declined in relevance: "Among the most formidable of the obstacles which the new Constitution will have to encounter may readily be distinguished the obvious interest of a certain class of men in every State to resist all changes which may hazard a diminution of the power, emolument, and consequence of the offices they hold under the State establishments." Another certain class of men has attached itself to the central government.

It makes little sense to think of these impressive concentrations of power and personnel as superstructures whose existence and purposes are largely derivative of the electorate, the class structure, the pressure group system, or whatever. Even if we ignore their functions, the more than one million Canadians who work for federal and provincial governments, and their dependents, constitute an immense component of Canadian society directly tied to government. When we do consider their functions of policy-making, service-provision, regulation, and protection, extending to the most specialized activities where government monopolizes the expertise in a given field, we are made aware that we live in a period of convulsive change in government-society relations. In the evolution of the division of labour between those who govern, and those who are governed, the energizing, proselytizing, and entrepreneurial role increasingly rests with those civil servants and politicians with the capacity to influence policy and its administration.

While the sheer fact of large numbers directly dependent on government should not be underestimated as a crucial, if elementary, factor in government survival, that contribution is multiplied by the ramifying effects of the institutional and organizational complexes in which these employees work and have their being. The ministries, departments, agencies, bureaus, and field offices to which they daily report constitute partially self-contained entities, valued for their own sake, and possessed of their own life and interests. Their minimum desire is for a steady level of activity. Typically, however, they seek to enlarge the scope of their functions. If the environment offers new opportunities for expansion in emergent problem areas they will compete with other bureaucracies for the prizes of status and growth offered by enhancement of their activity. If major challenges are made to their organizational identity, purpose, or cohesion they will fight back against unsympathetic political superiors and other menacing figures and forces in their environment. If their functions decline in social utility, or their expertise becomes obsolescent they will scan the horizon of alternative possibilities in an aggressive search for new justifications for continued existence. While they are subject to political control and direction they have impressive capacities to get their own way and to bend their political superiors to their will. Although their functions relate them to particular sectors of society, they are not puppets or simple reflections of the interests of the groups they control, regulate or service. "[B]oth the sector served and political leaders come to be forces in the environment which public servants must manage and manipulate so that they will demand or agree to expansion of the bureaucracy." Their basic strength resides in the expertise which makes them indispensable to their political superiors, and in the support of the external interests which have positively adapted to their policies. They represent a permanent, expansive aspect of government. They are the necessary instruments of an administered society which could not, without major disruption, survive their disappearance from the scene.

The presence in the Canadian federal system of eleven governments, each honeycombed with bureaucratic interests and desires of the nature just described, helps explain the expansion of each level of government, the frequent competition and duplication of activity between governments, and the growing impact of government on society. It is impossible to think clearly about Canadian federalism without devoting extensive attention to the one million Canadians parcelled out in eleven jurisdictions, and committed by loyalty, the terms of their employment, and self-interest to the particular government they serve.

These pyramids of bureaucratic power and ambition are capped by political authorities also possessed of protectionist and expansionist tendencies. The eleven governments of the federal system endow the incumbents of political office with the primary task of defending and advancing the basic interests of crucial sectors of the provincial or national economy and society. Each political office, particularly those of prime ministers and premiers, has a history which influences and constrains the succession of incumbents who briefly possess it. Thus, as André Bernard says: "No political leader in Quebec would ever dare voice a doubt about the sacrosanct objective of 'la survivance française en Amérique.' Survival of the French-Canadian people is an obligation, an article of faith. It has been so for 200 years. It is basic, fundamental." Since 1871 the political leaders of British Columbia have consistently pressed economic claims on Ottawa demanding compensation for the chronically alleged financial maltreatment they have suffered from the federal government. The special needs and expenses associated with the harsh facts of geography and a primary resource based economy have been reiterated in countless briefs. Other provinces also have "fairly durable and persisting interests" which reflect the relatively unchanging factors of society, economy, and basic position in the federal system. The claims derived from the preceding are nourished by the constantly refurbished memory of past grievances.

Provincial political elites not only seek to further the long-range interests of their society and economy, they also have "a vested interest in provincial status and power which the several provincial electorates perhaps do not share fully." Their policy determinations reflect a varying mix of goals for their provincial citizenry, and an institutional concern for the long-term survival of the political and bureaucratic power of government itself. On the other side of the bargaining table they encounter Ottawa, a larger version of their own expansionist tendencies, which, in the slightly jaundiced words of Claude Morin, "is quite simply loyal to a solidly-rooted historical tradition, the unmistakable outlines of which could already be discerned in John A. Macdonald's remarks at the time the federation was put together."

The inertia of the political and bureaucratic momentum of the governments they join inducts new recruits into prevailing definitions of the situation. This is instanced by the frequency with which staunch provincialists, from Joseph Howe onwards, become staunch federalists on entering the federal government. Thus, it is not surprising that the representatives of "French power" in Ottawa will seek solutions to French-English problems by policies which do not weaken the central government. They will try and make the federal government, and indeed the whole country a more congenial environment for francophones rather than opt for a solution which enhances the power of the government in Quebec City. It is also not surprising that such efforts are looked on with little favour by government elites in Quebec City. French Canadians in federal politics and in the federal civil service are conditioned to see the world through different eyes than their Quebec City counterparts. What is attractive to the latter is often a direct threat to the political and bureaucratic needs of the former. Profound governmental constraints minimize the possibility of ethnic solidarity across jurisdictional boundaries.

Federal and provincial governments are not neutral containers, or reflecting mirrors, but aggressive actors steadily extending their tentacles of control, regulation, and manipulation into society — playing, in Deutsch's terminology, a steering role — and thus fostering sets of integrated relationships between themselves and the various socioeconomic forces and interests in their jurisdictions. Governing elites view their task as the injection of provincial or federal meaning into society, giving it a degree of coherence and a pattern of interdependence more suited for government purposes than what would emerge from the unhindered working of social and market forces. Each government's policies pull the affected interests into relations of dependence and attachment to the power centre which manipulates their existence. Each government seeks policy coherence in order to minimize internal contradictions leading to the frustration of its own policies. The inadequacies of the theory and advice on which decision-makers rely produce major discrepancies between governmental ambition and actual achievement. The byzantine complexity of internal government structures, and the sluggishness of the diffuse bureaucratic instrumentalities on which policy-makers depend, create additional obstacles to the coherence in policy and society that each government seeks. Nevertheless, given these limitations each government transmits cues and pressures to the environment tending to group the interests manipulated by its policies into webs of interdependence springing from the particular version of socioeconomic integration it is pursuing. Provincial governments work toward the creation of limited versions of a politically-created provincial society and economy, and the national government works toward the creation of a country-wide society and economy.

Federal policies are responses to nation-wide considerations. From the perspective of Ottawa the provinces constitute concentrations of governmental power whose manipulation is difficult, but nevertheless must be attempted where necessary. In pursuing its mission as a national government from 1867 to the present, Ottawa has not hesitated to interfere with provincial policies by the disallowance of provincial legislation, and more recently by the adroit and extensive employment of the spending power. The mission of provincial political elites is necessarily more restricted, being territorially confined by provincial boundaries, often restrained by weaknesses of financial capacity, and, formerly, hampered by administrative shortcomings. Nevertheless, the British North America Act gives the provinces jurisdictional authority in functional areas of expanding significance, and, most important, gives them control of the natural resource base of their economy. While the jurisdiction of a province lacks the comprehensive coverage enjoyed by the government of a unitary state, it is a sufficiently impressive base of governmental power to elicit visions of futures to be pursued. It cannot be doubted, to cite only the more obvious examples, that Lesage, Smallwood, Douglas, W. A. C. Bennett, and Manning had coherent sets of public purposes for the provincial societies they governed. From their perspective the federal government and its policies constituted environmental uncertainties which had to be managed, exploited, or reduced, and in some cases bitterly attacked in the defence of the provincial futures whose creation they envisaged.

As they pursue their specific goals federal and provincial elites unwittingly serve the profound trend towards the increasing politicization of society. What Léon Dion calls the "political invasion of our daily lives . . . a new phenomenon in history," has a particular significance for a federal polity. In almost every conceivable aspect of our existence, from the workaday world of our daily occupation, to the private intimate worlds of sex and love, our conduct is affected by the larger, pervasive world of federal and provincial competition and cooperation. We are light years away from the relatively apolitical, nongovernmentalized societies of 1867. No national society existed in 1867, and provincial societies were expected to be relatively free from extensive government controls by the newly-created provincial governments. A century later we have governmentalized societies, both federal and provincial, interwoven with each other in relations of competitive interdependence.

The institutionalization of government, the construction of a sphere of political and bureaucratic existence differentiated from other spheres of collective life, automatically reduces the relative importance of nongovernment groups, interests and individuals in policy-making. There is impressive unanimity from students of Canadian government that members of the public are little more than spectators, mobilized by competing elites at three- to five-year intervals for electoral purposes, and then returned to their accustomed role as objects of government policy. "Canada," observes Richard Simeon, "combines the British tradition of a strong executive and centralized leadership with a *relative* freedom from mass pressure and popular constraint." Even bitter and well-publicized intergovernmental conflict may take place in the face of almost complete public indifference or ignorance, as Claude Morin asserts was true of the recent Ottawa-Quebec hostilities over the latter's role at international conferences.

Paradoxically, the institutionalization process which acts as a barrier to public influence on decision-making is the instrumentality for political and bureaucratic elites to bring society under ever more comprehensive government control and guidance. If socialism is about equality, contemporary Canadian federalism is about governments, governments that are possessed of massive human and financial resources, that are driven by purposes fashioned by elites, and that accord high priority to their own long-term institutional self-interest. We should not be surprised, therefore, to be told that in the early years of the Lesage regime "most governmental activity . . . was initiated by the government itself . . . ," to be reminded of the various federal government programmes introduced by political and bureaucratic elites in the absence of strong demands, and to read that the "demands on government have been in large part self-created." It is abundantly clear that the massive impact of government on society at the output stage does not require a prior massive impact of society on government at the input stage.

By and large, the above analysis also applies to Quebec. The Quebec government, like the others, attempts to mould society in terms of its conception of a desirable future. Here too bureaucrats and politicians have the same disproportionate capacity to influence policy evident in other jurisdictions. But important differences exist. In recent years the political system they manage has been repeatedly shaken by social transformations, often government induced. Further, the society to which elites respond is not simply the provincial segment of an English-speaking North American culture which, with variations, dominates the rest of the country and the neighbour to the south. Although clusters of French culture exist elsewhere in Canada, its primary concentration in the province of Quebec necessarily involves the government of that province in a host of specific national questions. The government of Quebec is not in the business of controlling and directing the provincial segment of a larger society, but of fostering and stimulating a "full-blown society" infused with nationalistic fervour by two centuries of minority status. This is a society in which the major groups, associations, and organizations increasingly "tend ... to fall back on the Quebec government."

The singular importance of provincial government in contemporary Quebec is partly a delayed compensation for the long era of negative government under Duplessis and his predecessors which bequeathed the modernizing governments of the past two decades a heritage of daunting problems. Also, the relative weakness of the francophone role in the private economic sector generates pressure to employ the majority-controlled provincial state to redress this no longer acceptable ethnic imbalance. Thus, although in contemporary Quebec, as elsewhere in Canada, the political debate centres on the precise nature of the leading role to be played by government, it is a debate with a difference. In recent years it has focussed with growing intensity on the fundamental question of the relationship of the people and government of Quebec with the rest of Canada. . . .

Thus far this paper has portrayed the federal political process from the perspective of political and bureaucratic actors in government. This section will look upwards, a revealing change of direction, from the perspectives of citizens, interest groups, and parties to show the impact of the federal system on the character of their political activity.

Our approach to the study of politics focusses disproportionately on the problems posed for governments by the transformation of society, and too little on the problems posed for society by the escalating demands of government. Society, constantly challenged by new public policies ranging from education, economy, and welfare to the basic questions of life, death, and human meaning devotes more and more resources to the task of responding to government. In a narrow, superficial sense this is most visible at the level of the taxpayer compelled to finance the numerous ill-conceived government ventures which litter the contemporary landscape of public choice. In recent years he has been burdened by the chaotic and unplanned introduction of automobile insurance in British Columbia, a system of railway passenger transportation whose escalating expenses produce less and less service, dramatic overruns on the Olympic installations in Montreal, and the burgeoning costs of the James Bay developments. . . .

These spectacular escapades, however, constitute only the tip of the governmental iceberg. A recent Ontario study found that the time from the submission of an application for subdivision approval to its final acceptance had increased from an average of 1.9 years in 1973 to 2.1 years in 1974 and 2.3 years in 1975. In general, the ever more elaborate regulatory role of government greatly increases "the overhead (compliance) costs of industry, trade unions and other groups in either protecting or extending their interests."

To those affected by its actions contemporary government is correctly viewed as both a potential resource and a threat. It is always a powerful presence in the environment to be exploited, attacked, or evaded as self-interest and citizen duty dictate. In the complex contest between provincial governments seeking control, and individuals and organized interests seeking a favourable environment, the latter may respond by exit, taking advantage of the gap between the limited geographic reach of particular governments, and the area of free movement which constitutes the federal system, to move to more congenial jurisdictions. Capital knows no loyalty. Its easy mobility across provincial and national boundaries exerts a strong pressure on each province not to deviate in its tax system from the other provincial systems with which it is in unavoidable competition, and on Canada not to impose a more burdensome or discriminatory system of taxes than exists in the United States. In British Columbia, polarized by a free enterprise versus socialism rhetoric for half a century, the claim that investment would dry up if the CCF-NDP formed the government has been a standard election threat by big business and the various partisan opponents of the left.

The social and economic interests of Canadian society, seeking their own advantage, work the federal system in their search for the optimum relationship with its double layer of governments. J. R. Mallory, writing of an earlier era, noted that powerful economic interests sought to stem collectivist inroads on their freedom by resort to extensive litigation to weaken the constitutional competence of the governments attempting to regulate them. Conversely, as Trudeau observed and deprecated, those interests seeking advantage and/or protection knocked on any government door, hoping to benefit from the confusion of jurisdiction and elicit a positive response, "regardless of the constitution," from whichever level of government would listen.

There is contemporary evidence that pressure groups attempt to influence the workings of the federal division of power by having the government closest to the centre of their organizational strength, and to which they have easiest access, handle the concerns affecting them. Thus the Quebec-based Confederation of National Trade Unions "attempted to weaken the federal government in order to strengthen the provincial governments, the Quebec government in particular. The [Canadian Labour Congress], on the other hand, has striven mightily to restore or preserve the authority of the federal government and to cajole it into regaining the initiative." ...

The impact of federalism is also evident in the workings of the party system. The general tendency in federal regimes, as Carl Friedrich observes, is that "parties tend toward paralleling the government setup.... Political science has recognized for some time that the organizational structure of parties tends to correspond to the governmental pattern under constitutional democracy. This is only natural, since it is one of the purposes of parties to gain control of the government; therefore, if the government is federally structured, parties must adapt themselves to such a structure."

In the contemporary era the structuring effect of federalism has generated a pronounced trend to the separation of federal and provincial party systems. This is manifested in tendencies towards distinct political careers at both levels, separate national and provincial organizations, and separate sources of party finance. Of particular significance is the development of public schemes of provincial election financing which reduce financial dependence on the national parties. The employment of the public resources of autonomous provincial governments to foster the autonomy of their party systems is an impressive illustration of federalism's capacity for self-reinforcement.

The federal system contributes to party system separation by its provision of discrete provincial arenas in which sectionally-based parties can capture power while weak in the country as a whole. The federal system also stimulates ideological differentiation between federal and provincial parties bearing the same name. This combines with divergent strategy requirements at the two levels to generate recurrent tensions between the federal and provincial branches of the party. The parties at different levels of the federal system exist in different socioeconomic environments, respond to different competitive situations, and are products of particular patterns of historical development, and historical accidents. They fight elections under different leaders, at different times, and on different issues before different electorates in separate jurisdictions endowed with distinctive constitutional responsibilities. Numerous voters respond to this catalogue of differences by deliberately switching their votes as they move from one arena to another, particularly where a third party with a limited or nonexistent federal presence is provincially strong, as in BC. The complicated translation of these differences into the strength or weakness of individual parties frequently results in striking dissimilarities between the federal and provincial party system in a particular province.

The circumstances in which provincial parties in power will support their federal counterparts almost entirely reflect strategic considerations. From the federal perspective incumbent national parties of whatever persuasion recognize that the intergovernmental conflict and collaboration involved in the working of contemporary federalism are only minimally affected by purely partisan considerations. "From the federal point of view, whatever parties are in power provincially will press provincial interests." And from the provincial point of view the same holds true of power-holding parties at the federal level....

The structuring effect of federalism on parties and interest groups has crucial consequences for the political system. The federal system was originally conceived as a layer of provincial governments representing territorial diversities, and a central government with responsibilities for creating the national society it was to serve. It has become a system of powerful governments, sustained by interest groups and parties which, with imperfections, mirror the governmental structure in which they exist. The chain of federal influence, commencing with the elemental fact of a federal constitutional system, has successfully exerted strong pressure to align parties, interest groups, and individual voters behind the distinct governments which are the essence of federalism. Federal and provincial governments, federal and provincial parties, and federal and provincial pressure groups reinforce each other and they reinforce federalism.

The fleshing out of the governmental structure of federalism by interest groups and parties contributes to the vitality of the system by attaching powerful supports to each level of government which resist any diminution of its authority. "[G]roups organized on a local or regional basis will tend to strengthen local awareness, local loyalties and local particularism," while nationally-organized groups foster "national awareness..., feelings of identification with the national institutions of government,... [and] heighten feelings of efficacy and involvement with those institutions and thus promote national integration." The symbiotic relationship between interest groups and the governments they interact with produces strong mutualities of interest in which each sustains and feeds on the other....

A federal system of governments, supported by parties and pressure groups which parallel the governmental structure, and infused with conflicting federal and provincial visions of economy and society held by competing political and bureaucratic elites, requires a language of political debate appropriate to its fundamental political concerns. Hence, the dominant political language since Confederation has been geared to the making of claims and counterclaims by the federal and provincial spokesmen for territorially-defined societies. In an indirect way, and with the passage of time, the federal language of political discourse became a vehicle for the standard normative controversies which concern modern political systems, questions dealing with equality, the socioeconomic rights of citizens, and social justice. Inevitably, however, the pressure of existing language contributed to the clothing of new controversies in federal garments and their emergence in claims on behalf of provincial communities and governments, or charter members, or founding races, or the national interest as defined by Ottawa.

Clearly, the political language of federalism, and the federal political system with which it is intertwined, have encouraged a politics in which provincial particularisms have been accorded special prominence. Provincial governments as the claimants for, and recipients of federal bounty, have acted as surrogates for the communities they govern. In the dialectical process of federal provincial controversies, the claims of provincial governments encounter the rival claims of the central government with its constitutional authority to speak for all Canadians, for the national community stretching from Bonavista to Vancouver Island. The political incentives for the federal government to couch its claims in the language of individual citizen rights and obligations engender a direct conflict with provincial claims on behalf of territorially-based communities, the reconciliation of which is worked out in the federal process....

The political language of federalism, a language for the conducting of political competition and cooperation between territorially-based groups and their governments, is necessarily hostile to the nation-wide politics of class.

The politics and language of class assume that the conditioning effects of capitalism have washed out identities and political perspectives based on socialization into provincial frames of reference. This has not yet happened. In spite of the auspicious depression circumstances of its birth, its early antipathy to the provinces, and its long-standing attempts to create a new politics and language of class at the national level, the CCF and its successor the NDP have made only minor dents in the nonclass language of federalism.

For nearly half a century left-wing academic analysis has stressed the allegedly inexorable logic of capitalist development in producing class polarization and a modern class-based politics, described as "creative politics" by its more recent exponents. Indeed, by constant repetition this perspective has become the time-honoured traditional language of a dissenting minority which updates the old arguments and the standard predictions decade after decade. Elections and surveys have been carefully monitored since the thirties in numerous attempts to detect the always imminent emergent trend of class mobilization and polarization, the assumed hallmarks of a maturing economy. The failure of reality to conform to the canons of this version of social science has evoked fulminations against federalism, and an adroit use of the concept of false consciousness. These have had minimal impact on the nonclass world view of elites and masses involved in the political world of federalism. The political language of territorially-based group competition derived from the federal system, and socialized into the consciousness of political actors since Confederation, has prevailed over the twentieth-century challenge from the weakly-developed language of class based on the economy.

Contrary to virtually all predictions, post-World War II Canadian politics has not displayed an irreversible trend to centralization, nor the manifestations of capitalist contradiction in polarized class politics, creative or otherwise. Instead, the provinces, aided by secular trends which have enhanced the practical significance of their constitutionally-based legislative authority, and by the deliberate improvement of their own bureaucratic power and capacity, have given a new salience to the politics of federalism and the territorially-based diversities it encompasses, reflects and fosters. The present crisis of Canadian federalism, indeed, is caused not by the politics of class, but by the passionate politics of territorially-based nationalism espoused by the incumbent government in Quebec City. In a logical sense the politics of the Quebec journey towards independence is simply an extended development of the traditional federal concept of provincial autonomy carried to an anti-federalist conclusion....

Success in grappling with the special burdens of governing a federal state does not come easily. The eleven governments of the provincial and country-wide societies of Canada require an effective coordinating capacity if each is not to frustrate the efforts of the others in their joint governing of the country.

The fact that the federal-provincial political arena is not restricted in scope to only a few matters of peripheral concern for society and economy enhances the importance of the task. Almost without exception, every crucial issue, including the constitutional framework of the country itself, eventually ends up at the conference table for resolution. "In few policy areas," according to Richard Simeon, "except perhaps defence, the post office or garbage collection — does one government act alone." ...

In these circumstances, contemporary intergovernmental coordination is not a simple matter of agreement between a handful of political leaders and their staff advisers. It requires the coordination of powerful bureaucracies with deep policy roots in their societies, and of "the publics that are implicated in their normal functioning." It requires, therefore, the containment of ineradicable tendencies to conflict between the federal vision of a society and economy, and ten competing provincial visions, each building on the pervasive links between government and its environment forged by its predecessors....

Parliamentary government and federalism have contributed to a flexible, nonideological, pragmatic style of politics which facilitates intergovernmental agreement. Federal politics, in particular, has always required political leaders with well-developed bargaining skills, capable of encompassing the profound diversities of the country in their appeals, politics and leadership. One of Mackenzie King's "robust convictions," doubtless born of long experience, was "his belief that the really important people in the world were the *conciliators*." ...

By implication this paper has suggested that to look at the literature of Canadian federalism historically makes clear how much has been a response to particular climates of academic and intellectual opinion, how much has been characterized by an anti-federalist mentality, and how the wish has too frequently fathered the thought. Studies of Canadian politics have suffered from a disciplinary mobilization of bias which grossly underestimates the autonomy of elites, the weight of government, and the moulding effect of institutions on political behaviour. A form of sociological reductionism common to North American political scientists has stressed society at the expense of the polity and either devalued, ignored, or denied an autonomous role for government. Democratic assumptions have elicited analyses which focus on the popular impact on government and neglect the reverse. Egalitarianism has had similar effects by undervaluing and underweighting the extent, significance, and unavoidability of elite discretion. Further, the search for class politics has entailed a stress on elections, an excessive interest in parties, and a deflection of attention from the overriding reality of government.

Developments in comparative politics have played a part in our miseducation. The evanescence and crumbling of political systems in the post-independence states of the Third World have contributed to a brutal awareness of the fragility of political structures incompatible with the historic social systems they confront. The study of the latter and their impact on the polity has elicited a strong sociological thrust in Third-World studies. However, the sociological perspective appropriately applied to the "soft states" of Africa,

Asia, and Latin America has been uncritically and inappropriately extended to the study of the highly-institutionalized political systems of the western world. . . .

. . . Accordingly, the enterprise of assessing the creative, formative, and coercive capacities of government, authority, and institutions requires us to overcome the biases of sociological reductionism, democratic mythology, egalitarian levelling, incorrect Third-World analogies, and the disciplinary errors to which they contribute. Success in the enterprise will provide much-needed understanding of "the reality of structures, the extent of their 'grip' over society, and the true importance of constitutions in shaping behaviour."

From Middle to Foremost Power: Defining a New Place for Canada in the Hierarchy of World Power

JAMES EAYRS

It is the argument of this essay that the term "middle power" no longer does justice to Canada's role in world affairs. Canada has become instead a "foremost power" — foremost in the dictionary definition of "most notable or prominent." I hope to show that this assertion is no chauvinistic trumpery, no Laurier-like extravaganza ("the twenty-first century belongs to Canada"), but rather a realistic assessment of Canadian capabilities in a world where the substance, and hence the distribution, of power have undergone swift and radical change.

"Power" is the master-concept of politics. As life is to biology, space to astronomy, deity to theology, so is power to relations among individuals, groups and nations. Its very centrality in its field has caused theorists to take power for granted, to take power as given. But in politics nothing should be taken for granted, nothing taken as given.

Let us review, therefore, the properties of power, of which three are basic. Power is *pervasive*; power is *elusive*; and power is *relative*. (Never dismiss platitudes; they often express essential truths.)

PERVASIVENESS OF POWER

What prose was for M. Jourdain ("Gracious me! For the last 40 years I have been speaking prose without knowing it."), power is for all of us. We may know power as its manipulators, we may know it as its victims, we may, like Jourdain, not know we know. But power is pervasive in our lives. Power is the ecology of politics. To talk of "power politics" is otiose, for there is no other kind.

Resistance to the notion of the pervasiveness of power is as pervasive as power itself. Saints, mystics, gurus of the hour or of the ages are often proclaimed by themselves and their disciples to be beyond the power principle, outside the power nexus.

Gandhi is widely cited as an example of a profoundly significant figure who refused to play the power game. Certainly the "half-naked, seditious

---

James Eayrs, "From Middle to Foremost Power: Defining a New Place for Canada in the Hierarchy of World Power," *International Perspectives* (May/June 1975), pp. 15-24. Reprinted by permission of the author and the publisher.

fakir" (as Churchill once described him) appeared to dwell in a kind of power counterculture — at loggerheads with power, at the antipodes from power. Certainly the saintly figure of the Mahatma in its ascetic's garb seemed even to his fellow Indians on first meeting to be (in Pandit Nehru's words) "very distant and different and unpolitical." How much more so must it have seemed to those worldly British politicians who — their exasperation rising as he remained beyond reach of the sort of argument to which politicians normally respond — tried to negotiate with him about the future of his country!

Gandhi's *satyagraha* — "clinging to truth" — demanded everything that power normally abhors. The shunning of duplicity. The turning of one's cheek. The avoiding of force even in the presence of a weaker adversary. No — the avoiding of force *especially* in the presence of a weaker adversary. And in the presence of a stronger? "I will come out into the open, and let the pilot see I have not a trace of evil against him [sic]." Such was Gandhi's bomber-defence system.

The strategy invites at worst derision, at best the comment made by Henry Kissinger about the only kind of pacifist he has the time of day for — "those who bear the consequences of non-violence to the end." "But," Kissinger adds, "even to them I will talk willingly merely to tell them that they will be crushed by the will of those that are strong, and that their pacifism can lead to nothing but horrible suffering."

Such an assessment gravely underrates the power of the Mahatma, which, skilfully deployed, made him the most influential politician — arguably — of our time. To interpret non-violent resistance as the rejection of power is to misunderstand the nature of power. The attraction of *satyagraha*, as of later strategies derived from it (notably Martin Luther King's), is precisely the expectation of potency. Gandhi never doubted it. "Working under this new law of non-violence," he wrote in 1920, "it is possible for a single individual to defy the whole might of an unjust empire." So it proved. Gandhi exaggerated only the novelty of *satyagraha*, which a Judean freedom-fighter had no less skilfully employed against the Romans 2,000 years before him.

PERVASION DENIED

Nations as well as individuals deny that power pervades. Especially newly-independent nations, which are characteristically reluctant to accept the fact that their hard-won freedom is no more than a licence to hunt in the jungle of power. They look on themselves as above the fray, beyond the struggle, reject the cynical aphorisms of the worldly philosophers — Kautilya's definition of an enemy as the state that is on one's border and of a friend as the state that is on the border of one's enemy, Hobbes's depiction of nations "in the state and posture of gladiators." George Washington for the young United States, Leon Trotsky for the young Bolshevik Republic, Raoul Dandurand for the newly-independent Dominion of Canada alike believed that the principles of their respective policies transcended the sordid statecraft of older, debauched societies.

These attitudes are much the same as those that try to claim for a Jesus or a Gandhi an immunity to power, and rest on the same confusion. What distinguishes them is not their exemption from having to play the game of power but rather their style of play. They have not renounced power, which is no more capable of renunciation by statesmen than gravity is capable of renunciation by spacemen. Theirs is not a renunciation at all, but an enunciation of a particular method of pursuing power — the method that strives after power not by the display or resort to bruising force but by the influence that good behaviour may exert upon opinion. It may not work; but that is another matter.

POWER ELUDES

Power pervades: there is no getting away from it. Power also eludes: there is no coming to grips with it. The elusiveness of power is beginning to preoccupy both practitioners and theorists, and about time, too!

> Our territory is large, our people are numerous, our geographical position is good.... It will be intolerable if after several decades we are not the greatest nation on earth.

> If we are six feet tall, the Russians are three feet tall, and the Chinese six inches tall.

> If one's line is correct, even if one has not a single soldier at first, there will be soldiers, and even if there is no political power, power will be gained.... The crux of the matter is line.

> One word of truth outweighs the whole world.

These four quotations — their authors, respectively, are Mao Tse-tung, U.S. Senator William Proxmire, Chou En-lai and Alexander Solzhenitsyn — are all statements about power, assessments of the constituents of power. They cannot all be correct. Those of Chou and Solzhenitsyn come close to saying the same thing, those of Chou and Mao are greatly at variance, while those of Mao and Proxmire are mutually incompatible.

The formulae of Mao and Proxmire do have something in common, however. Both proceed from geopolitical assumptions.

Geopolitical assumptions hold that power is a function of a nation's might, that the might of nations may be calculated more or less precisely, and that in consequence comparisons are possible, nations can be ranked and graded. The American humorist Russell Baker wrote a column — "Let's Hear It for No. 7" — in which he argued, tongue only half-in-cheek, that "countries that are No. 11 or No. 17" (he cites Denmark and Kenya) "don't have to spend all their income to get ready to wipe themselves out" and "as a result are often very pleasant countries." He does not want the United States to drop from No. 1 to No. 17, but sees distinct advantages in seventh place.

BASIS FOR CALCULATION
But how to tell that seventh place — or fourth or fifth or sixth? If might is amenable to calculation, what makes the mighty mighty, what makes them mightier yet?

Geopoliticians' answers differed. Some said mighty populations — the state with the biggest battalions. Others said mighty reserves — the state with the greatest bullion. Some said control of the seas, others control of the land. Some said control of the air, others control of the firmament: "If the Soviets control space, they can control earth" — thus John F. Kennedy in 1960 (making his pitch for the aerospace vote).

The ranking of Japan is a good example of the method, and even better of its limitations. Here power is seen to come not from the barrel of a gun but from the greatest GNP, in anticipation of which (this before the higher cost of a different kind of barrel) Herman Kahn foresaw the emergence of the Japanese super-state by the year 2000. For Edwin O. Reischauer (U.S. Ambassador to Japan during the Kennedy and Johnson Administrations), there is no need to wait so long: "Japan is the No. 2 power in the world."

How does he know? That being too difficult, what makes it so? If the key to Japanese power is export, the key to Japanese export is the qualities of those who make the product high in craftsmanship, low in cost—qualities once epitomized as those of the chrysanthemum and the sword: the sensibility of Japanese design, the zeal of Japanese application to the task at hand, be that overrunning Southeast Asia in the early 1940s or mass-assembling transistor television sets in the early 1970s. A *New York Times* correspondent puts it this way: "American officials and scholars have produced tomes trying to explain why the Japanese have done so well; it may be an oversimplification, but the fundamental reason is that they work like blazes." That does not explain why they work like blazes, but it may be better than no explanation at all.

Elusive as ever, power now seems to reside in the spirit of a people, in their mood and morale — aspects of might about which even neo-geopoliticians do well to hold their peace. "Great things need no firm foundation," the father of Zionism once remarked. "An apple must be placed on a table to keep it from falling. The earth hovers in the air. Thus I can perhaps found a secure Jewish state without a firm anchorage. The secret lies in movement. Hence I believe that somewhere a guidable aircraft will be discovered." (Herzl's metaphor of "a guidable aircraft," evoked some years before the Wright brothers took flight, is almost as remarkable at his forecast, in 1896, of the State of Israel more than a half a century before its birth.) Using a similar metaphor, a commentator accounted in 1905 for the success of British power in India: "The Indian empire is not a miracle in the rhetorician's sense but in the theologian's sense. It is a thing which exists and is alive, but cannot be accounted for by any process of reasoning founded on experience. It is a miracle, as a floating island of granite would be a miracle, or a bird of brass which flew and sung and lived on in mid-air. It is a structure built on nothing, without foundations, without buttresses [compare Herzl's "without a firm anchorage"] held in its place by some force the origin of which is undiscoverable and the nature of which has never been explained."

The modern illustration is surely Yugoslavia. Some wit once dismissed that country as a fifth-rate power. Asked for his impression of Belgrade, he replied: "Imagine a whole city illuminated with a 10-watt bulb." But the power of Yugoslavia is not to be measured by its wattage. "According to all rational calculations," A.J.P. Taylor has written, "Yugoslavia was the country most doomed to disintegrate in the storms of the twentieth century. It has few natural resources: little coal or iron and a territory largely composed of barren mountains. . . . Historical traditions, though strong, work against unity, not in its favour." Whence, then, derives its power? From defiance — from defying Stalin and succeeding. "Yugoslavia has been living on the strength of this defiance ever since."

The elusiveness of power may be seen not only in its possession by those who, on "rational calculations," have no right to it but also in its lack by those who, on calculations no less rational, have every right to it. Here is the cry of S. John Peskett in *The Times*, who, with the rest of us, has seen the assumptions of geopolitics, like so many sandcastle Gibraltars, washed away by the tide: "All the Queen's horses and all the Queen's men, plus the United States of America, the United Nations, NATO, and all the parachutists and glider troops we so busily train, cannot rescue a couple of hundred hostages and a few million pounds worth of aircraft from a handful of guerrillas half of whom are quarreling with the other."

RELATIVE TO USE
Power is pervasive, power is elusive. Power is also relative — relative not least to purpose. What you have of it depends on what you want to do with it.

The relativity of power is most simply illustrated by the distinction between the power to build and the power to destroy. The power to build — to create, to innovate, to improve — is hard to come by, arduous to exercise. It derives from resourceful diplomacy and nimble statecraft, sustained as these must be by a generous and patient citizenry. Rome was not built in a day; how much longer it takes to build a world free from poverty, ignorance, disease!

The power to destroy — to wreck, to frustrate, to sabotage — is, in contrast easy to come by, effortless to exercise. Little is required to smash some cherished project, to bring things tumbling down — only a rifle with a telescopic sight, an assassin hired by the hour. "I'm as important as the start of World War One," bragged Arthur Bremer to his diary when in Ottawa to try to kill his President. "I just need the little opening and a second of time."

The power exerted by these demolition experts — the Tepermans, so to speak, of the global village — can be very great. But it is the kind of power a blackmailer exerts over a wealthy victim — potent while it lasts, but of short duration and likely to end unpleasantly for both of them. It is the power wielded by a pyromaniac in a fireworks factory. It is the power displayed by the President of Libya, threatening retaliation unless the UN Security Council voted to his liking — "Otherwise we shall see what we shall see. We shall do what Samson did: destroy the temple with everyone inside it, including ourselves. Europe should look out for the catastrophe which is lying in wait for it."

Such are the properties of power. Were they fixed clearly in the minds of those who coined the expression "middle power" to describe Canada's place among the nations? I cannot prove it, but I doubt it.

OBSCURITY PREFERRED
For all that has been written about "Canada's role as a middle power" (and much has been written about it), its meaning remains obscure. Obscurity has, indeed, seemed preferable to clarity, Canadians resisting definition as an earlier generation resisted defining "Dominion status" for fear (as Lloyd George put it) of limiting their constitution "by too many finalities." "It is hard to say now precisely what a middle power is," John Holmes confessed in 1965; but that does not bother him. On the contrary: "I am all for accepting this ambiguity rather than insisting on a logical clarification." And again: "The more one tries to define [middle power], the more difficult and perhaps pretentious it appears to do so at all. Often it seems like describing the obvious. Definition spoils the special quality."

The origins of the term are as obscure as its meaning. If it was not used first in 1943, it was used first in 1944, for by 1945 "middle power" had come into widespread circulation. The year 1943 is when Canadians both in and out of government first gave thought to what their place in the postwar world might and ought to be. From the beginning, the prospect of divergence between that "might" and "ought" was both ominous and real. In 1943 Canada stood in the shadow of the United States and Britain. So long as a war remained to be won, such a position was not intolerable, might be construed as part of the Canadian war effort — unpleasant, but something to be put up with for the duration. But as a permanent stance for the postwar future it was out of the question, and Canadians began to say so.

Articulation of discontent was aroused by the threat of exclusion from the ruling circles of the first of the postwar international organizations. Word that Canada — of all countries — was to be left off the governing body of the United Nations Relief and Rehabilitation Agency sent shocks of anger around the foreign policy community. "We are still trying to run a democracy" (so, with notable asperity, the Government, as quoted in the Pearson memoirs, instructed its agent in Washington charged with arguing his country's case) "and there is some historical evidence to support the thesis that democracies cannot be taxed without representation. We have tried to lead our people in a full-out effort for the war, and we had hoped that we could continue to lead them in such a way as to get their support behind the provision of relief and maintenance for battle-scarred Europe in the postwar years. We will not be able to secure their support for such a programme if it, as well as the economic affairs of the world generally, are to be run as a monopoly by the four Great Powers."

UNITED STATES CRUCIAL

Of the four great powers, the United States was crucial for the Canadian case. If Washington would not offer sympathy and support for the aspirations of its friendly neighbour, who else could? But Washington's response left much to be desired. Our status was but dimly recognized, our stature underrated.

In 1925, an eminent American professor of international politics had placed Canada in the category of "other states of subordinate or doubtful rank." In 1939, President Franklin D. Roosevelt felt bound to telephone the Prime Minister to ascertain whether Canada was bound by a British declaration of war. In 1943, wags in Washington were saying that Canada was in the British Commonwealth Mondays, Tuesdays, Wednesdays, an ally of the United States Thursdays, Fridays, Saturdays, and only on Sundays a sovereign independent state. Canadians were not amused.

On 19 March 1943, the Prime Minister of Canada for the first time since the outbreak of the war was asked in Parliament to set forth his views on foreign policy as it might develop in the postwar world. Here was a subject on which Mackenzie King cared not at all to dilate: "The more [the] public . . . is diverted to questions about what is going to be the attitude of this country and that country at the peace table and [in] the postwar period, the less the country will be impressed with the fact that this war itself is not yet won." But something needed to be said, and what he chose to say was what he had said in the House of Commons as long ago as May 24, 1938:

> Our foreign and external policy is a policy of peace and friendliness, a policy of trying to look after our own interests and to understand the position of other governments with which we have dealings. It is a policy which takes account of our political connections and traditions, our geographical position, the limited numbers and the racial composition of our people, our stage in economic development, our own internal preoccupations and necessities — in short, a policy based on the Canadian situation. It is not and cannot be under these circumstances a spectacular headline policy; it is simply the sum of countless

daily dealings with other countries, the general resultant of an effort to act decently on every issue or incident that arises, and a hope of receiving the same treatment from others.

The authors of the volume in the *Canada in World Affairs* series for 1941-44 in which this passage is quoted allow themselves a restrained but telling comment: "Mr. King did not make any modification of this five-year-old statement to conform with the revolutionary development which had taken place in Canada's war potential and industrial production."

Indeed he did not. That would have been inconsistent with his style — a style which, when he came to enunciate principles of foreign policy, chose (to adapt the lyrics of a song of that era) "to eliminate the positive, latch on to the negative."

Even in 1938 — so it seems to one fair-minded and knowledgeable observer, Nicholas Mansergh — the statement overdrew the difficulties, stressing "the precariousness of Canada's export markets, but not the value of her exports; ... regional and cultural tensions within, but not the growing sense of unity; ... the conflicting pulls of geography and history to which indeed every 'settled' country is subject, but ... not the immense strength of Canada's position in the heart of the English-speaking world." In 1943 the statement greatly underrated the country's power. Canada's uranium alone might have been used to extract from the Anglo-American partners in atomic-energy production virtually any concession on postwar status. But that is not how its leaders chose to play their hand.

Still, it was plain folly to continue to be content with lisping their hope for decent treatment in a world about to gain knowledge of the holocaust and to witness Hiroshima. Such ultra-diffident diplomacy would lose Canada's case by default. Even Mackenzie King was soon compelled to realize as much. July 1943 finds him, for the first time, striving after a postwar status commensurate with wartime stature:

> A number of new international institutions are likely to be set up as a result of the war. In the view of the Government, effective representation on these bodies should neither be restricted to the largest states nor necessarily extended to all states. Representation should be determined on a functional basis which will admit to full membership those countries, large or small, which have the greatest contribution to make to the particular object in question.

Here is the germ of "the Canadian doctrine of the middle powers," for a moment's reflection upon its implications is sufficient to indicate how inadequate the "great power/small power" dichotomy had become. "The simple division of the world between great powers and the rest is unreal and even dangerous." Mackenzie King declared to Parliament in August 1944:

> The great powers are called by that name simply because they possess great power. The other states of the world possess power and, therefore, the capacity to use it for the maintenance of peace — in varying degrees ranging from almost

zero in the case of the smallest and weakest states up to a military potential not far below that of the great powers.

Somewhere on this spectrum of power lay Canada.

But where? Policy-makers developed a concern with ranking. "We are moving up in the International League," L.B. Pearson told a Toronto audience in March 1944, "even though we are not yet in the first division." And, in a letter written at that time, Pearson groped closer than anyone had thus far done to the concept of the "middle power":

> Canada is achieving, I think, a very considerable position as a leader, among a group of States which are important enough to be necessary to the Big Four but not important enough to be accepted as one of that quartet. As a matter of fact, the position of a "little Big Power" or "big little Power" is a very difficult one, especially if the "little Big Power" is also a "Big Dominion." The big fellows have power and responsibility, but they also have control. We "in-between States" sometimes get, it seems, the worst of both worlds. We are necessary but not necessary enough. I think this is being felt by countries like the Netherlands and Belgium as well as by ourselves. That is why these countries are not only looking towards the Big Powers, but are looking toward each other for support. There is, I think, an opportunity for Canada, if we desire to take it, to become the leader of this group.

Comparisons may be odious but, as time ran out on Canadian efforts to secure a position on the proposed United Nations Security Council, they became unavoidable. "Just as we are prepared to recognize the great difference in power and responsibility between Canada and the Soviet Union," Mackenzie King told the meeting of Commonwealth prime ministers on May 11, 1944, "[so] we should expect some recognition of the considerable difference between Canada and Panama." Reaffirming, against continued British opposition, its belief that powers other than the great powers should be represented on the Council, the Canadian Government repeated its conviction that their selection "should in some way be related to a dispassionate appraisal of their probable effective contribution to the maintenance of security." "You will, I am sure" — Mackenzie King thought it well to add for Churchill's benefit — "appreciate how difficult it would be for Canada, after enlisting nearly one million persons in her armed forces and trebling her national debt in order to assist in restoring peace, to accept a position of parity in this respect with the Dominican Republic or El Salvador."

Such perceptions were widely shared throughout the country. For some Canadians, indeed, their Government's disclaimer of topmost status — "Canada certainly makes no claim to be regarded as a great power" — seemed to be too bashful, too reserved. "A great world power standing beside Great Britain in the British Empire" was Howard Green's vision of our postwar future. "A country large enough to have world interests," was the assessment of the *Windsor Star*. And a leading Canadian publicist, pondering "A Greater Canada among the Nations," saw our role like this:

> Under the impact of war, Canada has moved up from her old status to a new stature. With her smaller population and lack of colonial possessions, she is not a major or world power like Britain, the United States or Russia. But with her natural wealth and human capacity she is not a minor one like Mexico or Sweden. She stands between as a Britannic Power of medium rank.

In short, a middle power. The term was officially employed for the first time in a despatch from the Department of External Affairs to heads of mission in the five capitals of the countries to which, on January 12, 1945, the Canadian Government made a final (and unavailing) appeal for representation on the Security Council; the exact phrase used was "a so-called middle power." The term was officially defined for the first time in a speech made by R.G. Riddell in 1947: "The Middle Powers are those which by reason of their size, their material resources, their willingness and ability to accept responsibility, their influence and stability are close to being great powers."

PROMOTION SOUGHT
The term "middle power" came into the vocabulary of diplomacy as part of a Canadian campaign to gain promotion from the status of a small power. But that is not the only purpose for which it may be used. It can also be an instrument of demotion. It lends itself not only to aggrandizement but to disparagement as well — as in the expression "merely a middle power."

An instance of how "middle power" may be used for the purpose of demotion and disparagement was reported from Moscow in 1955 on the occasion of Pearson's visit to the Soviet Union. At a reception at the Canadian Embassy for the diplomatic corps, the Canadian and Soviet foreign ministers exchanged some significant banter. "Mr. Molotov and I ought to understand each other," said Pearson joshingly. "We belong to the same trade union but he is a much more important member than I am." "Mr. Pearson is too modest," Molotov responded. "Canada is among the great powers." When Pearson jocularly compared Canada's position between the United States and the Soviet Union to that of the ham in a sandwich, Lazar Kaganovich chimed in to suggest that "a good bridge" was a better comparison. Nor was that the end of it. At a reception some days later, the Canadian Secretary of State for External Affairs found himself (according to one of the reporters present) "in the position of arguing that Canada is a small, rather frail country, while the Russians argued that Canada is a big, important one.... As Mr. Pearson pursued this line that Canada is a small nation, Molotov broke in. He said the Russians do not agree with the foreign minister. In the schools of his country, said Molotov, the children are taught to regard Canada as one of the world's major powers."

Not too much should be made of this exchange (it is not reported in Pearson's memoirs except for a fleeting reference to "flattering toasts to Canada"); it bears, indeed, a close resemblance to what George Kennan recalls as the "slightly disreputable" remarks which passed ritualistically between himself and assorted Latin American presidents some years before (" 'You, Mr. Kennan, are an official of the government of a great country; and I am only the President of an obscure little country'; 'Ah, Mr. President, that may be, but we are all aware that there is no connection between the size of a country and the amount of political wisdom it can produce'.") Much more significant is the deliberately depreciating analysis of Canada's place in the world put out from the Prime Minister's office on May 29, 1968, soon after Pierre Trudeau arrived there:

> Canada's position in the world is now very different from that of the postwar years. Then we were probably the largest of the small powers. Our currency was one of the strongest. We were the fourth or fifth trading nation and our economy was much stronger than the European economies. We had one of the very strongest navy [sic] and air forces. But now Europe has regained its strength. The Third World has emerged....
>
> These are the broad lines of the international environment in which Canada finds itself today. What are we proposing to do about it? We are going to begin with a thorough and comprehensive review of our foreign policy which embraces defence, economic and aid policies....

Without prejudging the findings of that review, it was nonetheless possible to state in a word what its objective ought to be. The word was "realism": "Realism — that should be the operative word in our definition of international aim. Realism in how we read the world barometer. Realism in how we see ourselves thriving in the climate it forecasts." And the first requirement of realism was that "we should not exaggerate the extent of our influence upon the course of world events."

In the course of public speaking over the next few months, the Prime Minister returned again and again to this opening theme. On December 18, 1968, asked by an interviewer if Canada should revert to its postwar role as a leader of the middle powers, Mr. Trudeau demurred:

> Personally I tend to discount the weight of our influence in the world.... I think we should be modest, much more modest than we were, I think, in the postwar years when we were an important power because of the disruption of Europe and so on. But right now we're back to our normal size as it is and I think we must realize that we have limited energy, limited resources and, as you said earlier, intellectual and [sic] manpower. Therefore, we must use modesty.... We shouldn't be trying to run the world.

On January 1, 1969:

> We're living in a world where the strategy is dominated by two powers. All we can do is talk a little bit about tactics but not much.

And on March 25, 1969 (to the National Press Club in Washington):

> I hope that we Canadians do not have an exaggerated view of our own importance.... We may be excused, I hope, if we fail to take too seriously the suggestions of some of our friends from time to time that our acts, or our failure to act — this or that way — will have profound international consequences or will lead to wide-scale undesirable results.

No one familiar with the role of a prime minister in the formulation of Canadian foreign policy will be surprised to learn that these ideas emerged relatively intact as the basic philosophy of the White Paper embodying the results of the foreign policy review when it appeared in 1970. Much has been written about *Foreign Policy for Canadians* — if the purpose was to spark discussion, it succeeded admirably in that purpose — to which there is no need to add. But one point must be made.

It was the Prime Minister's expectation and intention that the results of the review would endure. He believed that the review would outfit Canadians with a foreign policy that would do them for a couple of decades. "When you make a decision to review your foreign policy," Mr. Trudeau remarked in Calgary on April 12, 1969, "it will last for quite a while.... You only re-examine your foreign policy once in a generation. You can't switch every year, you can't switch after every election."

Here is a major error. You can switch, and you must. To stay put for so long is not just to risk being overtaken by events, it guarantees it.

MAJOR CHANGES
Between 1970 and 1975, three major changes have occurred within the international system that have drastically altered the pattern of power. Each is advantageous — or prospectively advantageous — to Canada.

The first is the emergence of what might be called "le défi OPEC" — that sudden accretion of wealth to the low-cost, oil-bearing countries of the Middle East that is currently netting their treasuries enormous "petrodollar" revenue.

It remains to be seen whether the assorted sheikhdoms and emirates that are the beneficiaries of this windfall can transmute their wealth to power, even whether they will enjoy the prosperity of Croesus or suffer the fate of Midas. (Shah Pahlavi and the late King Faisal show it can go either way.) Two consequences, however, are already clear.

One is that the power of oil-dependent industrial countries — all Western European states that lack access to North Sea sources and Japan — has been drastically reduced. The other is that the power of oil-sufficient industrial countries has been substantially increased — nowhere more so than in Canada, where oil is providentially found in conjunction with other sources of energy (notably coal).

RESOURCE POWER

A second major change of the past five years is the declining capacity of technology to confer power and the growing capacity of resources to confer it. To a world where population continues an exponential rate of climb towards demographic disaster, ultra-modern processes for the transmission and manipulation of data are more and more irrelevant and in less and less demand. Such a world requires computers, photocopiers and satellite communications systems less than it needs raw materials, minerals and — above all — food. Power is shifting from those who control the former to those who control the latter. A recent discussion of *The New Wealth of Nations* by Charles F. Gallagher identifies this trend:

> In a world of finite and dwindling physical assets the balance of market values has shifted, at least temporarily and perhaps for a very long period, from the ability of technology to create and develop new assets to the capacity of existing assets to command considerations that will permit the purchase of technology and the procurement of power. For long technology was joined to capital in a fruitful marriage, a happy coupling that developed material resources and created new assets. Today it is resources which have alienated the affections of capital and created conditions permitting the downgrading of technology to the status of a hand-maiden serving the new connubial union. In short, skills have been reduced to a position in which they are traded at a discount relative to goods. He who has the right materials is the better off than he who has the right training....

Because of the revaluation and redistribution of the chips of the game, we have a rearrangement in the classification of nations today.

If this is bad news for the Science Council of Canada, it is good news for the Government of Canada. It means that Canada is exceptionally well endowed to face the worst (short of nuclear war) the future may fling at mankind, exceptionally well equipped for what has been called "the desperate misadventure we are now engaged upon," as well-prepared as any people for those dismal "human prospects" envisaged by melancholiacs who forecast global breakdown. We have what it takes, since we have all it takes.

Canada has almost sinfully bestowed upon it the sources of power, both traditional and new. The technology is there, or waiting. (We need only decide how much technology to develop for ourselves, how much to buy from others.) The manpower is there, or waiting. (We need only decide how many millions more our country needs, then pick amongst the jostling clamourers according to the criteria of our choice.) The resources are there, or waiting, too — animal, vegetable *and* mineral. Hardly a month elapses without the revelation of some new bonanza in our larder. (We need only decide how fast to develop them, how much to charge for them.)

DECLINE OF U.S.

Finally — in part because of these two changes but only just in part — a third change that Peter Wiles has called "the declining self-confidence of the super-powers." These are super-powers now in name only. The decline in self-confidence is most striking in the United States — for reasons that require no elaboration. (The most telling thing about "Watergate" is that it could not have happened in the Soviet Union.) "No nation can pretend to be a super-power," writes C.L. Sulzburger about his country's recent compound fractures, "when its foreign policy suffers such blows as that of the United States in Southeast and Southwest Asia, when its economy reels, its unemployment zooms, its currency staggers, and when its leadership, symbolized by a Chief Executive who chooses that moment to take time off for golf, faces its crises in paralyzed confusion."

For Canadians to exult in American misfortune for its own sake would be the grossest form of *Schadenfreude*. Not for a moment do I suggest we should. I suggest only that we do so for our own sake.

It has not been good for Canada to have been obliged to exist so long in the shadow of a luminous imperial America, whose achievements in whatever field, measured by whatever standard, have so consistently outclassed our own. On the contrary, this condition has been a prescription for crippling neurosis. America's descent from the dizzy heights of power and responsibility which under successive administrations it has occupied since the era of the Marshall Plan offers Canada a chance to stand with more assurance in the light. Only a masochist could fail to welcome such an opportunity.

The opportunity is there, or waiting. "We live in a century," the Prime Minister of Canada remarked in the presence of the Premier of China, "where, increasingly, national greatness is measured not in terms of martial grandeur or even economic accomplishment but in terms of individual welfare and human dignity. No longer is military might or political hegemony the yardstick of achievement. The true test of a government is found in its ability to provide its people with a sense of worth, of accomplishment, of fulfilment." For the first time since 1945, it has become plausible to argue that Canada's chance of passing such a test is just as good as the United States — perhaps even better.

A recent attempt by Peter Dobell to re-rank Canada among the nations in accordance with these new realities promotes us from "middle power" to "minor great power." But such terms as "great power," whether minor or major, have, like "middle power" itself, lost all significance and meaning. I should be content with "foremost power" — if we produce a foreign policy to match.

3
THE DYNAMICS OF CULTURE

Elegy 9

DENNIS LEE

Here, as I sit and watch, the rusty leaves hang taut with
   departure.
The last few tourists pose by the Moore and snap their proof
   that they were also alive.
And what if there is no regenerative absence?
What if the void that compels us is only
a mood gone absolute?
We would have to live in the world.
What if the dreary high-rise is nothing but
banks of dreary high-rise, it does not
release the spirit by fraying its attachment,
for the excellent reason that there is no place else to go?
We would have to live in it, making our lives on earth.
Or else a man might go on day by day
in love with emptiness, dismayed each time he meets
good friends, fine buildings and grass in the acres of
   concrete, feeling the
city's erotic tug begin once more, perpetually
splayed alive by the play of his bungled desires,
though some do not salute the death of the body
before they have tested its life, but crippled they summon
   together
the fury from within, they tilt at
empite, empire, lethal adversary;

but I am one who came to
idolatry, as in a season of God,
taking my right to be from nothingness.

Across the square the crisp leaves blow in gusts, tracing
the wind's indignant lift in corners,
filling the empty pool.
People plod past through the raw air, lost in their overcoats.
I hunch down close to my chest and eat smoke.

But when the void became void I did
let go, though derelict for months
and I was easy, no longer held by its negative presence
as I was earlier disabused of many things in the world
including Canada, and came to know I still had access to
    them,
and I promised to honour each one of my country's failures
    of nerve and its sellouts.

To rail and flail at a dying civilisation,
to rage in imperial space, condemning
soviet bombers, american bombers — to go on saying
no to history is good.
And yet a man does well to leave that game behind, and go
    and find
some saner version of integrity,
although he will not reach it where he longs to, in the
vacant spaces of his mind — they are so
occupied. Better however to try.

But we are not allowed to enter God's heaven, where it is all a
drowsy beatitude, nor is God, the realm above our heads but
must grow up on earth.
Nor do we have recourse to void.
For void is not a place, nor
negation of a place.
Void is not the high cessation of the lone self's burden,
crowned with the early nostalgias;
nor is it rampant around the corner, endlessly possible.
We enter void when void no longer exists.

And best of all is finding a place to be
in the early years of a better civilisation.
For we are a conquered nation: sea to sea we bartered
everything that counts, till we have
nothing to lose but our forebears' will to lose.
Beautiful riddance!
And some will make their choice and eat imperial meat.
But many will come to themselves, for there is
no third way at last and these will
spend their lives at war, though not with
guns, not yet — with motherwit and guts, sustained
by bloody-minded reverence among the things which are,
and the long will to be in Canada.

The leaves, although they cling against the
wind do not resist their time of dying.
And I must learn to live it all again, depart again —
the storm-wracked crossing, the nervous descent, the barren
    wintry land,
and clearing a life in the place where I belong, re-entry
to bare familiar streets, first sight of coffee mugs,
reconnaissance of trees, of jobs done well or badly,
flashes of workday people abusing their power,
abusing their lives, hung up, sold out and
feeling their lives wrenched out of whack
by the steady brunt of the continental breakdown;
finding a place among the ones who live
on earth somehow, sustained in fits and starts
by the deep ache and presence and sometimes the joy of
    what is.

Freely out of its dignity the void must
supplant itself. Like God like the soul it must
surrender its ownness, like eternity it must
re-instil itself in the texture of our being here.
And though we have seen our most precious words
withdraw, like smudges of wind from a widening water-calm,
though they will not be charged with presence again in our
    lifetime that is
well, for now we have access to new nouns —
as water, copout, tower, body, land.

Earth, you nearest, allow me.
Green of the earth and civil grey:
within me, without me and moment by
moment allow me for to
be here is enough and earth you
strangest, you nearest, be home.

The Problem of a Canadian Literature

E.K. Brown

... There is a Canadian literature, often rising to effects of great beauty, but it has stirred little interest outside Canada. A few of our authors, a very few, have made for themselves a large and even enthusiastic audience in Britain or in the United States or in both. Among these the first in time was Thomas Chandler Haliburton, a Nova Scotian judge, who would not have relished the claim that he was a Canadian. A curious blend of the provincial and the imperialist, he ended his days in England, where long before he himself arrived his humorous sketches were widely read, so widely that Justin McCarthy has reported that for a time the sayings of his most ingenious creation, Sam Slick, were as well known as those of the more durably amusing Sam Weller. Haliburton's papers were also popular in the United States, and their dialectal humour and local colour have left a perceptible stamp upon New England writing. At the mid century, where Sam Slick was already a figure in English humour, *Saul*, a huge poetic drama by a Montreal poet, Charles Heavysege, had a passing vogue in Britain and in the United States, impressing Emerson and Hawthorne and inducing Coventry Patmore to describe it as "indubitably one of the most remarkable English poems ever written out of Great Britain." Its vogue was lasting enough for W.D. Lighthall, a Montreal poet of a later generation, to recall that "it became the fashion among tourists to Montreal to buy a copy of *Saul*." Today, along with Heavysege's other works, his *Count Filippo* and his *Jephthah's Daughter*, it is unknown within Canada and without. Even the songs and sonnets of Heavysege are absent from recent Canadian anthologies. At the turn of the century the animal stories of C. G. D. Roberts extended the range of North American writing in a direction it might naturally have been expected to take with equal success somewhat sooner — the imaginative presentation of the forms of wild life characteristic of this continent in their relationship to the frontiers of settlement. These tales, simple and at times powerful, continue to hold a high place in the rather isolated and minor kind of literature to which they belong; but there is no doubt that in our time they are more talked of than opened except by youthful readers. ...

More recently Canadian work of value comparable with that of Haliburton's sketches and Roberts's animal tales has become known outside the

---

Abridged from E.K. Brown, "The Problem of a Canadian Literature," *On Canadian Poetry* (Toronto: Ryerson Press, 1943), pp. 3-27. Reprinted by permission of McGraw-Hill Ryerson Limited.

country. There were the humorous papers of Stephen Leacock, the best of which have delighted not only Americans and Englishmen, and the peoples of other parts of the British Commonwealth, but also some Europeans. I can remember hearing M. André Maurois read to a group of students at the Sorbonne the charming study called "Boarding House Geometry"; and I never heard merrier laughter in Paris. The endless Jalna chronicles of Miss Mazo de la Roche maintain a large audience in Britain, and a sizable one in the United States; and in a more restricted group in the latter country the short stories and, to a less degree, the novels of Morley Callaghan are valued. I think that I have mentioned all the Canadians who have acquired considerable popularity or reputation as imaginative authors, either in the United States or in Great Britain. To the reader outside Canada such works as have been mentioned have not been important as reflections of phases in a national culture; the interest in the work has not spread to become an interest in the movements and the traditions in the national life from which the work emerged. Canadian books may occasionally have had a mild impact outside Canada; Canadian literature has had none.

Even within the national borders the impact of Canadian books and of Canadian literature has been relatively superficial. The almost feverish concern with its growth on the part of a small minority is no substitute for eager general sympathy or excitement. To one who takes careful account of the difficulties which have steadily beset its growth its survival as something interesting and important seems a miracle.

Some of these difficulties, those of an economic kind, may be easily and briefly stated. Economically the situation of our literature is, and always has been, unsound. No writer can live by the Canadian sales of his books. The president of one of our most active publishing companies, the late Hugh Eayrs, estimated that over a period of many years his profit on the sales of Canadian books was one per cent; and I should be surprised to learn that any other Canadian publisher could tell a much more cheerful tale, unless, of course, the production of text-books was the staple of his firm's business. Text-books make money in any country. In general the Canadian market for books is a thin one, for a variety of important reasons. The Canadian population is in the main a fringe along the American border: nine out of ten Canadians live within two hundred miles of it, more than half within a hundred miles. The one important publishing centre is Toronto; and a bookseller in Vancouver, Winnipeg or Halifax must feel reasonably sure that a book will be bought before he orders a number of copies which must be transported across thousands of miles. Books like *Gone with the Wind* and *The White Cliffs* — to keep to recent successes — he will order in quantity with confidence; but the distinguished work, the experimental novel, the collection of austere verse, the volume of strenuous criticism, is for him a luxury. The population of Canada is less than that of the State of New York; if our population were confined within an area of the same size the problem of distributing books would be soluble. Even if our fewer than twelve million people were confined within the huge triangle whose points are Montreal, North Bay and Windsor — enclosing an area comparable with that of the region of New England — the problem might be soluble. But it is hard to see how the cultivated minority is to be served when its centres are separated by hundreds if not thousands of miles in which not a single creditable bookstore exists.

Of the fewer than twelve million Canadians who are strung along the American border in a long thin fringe, almost a third are French-speaking. These read little if at all in any language except French, apart from a small, highly conservative minority which studies the classics and scholastic philosophy, and a rather larger minority which keeps abreast of books in English that treat of political and economic subjects. In French Canada the sense of cultural nationality is much stronger than in English Canada, but the nationality is French Canadian, not Canadian *tout court*. French Canada is almost without curiosity about the literature and culture of English Canada; most cultivated French Canadians do not know even the names of the significant English Canadian creative writers, whether of the past or of the present. Occasionally an important Canadian book is translated from the original into the other official language; but it is much more likely that the work of a French Canadian will be translated into English than that the work of an English Canadian will be translated into French. Louis Hémon was a *Français de France*, but it was because *Maria Chapdelaine* dealt with French Canada that a distinguished Ontario lawyer translated the novel into English, making one of the most beautiful versions of our time. W. H. Blake's translation of Hémon's book is a masterpiece in its own right; no French Canadian has as yet laboured with such loving skill to translate any book that deals with English Canada. A symbol of the fissure in our cultural life is to be found in the definition of sections in The Royal Society of Canada. Three sections are assigned to the sciences, one to mathematics, physics and chemistry, another to the biological sciences, and the third to geology and allied subjects; in these sections French and English fellows sit side by side. But in the two sections assigned to the humanities the French and English fellows are severely separate: in each the subjects run the impossible gamut from the classics to anthropology. It is not too much to say that the maximum Canadian audience that an English Canadian imaginative author can hope for is fewer than eight million people.

To write in the English language is to incur the competition of the best authors of Britain and of the United States. Every Canadian publisher acts as agent for American and British houses; and it is as an agent that he does the larger and by far the more lucrative part of his business. Every Canadian reviewer devotes a large part of his sadly limited space to comment on British or American books. Every Canadian reader devotes a large part of the time and money that he can allow for books to those which come from Britain and the United States. Some angry critics have contrasted the plight of Canadian literature with the eager interest that Norwegians take in the work of their own authors. It is obvious that the accident by which Canadians speak and read one of the main literary languages of the world is a reason why they are less likely to read native books than a Norwegian is, speaking and reading a language peculiar to his own country.

Our great distances, the presence among us of a large minority which is prevailingly indifferent to the currents of culture that run among the majority, the accident of our common speech with Britain and the United States — here are three facts with enormous economic importance for literature. The sum of their effect is the exceedingly thin market for the author who depends on Canadian sales. Unless an author gives all or most of his time to writing for popular magazines he can make very little indeed; and even the resort of the popular magazines is a precarious solution. There are few of these — they, too, are affected by the factors that have been mentioned. They are in almost ruinous competition with American magazines, they cannot pay very much, they print a good deal written outside Canada, and they live so dangerous an existence they commonly defer slavishly to the standards of their average readers.

The serious Canadian writer has a choice among three modes of combining the pursuit of literature with success in keeping alive and fed. He may emigrate: that was the solution of Bliss Carman, and many have followed in his train. He may earn his living by some non-literary pursuit: that was the solution of Archibald Lampman, and it has been widely followed. He may while continuing to reside in Canada become, economically at least, a member of another nation and civilization: that is the solution of Mr. Morley Callaghan. Each of these solutions is open to danger and objection.

The author who emigrates becomes an almost complete loss to our literature. It is probable that in the end, like Henry James or Joseph Conrad or Mr. T. S. Eliot, he will take out papers of citizenship in the country where he has found his economic security and to which he has transferred his spiritual allegiance. If he goes to Britain, the choice will not arise in this form, but he will be at best simply a citizen of the Empire ceasing to be an authentic Canadian. No one thinks of Grant Allen as a Canadian author nor did he so consider himself though he was born in Ontario. How the creative powers of a writer are affected by expatriation is much too vast a problem to receive adequate consideration here. Only this I should like to say: the expatriate will find it more and more difficult to deal vigorously and vividly with the life of the country he has left. Joseph Conrad did not write about Poland. When towards the end of his career Henry James read some of the early tales of Edith Wharton, before he had come to know her, he urged that she should be tethered in her own New York backyard. His own experience persuaded him that exile disqualified one from treating the life of one's own country without admitting one to the centre of the life in the country to which one had fled. If one compares the later novels of Edith Wharton, written after she had lost contact with New York, with the earlier ones which rose out of strong impacts that New York made upon her sensibilities, it is immediately evident that the colours and shapes are less vivid and definite, and that the works of her elder years are less significant. I should argue that Bliss Carman, our most notable exile, suffered a grave loss by passing his middle years in the United States, that he did not become an American writer, but merely a *déraciné*, a nomad in his imaginary and not very rich kingdom of vagabondia.

People often ask why an author cannot satisfy himself with the solution of Archibald Lampman. Lampman, after graduating from Trinity College, Toronto, entered the employ of the federal government as a clerk in the Dominion Post Office at Ottawa. Why, people inquire, cannot a writer earn his living as a clerk, or a teacher, or a lighthouse keeper and devote his leisure to literature? The answer to this question must be an appeal to experience. One of our most gifted novelists, Mr. Philip Child, once remarked to me that a writer must be the obsequious servant of his demon, must rush to write when the demon stirs, and let other things fall where they may. If you fob off the demon with an excuse, telling him to wait till you can leave the office, he will sulk, his visits will become rarer and finally he will not return at all. Temperaments differ; and some writers may, like Anthony Trollope, give fixed hours to authorship and the rest of the day to business and pleasure. Even the Trollopes of this world would prefer to be free from their unliterary employments, since it is not to manage a post-office that a Trollope came into this world. Temperaments less phlegmatic than Trollope's find even the mild yoke of the post-office too heavy for them. Lampman did. He had easy hours, from ten to four-thirty, work which did not exhaust, and long holidays; but he was irked by his employment and made desperate and always unsuccessful efforts to escape from it. One has only to read his letters to realize that he believed that his task-work was fatal to his full development, and one has only to read his poems to believe that there was something in Lampman that never did come to full fruition, something that would have led to deeper and wiser poetry than he did write except in snatches. It appears to me so obvious as to require no argument that whatever success a particular writer may have had in combining the practice of his art with the business of earning a living by work which is remote from letters, the notion that a whole literature can develop out of the happy employment of the odd moments of rather busy men is an unrealistic notion, and one that shows an alarming ignorance of the process by which great works are normally written....

There remains a third solution, Mr. Callaghan's solution. It is possible to write primarily for an American or a British audience. Most of Mr. Callaghan's novels and shorter tales are about the city in which he lives, Toronto; but it seems to me, and I speak as one who was born and brought up in that city, that Mr. Callaghan's Toronto is not an individualized city but simply a representative one. I mean that in reading Mr. Callaghan one has the sense that Toronto is being used not to bring out what will have the most original flavour, but what will remind people who live in Cleveland, or Detroit, or Buffalo, or any other city on the Great Lakes, of the general quality of their own milieu. If one compares Mr. Callaghan's Toronto with Mr. Farrell's Chicago, the point becomes very plain. When I pass through Mr. Farrell's Chicago, that part of the South Side which has been deserted by the Irish to be seized by the Negroes, the memory of what he has written of a life which has ceased to exist becomes very moving. When I walk through the parts of Toronto that Mr. Callaghan has primarily dealt with, the poor areas towards the centre and a little to the north-west of the centre, or the dingy respectability of the near east end, it is only with an effort that I remember that he has written of them at all. It is a notable fact that never once in all his novels does he use the city's name. Just as Mr. Callaghan uses his Canadian setting for its interest for a larger North American audience, so Miss Mazo de la Roche sets her emphasis on those exceedingly rare aspects of rural Ontario life which would remind an English reader of his own countryside and the kind of life that goes on in it. In the work of both writers an alien audience has shaped the treatment of Canadian life. Whether this peculiarity has injured the novelist's art as art, whether the characters and the setting are less alive and moving than the characters and setting in, let us say, Mr. Farrell's novels or Arnold Bennett's is not the immediate question; but there is not a scrap of doubt that the methods of Mr. Callaghan and Miss de la Roche have interfered with their presentation of Canadian life in the terms most stimulating and informing to Canadian readers. One of the forces that can help a civilization to come of age is the presentation of its surfaces and depths in works of imagination in such a fashion that the reader says: "I now understand myself and my milieu with a fullness and a clearness greater than before." Many a Russian must have said so after reading *Fathers and Sons* or *War and Peace*. It is difficult to believe that a Canadian will say this or anything of the sort after reading the work of Miss de la Roche or Mr. Callaghan....

The difficulties that have so far appeared, unlike as they are all have economic roots. It is time to turn to the psychological factors, implied in much that has been said, against which the growth of a Canadian literature must struggle.

Among these the most obvious, the most discussed, although *not* the most potent, is the colonial spirit. Long ago Harvard's President Felton doubted that Canada would come to much since a colony was doomed to be second-rate. In a later generation an American who knew us much better than Felton and who wished us well, William Dean Howells, used almost the same language. In *Their Wedding Journey* he conducts his couple from Niagara Falls by way of Kingston and Montreal to the east coast, giving sharp little pictures of the Canadian towns; he concludes that in comparison with the free nation to which they belong this colony is second-rate in the very quality of its life. Just a year or so ago the Halifax novelist, Mr. Hugh MacLennan, gave to one of the colonially minded characters in *Barometer Rising* the same thought: "I've wasted a whole lifetime in this hole of a town. Everything in this country is second-rate. It always is in a colony." These are probably independent judgments. What do they mean? That a colony lacks the spiritual energy to rise above routine, and that it lacks this energy because it does not adequately believe in itself. It applies to what it has standards which are imported, and therefore artificial and distorting. It sets the great good place not in its present, nor in its past nor in its future, but somewhere outside its own borders, somewhere beyond its own possibilities.

The charge that English Canada is colonial in spirit is the most serious of all the many charges that French Canada brings against us. Speaking in the 1942 session of the Canadian House of Commons, Mr. Louis Saint Laurent, the leading French member of the government, illustrated what he meant by our colonialism when he cited an interchange that is supposed to have occurred within the last few years between the two living ex-prime ministers of Canada. One said to the other, on the eve of his departure to live in England: "I am glad to be going *home*," and the other replied: "How I envy you!" For these two men — if the interchange did occur — Canada was not the great good place; and every French Canadian would regard their sentiments as justifying his practice of referring to us not as *Canadiens Anglais*, but merely as *Anglais*, or when his blood is up, as *maudits Anglais!* Colonialism of this kind is natural to emigrants. One can easily forgive Sir Daniel Wilson, although he spent almost his entire active career in Canada, for wishing to lie in Scottish earth; and yet for a Canadian who knows what Scotland is like in November it is an awe-inspiring thought that Sir Daniel on one of our autumn days, full of the crashing scarlet glories of the Canadian forests or the mellow radiance of our Indian summers, wished to be amid the "sleety east winds" of his native land. What is odd, and unsatisfactory, is the perpetuation of this kind of colonialism in the descendants of emigrants even to the third and fourth generation. It is clear that those who are content with this attitude will seek the best in literature, where they seek the best in jam and toffee, from beyond the ocean. That anything Canadian could be supremely good would never enter their heads....

In the contemporary world autonomy is the most luxurious of privileges, one which this anxious country cannot now afford and will not be able to afford in any measurable future. It is not an unmixed good. Autonomy almost always breeds chauvinism, and usually brings as an immediate consequence an unwholesome delight in the local second-rate. Its advent opposes strong obstacles to international currents of art and thought. This is to be set firmly against the notion that out of autonomy all good things soon issue. Still it must be appreciated just as clearly that dependence breeds a state of mind no less unwholesome, a state of mind in which great art is most unlikely to emerge or to be widely recognized if it did. A great art is fostered by artists and audience possessing in common a passionate and peculiar interest in the kind of life that exists in the country where they live. If this interest exists in the artist he will try to give it adequate expression; if it exists in the audience they will be alert for any imaginative work which expresses it from a new angle and with a new clearness. From what was said a moment ago it will be obvious that in a colonial or semi-colonial community neither artist nor audience will have the passionate and peculiar interest in their immediate surroundings that is required. Canada is a state in which such an interest exists only among a few. I have pointed out how Mr. Callaghan and Miss de la Roche have written as they could not have written if they had possessed such interest. It is the same with Canadian readers. A novel which presents the farms of the prairie, or the industrial towns of south-western Ontario, or the fishing villages in the Maritime Provinces will arouse no more interest in the general reader than a novel which is set in Surrey or in the suburbs of Chicago. Canadian undergraduates are much less likely than Americans to write stories about their immediate environment: their fancies take them to nightclubs in Vienna (rather than Montreal), islands in the South Seas (rather than the St. Lawrence), foggy nights in London (rather than Halifax). It is almost impossible to persuade Canadians that an imaginative representation of the group in which they live could clarify for the reader his own nature and those of his associates. To the typical Canadian reader such a notion is arty folly. I give this as a fact; and I offer as a partial interpretation, at least, that most Canadians continue to be culturally colonial, that they set their great good place somewhere beyond their own borders.

Somewhere beyond their borders — not necessarily beyond the seas. Canada is colonial not only in its attitude towards Britain, but often in its attitude toward the United States. It is true that the imprint of a London publisher, or of a British university press is a more impressive guarantee of a book or an author than any Canadian sponsorship, even a Governor-General's. When the late Lord Tweedsmuir remarked that a Canadian's first loyalty should be towards Canada (rather than towards Britain or towards the empire) it was believed in some circles, and these not the least cultivated, that he had been guilty, as one journalist phrased it in cynical fun, of "disloyalty towards himself." It was inevitable that a Scottish man of letters should think in such terms, Scotland being almost wholly free from the spirit of colonialism. Pleas that we should seek to free ourselves from our colonial feelings towards Britain are met with cries of "ingrate!" or "traitor!" There can, of course, be no question of such open and violent objection against efforts to free us from a colonial attitude towards the United States. Our colonialism in relation to the United States is unavowed, but it is deep. The praise of a couple of New York reviewers will outweigh the unanimous enthusiasm of Canadian journals from coast to coast. There is every reason to suppose that as Canadian feeling becomes more and more friendly towards the United States, as it has done during the past quarter century, our cultural dependence on the Americans will grow. If it does, our literature may be expected to become emphatically regionalist; of the dangers of regionalism something will be said a little later.

One consequence of our colonial or dominion status, and of our growing dependence on the United States and growing sense of security in American power, claims special note. Taking stock of our literature in 1891, and thinking in particular of the lack of national feeling or thought in it, Archibald Lampman wrote: "The time has not come for the production of any genuine national song. It is when the passion and enthusiasm of an entire people, carried away by the excitement of some great crisis, enters into the soul of one man specially gifted, that a great national poem or hymn is produced. We have yet to reach such an hour, and we may pray that it will not come too soon or too late." In the earlier years of the Confederation, when there was still some suspicion of the friendliness of the United States, Canadians felt that they had a strong defence in the force and prestige of England; and in later times the force and prestige of the United States as well has been conceived as an assurance that Canada need not fear aggression. There has been no moment in our history comparable with what England knew on the eve of the Elizabethan efflorescence, when the Armada approached her shores, or at the height of the Romantic achievement, when Napoleon gathered his forces at Boulogne, or in the early summer of 1940, when the salvation of the country depended upon itself alone. Nor has Canada known an internal crisis at all comparable to the War between the States. It is probable that, as Lampman supposed, a national crisis of supreme intensity would call forth emotions of such a strength and purity as to issue in a significant expression in the arts. We are probably as far, or almost as far from such a crisis in 1944 as in 1891. The only tension to become impressively more dangerous is that between the French and the other strains in the Canadian population; and this tension, alarming as it is, stopped far short of crisis on the two occasions when it has become acute, 1917 and 1942. The essential orderliness and forbearance of the Canadian character allows one to believe that the interracial tension will not escape from control. On some other issue at some time not yet to be foreseen the passion and enthusiasm to which Lampman looked will surge up and there will ensue a fierce coming of emotional age. Our Whitman is in the future.

A more powerful obstacle at present to the growth of a great literature is the spirit of the frontier, or its afterglow. Most Canadians live at some distance from anything that could even in the loosest terms be known as a material frontier; but the standards which the frontier-life applied are still current, if disguised. Books are a luxury on the frontier; and writers are an anomaly. On the frontier a man is mainly judged by what he can do to bring his immediate environment quickly and visibly under the control of society. No nation is more practical than ours; admiration is readily stirred, even more readily than south of the border, by the man who can run a factory, or invent a gadget or save a life by surgical genius. This kind of admiration is a disguised form of the frontier's set of values. No such admiration goes out to any form of the aesthetic or contemplative life. The uneasiness in the presence of the contemplative or aesthetic is to be ascribed to the frontier feeling that these are luxuries which should not be sought at a time when there is a tacit contract that everyone should be doing his share in the common effort to build the material structure of a nation. That a poem or a statue or a metaphysic could contribute to the fabric of a nation is not believed. In a gathering of ruminative historians and economists, speaking their mind one evening in Winnipeg years before the war was imminent, the unanimous opinion was that a destroyer or two would do more than a whole corpus of literature to establish a Canadian nationality. The dissent of two students of literature was heard in awkward silence. If there were any belief in the national value of art or pure thought, the strong desire of the frontiersman that what is being built should eclipse all that was ever built before would make a milieu for art and thought that would at the root be propitious.

In a disguised form of frontier life what function can the arts hold? They are at best recreative. They may be alternatives to the hockey match, or the whiskey bottle, or the frivolous sexual adventure as means of clearing the mind from the worries of business and enabling it to go back to business refreshed. The arts' value as interpretation is lost in the exclusive emphasis on their value as diversion, and even their value as diversion is simplified to the lowest possible form — a work of art must divert strongly and completely. It must divert as a thriller or a smashing jest diverts, not as an elaborate and subtle romance or a complicated argument diverts. In a word, Canada is a nation where the best-seller is king, as it is on the frontier.

A third factor telling against the appreciation of art is our strong Puritanism. Every foreign observer notes with amazement, both in our French and in our English books, the avoidance of the themes that irk the Puritan, or the language that now irks him more. Canada has never produced a major man of letters whose work gave a violent shock to the sensibilities of Puritans. There was some worry about Carman, who had certain qualities of the *fin de siècle* poet, but how mildly he expressed his queer longings! Mr. Callaghan has fallen foul of the censors of morals in some of our more conservative cities, and even among those of his own Roman Catholic faith a novel as *Such Is My Beloved* has had an uneasy path; but how cautious in the description of sordor and how chastened in language he has always been! Imagination boggles at the vista of a Canadian Whitman, or Canadian Dos Passos. The prevailing literary standards demand a high degree of moral and social orthodoxy; and popular writers accept these standards without even such a rueful complaint as Thackeray made in warning that he could not draw his Pendennis as a full man, since no hero of an English novel intended for the general public had been drawn in full since Fielding went to his grave....

If Puritanism operated simply to restrain the arts within the bonds of moral orthodoxy, its effects, though regrettable, would be much less grave than they now are. Puritanism goes beyond the demand for severe morality: it disbelieves in the importance of art. It allows to the artist no function except watering down moral ideas of an orthodox kind into a solution attractive to minds not keen enough to study the ideas in more abstract presentations. At its most liberal Puritanism will tolerate, a little uneasily, the provision through the arts of an innocent passing amusement which is expected to leave no deep trace on character. To popularize orthodox morality and to provide light, clean fun — that is the very limit of what the arts can be allowed to do without alarming the Puritan mind. For the Puritan a life devoted to one of the arts is a life misused: the aesthetic life is not a form of the good life. That profane art, both for artist and for audience, may provide the contemplation of being, may offer an insight into the life of things, is for the Puritan mist and moonshine.

Puritanism is a dwindling force, and the time is not far off when it will no longer exercise its ruinous restraint upon the themes or language of a Canadian writer who is addressing the general public. Regionalism, another force which tells against the immediate growth of a national literature, cannot be expected to dwindle so fast. Canada is not an integrated whole. The Maritime Provinces recall the days — only seventy-five years in the past — when they were separate colonies; Nova Scotia, for instance, has re-established its colonial flag, dating from the eighteenth century and flying now from the Province House at Halifax; French Canada is a civilization apart; Ontario unconsciously accepts itself as the norm of Canadian life; the Prairie Provinces are steeped in their special vivid western past; and British Columbia has a strong sense of its pre-confederation life and of its continuing separate identity. Geography confirms the influence of history. Ontario is separated from the Maritime Provinces by the solid enclave of Quebec; between the populous southern part of Ontario and the prairies the Laurentian shield interposes another huge barrier; and this barrier is no stronger, if broader, than the Rocky Mountains create between the prairies and the coastal province of British Columbia. There is little doubt that the Fathers of Confederation, or the majority of the leaders among them, expected and planned for a much more unified whole than has so far come into being. In time of war the tendency to self-aggrandizement on the part of the Provinces is arrested, and even reversed; but there is ground for fearing that the return to peace will start it into vigorous being once more. Among most Canadians there is little eagerness to explore the varieties of Canadian life, little awareness how much variety exists, or what a peril that variety is, in time of crisis, to national unity. It may be that the next important stage of Canadian literature will be strongly particularist and regionalist: one remembers what a force regionalism was in American literature in the years after the Civil War.

Regionalist art may be expected to possess certain admirable virtues.

One of these is accuracy, not merely accuracy of fact, but accuracy of tone; and throughout our literature there has been a disposition to force the note, to make life appear nobler or gayer or more intense than Canadian life really is in its typical expressions. It would help us towards cultural maturity if we had a set of novels, or sketches, or memoirs that described the life of Canadian towns and cities as it really is, works in which nothing would be presented that the author had not encountered in his own experience. It should also be acknowledged that a warm emotion for one's *petit pays* can lead to very charming art, as in Stephen Leacock's humorous transposition of an Ontario town in his *Sunshine Sketches*. In the end, however, regionalist art will fail because it stresses the superficial and the peculiar at the expense, at least, if not to the exclusion, of the fundamental and universal. The advent of regionalism may be welcomed with reservations as a stage through which it may be well for us to pass, as a discipline and a purgation. But if we are to pass through it, the coming of great books will be delayed beyond the lifetime of anyone now living.

What I have been attempting to suggest with as little heat or bitterness as possible is that in this country the plight of literature is a painful one. People who dislike to face this truth — and most Canadians do — have many easy answers. One is that Canadians have been so busy making a new world that it is harsh and unrealistic to expect that they might have written a large number of important books, read them with strong and general interest, and set a distinctive literary tone for their civilization. To this answer one may retort by pointing to what had been achieved in the United States a century ago, calling the roll of the names of those Americans who had written works of the first order, of national and international importance, by 1844 — Edwards, Franklin, Jefferson, Irving, Cooper, Poe, Hawthorne and Emerson. In certain other ways the American environment up to 1844 was more hospitable to literature than ours has been up to the present time; but there can, I think, be no doubt that Americans were in the century and a half preceding 1844 just as busy building the material structure of a nation as we have ever been. Another easy answer is often put in such terms as these: "If a Dickens begins to write in Canada we shall greet him with a cheer, we shall buy his books by the scores of thousands, get him appointed to the Senate of Canada, and request the Crown to give him an O.M. Meanwhile, don't bother us with your complaints. You can't point to a single man of anything approaching the calibre of Dickens who has written in this country. We have neglected no one of great importance. Wait till our Dickens comes along, and then we'll prove to you that we know how to honour a great writer." The line taken here depends on the belief that literature is an autonomous thing, a succession of single great men, each arising accidentally, each sufficient to himself. On this view you will get your great literature when you get your great men of letters, and meanwhile there is no problem worth discussing.

Thinking of this sort ignores a fundamental fact: that literature develops in close association with society. I should not deny that a single man of genius might emerge and express himself more or less fully in a society which was inhospitable to literature; but I find it significant that the most original of our poets, E. J. Pratt, has maintained:

> The lonely brooding spirit, generating his own steam in silence and abstraction, is a rare spirit, if indeed he ever existed, and as far as one may gather from scientific discussions on the point, there is no biological analogy for this kind of incubation. Rather, the mountains come to birth out of the foothills, and the climbing lesser ranges. The occasional instance cited in literary history, of personal isolation ignores the context of spiritual companionship with books and causes and movements.

The ways of genius cannot be fully predicted; but the "occasional instance," the single man of genius, is not a literature and does not bring a literature into being. No doubt if a Browning or a Yeats were to write in Canada and to make himself felt in Canada, the effect on Canadian literature would be considerable. But the stimulus such a writer could give, great though it would be, and much as it may be wished for by all who hope for the growth of a great literature in this country, would be a passing stimulus, unless it were assisted by social conditions friendly to creative composition. A great literature is the flowering of a great society, a vital and adequate society. Here I must reluctantly take leave of the subject, for it is not in the province of a student of letters to say how a society becomes vital and adequate.

In the observations I have offered it will be thought by many Canadians that the note of pessimism, or at least of rigour, is too strong. On the side of hope and faith it should be said that the future of Canada is almost singularly incalculable: none of the factors that now tell so strongly against the growth of our literature is necessarily eternal, and many of them are likely to diminish in force. Every reflective Canadian must feel a mixture of disturbance and delight in our inability to foresee even the main stresses of the Canada that will exist a hundred years from now.

Survival

Margaret Atwood

I started reading Canadian literature when I was young, though I didn't know it was that; in fact I wasn't aware that I lived in a country with any distinct existence of its own. At school we were being taught to sing "Rule, Britannia" and to draw the Union Jack; after hours we read stacks of Captain Marvel, Plastic Man and Batman comic books, an activity delightfully enhanced by the disapproval of our elders. However, someone had given us Charles G. D. Roberts' *Kings in Exile* for Christmas, and I snivelled my way quickly through these heartwrenching stories of animals caged, trapped and tormented. That was followed by Ernest Thompson Seton's *Wild Animals I Have Known*, if anything more upsetting because the animals were more actual — they lived in forests, not circuses — and their deaths more mundane: the deaths, not of tigers, but of rabbits.

No one called these stories Canadian literature, and I wouldn't have paid any attention if they had; as far as I was concerned they were just something else to read, along with Walter Scott, Edgar Allan Poe and Donald Duck. I wasn't discriminating in my reading, and I'm still not. I read then primarily to be entertained, as I do now. And I'm not saying that apologetically: I feel that if you remove the initial gut response from reading — the delight or excitement or simply the enjoyment of being told a story — and to try to concentrate on the meaning or the shape or the "message" first, you might as well give up, it's too much like all work and no play.

But then as now there were different levels of entertainment. I read the backs of Shredded Wheat boxes as an idle pastime, Captain Marvel and Walter Scott as fantasy escape — I knew, even then, that wherever I lived it wasn't *there*, since I'd never seen a castle and the Popsicle Pete prizes advertised on the comic book covers either weren't available in Canada, or cost more — and Seton and Roberts as, believe it or not, something closer to real life. I *had* seen animals, quite a few of them; a dying porcupine was more real to me then a knight in armour or Clark Kent's Metropolis. Old mossy dungeons and Kryptonite were hard to come by where I lived, though I was quite willing to believe they existed somewhere else; but the materials for Seton's stick-and-stone artefacts and live-off-the-land recipes in *Wildwood Wisdom* were readily available, and we could make them quite easily, which we did. Most of the recipes were somewhat inedible, as you'll see if you try

---

Abridged from Margaret Atwood, "Survival" and "The Casual Incident of Death," *Survival: A Thematic Guide to Canadian Literature* (Toronto: House of Anansi Press, 1972), pp. 29-42, 165-74. Reprinted by permission.

Cat-tail Root Stew or Pollen Pancakes, but the raw ingredients can be collected around any Canadian summer cottage.

However, it wasn't just the content of these books that felt more real to me; it was their shapes, their patterns. The animal stories were about the struggle to survive, and Seton's practical handbook was in fact a survival manual: it laid much stress on the dangers of getting lost, eating the wrong root or berry, or angering a moose in season. Though it was full of helpful hints, the world it depicted was one riddled with pitfalls, just as the animal stories were thickly strewn with traps and snares. In this world, no Superman would come swooping out of the sky at the last minute to rescue you from the catastrophe; no rider would arrive post-haste with a pardon from the King. The main thing was to avoid dying, and only by a mixture of cunning, experience and narrow escapes could the animal — or the human relying on his own resources — manage that. And, in the animal stories at any rate, there were no final happy endings or ultimate solutions; if the animal happened to escape from the particular crisis in the story, you knew there would be another one later on from which it wouldn't escape.

I wasn't making these analytical judgments at the time, of course. I was just learning what to expect: in comic books and things like *Alice in Wonderland* or Conan Doyle's *The Lost World*, you got rescued or you returned from the world of dangers to a cozy safe domestic one; in Seton and Roberts, because the world of dangers was *the same* as the real world, you didn't. But when in high school I encountered — again as a Christmas present — something labelled more explicitly as Canadian Literature, the Robert Weaver and Helen James anthology, *Canadian Short Stories*, I wasn't surprised. There they were again, those animals on the run, most of them in human clothing this time, and those humans up against it; here was the slight mistake that led to disaster, here was the fatal accident; this was a world of frozen corpses, dead gophers, snow, dead children, and the ever-present feeling of menace, not from an enemy set over against you but from everything surrounding you. The familiar peril lurked behind every bush, and *I knew the names of the bushes*. Again, I wasn't reading this as Canlit, I was just reading it; I remember being elated by some stories (notably James Reaney's "The Bully") and not very interested in others. But these stories felt real to me in a way that Charles Dickens, much as I enjoyed him, did not.

I've talked about these early experiences not because I think that they were typical but because I think that — significantly — they weren't: I doubt that many people my age had even this much contact, minimal and accidental though it was, with their own literature. (Talking about this now makes me feel about 102, because quite a lot has changed since then. But though new cirricula are being invented here and there across the country, I'm not convinced that the *average* Canadian child or high school student is likely to run across much more Canadian literature than I did. *Why* this is true is of course one of our problems.)

Still, although I didn't read much Canadian writing, what I did read had a shape of its own that felt different from the shapes of the other things I was reading. What that shape turned out to be, and what I felt it meant in terms of this country, became clearer to me the more I read; it is, of course, the subject of this book.

I'd like to begin with a sweeping generalization and argue that every country or culture has a single unifying and informing symbol at its core. (Please don't take any of my oversimplifications as articles of dogma which allow of no exceptions; they are proposed simply to create vantage points from which the literature may be viewed.) The symbol, then — be it word, phrase, idea, image, or all of these — functions like a system of beliefs (it *is* a system of beliefs, though not always a formal one) which holds the country together and helps the people in it to co-operate for common ends. Possibly the symbol for America is The Frontier, a flexible idea that contains many elements dear to the American heart: it suggests a place that is *new*, where the old order can be discarded (as it was when America was instituted by a crop of disaffected Protestants, and later at the time of the Revolution); a line that is always expanding, taking in or "conquering" ever-fresh virgin territory (be it The West, the rest of the world, outer space, Poverty or The Regions of the Mind); it holds out a hope, never fulfilled but always promised, of Utopia, the perfect human society. Most twentieth century American literature is about the gap between the promise and the actuality, between the imagined ideal Golden West or City Upon a Hill, the model for all the world postulated by the Puritans, and the actual squalid materialism, dotty small town, nasty city, or redneck-filled outback. Some Americans have even confused the actuality with the promise: in that case Heaven is a Hilton hotel with a coke machine in it.

The corresponding symbol for England is perhaps The Island, convenient for obvious reasons. In the seventeenth century a poet called Phineas Fletcher wrote a long poem called *The Purple Island*, which is based on an extended body-as-island metaphor, and, dreadful though the poem is, that's the kind of island I mean: island-as-body, self-contained, a Body Politic, evolving organically, with a hierarchical structure in which the King is the Head, the statesmen the hands, the peasants or farmers or workers the feet, and so on. The Englishman's home as his castle is the popular form of this symbol, the feudal castle being not only an insular structure but a self-contained microcosm of the entire Body Politic.

The central symbol for Canada — and this is based on numerous instances of its occurrence in both English and French Canadian literature — is undoubtedly Survival, *la Survivance*. Like the Frontier and The Island, it is a multi-faceted and adaptable idea. For early explorers and settlers, it meant bare survival in the face of "hostile" elements and/or natives: carving out a place and a way of keeping alive. But the word can also suggest survival of a crisis or disaster, like a hurricane or a wreck, and many Canadian poems have this kind of survival as a theme; what you might call "grim" survival as opposed to "bare" survival. For French Canada after the English took over it became cultural survival, hanging on as a people, retaining a religion and a language under an alien government. And in English Canada now while the Americans are taking over it is acquiring a similar meaning. There is another use of the word as well: a survival can be a vestige of a vanished order which has managed to persist after its time is past, like a primitive reptile. This version crops up in Canadian thinking too, usually among those who believe that Canada is obsolete.

But the main idea is the first one: hanging on, staying alive. Canadians are forever taking the national pulse like doctors at a sickbed: the aim is not to see whether the patient will live well but simply whether he will live at all. Our central idea is one which generates, not the excitement and sense of adventure or danger which The Frontier holds out, not the smugness and/or sense of security, of everything in its place, which The Island can offer, but an almost intolerable anxiety. Our stories are likely to be tales not of those who made it but of those who made it back, from the awful experience — the North, the snowstorm, the sinking ship — that killed everyone else. The survivor has no triumph or victory but the fact of his survival; he has little after his ordeal that he did not have before, except gratitude for having escaped with his life.

A preoccupation with one's survival is necessarily also a preoccupation with the obstacles to that survival. In earlier writers these obstacles are external — the land, the climate, and so forth. In later writers the obstacles tend to become both harder to identify and more internal; they are no longer obstacles to physical survival but obstacles to what we may call spiritual survival, to life as anything more than a minimally human being. Sometimes fear of these obstacles becomes itself the obstacle, and a character is paralyzed by terror (either of what he thinks is threatening him from the outside, or of elements in his own nature that threaten him from within). It may even be life itself that he fears; and when life becomes a threat to life, you have a moderately vicious circle. If a man feels he can survive only by amputating himself, turning himself into a cripple or a eunuch, what price survival?

Just to give you a quick sample of what I'm talking about, here are a few capsule Canadian plots. Some contain attempts to survive which fail. Some contain bare survivals. Some contain crippled successes (the character does more than survive, but is mutilated in the process).

Pratt:	*The Titanic*: Ship crashes into iceberg. Most passengers drown.
Pratt:	*Brébeuf and His Brethren*: After crushing ordeals, priests survive briefly and are massacred by Indians.
Laurence:	*The Stone Angel*: Old woman hangs on grimly to life and dies at the end.

Carrier: *Is It The Sun, Philibert?* Hero escapes incredible rural poverty and horrid urban conditions, almost makes it financially, dies when he wrecks his car.

Marlyn: *Under The Ribs of Death*: Hero amputates himself spiritually in order to make it financially, fails anyway.

Ross: *As For Me and My House*: Prairie minister who hates his job and has crippled himself artistically by sticking with it is offered a dubious chance of escape at the end.

Buckler: *The Mountain and the Valley*: Writer who has been unable to write has vision of possibility at the end but dies before he can implement it.

Gibson: *Communion*: Man who can no longer make human contact tries to save sick dog, fails, and is burned up at the end.

And just to round things out, we might add that the two English Canadian feature films (apart from Allan King's documentaries) to have had much success so far, *Goin' Down the Road* and *The Rowdyman*, are both dramatizations of failure. The heroes survive, but just barely; they are born losers, and their failure to do anything but keep alive has nothing to do with the Maritime Provinces or "regionalism." It's pure Canadian, from sea to sea.

My sample plots are taken from both prose and poetry, and from regions all across Canada; they span four decades, from the thirties to the early seventies. And they hint at another facet of Survivalism: at some point the failure to survive, or the failure to achieve anything beyond survival, becomes not a necessity imposed by a hostile outside world but a choice made from within. Pushed far enough, the obsession with surviving can become the will *not* to survive.

Certainly Canadian authors spend a disproportionate amount of time making sure that their heroes die or fail. Much Canadian writing suggests that failure is required because it is felt — consciously or unconsciously — to be the only "right" ending, the only thing that will support the characters' (or their authors') view of the universe. When such endings are well-handled and consistent with the whole book, one can't quarrel with them on aesthetic grounds. But when Canadian writers are writing clumsy or manipulated endings, they are much less likely to manipulate in a positive than they are in a negative direction: that is, the author is less likely to produce a sudden inheritance from a rich old uncle or the surprising news that his hero is really the son of a Count than he is to conjure up an unexpected natural disaster or an out-of-control car, tree or minor character so that the protagonist may achieve a satisfactory *failure*. Why should this be so? Could it be that Canadians have a will to lose which is as strong and pervasive as the Americans' will to win?

It might be argued that, since most Canlit has been written in the twentieth century and since the twentieth century has produced a generally pessimistic or "ironic" literature, Canada has simply been reflecting a trend. Also, though it's possible to write a short lyric poem about joy and glee, no novel of any length can exclude all but these elements. A novel about unalloyed happiness would have to be either very short or very boring: "Once upon a time John and Mary lived happily ever after, The End." Both of these arguments have some validity, but surely the Canadian gloom is more unrelieved than most and the death and failure toll out of proportion. Given a choice of the negative or positive aspects of any symbol — sea as life-giving Mother, sea as what your ship goes down in; tree as symbol of growth, tree as what falls on your head — Canadians show a marked preference for the negative.

You might decide at this point that most Canadian authors with any pretensions to seriousness are neurotic or morbid, and settle down instead for a good read with *Anne of Green Gables* (though it's about an orphan . . .) But if the coincidence intrigues you — so many writers in such a small country, and *all with the same neurosis* — then I will offer you a theory. Like any theory it won't explain everything, but it may give you some points of departure.

Let us suppose, for the sake of argument, that Canada as a whole is a victim, or an "oppressed minority," or "exploited." Let us suppose in short that Canada is a colony. A partial definition of a colony is that it is a place from which a profit is made, but *not by the people who live there*: the major profit from a colony is made in the centre of the empire. That's what colonies are for, to make money for the "mother country," and that's what — since the days of Rome and, more recently, of the Thirteen Colonies — they have always been for. Of course there are cultural side-effects which are often identified as "the colonial mentality," and it is these which are examined here; but the root cause for them is economic.

If Canada is a collective victim, it should pay some attention to the Basic Victim Positions. These are like the basic positions in ballet or the scales on the piano: they are primary, though all kinds of song-and-dance variations on them are possible.

The positions are the same whether you are a victimized country, a victimized minority group or a victimized individual.

BASIC VICTIM POSITIONS

Position One
To deny the fact that you are a victim.

This uses up a lot of energy, as you must spend much time explaining away the obvious, suppressing anger, and pretending that certain visible facts do not exist. The position is usually taken by those in a Victim group who are a little better off than the others in that group. They are afraid to recognize they are victims for fear of losing the privileges they possess, and they are forced to account somehow for the disadvantages suffered by the rest of the people in the group by disparaging them. As in: "*I* made it, therefore it's obvious we aren't victims. The rest are just lazy (or neurotic, or stupid); anyway it's their own fault if they aren't happy, look at all the opportunities available for them!"

If anger is felt by Victims in Position One, it is likely to be directed against one's fellow-victims, particularly those who try to talk about their victimization.

The basic game in Position One is "Deny your Victim-experience."

Position Two
To acknowledge the fact that you are a victim, but to explain this as an act of Fate, the Will of God, the dictates of Biology (in the case of women, for instance), the necessity decreed by History, or Economics, or the Unconscious, or any other large general powerful idea.

In any case, since it is the fault of this large *thing* and not your own fault, you can neither be blamed for your position nor be expected to do anything about it. You can be resigned and long-suffering, or you can kick against the pricks and make a fuss; in the latter case your rebellion will be deemed foolish or evil even by you, and you will expect to lose and be punished, for who can fight Fate (or the Will of God, or Biology)?

Notice that:
1. The explanation *displaces* the cause from the real source of oppression to something else.
2. Because the fake cause is so vast, nebulous and unchangeable, you are permanently excused from changing it, *and also* from deciding how much of your situation (e.g. the climate) is unchangeable, how much can be changed, and how much is caused by habit or tradition or your own need to be a victim.
3. Anger, when present — or scorn, since everyone in the category is defined as inferior — is directed against both fellow-victims and oneself.

The basic game in Position Two is Victor/Victim.

Position Three
To acknowledge the fact that you are a victim but to refuse to accept the assumption that the role is inevitable.

As in: "Look what's being done to me, and it isn't Fate, it isn't the Will of God. Therefore I can stop seeing myself as a *fated* Victim."

To put it differently: you can distinguish between the *role* of Victim (which probably leads you to seek victimization even when there's no call for it), and the *objective experience* that is making you a victim. And you can probably go further and decide how much of the objective experience could be changed if you made the effort.

This is a dynamic position, rather than a static one; from it you can move on to Position Four, but if you become locked into your anger and fail to change your situation, you might well find yourself back in Position Two.

Notice that:
1. In this position the real cause of oppression is for the first time identified.
2. Anger can be directed against the real source of oppression, and energy channelled into constructive action.
3. You can make real decisions about how much of your position can be changed and how much can't (you can't make it stop snowing; you can stop blaming the snow for everything that's wrong).

The basic game of Position Three is repudiating the Victim role.

Position Four
To be a creative non-victim.

Strictly speaking, Position Four is a position not for the victims but for those who have never been victims at all, or for ex-victims: those who have been able to move into it from Position Three because the external and/or the internal causes of victimization have been removed. (In an oppressed society, of course, you can't become an ex-victim — insofar as you are connected with your society — until the entire society's position has been changed.)

In Position Four, creative activity of all kinds becomes possible. Energy is no longer being suppressed (as in Position One) or used up for displacement of the cause, or for passing your victimization along to others (Man kicks Child, Child kicks Dog) as in Position Two; nor is it being used for the dynamic anger of Position Three.

And you are able to accept your own experience for what it is, rather than having to distort it to make it correspond with others' versions of it (particularly those of your oppressors).

In Position Four, Victor/Victim games are obsolete. You don't even have to concentrate on rejecting the role of Victim, because the role is no longer a temptation for you.

(There may be a Position Five, for mystics; I postulate it but will not explore it here, since mystics do not as a rule write books.)

I devised this model not as the Secret of Life or the answer to everything (though you can apply it to world politics or your friends if you like), but as a helpful method of approaching our literature. It's a model about Victims for the simple reason that I found a superabundance of victims in Canadian literature. If I'd been looking at the nineteenth century English novel I'd have devised a table called Characteristics of Gentlemen; or if I'd been investigating American literature I would have found myself thinking about picaresque anti-heroes; or if I'd been examining German Romantic literature the result would probably have been a diagram of Doppelgängers. But stick a pin in Canadian literature at random, and nine times out of ten you'll hit a victim. My model, then, is a product of my Canadian literary experiences, not a Procrustean bed dreamed up in advance on which Canlit is about to be stretched. Now that I've traced its main outlines, I'll indicate briefly how I intend to use — and not to use — the model.

First, three general points about the model:

- As I said, this is a verbal diagram: it is intended to be suggestive rather than totally accurate. But experience is never this linear: you're rarely in any Position in its pure form for very long — and you may have a foot, as it were, in more than one Position at once.
- What happens to an individual who has reached Position Three in a society which is still in Positions One or Two? (Not very nice things, usually.) Or, what happens to an individual who is a victim — like a Black in America — in a society which as a whole *is not* being oppressed by another society? (Again, not very nice things.) If, for instance, your society is in Position Two, perhaps you can't move through Position Three into Position Four except by repudiating your society, or at least its assumptions about the nature of life and proper behaviour. This may eventually make Position Four unreal for you: can you fiddle happily while Rome groans?
- I've presented the model as though it were based on individual rather than social experience. Perhaps the terms would shift slightly if you were to substitute "we" or "our class" or "our country" for "I," and you'd then get a more complicated analysis of Canadian colonialism. My approach is more modest: it sketches a perspective from which Canadian *Literature* makes a surprising amount of sense.

Now, the model as it applies to writing:

- I assume that *by definition* (mine, and you don't have to believe me) an author is in Position Four at the moment of writing, that is, the moment of creation — though the subject of his book may be Position Two, and the energy for it may come from Position Three. In the rest of his life he shifts around, like everyone else. (The analogous Position Four moment for the reader is not the time it takes to read a book, but the moment of insight — the time when the book makes sense or comes clear.) And apart from that comment, I don't want to speculate about the state of authors' souls. Instead, just as in the Preface I proposed the fiction that the literature was being written by Canada, I here propose to regard novels and poems as though they were expressions of Positions, not of authors.
- This method will, I hope, articulate the skeleton of Canadian literature. It will let you see how the bones fit together, but it won't put flesh on them. That is, the method provides a static dissection, rather than a dynamic ex-

amination of a process-in-motion. (A "static" model facilitates classification. Trying out a dynamic model would also be interesting.)
- Because I'm not handing out gold stars, I'll try not to do much evaluating — praising or censuring — of books according to this model. Although in real life Position Four may be preferable to Position Two, I do find a consistent and tough-minded Position Two poem preferable to a sloppy and unearned Position Four one. But I'll let you do that kind of evaluation for yourself.

You might try to decide whether, in any given work, the actual conditions of the characters' lives are sufficient to account for the doom and gloom meted out to them. Bare Survival isn't a central theme by accident, and neither is the victim motif; the land *was* hard, and we have been (and are) an exploited colony; our literature is rooted in those facts. But you might wonder, in a snowstorm-kills-man story, whether the snowstorm is an adequate explanation for the misery of the characters, or whether the author has displaced the source of the misery in their world and is blaming the snowstorm when he ought to be blaming something else. If so, it is a Position Two story: quite apart from the subject matter, it expresses a premature resignation and a misplaced willingness to see one's victimization as unchangeable.

And I'll point out too that a book can be a symptom or reflection of a Position (though not necessarily a bad book); or it can be a *conscious examination* of it (though not necessarily a good one). The latter seems less fatalistic, a conscious examination of victim experience — including the *need* to be a victim — suggests a more realistic desire to transcend the experience, even if that is not made explicit in the book.

I've laid out the skeleton of Canadian literature in a way that was easy for me to manage and I hope will be easy for you to follow. The key patterns themselves are arranged in four groups. Chapters Two, Three and Four (the first group) deal with the patterns Canadian literature has made of what white people found when they arrived here: the land, the animals, and the Indians. Chapters Five, Six, Seven and Eight deal with what Canadian literature has made of its "ancestor" figures. Chapters Nine and Ten cope with two representative figures — the Canadian Artist, who is usually male, and the Canadian Woman, who is usually female — and explore some of the reasons for their rather curtailed anatomies. And Chapters Eleven and Twelve provide some rays of light, in the shape of bonfires and insights.

You will need the rays of light because the surrounding gloom sometimes gets pretty dense; a lot of our literature (as you may have suspected) is either an expression or an examination of Position Two: "I am a victim but there is nothing I can do about it." However, a writer's job is to tell his society not how it ought to live, but how it does live.

But before you plunge in here are some cheering thoughts:

- Although negative stances towards theme and image predominate, there are also examples of escapes, positive changes, and revelations.
- Much of our literature is a diagram of what is *not* desired. Knowing what you don't want isn't the same as knowing what you do want, but it helps.
- Naming your own condition, your own disease, is not necessarily the same as acquiescing in it. Diagnosis is the first step.

Armed with these maxims, you should be proof against some of the murkier depths that lie ahead.

The Casual Incident of Death

MARGARET ATWOOD

...I would now like to examine several problems that arise in connection with the literary Hero, more specifically with the attempts to create Heroes based on historical figures. The Explorer of course is a kind of "heroic" figure, but he is not essentially connected with any society or group of people; he is a loner, whereas the Hero has traditionally been the champion of a society, fighting its enemies on its behalf.

Let me elucidate what I mean by "Hero." Imagine a writer who wishes to write something — suppose it is to be a play or a long poem or an opera — in an epic or tragic mode; not a satire, a romance or a comedy. He knows that for the kind of play he has in mind a hero is necessary. His hero must struggle against obstacles, as heroes traditionally do; the struggle must be meaningful, it must have significance for people other than the hero himself, he must be fighting on behalf of his own group or nation. If the hero is allowed to win, his victory must save a people also; St. George defeats the Dragon, Beowulf kills Grendel, Odysseus kicks out the false suitors, and folks can sleep at night. If he has to die, his death must still be in some way redemptive; he must take some of his enemies down with him and help to make a victorious or at least a safe future possible. Traditionally the hero must have a tragic flaw or two; he may be a man destroyed by his own pride, like Oedipus, or by his own indecisiveness, like Hamlet, but he must also have great virtues. Above all he must be central, significant: issues and kingdoms depend on his rise and fall.

Now imagine that this writer is searching for his hero in the twentieth century. The twentieth century alters things: it is the century of Everyman, or so we are told. It does not believe readily in heroes, though it is fond of villains. Our writer must concoct a fictional hero — a rock singer or some such — or he may fall back on historical drama and write a play about Sir Thomas More or Elizabeth the First or Abraham Lincoln or George Washington or Benjamin Franklin; this way he will make a lot of money. His dilemma is not insoluble.

Let us further suppose that our writer is Canadian, and that he wishes to set his drama or poem in Canada. Let's throw caution to the winds and imagine he wants to use real historical material. Now he has problems. These problems are connected with the patterns of Canadian history, and the related and perhaps even resultant patterns of the Canadian psyche. That is, his subject will depend on what kinds of figures are made available to him by his country's history, and his approach to his subject will depend on the habits of thought and feeling made available to him by his culture. What, then, have our writers made of our historical "great men?"

The traditional hero is defined by the purpose and quality of his death. The title of this chapter is from Pratt's poem *Brébeuf and His Brethren*; it sums up the Canadian way of death. The American way of death, as demonstrated by both history and literature, is death by violence: assassination, lynching, murder, an upsurge of individual or mass maniacal destructiveness in defiance of law. The defiance of law was itself sanctioned by the Revolution, the overthrow of traditional authority, and Americans have been rebelling against authority ever since: outlaws are heroes.

The English way of death, insofar as there is a single one, is death by history; that scene on the battlefield or in the Tower or on the scaffold, just before the axe falls, appears to be essential to a good English historical movie. Shakespeare was fond of death by history; so was Charles Dickens. Such deaths are seen in the perspective of an interrelated series of social events: clashes of factions and ideals, struggles for power on a monumental scale. Those who die know why they are dying.

The Canadian way of death is death by accident. Death by Nature has been discussed already in Chapter Two; those that drown, freeze or fall off mountains are usually seen as victims, of circumstance or of the environment, both by their authors and by the characters within the poem or novel. The victims may acquire a certain stature by their courage and dignity in the face of death, but the deaths themselves are senseless and accomplish nothing. In *The Bush Garden*, Northrop Frye speaks of such deaths as pointless and useless. But what about cases in which a man, defending an ideal or a social group — that is, under circumstances which ought to give his death "heroic" stature — is killed by other men? Are such deaths any less "accidental," any less "casual," do they have a point, are they useful?

Pratt's *Brébeuf and His Brethren* is the story of an heroic attempt that ends in failure: Brébeuf is tortured and killed, as are many of the other priests; the Mission they have built so laboriously is destroyed, and "the remnant of a nation" staggers back to Québec City. Pratt sees fit to end the poem with a section called "The Martyrs' Shrine," which is a tentative effort to ascribe some sort of positive result to the deaths undergone by the Jesuits: the Mission is rebuilt three hundred years later, the dead rise, more or less, from the grave:

> Near to the ground where the cross broke under the hatchet,
> And went with it into the soil to come back at the turn
> Of the spade with the carbon and calcium char of the bodies,
> The shrines and altars are built anew; the Aves
> And prayers ascend, and the Holy Bread is broken.

Pratt does all that can be done, but the material he is working with undercuts any attempt to make Brébeuf's death that of a traditional hero: we know that the Mission is, in fact, a sort of tourist attraction, and Brébeuf would probably turn over in his grave if he could see the end result of his ordeal: is *that* all, we cannot help asking. It's a bit of an anticlimax. And although the Indians lost eventually, Brébeuf's death did not save *his* society: the French Catholics lost too.

There is a similar irresoluteness about the ending of Don Gutteridge's long narrative poem, *Riel*. Riel is the perfect all-Canadian failed hero — he's French, Indian, Catholic, revolutionary and possibly insane, and he was hanged by the Establishment — and as such has inspired a number of works, among them a play (John Coulter's *The Trial of Louis Riel*) and an opera, Harry Somers' and Mavor Moore's *Riel*. Gutteridge writes in the tradition of Pratt, using a similar technique, interspersing original narrative and lyrical passages with historical documents, some imagined, some real and left intact. In the symbolism of the poem Riel stands for the authentic life of the land, Sir John A. Macdonald for the attempt to impose on the land an artificial structure alien to it, building a "carefully contrived nation of blocks." His famous railway is an act of aggression against the land and the native languages, French and Indian; it is "straight as a gun-barrel," "a steel tongue intoning / its single word." Among the "documents" are a letter from "Sergeant ....," a member of the expedition sent by Sir John A. against Riel; he experiences difficulties with the journey similar to Brébeuf's camping-trip problems:

> At Lake Superior, not only the shale and boulders of the great cliffs blocked our way, but the pines, hundreds of years old, seemed for no apparent reason to have collapsed across the "road," almost as if we were intruders. And for weeks we cut and pulled and dragged our fatigued bones through the most abominable bushland known to man....

These men are in fact intruders; Nature and Riel alike attempt to reject them. But the soldiers and Sir John A. win, the railroad goes through, and "metal" squares and rectangles replace the "wood" and the curved season-shaped natural rhythms of the prairie. (This is, you'll notice, reminiscent of the Settler-versus-Land imagery we noticed in Chapter Five.)

Riel, the man who wished to secede from Sir John's monolithic vision and found a Métis state, falls before an almost faceless authority like an old city block before a highrise developer. "Riel had forfeited his life," Gutteridge quotes from *The Mail*, "and as it valued law and order in the North-West...the Administration was bound to make an example of him." Riel is as much a man with a "mission" as is Brébeuf (he thinks of himself as a prophet, he is much obsessed by his adopted middle name, David), and he is seen as a small David battling the Goliath of Ottawa (the metaphor for his resolution is "this flowing: coiled inside, like a smooth stone"). The difference between the Bible and Canada is that in the Bible God helps, miracles happen, David wins. But Riel's defeat is absolute, and unlike Brébeuf he doesn't even get to be a tourist attraction. The poem ends with his death:

176 / The Dynamics of Culture

> Well, the God damned son of a bitch is gone at last!
> Yeah, the son of a bitch is gone for certain now.
> Along the banks of the ancient Ottawa
> The grey towers stand.

This confrontation, individual against the impersonal "grey towers" of the "Administration," authentic people against imposed culture, attempted revolution foiled by the Mounties, is repeated over and over in Canadian history and in the historical narratives based on it.

Not all Canadian history took place in the nineteenth century, but the twentieth century patterns which writers choose — or which history chooses for them — are remarkably similar. A recent and remarkable play, Carol Bolt's *Buffalo Jump*, tells the story of one of Riel's successors-in-spirit, Red Evans (a composite hero based on two historical figures) and his fight against R. B. Bennett, reincarnation of Sir John A., and his Goliath Mounties.

Evans is a union organizer who leads a march through Vancouver and later a railway odyssey across Canada in an attempt to gain improved conditions for relief-camp workers during the Depression. His men make it only as far as Regina, where Bennett orders the Mounties to get them. The confrontation scene between Evans and Bennett, West and East again, could be straight out of *Riel*: while Evans and his delegation are presenting their case, Bennett sits down behind a model of the Parliament Buildings so that his face is hidden. Those grey towers again. The overall shape of the play is Canadian pure and simple: courageous struggle against overwhelming odds, followed by defeat at the hands of an impersonal giant. It's perhaps significant that the only group of people who are nice to the strikers — the citizens of Golden — are played as characters in an operatic farce. Goodness in such a vision is too good to be true. The play ends with the Regina riot, and the last characters on stage are the victorious Mounties.

I believe that in all three of the examples before us there is an uneasiness, an uncertainty of focus, which at its best can be a teasing ambiguity but at its worst is confusion; and although the confusion may have existed on the part of the authors, it will be magnified if the reader approaches these works looking for a "great man" Hero. Here are some tentative suggestions which may indicate, if not the ultimate reasons for these two kinds of confusion, at least their nature.

Canadian history defeats attempts to construct traditional society-saving or society-changing heroes. The imaginative pattern we've been observing is one of useless individual death, coupled with the defeat of the protagonist's society and the absence of social consequence or significance. All Canadian revolutions are failed revolutions, and our writer, searching the past for Hero materials, will find himself almost inevitably writing a drama in which an individual defending the rights of a small group finds himself up against faceless authority — the Establishment, embodied usually by the Mounties — and is overcome by it. His death or defeat does not save his group: Riel is hanged and the Métis perish as a people, Brébeuf dies for his faith and the English Protestants win eventually; the same is true of Dollard and the defence of the Long Sault (see Lampman's poem "At the Long Sault"). William Lyon Mackenzie loses and so does his cause. The two historical moments at which mild congratulation might seem in order — the War of 1812 and the building of the trans-Canada railroad (or, for that, substitute Confederation; both symbolize the unifying of the country) — cannot sustain elation in the face of the irony of history: Canada repels invasion in 1812 and the Yanks take over anyway; Macdonald pulls the country together and now it's about to fall apart.

Canadian history and the Canadian imagination, then, conspire to make a plausible heroic death — a death that accomplishes something, means something in terms of its society — almost impossible. The works of literature built on history reflect this near impossibility, though authors may strain for the desired "traditional" significance. Frequently, however, they bow to the inevitable and write about the Hero-as-loser or -victim, almost despite themselves.

Canadians don't know which side they're on. This remark applies to situations such as those in *Riel* and *Buffalo Jump* in which would-be revolutionaries confront the Mounties and lose. Both of these works suffer from a confusion about the nature and moral position of authority which is in fact a confusion in the Canadian psyche itself. Author and audience sympathies in both cases are with the rebels; but if the rebels had won, what then? Canadians — and not only Canadian Prime Ministers — are terrified of having authority undermined, monolithic federalism shaken. A house divided against itself cannot stand, we mutter endlessly. If the railroad hadn't gone through, the Americans would have got the West; if the country falls apart, who will inherit the pieces?

Canada has from the beginning defined itself as a place where revolutions are really rebellions, against lawful authority — which, as we noted in Chapter Five, is seen as the social form of a divine order. This may work in positive or negative ways (no one riots, for instance, when things like Civil Rights get suspended) but the fact remains that it's hard for Canadians to see the Mounties — symbol of "lawful authority" — as the enemy pure and simple. (Canada must be the only country in the world where a policeman is used as a national symbol; the Canadian contestant in Miss Universe contests invariably wears a cute Mountie uniform. Maybe the only alternative would be a beaver uniform, and dressing up like a Mountie beats dressing up like a peach or a potato, as do Misses Georgia and Idaho; still....)

But if the enemy in its lawful authority is not really an enemy but a necessary and mitigated evil, a fact of life, then the construction of "revolutionary" heroes becomes difficult; you get not so much a hero as one who has allowed himself to be a victim of idiot circumstance, like a man who goes swimming in a thunderstorm. The order of the universe, one half of our schizophrenic Canadian consciousness can't help feeling, will of course strike him down.

His death may be a death-by-accident (as befits a Canadian hero), like that of Chartier the mad bomber, who tried to blow up the Parliament Buildings but only succeeded in blowing up himself, by mistake, and, ignominiously, in the john. But the half of the Canadian psyche that distrusts and fears any attempt to overthrow even a repressive authority will see such deaths as proper and meaningful retribution; while the other half, the one which is on the side of the underdog because it identifies with the *victims* of repressive authority, will see the death as pointless because wasted: the death hasn't accomplished the revolution. But then, the first half of the psyche never meant it to. Canadian rebellions have never become revolutions precisely because they have never received popular support. "Prophets" here don't get very far against the Civil Service; which is of course the hidden Clark Kent side of that romantic red-coated collective superhero on the Musical-Ride horse.

The attempt to create a traditional individual hero may be misguided in Canada. Demanding that we have "Heroes" may be like demanding that we have a Frontier of our very own, or like putting down all Canadian books because they aren't *Moby Dick*: it may be just a symptom of a colonial state of mind. The attempt to write up "great man" Heroism in Canada may parallel the Lake-District-in-Algonquin-Park approach to Nature: insisting that Nature here should be what Wordsworth saw. The "great man" — and possibly also the "anti-hero" and the "representative little man," like Willy Loman in *Death of a Salesman* — may well be foreign models, and outmoded ones at that, which don't grow authentically when transplanted. But the attempt may still break ground, if only by demonstrating that the foreign model doesn't work very well here.

Several critics, including Northrop Frye and Robin Mathews, have suggested that the pull of the native tradition is not in the direction of individual heroes at all, but rather in the direction of collective heroes. This can be seen even in the examples we've chosen. Brébeuf is not the *only* individual to undergo ordeals and martyrdom: there are also the "Brethren," and a lot of the poem's time is spent on them. The spotlight is diffused, not focussed. Similarly, in *Riel* an apparently disproportionate amount of space is given over to the description of a Métis buffalo hunt: it's the people, not just Riel, who exist and resist. And in *Buffalo Jump* the real "hero" is not Red Evans by himself — he comes through merely as a catalyst — but the men on the march. These collective heroes are as capable of failure as individual ones, and these three examples do in fact fall; the point is that it is they, rather than individual "great men," who are the real emotional focus.

A favourite epic theme has been the building of the railroad across Canada. Pratt has a poem on it, *Towards the Last Spike*, and there are Pierre Berton's popular prose treatments, *The National Dream* and *The Last Spike*. Again, building the railroad is not seen as the achievement of a single individual. Sir John A. Macdonald may be a focus, but the railroad is actually *built* by a large group of men, and it is thus that Pratt handles the "heroic" act. The passengers on the Titanic, the seamen of *The Roosevelt and the Antinoe*, the men at Dunkirk — these are the collective heroes in three other poems by Pratt. In looking for individual, or individualist, heroes in Canadian literature we may be looking for the wrong thing in the wrong place.

This has obvious literary and social advantages and disadvantages. The collective hero can be an expression of a closed and ingrown garrison mentality or of a living community; collective action has been necessary for survival but it may also stifle individual growth. And in literature, it can generate moments of emotion which are different *in kind* from those generated by individual heroes; the death of a battalion or a shipload is different from the death of a general. The collective hero may also be crucial to any analysis of the "way out" of the Canadian victim situations we've been defining.

Pushed a step further, the Canadian tendency to favour collective heroes rather than individual ones leads to a positive and deliberate undercutting of individual heroics. For instance, the first re-imagined historical moment in Dennis Lee's *Civil Elegies* goes like this:

> ....casting back I saw
> regeneration twirl its blood and the rebels riding
> riderless down Yonge Street, plain men much
> goaded by privilege — our other origin, and cried
> "Mackenzie knows a word, Mackenzie
> knows a meaning!" but it was not true. Eight hundred-odd steely Canadians
> turned tail at the cabbage patch when a couple of bullets fizzed
> and the loyalists, scared skinny by the sound of their own gunfire,
> gawked and bolted south to the fort like rabbits,
> the rebels for their part bolting north to the pub: the first
> spontaneous mutual retreat in the history of warfare.
> Canadians, in flight.

Here Mackenzie, posing as Hero, fails to deliver the goods, and *both* sides lose — a typically Canadian record, that (ordinarily there's at least *one* winner).

A similar pattern can be found in Roch Carrier's *La Guerre, Yes Sir!* The ostensible "Hero" is a dead man in a coffin. He has died in the Second World War, and the people in his small Québec village believe him to be a glorious military hero, though at home he was a n'er-do-well. Actually he died by accident: not even an ignominious death, but a silly one. He didn't want to wait in line at the toilet, went behind a bush instead, and was blown up by a stray landmine. But his death does accomplish something: it unites the people of his village in opposition to the English soldiers who are supervising his funeral. They attack the soldiers in an attempt to recapture the coffin, after the soldiers have terminated the wake.

Again neither side wins, exactly. The soldiers depart eventually, carrying the coffin of their own dead Anglais anti-hero, killed by mistake during the skirmish; the villagers have survived. The point is that there is no individual leader or hero: *all* the villagers participate in the fight, even though they've been fighting among themselves earlier. The assumed hero is both dead and a sham; it's the collective that's alive.

When you've recognized a pattern or a tradition, the best course is not to bemoan the fact that it is what it is (tough that we can't write *Hamlet*, we aren't the English Renaissance; tough that we can't have American alienated heroes, we go in for collectives) but to explore the possibilities for using that pattern in as many significant ways as possible. For playwrights and directors, I think the possibilities for collective plays about collective heroes are very exciting. (So did Brecht.) There was a play put on in Toronto in 1972, *Fanshen* by Rick Salutin, which was about the Chinese Revolution and the necessity for the revolution's being made by all the individuals in the society, working together. The play wasn't just about China.

In Defence of North America

GEORGE GRANT

To exist as a North American is an amazing and enthralling fate. As in every historical condition, some not only have to live their fate, but also to let it come to be thought. What we have built and become in so short a time calls forth amazement in the face of its novelty, an amazement which leads to that thinking. Yet the very dynamism of the novelty enthralls us to inhibit that thinking.

It is not necessary to take sides in the argument between the ancients and moderns as to what is novelty, to recognize that we live in novelty of some kind. Western technical achievement has shaped a different civilization from any previous, and we North Americans are the most advanced in that achievement. This achievement is not something simply external to us, as so many people envision it. It is not merely an external environment which we make and choose to use as we want — a playground in which we are able to do more and more, an orchard where we can always pick variegated fruit. It moulds us in what we are, not only at the heart of our animality in the propagation and continuance of our species, but in our actions and thoughts and imaginings. Its pursuit has become our dominant activity and that dominance fashions both the public and private realms. Through that achievement we have become the heartland of the wealthiest and most powerful empire that has yet been. We can exert our influence over a greater extent of the globe and take a greater tribute of wealth than any previously. Despite our limitations and miscalculations, we have more compelling means than any previous for putting the brand of our civilisation deeply into the flesh of others.

To have become so quickly the imperial centre of an increasingly realised technological civilisation would be bewildering for any human beings, but for North Americans particularly so. From our beginnings there has been an ambiguity for us as to who we are. To the Asians as they suffer from us, we must appear the latest wave of dominating Europeans who spread their ways around the world, claiming that those ways were not simply another civilisation, but the highest so far, and whose claim was justified in the fact of power, namely that it could only be countered by Asians who accepted the very forms which threatened them. To the Europeans also we appear as spawned by themselves: the children of some low class servants who once

---

Abridged from George Grant, "In Defence of North America," *Technology and Empire: Perspectives on North America* (Toronto: House of Anansi Press, 1969), pp. 15–40. This is an edited version of the essay. Reprinted by permission.

dared to leave the household and who now surprisingly appear as powerful and dominating neighbours masquerading as gentry, whose threat can only be minimised by teaching them a little culture. They express contempt of us as a society barren of anything but the drive to technology; yet their contempt is too obviously permeated with envy to be taken as pure.

In one sense both the Asians and Europeans are correct. Except for the community of the children of the slaves and the few Indians we have allowed just to survive, we are indeed Europeans. Imperially we turn out to the rest of the world bringing the apogee of what Europeans first invented, technological civilisation. Our first ways, in terms of which we met the new land, came with us from Europe and we have always used our continuing contact with the unfolding of that civilisation. To this day many of our shallow intellectual streams are kept flowing by their rain. It was exiled Europeans with the new physical theory who provided us with our first uses of atomic energy. Our new social science may fit us so perfectly as to seem indigenous; but behind Parsons is Weber, behind Skinner, Pavlov, behind social work and psychiatry Freud. Even in seeking some hope against the inhuman imperial system and some less sterile ground of political morality than a liberalism become the end of ideology, many of the most beautiful young turn for their humanism to so European a thinker as Marcuse. In a field as un-American as theology, the continually changing ripples of thought, by which the professionals hope to revive a dying faith, originate from some stone dropped by a European thinker.

Yet those who know themselves to be North Americans know they are not Europeans. The platitude cannot be too often stated that the U.S. is the only society which has no history (truly its own) from before the age of progress. English-speaking Canadians, such as myself, have despised and feared the Americans for the account of freedom in which their independence was expressed, and have resented that other traditions of the English-speaking world should have collapsed before the victory of that spirit; but we are still enfolded with the Americans in the deep sharing of having crossed the ocean and conquered the new land. All of us who came made some break in that coming. The break was not only the giving up of the old and the settled, but the entering into the majestic continent which could not be ours in the way that the old had been. It could not be ours in the old way because the making of it ours did not go back before the beginning of conscious memory. The roots of some communities in eastern North America go back far in continuous love for their place, but none of us can be called autochthonous, because in all there is some consciousness of making the land our own. It could not be ours also because the very intractibility, immensity and extremes of the new land required that its meeting with mastering Europeans be a battle of subjugation. And after that battle we had no long history of living with the land before the arrival of the new forms of conquest which came with industrialism.

That conquering relation to place has left its mark within us. When we go into the Rockies we may have the sense that gods are there. But if so, they cannot manifest themselves to us as ours. They are the gods of another race, and we cannot know them because of what we are, and what we did. There can be nothing immemorial for us except the environment as object. Even our cities have been encampments on the road to economic mastery.

It may be that all men are at their core the homeless beings. Be that as it may, Nietzsche has shown that homelessness is the particular mark of modern nihilism. But we were homeless long before the mobility of our mobilised technology and the mass nihilism which has been its accompaniment. If the will to mastery is essential to the modern, our wills were burnished in that battle with the land. We were made ready to be leaders of the civilisation which was incubating in Europe.

The very use of the word "autochthonous" raises another way in which we are not Europeans. Living undivided from one's own earth: here is not only a form of living which has not been ours but which is named in a language the echoes of which are far from us. The remoteness of "chthonic" from us measures our separation from Europe. Greece lay behind Europeans as a first presence; it has not so lain for us. It was for them primal in the sense that in its perfected statements educated Europeans found the way that things are. The Greek writings bared a knowledge of the human and non-human things which could be grasped as firmness by the Europeans for the making of their own lives and cities. Most important, Plato and Aristotle presented contemplation as the height for man. Until Nietzsche, Socrates was known as the peak of Greekness.

To say this does not deny that there was for Europeans another primal — Christianity. Indeed the meeting of these two in men's lives, the manifold attempts to see them as one, to bring together contemplation and charity, the fact that they were seen by some to be antithetical and so either one or the other condemned, the way that each was interpreted and misinterpreted in terms of the other and each used against the other in the building of a civilisation which was new and which was neither, these inter-relations formed the chief tension out of which Europe was shaped. It is still possible for some Europeans to live in one or the other as primal although they are part of a civilisation which is so alien from both.

The degree to which the Greek was primal for Europeans can be seen in the fact that those theoretical men, from Machiavelli to Nietzsche, who delineated what modern Europe was to become when it was no longer explicitly Christian, made an increasing appeal to the Greeks as primal, while Christianity became for them either a boring, although necessary, convention, or an avowed enemy. Even as their delineation was founded on an increasingly radical criticism of Greek thought, they claimed to be rediscovering a more authentic account of what the ancients had meant than that held by their immediate predecessors; thus Machiavelli against the theologians, Rousseau against the English, Nietzsche against Rousseau and Hegel. Even such a modern revolutionary as St. Just justified his use of terror by an appeal to classical sources. The ways of modern Europe have often been described as a species of secularised Christianity. However, the ambiguity remains: the formulations of modernity have often been made by men who claimed to be returning behind Christianity to the classics, and yet laid out a fundamental criticism of the classical accounts of science, art, politics, etc. And that criticism seems to have been influenced by the hidden depths of Biblical religion.

Members of the civilisation which initiated modern technology often now express a fear of the Americanisation of Europe, and state that fear in their identification of the U.S. with the pure will to technique. This may be an expression of their deeper fear that their own society in becoming sheerly modern has at last and perhaps finally lost touch with its primal and therefore perhaps with contemplation itself, and that thereby Europe, in its particularity, is no more.

For us the primal was much different. It was the meeting of the alien and yet conquerable land with English-speaking Protestants. Since the crossing of the ocean we have been Europeans who were not Europeans. But the Europeanness which remained for us was of a special kind because Calvinist Protestantism was itself a break in Europe — a turning away from the Greeks in the name of what was found in the Bible. We brought to the meeting with the land a particular non-Mediterranean Europeanness of the seventeenth century which was itself the beginning of something new.

To understand North America it is necessary to understand those Protestants and to understand particularly their connection to the new physical and moral science which were coming into being in Europe. Why was it that the new physical and moral sciences, although not initiated by Calvinists, found a particularly ready acceptance among them, especially among the Dutch and the English? Weber enucleated the central practical relation between capitalism and the Calvinists as the worldly asceticism of the latter. His exposition of the essentials of that relationship is true despite its mistakes in detail and his lack of theoretical depth. Marxist historians have taken up the subject and written clearly of the relation between the new capitalism and Puritanism, particularly as the two were linked together in the parliamentary party during the English civil war.

Because they were concentrating on the practical relation between religion and society, neither Weber nor the Marxists were concerned with the deeper level of the matter, which is the connection between Protestant theology and the new sciences. For example, more fundamental than the practical connections between capitalism, the parliamentary party and Protestantism, lies the fact that the refugee Protestant theologians from the continent espoused so immediately the Baconian account of science and worked to make it influential in England. It is only possible to write here generally about the relation between Protestant theology and the new science. It sprang initially from one negative agreement: both the theologians and the scientists wished to free the minds of men from the formulations of mediaeval Aristotelianism, though for different reasons. Because of our present education, the criticism by the 17th century scientists of the traditional doctrines is well known. They criticised the mediaeval teleological doctrine with its substantial forms as preventing men from observing and understanding the world as it is. The criticism by the theologians is less well known and less easily understandable in an age such as ours. They attacked the mediaevel teleological doctrine as the foundation of what they called "natural" theology, and that theology was attacked because it led men away from fundamental reliance on Christian revelation. The teleological doctrine did this because it encouraged men to avoid the surd mystery of evil by claiming that final purpose could be argued from the world. Such mitigation led men away from the only true illumination of that mystery, the crucifixion apprehended in faith as the divine humiliation.

But beyond this common negative attack on the mediaeval science, there was in the theology of the Calvinist Protestants a positive element which made it immensely open to the empiricism and utilitarianism in the English edition of the new sciences. Troeltsch has described that element and its consequent openness: "Calvinism, with its abolition of the absolute goodness and rationality of the Divine activity into mere separate will-acts, connected by no inner necessity and no metaphysical unity of substance, essentially tends to the emphasising of the individual and empirical, the renunciation of the conceptions of absolute causality and unity, the practically free and utilitarian individual judgement of all things. The influence of this spirit is quite unmistakably the most important cause of the empirical and positivist tendencies of the Anglo-Saxon spirit, which today find themselves in it as compatible with strong religious feeling, ethical discipline and keen intellectuality as they formerly did in Calvinism itself." "Today" for Troeltsch was before 1914, so that "strong religious feeling, ethical discipline and keen intellectuality" must be taken as an account of the English-speaking bourgeois world before the adventures and catastrophes of the last half century, before the total collapse of Calvinism as an explicit social force. Indeed as Calvinism was more present in North America than in England as the dominant public religion, Troeltsch's words apply more forcibly to this continent than to the home of Puritanism. . . .

When one contemplates the conquest of nature by technology one must remember that that conquest had to include our own bodies. Calvinism provided the determined and organised men and women who could rule the mastered world. The punishment they inflicted on non-human nature, they had first inflicted on themselves.

Now when from that primal has come forth what is present before us; when the victory over the land leaves most of us in metropoloi where widely spread consumption vies with confusion and squalor; when the emancipation of greed turns out from its victories on this continent to feed imperially on the resources of the world; when those resources cushion an immense majority who think they are free in pluralism, but in fact live in a monistic vulgarity in which nobility and wisdom have been exchanged for a pale belief in progress, alternating with boredom and weariness of spirit; when the disciplined among us drive to an unlimited technological future, in which technical reason has become so universal that it has closed down on openness and awe, questioning and listening; when Protestant subjectivity remains authentic only where it is least appropriate, in the moodiness of our art and sexuality, and where public religion has become an unimportant litany of objectified self-righteousness necessary for the more anal of our managers; one must remember now the hope, the stringency and nobility of that primal encounter. The land was almost indomitable. The intense seasons of the continental heartland needed a people who whatever else were not flaccid. And these people not only forced commodities from the land, but built public and private institutions of freedom and flexibility and endurance. Even when we fear General Motors or ridicule our immersion in the means of mobility, we must not forget that the gasoline engine was a needfilled fate for those who had to live in such winters and across such distances. The Marxists who have described the conquest of the continent as an example of capitalist rape miss the substance of those events, as an incarnation of hope and equality which the settlers had not found in Europe. Whatever the vulgarity of mass industrialism, however empty our talk of democracy, it must not be forgotten that in that primal there was the expectation of new independence in which each would be free for self-legislation, and for communal legislation. Despite the exclusion of the African, despite the struggles of the later immigrant groups, the faith and institutions of that primal encounter were great enough to bring into themselves countless alien traditions and make these loyal to that spirit. To know that parents had to force the instincts of their children to the service of pioneering control; to have seen the pained and unrelenting faces of the women; to know even in one's flesh and dreams, the results of generations of the mechanising of the body; to see all around one the excesses and follies now necessary to people who can win back the body only through sexuality, must not be to forget what was necessary and what was heroic in that conquest....

At home the ruling managers move "towards the year 2000." It might seem here that the practical primal has become no more than the unalloyed drive to technological mastery for its own sake. It is this interpretation which allows certain Europeans to consider us a wasteland with nothing seriously human amongst us but that self-propelling will to technology. But this interpretation underestimates the very effectiveness of North America in the world, in its forgetting that it is men who make that drive. What makes the drive to technology so strong is that it is carried on by men who still identify what they are doing with the liberation of mankind. Our ruling managers are able to do what they do just because among sufficient of them technology and liberalism support each other as identified. It is this identification which makes our drive to technology still more dynamic than the nihilistic will to will which is emptied of all conceptions of purpose. It may be (to use the indicative would be claiming to have grasped the very heart of what is) that this drive to practicality moves to become little more than a will to mastery governing the vacuous masses. But that is not yet how we understand our present. The identification in our practicality of masterful interference and the building of a human world still filters through the manifold structures of managerial and scientific elites to be the governing faith of the society. All political arguments within the system, the squalls on the surface of the ocean (for example that about the rights of property in relation to the common good, between the freedom for some and the freedom for all) take place within the common framework that the highest good is North America moving forward in expansionist practicality. To think outside this faith is to make oneself a stranger to the public realm....

To such comprehension the technological society is only in detail a terra incognita, as in its rushing change new problems arise which cannot always be predicted in advance. We therefore require the clearest minds to predict by understanding those which are on the horizon and to sort them out by calculation with courage. As we move "towards the year 2000" we need all the institutes of urban studies and of race relations, all the centres of economic development and psychological adjustment we can get. We will have to see how cities need not set affluence and squalor, private competence and public disorganization against each other; how all can reach a level of educational competence to inherit the hope; how the young can be shown purpose in the midst of enormous bureaucracies; how banality need not be incumbent on mass culture; how neuroses and psychoses, which are so immediately destructive when power is great, can be overcome by new understandings of psychology and sociology, etcetera, etcetera. Add to these the international problems of how underdeveloped countries can be brought to share in the new possibilities by accepting the conditions of modernisation, how the greed of already modern societies does not hold the others in slavery, how mass breeding with modern medicine does not overwhelm them and us before modernisation can be accomplished, above all how the new military techniques do not explode us all before we have reached an internationalism appropriate to the age of reason. But these are difficulties of detail, requiring our best calculation to avoid, but not vitiating intrinsically the vision of the technological society as a supreme step in our liberation. Behind them lie the comprehension of this great experience in the minds of our dominant majority as self-evidently good, that for which man has struggled in evolution since his origins in pain and chance, ignorance and taboo.

Indeed the loud differences in the public world — what in a simpler mind nineteenth century Europe could be described as the divisions between left and right — are carried on within this fundamental faith. The directors of General Motors and the followers of Professor Marcuse sail down the same river in different boats. This is not to say anything as jejune as to deny the obvious fact that our technological society develops within a state capitalist framework and that that will have significant effect on what we are and what we will become, particularly in relation to other technological societies developed under other structures. But amid the conflict of public ideologies it is well to remember that all live within a common horizon. Those of the "right," who stand by the freedoms of the individual to hold property and for firmer enforcement of our present laws, seem to have hesitation about some of the consequences of modernity, but they do not doubt the central fact of the North American dream — progress through technological advance. It may be indeed that, like most of us, the "right" want it both ways. They want to maintain certain moral customs, freedoms of property and even racial rights which are not in fact compatible with advancing technological civilisation. Be that as it may, the North American "right" believes firmly in technical advance. Indeed its claim is that in the past the mixture of individualism and public order it has espoused has been responsible for the triumphs of technique in our society.

Equally those of the "left" who have condemned our social arrangements and worked most actively to change them have based their condemnation in both the 1930s and 1960s on some species of Marxism. This is to appeal to the redemptive possibilities of technology and to deny contemplation in the name of changing the world. Indeed domestic Marxists have been able as a minority to concentrate on the libertarian and Utopian expectations in their doctrines because unlike the Marxists of the East they could leave the requirements of public order to others. But however libertarian the notions of the new left, they are always thought within the control of nature achieved by modern techniques. The liberation of human beings assumes the ease of an environment where nature has already been conquered. For example, at the libertarian height of Professor Marcuse's writings (*Eros and Civilization*), he maintains that men having achieved freedom against a constraining nature can now live in the liberation of a polymorphous sexuality. The orgiastic gnosticism there preached always assumes that the possibilities of liberation depend on the maintenance of our high degrees of conquest. Having first conquered nature we can now enjoy her. His later *One Dimensional Man* is sadder in its expectations from our present situation, but technology is still simplistically described and blessed, as long as it is mixed with the pursuit of art, kind sexuality and a dash of Whiteheadian metaphysics.

Even the root and branch condemnation of the system by some of the politicised young assumes the opportunities for widespread instant satisfaction which are only possible in terms of the modern achievements. They want both high standards of spontaneous democracy and the egalitarian benefits accruing from technique. But have not the very forms of the bureaucratic institutions been developed as necessary for producing those benefits? Can the benefits exist without the stifling institutions? Can such institutions exist as participatory democracies? To say yes to these questions with any degree of awareness requires the recognition of the fact that the admired spontaneity of freedom is made feasible by the conquering of the spontaneity of nature. In this sense their rejection of their society is not root and branch. They share, with those who appear to them as enemies, the deeper assumptions which have made the technological society.

Indeed the fact that progress in techniques is the horizon for us is seen even in the humane stance of those who seek some overreaching vision of human good in terms of which the use of particular techniques might be decided. Who would deny that there are many North Americans who accept the obvious benefits of modern technique but who also desire to maintain firm social judgement about each particular method in the light of some decent vision of human good? Such judgements are widely attempted in obvious cases, such as military techniques, where most men still ask whether certain employments can ever serve good. (This is even so in a continent whose government is the only one so far to have used nuclear weapons in warfare.) At a less obvious level, there are still many who ask questions about particular techniques of government planning and their potency for tyranny. Beyond this again there are a smaller number who raise questions about new biochemical methods and their relation to the propagation of the race. As the possible harm from any new technique is less evident, the number of questioners get fewer. This position is the obvious one by which a multitude of sensible and responsible people try to come to terms with immediate exigencies. Nevertheless the grave difficulty of thinking a position in which technique is beheld within a horizon greater than itself, stems from the very nature of our primal, and must be recognized.

That difficulty is present for us because of the following fact: when we seek to elucidate the standards of human good (or in contemporary language "the values") by which particular techniques can be judged, we do so within modern ways of thought and belief. But from the very beginnings of modern thought the new natural science and the new moral science developed together in mutual interdependence so that the fundamental assumptions of each were formulated in the light of the other. Modern thought is in that sense a unified fate for us. The belief in the mastering knowledge of human and non-human beings arose together with the very way we conceive our humanity as an Archimedean freedom outside nature, so that we can creatively will to shape the world to our values. The decent bureaucrats, the concerned thinkers and the thoughtful citizens as much conceive their task as creatively willing to shape the world to their values as do the corporate despots, the motivations experts and the manipulative politicians. The moral discourse of "values" and "freedom" is not independent of the will to technology, but a language fashioned in the same forge together with the will to technology. To try to think them separately is to move more deeply into their common origin.

Moreover, when we use this language of "freedom" and "values" to ask seriously what substantive "values" our freedom should create, it is clear that such values cannot be discovered in "nature" because in the light of modern science nature is objectively conceived as indifferent to value. (Every sophomore who studies philosophy in the English-speaking world is able to disprove "the naturalistic fallacy," namely, that statements about what ought to be cannot be inferred solely from statements about what is.) Where then does our freedom to create values find its content? When that belief in freedom expresses itself seriously (that is politically and not simply as a doctrine of individual fulfilment) the content of man's freedom becomes the actualising of freedom for all men. The purpose of action becomes the building of the universal and homogenous state — the society in which all men are free and equal and increasingly able to realise their concrete individuality. Indeed this is the governing goal of ethical striving, as much in the modernising east as in the west. Despite the continuing power in North America of the right of individuals to highly comfortable and dominating self-preservation through the control of property, and in the communist bloc the continuing exaltation of the general will against all individual and national rights, the rival empires agree in their public testimonies as to what is the goal of human striving....

Indeed the situation of liberalism in which it is increasingly difficult for our freedom to have any content by which to judge techniques except in their own terms is present in all advanced industrial countries. But it is particularly pressing for us because our tradition of liberalism was moulded from practicality. Because the encounter of the land with the Protestants was the primal for us, we never inherited much that was at the heart of western Europe. This is not to express the foolish position that we are a species of Europeans-minus. It is clear that in our existing here we have become something which is more than European — something which by their lack of it Europeans find difficult to understand. Be that as it may, it is also clear that the very nature of the primal for us meant that we did not bring with us from Europe the tradition of contemplation. To say contemplation "tout court" is to speak as if we lacked some activity which the Ford Foundation could make good by proper grants to the proper organisations. To say philosophy rather than contemplation might be to identify what is absent for us with an academic study which is pursued here under that name. Nevertheless, it may perhaps be said negatively that what has been absent for us is the affirmation of a possible apprehension of the world beyond that as a field of objects considered as pragmata — an apprehension present not only in its height as "theory" but as the undergirding of our loves and friendships, of our arts and reverences, and indeed as the setting for our dealing with the objects of the human and non-human world. Perhaps we are lacking the recognition that our response to the whole should not most deeply be that of doing, nor even that of terror and anguish, but that of wondering or marvelling at what is, being amazed or astonished by it, or perhaps best, in a discarded English usage, admiring it; and that such a stance, as beyond all bargains and conveniences, is the only source from which purposes may be manifest to us for our necessary calculating.

To repeat, western Europe had inherited that contemplation in its use of it theologically, that is, under the magistery of revelation. Within that revelation charity was the height and therefore contemplation was finally a means to that obedient giving oneself away. Nevertheless it was necessary for some to think revelation and the attempt to do so led theologians continually back to the most comprehensive thinkers that the west had known. Augustine spoke of "spoiling the Egyptians" but in that use of philosophy to expound revelation, the spoilers were often touched by that which they would use as something they could not use. In that continual tasting of the Greeks, some men were led back to thought not determined by revelation, and therefore to a vision of contemplation not subservient to charity, but understood as itself the highest. As has been said earlier, the Calvinists claimed to be freeing theology from all but its Biblical roots and cut themselves off from pure contemplation more than did any other form of European theology — Catholic or Jewish, Lutheran or even Anglican. For the Calvinist, theology was a prophetic and legal expounding of a positively conceived revelation, the purpose of which was to make its practical appeal to men. Thus being in our origins this form of Protestant, thrown into the exigencies of the new continent, we did not partake of the tradition of European contemplation. And as we moved from that Calvinism to modernity, what was there in the influence of liberalism which could have made us more open to that contemplation? Indeed for lack of contemplation, American intellectual patriots have had to make the most of Emerson and Adams, James and Pierce.

I know how distant from North Americans is the stance of contemplation, because I know the pervasiveness of the pragmatic liberalism in which I was educated and the accidents of existence which dragged me out from it. To write so may seem some kind of boasting. But the scavenging mongrel in the famine claims no merit in scenting food. Perhaps for later generations of North Americans it is now easier to turn and partake in deeper traditions than they find publicly around them. The fruits of our own dominant tradition have so obviously the taste of rot in their luxuriance. It may be easier for some of the young to become sane, just because the society is madder. But for myself it has taken the battering of a lifetime of madness to begin to grasp even dimly that which has been inevitably lost in being North American. Even to have touched Greekness (that is to have known it not simply as antiquarianism) required that I should first have touched something in Europe which stayed alive there from before the age of progress through all its acceptance of that age. By touching Europe I do not mean as a fascinating museum or a place of diversion, but to have felt the remnants of a Christianity which was more than simply the legitimising of progress and which still held in itself the fruits of contemplation. By that touching I do not mean the last pickings of authentic theology left after the storms of modern thought (though that too) but things more deeply in the stuff of everyday living which remain long after they can no longer be thought: public and private virtues having their point beyond what can in any sense be called socially useful; commitments to love and to friendship which lie rooted in a realm outside the calculable; a partaking in the beautiful not seen as the product of human creativity; amusements and ecstasies not seen as the enemies of reason. This is not to say that such things did not or do not exist in North America (perhaps they cannot disappear among human beings) but their existence had been dimmed and even silenced by the fact that the public ideology of pragmatic liberalism could not sustain them in its vision. The remnants of that which lay beyond bargaining and left one without an alternative still could be touched even amidst the degeneracy of Europe's ruin. They generally existed from out of a surviving Christianity or Judaism (neither necessarily explicit) which pointed to a realm in which they were sustained. I remember the surprise — the distance and the attraction — of letting near one at all seriously a vision of life so absent in day to day North America. I remember how such a vision inevitably jeopardised one's hold on North America: how it made one an impotent stranger in the practical realm of one's own society. But the remnants of such a Europe were only one remove from what was one's own. It was the seedbed out of which the attenuated Christianity of our secularised Calvinism had come. To touch the vestiges of this fuller Christianity was a possible step in passing to something which was outside the limits of one's own.

Indeed until recently the very absence of a contemplative tradition spared us the full weight of that public nihilism which in Europe flowered with industrial society. The elimination of the idea of final purpose from the scientific study of the human and non-human things not only led to the progress of science and the improvement of conditions but also had consequences on the public understanding of what it was to live. But this consequence was not so immediately evident in our practical culture as it was to Europeans. We took our science pragmatically as if its effect on us could be limited to the external. Thus it was possible for us to move deeply into the technological society, while maintaining our optimism and innocence.

In the public realm, this optimism and innocence delayed the appearance amongst us of many of those disorders which in Europe were concurrent with that nihilism. It is well to remember that large sections of our population resisted the call to imperialism by the economic and political powers of the eastern seaboard, even when they welcomed the technological expansion which made it inevitable. Europeans (particularly the English) would do well to remember, now that they live in the full noon of that imperialism, how hard they worked to drag North American democracy to wider imperial pursuits. Until recently there have not appeared amongst us those public atheisms of the left and of the right which were central to the domestic violence of Europe in this century. The propertied classes of the right have remained uneducated until recently and so kept longer within the respectable religion of their tradition than did their counterparts in Europe. Liberals have ridiculed as hypocrisy the continuing religion among the propertied and even among the bureaucratic. When such traditions have gone those ridiculers may miss the restraints among their rulers that were part of such traditions. For can there be any doubt that the bureaucratic "right" must be more powerful in advanced societies than the left? For the last hundred years our optimism has been reaffirmed by generations of new immigrants who, whatever their trials, found in the possibilities of the new land the opportunity of affluence and freedom on its practical terms. This continuous entry of new families and new peoples busy fighting to partake in the North American dream perpetuated the vitality of the modern.

Even as the language of Europe's "agony" began to penetrate our institutions of the intellect, we were able to use that language as if it could be a servant of our optimistic practical purposes. To repeat, what would North American rhetoric be without the word "values"? But even those who use the word seriously within theoretical work seem not to remember that the word was brought into the centre of western discourse by Nietzsche and into the discourse of social science through Nietzsche's profound influence upon Weber. For Nietzsche the fundamental experience for man was apprehending what is as chaos; values were what we creatively willed in the face of that chaos by overcoming the impotence of the will which arises from the recognition of the consequences of historicism. Nietzsche's politics (and he affirmed that the heart of any philosophy can be seen in its political recommendations) stated that democracy and socialism were the last debasements brought into the world by Christianity as it became secularised. The universal and homogeneous state would be made up of "last men" from whom nobleness and greatness would have departed. Because of our firm practicality, North American social scientists have been able to use the language of values, fill it with the substantive morality of liberalism and thereby avoid facing what is assumed in the most coherent unfolding of this language. The writings of Lasswell and Parsons were hymns to that innocent achievement. It has been wonderful to behold legions of social scientists wising up others about the subjectiveness of their values while they themselves earnestly preached the virtues of industrial democracy, egalitarianism, and decent progressive education; espousing, in other words, that liberalism which sees the universal and homogeneous state as the highest goal of political striving. They took their obligations to the indigenous traditions more seriously than those to the theoretical consequences of their sciences.

Such a position could not last. The languages of historicism and values which were brought to North America to be the servants of the most advanced liberalism and pluralism, now turn their corrosive power on our only indigenous roots — the substance of that practical liberalism itself. The corrosions of nihilism occur in all parts of the community. Moreover, because our roots have been solely practical, this nihilism shares in that shallowness. The old individualism of capitalism, the frontier and Protestantism, becomes the demanded right to one's idiosyncratic wants taken as outside any obligation to the community which provides them. Buoyed by the restless needs of affluence, our art becomes hectic in its experiments with style and violence. Even the surest accounts of our technomania — the sperm-filled visions of Burroughs — are themselves spoken from the shallowness they would describe. Madness itself can only be deep when it comes forth from a society which holds its opposite. Nihilism which has no tradition of contemplation to beat against cannot be the occasion for the amazed reappearance of the "What for? Whither? and What then?" The tragedy for the young is that when they are forced by its excesses to leave the practical tradition, what other depth is present to them in which they can find substance? The enormous reliance on and expectation from indigenous music is a sign of the craving for substance, and of how thin is the earth where we would find it. When the chthonic has been driven back into itself by the conquests of our environment, it can only manifest itself beautifully in sexuality, although at the same time casting too great a weight upon that isolated sexuality.

For those who stay within the central stream of our society and are therefore dominant in its institutions, the effect of nihilism is the narrowing to an unmitigated reliance on technique. Nietzsche's equivocation about the relation between the highest will to power and the will to technology has never been part of the English speaking tradition. With us the identity was securely thought from the very beginning of our modernity. Therefore as our liberal horizons fade in the winter of nihilism, and as the dominating amongst us see themselves within no horizon except their own creating of the world, the pure will to technology (whether personal or public) more and more gives sole content to that creating. In the official intellectual community this process has been called "the end of ideology." What that phrase flatteringly covers is the closing down of willing to all content except the desire to make the future by mastery, and the closing down of all thinking which transcends calculation. Within the practical liberalism of our past, techniques could be set within some context other than themselves — even if that context was shallow. We now move towards the position where technological progress becomes itself the sole context within which all that is other to it must attempt to be present.

We live then in the most realised technological society which has yet been; one which is, moreover, the chief imperial centre from which technique is spread around the world. It might seem then that because we are destined so to be, we might also be the people best able to comprehend what it is to be so. Because we are first and most fully there, the need might seem to press upon us to try to know where we are in this new found land which is so obviously a "terra incognita." Yet the very substance of our existing which has made us the leaders in technique, stands as a barrier to any thinking which might be able to comprehend technique from beyond its own dynamism.

Our Two Cultures

PATRICIA SMART

One suspects our ancestors to have been possessed of a kind of divine madness to have undertaken the voyages they did to a country Jacques Cartier described as "the land God gave to Cain." But it was a madness that as another Frenchman in our own century, André Breton, commented: "took root, and has lasted"... and produced a culture or cultures that have begun to return full circle to their origins.

> Mon pays a franchi ses frontières
>   d'exil
> Mon pays vient parler sur la place du monde

writes Gatien Lapointe, whose death last fall at the early age of 52 was mourned by all lovers of Quebec poetry.

If you are familiar with Canadian literature, you know that there is now confidence and a joy of affirmation in the writing of both our major cultures. Such confidence was fought for slowly and painfully in both Quebec and English Canada by the nationalist generation of the 1960s, a generation that had to prove in spite of all appearances to the contrary that it did have a heritage and a culture (or rather two heritages and two cultures) and a present and future reflected in the mirrors its writers were placing before it. Mirrors have a way of becoming prisons, however, unless there is sharing and growth through contact with what is outside oneself. "In order to flower," writes another Quebec poet, Gaston Miron, "poetry needs a land, a space, a light, a milieu where it can put down roots, and a great deal of friendship."

I want to reflect on the land, the space, the milieux where our two literatures have put down their roots and make some tentative suggestions about the different ways the writers of the two cultures have inhabited the territories of the real, the imaginary and of language. Linked to each other willy-nilly since the conquest in which both Wolfe and Montcalm lost their lives, we have transposed our battles and our psychological borders even onto the names we have called ourselves. From the clearly demarcated names of *les Anglais* and *les Canayens* (the English and the Canadians) used by both races until 1840, we have moved through a variety of hyphenated and non-hyphenated attempts to name ourselves, our relationship and our sense of belonging to an often contested territory.

Abridged from Patricia Smart, "Our Two Cultures," *Canadian Forum* (December 1984), pp. 14-19. Reprinted by permission of the author.

History makes strong claims on the Canadian and *Québécois* consciousness: we have never, I think, seen ourselves as a generation of new Adams (or Eves) operating in virgin territory and in total rupture from tradition. And so, in a country where in 1984 official bilingualism — the dream of our departed Prime Minister Pierre Elliot Trudeau — has been met with resistance strong enough to have brought the Manitoba legislature to a standstill, it is tempting to fall back in defense of bilingualism on the historically-validated description of French and English as our "two founding cultures." This term, however, is rejected by many Western Canadians, whose ancestors arrived after the geographical chess game that split that nation in two; and it is rejected with greater justification by the native peoples of the country, whose own claims rest on a more ancient historical imperative.

To speak simply of French-Canadian and English-Canadian cultures has the practical advantage of including the important members of each culture who live and write within the territory of the other — Gabrielle Roy, Antonine Maillet, Mordecai Richler and Leonard Cohen, to name only a few — but events in Quebec have coloured these terms in a decidedly federalist hue. The terms now used by many writers and intellectuals to describe the two cultures are "Quebec" and "Canada," but these too are ambiguous, for it is never quite clear whether they are meant to refer to the situation of a part within the larger whole, or to two mutually exclusive territories of the imagination which may well regard each other with affection, but do not overlap.

For compromisers like myself, who I like to think are also realists, it is perhaps most useful to speak of Quebec or *Québécois* and English-Canadian culture: for these are the two major groups which have historically battled and out of necessity have compromised, and who have passed from generation to generation the visions that have shaped our two literatures.

What are these visions or cultural traditions? How have they regarded each other? Do they contain within them any basis for the comparison of *Québécois* and English-Canadian literature? An astonishingly small amount of work has been done in the area of comparative Quebec and English-Canadian literature, for reasons that differ, I think, depending on the critic's culture of origin. For many English-Canadian critics, the border between the two cultures has traditionally not existed, and the Quebec tradition has simply been assimilated into the larger Canadian whole — an act easier to achieve on paper than it has been in historical reality. The rarity of comparative studies coming from within Quebec is on the surface simply a question of other priorities — Quebec itself, but also Europe, the United States, Latin America come first. Anywhere but English Canada, one is sometimes tempted to think. When articles on English-Canadian culture do appear in Quebec, they are likely to be headed by a title like "Does English Canada really exist?," betraying a commonly-held belief that English Canada is culturally only a region of the United States. Paradoxically then, one could say that the relationship between conqueror and conquered is reversed in the cultural sphere, and it is most often the English Canadian who expends his or her energy envying and admiring the passion, the militancy, the theoretical sophistication, the collective character of Quebec literature, while remaining unsure of his or her own discourse and guilt-ridden about the power relationships that exist in the political realm.

Critics who have reflected on the two cultures have proposed a number of geometric symbols meant to characterize their relationship — parallel lines, the "horizontality" of English Canada as opposed to the "verticality" of Quebec, a spiral staircase, an ellipse, a double helix, a lattice-work fence. But like criticism itself, especially comparative criticism, these figures remain abstract and aloof from the historical contingencies that have defined our cultures and their relationship. Looking toward the literature itself, we find a clearer sense of the images we have had of each other. Here we enter the realm of stereotypes, but with the knowledge that stereotypes grow out of a reality imposed by history, and can be played with by imaginative writers to reveal us to ourselves and create new perceptions.

In Quebec and English-Canadian literature before 1960, I think we are dealing in stereotypes rarely opened out to reveal the push-pull ambiguities that have linked our cultures in a hostile kind of togetherness. In traditional Quebec literature, from Patrice Lacombe's 1846 novel *La Terre paternelle* through the classic novels of the land *Maria Chapdelaine, Menaud, maître-draveur*, and *Trente arpents* to Gabrielle Roy's urban masterpiece *Bonheur d'occasion*, the English is the conqueror, the invader, the rich industrialist insensitive to the language and culture he is destroying through his economic expansionism. Traditional English-Canadian literature, to the extent that it deals with the *Québécois* at all, presents the other side of the same coin — the loggers in Connor's *The Man from Glengarry*, the *habitants* in the poetry of William Henry Drummond, *mutatis mutandis*, the French Canadians in MacLennan's *Two Solitudes*, are basically charming folkloric remnants of a culture doomed to be left behind in the march of Anglo-Saxon progress.

In the two literatures since 1960, however, these stereotypes begin to open up and reveal the vertiginous underside of ourselves revealed in the mirror of the other. I want to look at four of these images — taken from works by Hubert Aquin, Jacques Godbout, Margaret Atwood and Nicole Brossard — and attempt to extract from them some insights into the changes in the English-Canadian-*Québécois* relationship over the last 20 years.

In Aquin's 1965 novel *Prochain épisode*, the Quebec revolutionary seeking his own identity and union with his beloved woman-country sets out to kill the Other, the enemy, but finds in him the benevolent and cultured conqueror, the enemy-brother with whom fusion would equal death but also mystical ecstasy. This Other is perceived by the *Québécois* — and this is a theme to which I will return — as powerful and attractive in the way he inhabits space:

> the pleasure of inhabiting a house can, then, resemble the overwhelming sense of awe and comfort I feel in this large and majestic drawingroom. H. de Heutz inhabits a second universe which has never been accessible to me, as I pursue my chaotic exile in a series of hotels that are never home to me.

Aquin's image of the relation between the two cultures is one of fascination, struggle and finally of stasis, as in the baroque sculpture of two warriors "reaching towards each other in complementary postures, immobilized by a sort of cruel embrace, a duel to the death that bathes the dark piece of furniture in radiant light." It is an image which may well return to haunt us, but which at present, in the post-referendum atmosphere of the 1980s, seems to belong to a bygone age.

About 15 years after *Prochain épisode*, a more grotesque and carnavalesque image is proposed almost simultaneously by writers central to each of the two cultures. Both Margaret Atwood in her 1978 volume *Two-Headed Poems* and Jacques Godbout in his 1981 novel *Les têtes à Papineau* describe English Canada and Quebec as Siamese twins joined by the head, on whom radical surgery is impossible. The Siamese twin image is perhaps more despairing than Aquin's in its sense of an inescapable biological, geographical and historical fatality, a monstrous farce into which we were born; but it is more liberating as well in its suggestion that the situation can best be dealt with by laughter and acceptance of our grotesque but real natures. Godbout's image is in fact internal to Quebec: his Siamese twins are not precisely English Canada and Quebec, but rather the English and French sides of the *Québécois* psyche — a two-headed monster, named Charles-François (read *Canadien-français*) Papineau. Joined at the neck, Charles and François are basically content with each other, but are told by ideology and modern technology that their two-headedness is unacceptable. In the course of the novel they allow themselves to be convinced by an English-Canadian surgeon — trained of course in the United States — to submit to an operation meant to fuse their heads into one. The result is a triumph of technology over culture: the two heads are in fact fused and life goes on, but the resulting one-headed creature, Charles F. Papineau, can no longer speak French and works in a laboratory at English Bay in Vancouver. Better perhaps, Godbout seems to be suggesting, to accept that the 50/50 division of the French-Canadian vote in Quebec's 1980 referendum on independence is a true reflection of the culture's duality, and to learn to live with the ambiguities it involves. And yet the ending is doubly ambiguous, for Charles and François' downfall can also be seen as a result of their trust in English-Canadian power and technology.

Margaret Atwood's *Two-Headed Poems* are less science-fictionally prophetic than Godbout's novel, but equally wary of splitting the two-headed monster, which for Atwood is Canada:

> Why fear the knife that could sever us.
> unless it would not cut skin but brain?

Like Godbout, Atwood plays with the familiar stereotypes — the *Québécois* as "one big happy family" and the English Canadians as the unwanted neighbours, the uncultured merchants and technocrats of the country. What is interesting in her portrayal, I think, is the reversal of the colonizer-colonized relationship I referred to earlier — the silencing of the English Canadian as he or she finds herself trapped in the stereotype dictated by the other culture. How is dialogue possible, or even an articulation of one's own voice, when that voice is heard by the other as:

> a language for ordering the slaughter and gutting of hogs, for counting stacks of cans. Groceries are all you are good for. Leave the soul to us.

In spite of the cool irony of its surface, Atwood's poem is a moving plea for dialogue and an avowal of the feeling of paralysis experienced by the English Canadian in the face of *Québécois* indifference:

> These words slow us, stumble
> in us, numb us, who
> can say even Open
> the door, without these diffident
> smiles, apologies?"
>
> If I were a foreigner, as you say
> instead of your second head,
> you would be more polite...
>
> But we are not foreigners
> to each other; we are the pressure
> on the inside of the skull, the struggle among
> the rocks for more room,
> the shove and giveaway, the grudging love
> the old hatreds.

Compared with the despairing passion of Aquin's two warriors image, the humour and self-mockery in Godbout's and Atwood's Siamese twin image can be seen as a step forward in the relation between the two cultures. But we are still trapped in the head, in the brain — in the attempt at "reasonable" dialogue between the two cultures that has never really succeeded. And so we have, as Atwood herself states:

> not a debate
> but a duet
> with two deaf singers.

The implication of this image, whether or not Atwood is conscious of it, is that the Siamese twins should forget their debate and concentrate on their songs — their own songs and poems and stories and not the stereotypical voice and image imposed on them by the other. The debate between *Qué-*

bécois and English Canadian has in fact never really taken place in Canada — the striking difference between the charismatic photographs of Quebec premier René Lévesque used in the Quebec media and the angry demagogical ones chosen by English-Canadian newspapers and television is only one example of the chasm between the cultures on the level of political debate. But debate functions according to the rules of logic, and there has never been anything logical about the Canadian attempt to achieve equality between the majority English and the minority French.

If there is a solution it can only be found in paradox, and in the final literary image I want to propose as an emblem of our two cultures there is a paradoxical turning away from each other that becomes an image of sharing between two autonomous partners. Nicole Brossard's image is not consciously proposed as an emblem of the two cultures, for like Jacques Godbout and other *Québécois* writers she has freed herself from the gaze of the other culture and is writing about her own primary concern: the question of the emerging voice of women. The paradox, I think, as far as Quebec and English Canada are concerned, is that in recent years there has been an unprecedented sharing between women writers and critics of the two cultures, and that this dialogue has been built not on the conscious desire to link the two cultures as such, but on the excitement of examining within the specificity of our separate cultural contexts what we have to say to each other as women. It seems appropriate then to transpose onto the larger cultural sphere Brossard's striking image of two women standing back to back but touching each other:

> It feels like panic, confusion,
> this impossible romance of being
> face to face, this juggling of
> acrobatic bodies, this Berlin
> wall I can lean against,
> this shivering in the back
>   it is marvellous: you
> can see everywhere at once.
> She can read my thoughts while
> I have my back turned she is
> amazed at my amazement....

In contrast with the geometric images proposed by the literary critics and with earlier images of aborted dialogue proposed by the writers, this image is real, incarnate and loving. And why not an image of two women as emblematic of the two cultures, given the importance of women for somewhat different cultural reasons in both English-Canadian and *Québécois* literature? Why not a bodily image, given the coming down to earth, the breaking out of the rigid garrison mentality, that has characterized both our literatures in recent years? Brossard's image is one of touching but not of fusion, of separate identities respected and shared as both partners look not at each other, but — supporting each other — out to the world. Transposed, it becomes an image of two nations and two projects, an adjacent but not a common space, a border shared in which both cultures find strength in difference.

And that, I think, is the present situation of the *Québécois* and English-Canadian cultures: involved in a process of integrating into their images of self the voices of women and of the world around them, they are beginning to find new modes of dialogue that subvert the old logic of political boundaries. No longer attached by the head, they are beginning to find ways of speaking to each other with a more bodily intelligence which does not exclude the heart or the shared history of their becomings. Special issues devoted to English-Canadian literature in two major Quebec literary periodicals this year are one sign among many of this new mood.

If there is, as I have suggested, a more detached and positive relationship developing between the two cultures, its effect is likely to be felt as well in the area of comparative literary criticism. To date, with one possible exception, the only book-length comparative studies that exist have been thematic and sociological in their methodology and undeniably if unconsciously federalist in their underlying ideology. Unrelenting in their search for similarities in the themes, literary genres and value systems of the two cultures, they have deformed both traditions by ignoring the fundamental differences in their ideological context and literary reference points. The exception, E.D. Blodgett's *Configuration: Essays on the Canadian Literatures* (1982), makes the important statement in its introduction:

> not only that all literary theory is ideological, but that any literary theory that tries to resolve the problems of nation-states that are at least bilingual in an official sense must be clear about its ideology:

Further, states Blodgett, "any literary framework that assumes equality of status between [the two major] cultural groups [in Canada] mistakes the nature of the relationship." Blodgett's own essays, however, concentrate on the plurality of Canadian immigrant literatures, European influences and uses of literary genre rather than on any real attempt to relate the *Québécois* and English-Canadian literary traditions as such.

My own suggestion as to a mode of comparison that might allow recognition of the difference between the two cultures would be an approach centered on the ways that *Québécois* and English-Canadian writers have inhabited space: the territories of reality, the imagination and language. A comment made to me by a *Québécois* friend who had tried to read the work of Margaret Laurence helped to crystalize the sense I have had of our fundamental difference: "I tried to get into her novels," he said, "but they were too real." Implicit in his comment, I think, was the question "Where is the fantasy? the dream? the excursion to the borders of madness to which my own culture has accustomed me? Where is the explosion of language that subverts the referential relationship of literature to reality and therefore subverts reality itself?"

It is not my intention to deny the importance of post-modernist writers in English Canada — Robert Kroetsch, Rudy Wiebe, Daphne Marlatt, Jack Hodgins and others — and their conscious play with inversions of the relationship between reality and fiction. But I cannot escape my instinctive feeling that if there is one contemporary writer who has been regarded as typical of the English-Canadian sensibility it is Margaret Laurence and that she, as well as other major English-Canadian writers like Robertson Davies, Timothy Findley and even Margaret Atwood, are part of a tradition of realism that distinguishes them from the central tradition of *Québécois* writing. This distinction between realism and something else — utopia? despair? revolution? desire? fascination with language? — seems to me to be the essential category to be addressed if we hope to relate the two cultural traditions in any meaningful way.

By realism I mean not only an attitude with regard to narrative structures and language, which in spite of questioning and experimentation remain basically intact in English-Canadian fiction, but also a fundamentally optimistic and pragmatic relationship to society that is present in most English-Canadian writing. Teaching a novel by Margaret Atwood opposite one by Hubert Aquin or Marie-Claire Blais in a comparative Canadian-Quebec literature course, for example, leads one inescapably to the observation that for Atwood — in spite of her lucid and ironic exposure of societal and sexual injustice and her consciousness of the games of language — there is an underlying realist and essentially moralistic vision of a correctible society; while in Aquin and Blais there is a more extreme and passionate vision of the inescapable fact of death or of the necessity of total revolution.

The same structural and ideologically-based contrasts would be possible between most of the major writers of the two traditions. In the work of poets like Roberts, Lampman, F.R. Scott, Dorothy Livesay, Earl Birney and Al Purdy language is taken for granted and used as a means of entry into reality, while for Emile Nelligan, Saint-Denys Garneau and even for a political poet like Gaston Miron, a primary focus is not reality but the voyage within language itself. Is it purely accidental that landscape has been an essential category in English-Canadian poetry and literary criticism, and not in the Quebec tradition? Whether it has inspired terror or love, or has been regarded as a force to be learned from, the land has existed in English-Canadian poetry as an external reality drawing the poet out of him or herself, while in Quebec poetry it has been on the contrary a symbolic projection of self or of the quest for national identity. A comment made by Jacques Godbout on the two cultural traditions helps to clarify this relationship between landscape and realism. If you asked the average English Canadian to name a painting that represents his culture, Godbout said, he or she would choose a Group of Seven painting. If you asked a *Québécois* the same question, he or she would choose a painting by Jean-Paul Lemieux — that is, a representation of a solitary individual in the foreground against the vaguely outlined backdrop of a desolate landscape.

Despite the parallel developments of the novel genre that have been traced by critics like Ronald Sutherland — from rural to small town to urban, from alienation to liberation — the same contrasts based on attitudes to reality (and here I mean social reality) are possible between the two traditions. Seen in contrast with the Quebec *roman de la terre*, which is closed and circular in structure and unrelentingly patriarchal in its value system, the English-Canadian novel of the land appears open in structure and in its vision of accommodating technological and social change. Abe Spalding in Grove's *Fruits of the Earth* is undoubtedly a patriarch, but he is chastened and changed by his daughter's rebellion and by the necessary modernization of his agricultural way of life; while the Quebec *cultivateur* clings to patriarchal tradition and sees his world disappear, choosing (or being forced to) defeat rather than compromise. Even a novel like Sinclair Ross' *As for Me and My House*, which has often been regarded as typical of the victimization of the Canadian protagonist in the face of nature and a hostile society, seems open in its narrative structure and vision of the couple and society when compared with a Quebec analogue like *Poussière sur la ville* by André Langevin. The ambiguities of Ross' novel have been much debated, but it is surely significant that it is narrated not by the protagonist but by his wife, and that in spite of the lack of communication between husband and wife that constitutes the novel's subject, it concludes with the hope of renewed dialogue between them and the possibility of their leaving the small Western town where their misfortunes have taken place to begin again elsewhere.

In Langevin's novel, also situated in a hypocritical small town, the narrator's wife is seen only from his point of view, and her suicide constitutes a symbolic gesture suggesting the necessary explosion of a closed order. Unlike Ross' Western Canadian couple, the *Québécois* protagonist is denied the luxury of mobility: at the novel's end he remains in the town, conscious that his struggle must be played out within the limits of the enclosed space that defines his world. Such contrasts, rooted in the way the underlying ideological space of the two cultures has shaped literary structures, would also help to explain why women have had more room to exist as autonomous individuals within the English-Canadian tradition than in Quebec, where women writers from the 19th century on often seem to be writing as if they were attempting through words to break down the walls of a prison.

If we were to examine the different philosophical traditions that have shaped the cultures of English Canada and Quebec, we would discover a further dimension and explanation of these basic contrasts. Reduced to their simplest level, they seem to me to be encapsulated in a well-known motto of our federalist French-Canadian Prime Minister: "Reason over passion," or Canada over Quebec. There has in fact been in English-Canadian cultural history an overriding belief in reason, in the possibilities of compromise, in the simultaneously progressive and conservative nature of a tradition that believes reality is manageable, changeable and open to the future. On the *Québécois* side, certainly because of the colonizer-colonized relationship and also because of the absolutist character of Roman Catholic religious tradition, there has been on the contrary a traditional refusal or inability to compromise with the real. Space is basically inhabitable in English-Canadian literature, while in Quebec literature it is a prison to be exploded through the play of language and the imaginary.

Is is purely coincidental that in addition to the differences of ideology, religious tradition and historical circumstance that account for these contrasts there is a fundamental difference in the *real* space inhabited by the two literatures? The geographical space of traditional Quebec literature is enclosed, diminished, a degraded version of the huge geographical canvas occupied by New France that for many generations in Quebec was seen with nostalgia as the myth of a Paradise lost through the British conquest. The space of English-Canadian literature, on the other hand, is open, eclectic, often disorienting in its regional disparity, a space that is possessed and even taken for granted by its literary inhabitants, and that allows for exploration and expansion. Unlike the *Québécois* the English-Canadian has had the luxury of being what poet Al Purdy calls a "transient," running and running without ever leaving home:

> Riding the boxcars out of Winnipeg in a morning
>   after rain so close to
> the violent sway of fields it's
> like running and running
> naked with summer in your mouth...
> After a while there is no arrival and
> no departure possibly any more
> you are where you were always going
> and the shape of home is under your fingernails.

To return to the image used by Hubert Aquin in *Prochain époside*, the English Canadian has taken for granted "the pleasure of inhabiting a house," while the *Québécois*, pursuing his "chaotic exile in a series of hotels that are never home to [him]," has learned to challenge the structures of the real and to seize possession of language....

Sharing the Continent

NORTHROP FRYE

Practically all Canadians have friends or relatives in the United States, and have spent a good deal of time there. Hence it is generally assumed, in both countries, that English-speaking Canadians, at least, cannot be told apart from Americans. This was a view that I held myself until I spent a couple of years in England as a student. Then I realized that there was a difference, but I found it hard to put the difference into words, and because our civilization is tied up in words, we are apt to think that whatever we can't verbalize is unreal. After that, I began an academic career, and have taught briefly at several American universities. My American students often ask me if I notice much difference between teaching them and teaching Canadians in Toronto. They usually expect the answer to be no, but my answer is yes. Here is, perhaps, something that it is possible to put into words. American students have been conditioned from infancy to think of themselves as citizens of one of the world's great powers. Canadians are conditioned from infancy to think of themselves as citizens of a country of uncertain identity, a confusing past, and a hazardous future. Nine-tenths of the time the responses of my American students are identical with those of Canadian students, but the tenth time I know that I'm in a foreign country and have no idea what the next move is. The sensation must be rather similar to that of a Dane in Germany or a Finn in Russia; or, on a smaller scale, of a Welshman in England. What I should like to try to do here is to define the areas of likeness and of difference a little more precisely. The history and the geography of the two countries have been so different that the cultural response to them has to be different too.

I begin with the geographical differences. Some years ago I first saw Herbert Marcuse's *One-Dimensional Man* in a bookshop, and what came into my mind was a quite irrelevant reflection: "I wonder what he'd say if he had to live in a one-dimensional country?" For Canada, through most of its history, has been a strip of territory as narrow as Chile, besides being longer and more broken up. In the United States, the general historical pattern has been based on a north-south axis with a western frontier that moved gradually across mountains and rivers and prairies to the Pacific. In Canada there is a single gigantic east-west thrust down the St. Lawrence, up the Great Lakes, and across the prairies, then through whatever holes a surveyor could find in the Rockies to the west coast. Consider the emotional difference

---

Northrop Frye, "Sharing the Continent," *Divisions on a Ground: Essays on Canadian Culture* (Toronto: House of Anansi Press, 1982), pp. 57–70. Reprinted by permission.

between coming to the United States by ship from England and coming to Canada. The United States presents a fairly symmetrical coastline, with relatively few islands, apart from a minor group in the mouth of the Hudson, and one is reminded of the old remark about Columbus' discovering America: "How could he have missed it?" One enters Canada through the Strait of Belle Isle into the Gulf of St. Lawrence, where five Canadian provinces surround us, with enormous islands and glimpses of a mysterious mainland in the distance, but in the foreground only sea and sky. Then we go down the waterway of the St. Lawrence, which in itself is only the end of a chain of rivers and lakes that starts in the Rockies. The United States confronts the European visitor; Canada surrounds and engulfs him, or did until the coming of the airplane.

In the United States, the frontier has been, imaginatively, an open-ended horizon in the west; in Canada, wherever one is, the frontier is a circumference. Every part of Canada is shut off by its geography, British Columbia from the prairies by the Rockies, the prairies from the Canadas by the immense hinterland of northern Ontario, Quebec from the Maritimes by the upthrust of Maine, the Maritimes from Newfoundland by the sea. A generation ago, Huge MacLennan took a phrase from Rilke, "two solitudes," as the title for a novel about the mutual isolation of English and French in Montreal. But everywhere in Canada we find solitudes touching other solitudes: every part of Canada has strong separatist feelings, because every part of it is in fact a separation. And behind all these separations lies the silent north, full of vast rivers, lakes and islands that, even yet, very few Canadians have ever seen. The Mississippi, running north to south through the middle of the country, is a symbol of the American frontier and its steady advance into the sunset. The largest river in Canada, the Mackenzie, pouring slightly into the Arctic Ocean at what seems the end of the earth, is a symbol of the *terra incognita* in Canadian consciousness, or what Rupert Brooke called the "unseizable virginity" of the Canadian landscape. Or, as another British visitor, Wyndham Lewis, remarked: "this monstrous, empty habitat must continue to dominate this nation psychologically, and so culturally."

In looking at two countries as closely related to Canada and the United States, no difference is unique or exclusive: we can point to nothing in Canada that does not have a counterpart, or many counterparts, south of its border. What is different is a matter of emphasis and of degree. In the United States exploration and the building of railways have naturally been of central importance in the imagination of the country. In Canada they have been obsessive. The Confederation of 1867 depended on the building of a railway from one ocean to the other: the political necessity to keep the CPR entirely within Canada meant that the railway had to be built in the face of almost unimaginable natural obstacles. The CPR remained a private corporation, but the great difficulty of establishing communication in Canada meant that Canada became accustomed very soon to nationalized railways, broadcasting corporations, film boards, air lines, and similar efforts of deficit financing. Canadian culture has reflected the same preoccupations. The first wave of exploration was mainly religious and economic, carried on by missionaries and *voyageurs* and fur-traders, along with the explorers who worked in their interests. The second wave was technological and scientific, an age of railway building and geological surveys. The third wave was cultural, and was spearheaded by painters, from the earliest travelling and military artists of the nineteenth century, Krieghoff, Paul Kane, Thomas Davies, to the Group of Seven and their contemporaries a generation ago.

A strong documentary interest in painting, in films, even in literature, is an obvious and distinctive feature of Canadian culture, and it follows the tradition of the early explorers and missionaries, of the Jesuit Relations and the reports of the Hudson's Bay Company. But it is painting in particular that expresses this interest: painting, the art that began in the deep caves of paleolithic times, has always had something of an unborn world about it, the projecting on nature of colours in the dark, this last phrase being the title of a Canadian play by James Reaney. Painting is in the front line of imaginative efforts to humanize a non-human world, to fight back, in a sparsely-settled country, against a silent otherness that refuses to assimilate to anything human.

A fascination with landscape is the dominant feature of Canadian painting down to about 1930. Even in later and more abstract painters, Riopelle, for example, it seems to me that there is a strong basis of landscape in the underlying vision. The exploring and pioneering aspect of this is clearest in Tom Thomson, Emily Carr, and the Group of Seven, where we are still very largely in the Canada of the blazed trail and the canoe. The painter keeps shifting our eye from the foreground into the opening in the woods, the bend of the river, the break through the distant hills. The use of expressionist and fauve techniques, with powerful colour-contrasts exploding against one another, suggests a natural world that is unconscious of man and is absorbed in an internecine battle of titans. In historical perspective another element emerges which is much more sinister than simply the unblinking stare of a stark "solemn land," as J.E.H. MacDonald called one of his best known paintings. Just as, in a crowded country like Great Britain, the practice of archaeology is a matter of keeping one jump ahead of the bulldozer, so these precious records of nature in her "unspoiled" loveliness of snow and rock and red sumach and maple seem to be hastily jotted notes of a hunted refugee, set down before civilization arrives and turns the scene into one more garbage dump.

Literature during this period did not fare so well as painting, because this long-range perspective in literature is very apt to turn rhetorical, in a rather bad sense. Thus Charles G.D. Roberts:

> Awake, my country, the hour is great with change!
> Under this gloom which yet obscures the land,

> From ice-blue strait and stern Laurentian range
>   To where giant peaks our western bounds command,
> A deep voice stirs...
>   ("An Ode for the Canadian Confederacy").

I quote this because it is typical of what made so much Canadian poetry of a century ago immature and colonial. The poet is not expressing his feelings but talking about the feelings he thinks he ought to have, and the clue to his poetic insincerity is the remote surveying vision that is really focussed on nothing but a map. In other contexts this kind of rhetoric turns didactic, as in Bliss Carman's rather forced praises of the strenuous life. No poets of this period gave us the sense of an inward struggling nature that Thomson and Emily Carr do, except for some brilliant flashes in one writer, Isabella Crawford, who died unknown at 37. English-Canadian poetry had to wait for E.J. Pratt to convey the real sense of this centrifugal and linear rhythm in Canadian life. His themes are those that are most closely connected with this rhythm: the martyrdom of the Jesuit missionaries, the building of the CPR, the stories of whale hunts and shipwrecks that bring out the sense of a beleaguered and surrounded garrison.

I have been speaking of one direction in the Canadian imagination: the direction that followed the east-west Laurentian movement and responded emotionally to the national motto *a mari usque ad mare*. This was both a romantic and a conservative movement: romantic because it sought the new and the unknown, conservative because its original impetus was in Europe. The Confederation that took shape around a transcontinental railway was part of a global chain of communication that started in London and linked together all the pieces of an empire on which the sun never set. But as settlement in the country advanced, a more longitudinal and north-south consciousness developed. This perspective focussed on the American connection rather than the British Empire, and tended to see the country as a series of northern spurs of the United States. When I was growing up in the Maritime Provinces during the nineteen-twenties, there was a strong political loyalty to Confederation, but an even stronger sense that Boston was our real capital, and that the Maritimes formed the periphery of New England, or what was often called "the Boston states." In the nineteenth century, at least, the Liberal party reflected the north-south North American outlook, as the Conservative party reflected the Laurentian one.

Once again it is painting that gives us the clearest sense of the contrast. If we turn from the Group of Seven to the Quebec landscape painters, to Maurice Cullen, Suzor-Côté, Clarence Gagnon and the very little of Morrice that was done in Canada, we are in a world of softer and gentler outlines where the sense of being lived in shows through. The painter's eye is more restricted and at the same time more precise. The landscape is receding from a human eye, not absorbed in itself. Quebec is the only part of Canada which has been settled long enough for a sense of imaginative digestion, so to speak, to emerge. When E.J. Pratt spoke of a kind of poetry he disapproved of, a poetry that avoided social issues and cultivated an easy self-indulgence, he described it in the pictorial metaphor of "still life." In his use of this phrase there is, perhaps, something of that odd fear of catching nature's eye that is very characteristic of that stage in Canadian development. It is significant, first, that the best still-life painter in the earlier period, Ozias Leduc, lived and died in Quebec, and, second, that the still-life perspective, where the imagination has completely surrounded the subject, begins to emerge rather later than the Group of Seven, with David Milne, and further west, Lemoine Fitzgerald.

What has been gradually revealed in this development is the fact that cultural movements are different in direction and rhythm from political and economic ones. Politically and economically, the current of history is toward greater unity, and unity in this context includes uniformity. Technology is the most dramatic aspect of this development: one cannot take off in a jet plane and expect a radically different way of life in the place where the plane lands. But culture has something vegetable about it, something that increasingly needs to grow from roots, something that demands a small region and a restricted locale. The fifty states of the Union are not, in themselves, a cultural entity: they are a political and economic entity that provides a social background for a great variety of cultural developments. We speak for convenience of American literature, but its real cultural context usually turns out to be something more like Mississippi or New England or Chicago or an expatriate group in Paris. Even in the much smaller Great Britain we have Thomas Hardy largely confined to "Wessex," Dylan Thomas to South Wales, D.H. Lawrence to the Midlands. Similarly in Canada: as the country has matured, more and more of its local areas have come to life imaginatively.

This fact has given French Canadian writers, in particular, one considerable advantage. The French Canadian poet or novelist knows that he is contributing to the articulateness of a beleaguered language, hence he need have no doubt about his social function or the importance of being a writer in such a situation. He has no competitors closer than European France, and they live in a very different social context. The English Canadian writer has not had this advantage, and the tedium of a permanent identity crisis has afflicted English Canada for a century. Soon after the Second World War, French Canada entered what has been called the quiet revolution, an awareness of belonging both to itself and to the modern world, which shook off most of the isolating features that had been previously restricting its cultural life. I think it was partly a response to the French act of self-definition that made for a sudden and dramatic emergence of English Canadian culture after about 1960. Since then there has been a tremendous cultural explosion, in literature and painting particularly, which has produced a mood that is often called cultural nationalism.

This is a most misleading phrase, and for two reasons. First nationalism suggests something aggressive, like a nineteenth-century jingoist waiting for the next war to start, or a twentieth-century third-world revolutionary. But culture in itself seeks only its own identity, not an enemy: hostility only confuses it. Second, contemporary Canadian culture, being a culture, is not a national development but a series of regional ones, what is happening in British Columbia being very different from what is happening in New Brunswick or Ontario. Even there we find an increasing decentralization: one reason why Montreal has been so lively a cultural centre is that there are a good many Montreals, each one with its own complexities and inner conflicts. Then again, while a certain amount of protection may be needed for Canadian writers and artists, cultural products are export products. If we look at, say, the literature that has come out of Ireland during the last century, we can see that culture, like a grain or wine crop, is produced in a local area but is not necessarily consumed there.

Politically, economically and technologically, the world is uniting; Canada is in the American orbit and will remain so for the foreseeable future. Canadians could not resist that even if they wanted to, and not many of them do want to. Culturally, both nations should run their own show, and the way to run a cultural show is to let a thousand flowers bloom, in Mao's phrase. Things go wrong when cultural developments are hitched on to economic or technological ones. That gives us, on this continent, a sub-culture dominated by advertising and distributed through the mass media. The influence of this in our lives is often spoken of, both inside and outside the United States, as an Americanizing influence. Ten years ago, during the centenary of Confederation, a sour little joke was circulating in Canada to the effect that what had been aimed at in Canada was a combination of British political institutions, American economic buoyancy and French culture, and that what we had, after a century, was French politics, British economic buoyancy, and American culture. However, the growth of an anonymous, mass-produced, mindless sub-culture is American only to the extent that the United States is the world's most highly industrialized society. Its effect on genuine American culture is quite as lethal as its effect everywhere else, and its main features are as Japanese or German or Russian as they are American.

Things go wrong in the opposite direction when economic or political developments are hitched on to cultural ones, as has happened in the Quebec separatist movement. It is a part of M. Levesque's sales pitch to speak of separation as inevitable, and to compare it with the American Revolution. It seems to me a retrograde and counter-historical movement, both in its neo-colonial attitude to France and in its arrogant attitude to French Canadians outside Quebec. As for the American analogy, what was of permanent importance there was not the separation from Britain but the principle of *e pluribus unum*: politically and economically, the colonies had to unite, though culturally there was no reason why Massachusetts and Virginia should not be quite different. Separatism in Quebec is an intellectuals' movement, a *trahison des clercs*: it has dominated the communications media for some years, and by-passes economic issues with a simple emotional construct in which Confederation equals bondage and separation freedom. As an intellectuals' movement, even a revolutionary one, it may settle for a purely symbolic separation: if it goes beyond that, whatever is distinctive in the culture of Quebec will be its first casualty.

My reasons for thinking so take me into the second group of conditioning differences from the United States, the historical ones. The pattern of Canadian history has been almost the opposite of the pattern of American history. The United States had a War of Independence against a European power in the eighteenth century, and a civil war on its own soil a century later. Canada had a civil war of European powers on its own soil in the eighteenth century, and a movement of independence against its American partner in the nineteenth. This started with the invasion of 1775 and continued in the war of 1812, which had very little point as a war with Britain, but was in many respects a war of independence for Canada. I discover that Americans, while they know about the bombardment of Washington and the battle of New Orleans, are often hardly aware that this war involved Canada at all, much less that the bombardment of Washington was a reprisal for the burning of what is now Toronto. All through the nineteenth century, up to and beyond Confederation, there continued to be a certain edginess about the aggressive expansion of America, as it came through in Fenian raids and boundary disputes, and Confederation itself completed what the American invasions had begun, the sense that there was an identity on the north side of the border that could be brought into being only by some kind of political unity.

Another historical contrast is even more important. The United States reached its peak of articulateness in the latter part of the eighteenth century, the age when it became a nation, the age of Washington, Adams, Jefferson, and Franklin. The United States is today the oldest country in the world: that is, no other nation has lasted so long with so relatively little social change. The party now in power is the world's oldest political party, and the American flag is one of the world's oldest flags. Canada, by contrast, had no eighteenth century. It started with the expansion of French Canada in the seventeenth century, and started again with the influx of defeated Tories into Ontario and the Maritimes after the Revolution, going directly from Baroque to Romantic expansion, but never achieving the moment of self-definition that the United States achieved.

It would be a great mistake to exaggerate the strength of the British connexion in Canada, even in the nineteenth century. There was a great deal of superficial loyalty, or at least a good many expressions of it, but there was also much resentment, and a feeling that colonials would have been treated with more respect in London if, like Americans, they had represented an independent nation. Some years ago a book appeared in Quebec called *White Niggers of America*, meaning the French Canadians, an expression of strong separatist feelings in Quebec, but the same metaphor had been used over a century earlier by the deeply conservative Haliburton of Nova Scotia, who makes his Sam Slick remark that a colonial and a freed black slave differed in nothing but colour: they had theoretical rights but no power to enforce them.

It would, I think, make for a clearer sense of Canada if we thought of it, not as British North America, but as a country that grew out of a Tory opposition to the Whig victory in the American Revolution, thus forming, in a sense, something complementary to the United States itself. This may sound like a very English-based view of Canadian history, but I am not sure that it is. Not long after the British conquest came the French Revolution with its strongly anti-clerical bias. The clergy remained the ideologically dominant group in Quebec down to a generation ago, and the clergy wanted no part of the French Revolution or anything it stood for. Quebec still flies the pre-revolutionary flag of lilies. Nor, from that clergy's point of view, was the American Revolution really so different from the French one. But apart from the clerical influence, French Canada had excellent and foresighted reasons for accepting a conservative *modus vivendi* which, from the Quebec Act in the eighteenth century to Confederation in the nineteenth, had as its central idea the uniting of a French and an English community on a basis that guaranteed some cultural integrity for both.

Historically, the Tories stood for the supremacy of the crown and the established church, and for a society closely connected with the land. Conservatives in both Britain and Canada are called Tories, but the real Tories were pre-Conservative: they revolved around a domestic economy and a personal relationship to the working class that was destroyed by the Industrial Revolution. Expressions of Canadian opposition to American ideology, all through the nineteenth century, attack from the left quite as often as from the right. One writer, in 1841, spoke of "the United States, where from the great mixture of races, British feelings and British connexion have given way before a flood of undefinable notions about liberty and equality, mixed with aristocratic wealth, slavery, and bigotry in religion." I quote this not because it is profound but because it is commonplace; and we notice that what the writer dislikes is not only American democracy but American oligarchy, the inequalities of wealth and opportunity. It is not surprising, then, that so many of Canada's intellectuals, both English and French, should be one form or another of Tory radical, One of these, and also one of the ablest commentators on the Canadian scene, George Grant, writes near the end of his *Lament for a Nation*:

> The impossibility of conservatism in our era is the impossibility of Canada. As Canadians we attempted a ridiculous task in trying to build a conservative nation

in the age of progress, on a continent we share with the most dynamic nation on earth. The current of modern history was against us.

Yet before we write off Canada as an abortive and quixotic culture that has failed to break through the heavy snow-crust of a technological world, it might be worth asking what there is, in this Tory devotion to crown and church and land, that can be translated into terms of the nineteen-seventies. Human ideas have an extraordinary power of metamorphosis, and many things that are outdated or absurd in their original context may reappear later in a very different aspect. For instance, no church has ever been established in Canada, but there has been a much closer connexion between church and state, especially in education, which has given Canadian culture a distinctive colouring. Again, there may be advantages in having the personal symbol of the Queen instead of the impersonal one of the flag, which Canada did not have until recently, and would hardly miss if it still did not. But I think something rather different is involved here, which I shall illustrate by an example. When I first came to Toronto, in 1929, it was a homogeneous Scotch-Irish town, dominated by the Orange Order, and greatly derided by the rest of Canada for its smugness, its snobbery, and its sterility. The public food in restaurants and hotels was of very indifferent quality, as it is in all right-thinking Anglo-Saxon communities. After the war, Toronto took in immigrants to the extent of nearly a quarter of its population, and large Greek, Italian, Portuguese, Central European, West Indian communities grew up within it. The public food improved dramatically. More important, these communities all seemed to find their own place in the larger community with a minimum of violence and tension, preserving much of their own cultures and yet taking part in the total one. It has always seemed to me that this very relaxed absorption of minorities, where there is no concerted effort at a "melting pot," has something to do with what the Queen symbolizes, the separation of the head of state from the head of government. Because Canada was founded by two peoples, nobody could ever know what a hundred per cent Canadian was, and hence the decentralizing rhythm that is so essential to culture had room to expand.

Still more important is the Canadian sense of the close relation of the people to the land. Everywhere we turn in Canadian literature and painting, we are haunted by the natural world, and even the most sophisticated Canadian artists can hardly keep something very primitive and archaic out of their imaginations. This sense is not that of the possession of the land, but precisely the absence of possession, a feeling that here is a nature that man has polluted and imprisoned and violated but has never really lived with.

Canada does not have quite so heavy a burden of guilt toward red and black peoples as the United States, and the French record with the Indians was rather better than the British or Spanish record. Even so there is little to be proud of: in Newfoundland, for instance, a gentle and inoffensive people, the Beothuks, were exterminated as casually as though they were mosquitoes. But still the main focus of guilt in Canada seems to fall on the rape of nature. The deaths of animals seems to have an extraordinary resonance in Canadian literature, as though the screams of all the trapped and tortured creatures who built up the Canadian fur trade were still echoing in our minds. One of the silliest of Tory fetishes, the preserving of game, seems to be taking a very different role in the Canadian imagination.

The seventeenth-century invaders of both countries brought with them the Cartesian ego, the sense of man as a perceiving subject, totally different from everything else in nature by virtue of his consciousness. It was a long time before the philosophers got around to realizing that egocentric consciousness is primarily a consciousness of death, but the poets had always known that: even the nineteenth-century rhetorical poets I spoke of wrote their best poetry in elegiac or nostalgic or other moods that were close to the sense of death. The narrative poets gave us stories of death in log jams, on glaciers, in hunting expeditions where the hunter seems to identify with his victim. This was not of course confined to Canada: one thinks of Whitman, who also wrote his best poetry about death and his worst rhetoric about democracy. But it was so strong in Canada as to give most of its serious literature, especially its poetry, a very sombre cast.

In 1948 a group of Quebec artists, headed by Paul-Emile Borduas, produced a surrealist manifesto called *Refus Global*, which seems to me a most important break-through in Canadian culture, not because of what it said, which was naive and confused enough, but because it was a sign that the old antithesis between a conscious mind and an unconscious nature was breaking down. For Borduas, the human mind contained an It as well as an I or ego, and this It was what he felt needed expression. In more recent painting, in the quasi-realism of Alex Colville and Christopher Pratt, in the ghostly figures of Jean-Paul Lemieux, there is often a feeling of loneliness and emptiness, as though the conscious mind were deliberately draining itself of its contents, and waiting for something else to move in. Meanwhile an interest in Indian and Eskimo art, with all their nature-spirits, has grown into a fascination, and many of our younger poets — Susan Musgrave, John Newlove, Gwendolyn MacEwen — write as though Indians and Eskimos were our direct cultural ancestors whose traditions continue in them and in us. In fiction, there are some curious stories, such as Margaret Atwood's *Surfacing* and Marian Engel's *Bear*, of heroines turning away from their civilized heritage toward an identity with nature. It seems clear that for Canadian culture the old imperialist phrase "going native" has come home to roost. We are no longer an army of occupation, and the natives are ourselves.

The first half of the twentieth century saw a bitter dispute between democratic and Marxist conceptions of the best way to minimize the exploitation of man by man. Nobody seemed to notice that both sides were exploiting nature with equal recklessness. It seems to me that the capitalist-socialist controversy is out of date, and that a détente with an outraged nature is what is important now. Canada is still a place of considerable natural resources, but it is no longer simply a place to be looted, either by Canadians or by non-Canadians. It is of immense importance to the United States itself that there should be other views of the human occupation of this continent, rooted in different ideologies and different historical traditions. And it is of immense importance to the world that a country which used to be at the edge of the earth and is now a kind of global Switzerland, surrounded by all the world's great powers, should have achieved the repatriating of its culture. For this is essentially what has happened in the last twenty years, in all parts of Canada: and what was an inarticulate space on a map is now responding to the world with the tongues and eyes of a matured and disciplined imagination.

SECTION TWO
REGIONAL IDENTITIES

INTRODUCTION

Eli Mandel

The first section of this introduction to Canadian Studies concerns itself with one of the insistent, recurring questions in the study of Canada, the nature of a Canadian identity. At the same time it seeks to locate a methodology for asking such a question by way of a multi-perspective, multi-disciplinary approach. This is done in the belief that the obsessive and passionate questioning of the nature and quality of its own social and historical existence, from a variety of viewpoints, reflects the actual processes of discovery and definition that not only define the nation but bring it to heightened self-consciousness and awareness. Multi-faceted, this methodology mirrors a postmodern nation that, in the language of contemporary critical theory, in the very act of coming to presence asserts itself as absence.

It is this very complexity and diversity of approach that has seemed a major deficiency in Canadian Studies to some scholars who long for the certainties and rigours of established disciplines. Yet it has seemed to us just the opposite: much of the character and quality of this country is not only an expression of diversity but can only be understood in such terms. Margaret Laurence concludes a moving and vivid meditation on the particularities of place with a definition and celebration of her world: "which gave me my own lifework to do, because it was here that I learned the sight of my own particular eyes."

The logic of that "local pride" shifts the burden of the discussion of identity from its national to its regional perspective and consequently to more and more particular manifestations of regionalism. The question that immediately comes to mind is where to locate a discussion on apparently constantly shifting ground. It seemed evident to us that the beginning had to be the conceptual framework of region itself. And so we begin with William Westfall's lucid discussion "On the Concept of Region in Canadian History and Literature." Beginning with the challenge to nation-building schools of history, and the implied oversimplification and abstraction of the "empirical data of the historical record," Westfall notes a move to concepts of limited identities, the study of pluralism, and the attempt to reconstruct history along regional lines. Perhaps the most important distinction, certainly the most useful, in this conceptual move is Northrop Frye's distinction between identity and unity, between regional imaginative and national political concerns. Frye's distinction locates regions without cultural boundaries, the shape of which goes a long way toward explaining the boundaries and interests of the discussion that follows throughout this section on regional identities.

Westfall continues to discuss major attempts to formulate historical and literary accounts of regions and regionalism. He articulates the rationale and the deficiencies of environmental approaches and examines the more sophisticated analyses of formal and functional regions. In literary history, this distinction manifests itself in an increasingly internalized account, that is, a mythic reading of regional definitions. "Complexity and change," concludes Westfall, "must be recognized in any analytical approach to regions in Canadian studies." His article is a strong defence of both the diversity and pluralism of Canadian society and a plea for the integration of the various levels of regional analysis in Canadian Studies. In the light of his conceptual framework, certain kinds of analysis and approaches are called for.

His article is immediately followed by William Wonders's sophisticated analysis, in geographical terms, of "Canadian Regions and Regionalisms: National Enrichment or National Disintegration." As the title indicates, Wonders frames his discussion as one of the major tensions of Canadian life. Examining the very considerable diversity of geographers' regions, he concludes that they are "geographical facts of life" and are reflected in most fields, quite properly involving a diversity of scholars. Despite the centrifugal threat of the regions to the state itself, for "every Canadian," Wonders says, citing the last Minister of Regional Economic Expansion, "his region is his universe."

In the light of the conclusions by Wonders and Westfall, it seemed appropriate, and indeed necessary, that the discussion of regional identities include not only economic, political, and historical analyses of specific regions, but that some sense of cultural identities as well be given. Accordingly, the collection is divided into five regional areas: Quebec, the Maritimes, Ontario, the West and the North. Roughly speaking, these represent the major environmental regions of the country, but as Westfall argues, they cannot be limited environmentally.

Dramatic parts of the discussion around regional identities springs from the sharp contrast between the vivid localism of the poetic entries and the cool objectivity of the analytic pieces by the scholars. This is not to pass a value judgment on either but to illuminate two quite different ways of thinking about the problem of regions. For example, Michèle Lalonde's "Speak White" (the title surely is meant to call to mind Pierre Vallières's notorious *White Niggers of America*, itself calling to mind a radical critique of the colonists of Algeria, Franz Fanon's *The Wretched of the Earth*) plays off English as the imperial language, the boss's language, against French, the language of the defeated. It is an impassioned identification of a place, people, and a culture. Compare the poem with the two succeeding articles, "The Development of Ideologies in Quebec," by the important sociologist Marcel Rioux and "Has the Quiet Revolution Finally Ended?" by Ramsay Cook, a distinguished historian.

"What ideas did the Quebecois, that is, the Francophone majority, have of themselves and their society?" asks Rioux — a perfectly legitimate question, and certainly a question that enables one to work out a regional identification, as Rioux does. "Quebecers," says Cook, "show signs of losing faith — for a second time." His assessment of the political situation in Quebec today is — from the point of view of the Quebec nationalist — dismal. But then Cook, of course, is not a nationalist. It is, perhaps a sentimental preference, and an unnecessary comparison, to say that both the sociologist's analysis and the historian's political assessment, lucid and informative as they are, offer us far less insight into the heart of Quebec than the brief glimpse given in Lalonde's poem. Yet if the Quebec problem is to be located anywhere, surely it is in cultural distinctions, in, as Lalonde knows, with a poet's instinct, language.

In succeeding sections, "The Maritimes" and "Ontario," the differences between cultural identification and analytical analysis become sharper, and perhaps even troubling. On the Maritimes, for example, the distinguished novelist Hugh MacLennan writes with a sure hand about an island culture, about the seas and the hills, about the people who came there with their sense of fate and doom about them, and about what it is men can love and know. The sense that the island culture has been identified is very strong, perhaps because MacLennan has narrowed the question so, or because he reaches no farther than the island. As he says, "Continents are much alike, and a man can no more love a continent than he can love a hundred million people." His narrowness permits an identification. J.M. Beck, in "An Atlantic Regional Political Culture: A Chimera," concludes that there are only, at best, four provincial cultures; the larger, the Maritime, is an illusion. The difficulty lies in the terms. There are reasons to believe the notion of the province as a region is inadequate. The world of Margaret Laurence is after all Manawakaw, a town, not a province, though it might very well include something as vast as the Prairies.

The difficulty appears when we pose the question in terms so large as "Ontario," a problem Robert Drummond wrestles with in his article "Is There an Ontario Identity?" His analysis is socio-historical and political, with occasional glances at other possibilities. On the whole, one has to conclude that despite a valiant attempt to answer the question, Drummond finally yields to the flux that is the contemporary scene of the province. New immigrant voices undercut whatever stability he had hoped to discern. Meanwhile, back in Stratford, Ontario, at least in memory, James Reaney plays about with the literary, historical, mythic associations of a river poem, "To the Avon River Above Stratford, Canada." It is a naming poem from his award winning collection "Twelve Letters to a Small Town," which self-reflexively discovers the significance of the naming process, that is, a means of identification. Stratford is raised to the level of its existence as a pun, a renamed place of literature and story and drama and deep myth that forms a boy's memories and his world. Just as for Margaret Laurence the world comes into existence through perception, for Reaney it lives in its vivid particularity through language. Language is the region of his mind that he dwells in always.

Whatever the dilemmas of placing, categorizing, or defining that we encounter in attempting to discern the regions of Canada, it is interesting to note that as we move farther west, we move to a surer sense of regional identity, at least as it is articulated here, than elsewhere. The explanations are not easy to come by, but there are some suggestions in Robert Kroetsch's "On Being An Alberta Writer" and in Douglas Francis's "Changing Images of the West." Both suggest the increasing mythicization of the West has a good deal to do with it. Kroetsch makes the daring leap that it is even the abandonment, the absence that speaks to us — of presence. Paradoxically, the country without a mythology, as it has been called, calls forth the deepest sense of identity. In its very absences, in its long silences about its deepest yearnings, in its refusal to be named, it calls forth the ultimate passion — the passion for identity.

Kroetsch writes, "Where I had learned the idea of absence, I was beginning to learn the idea of trace. There is always something left behind. That is the essential paradox. Even abandonment gives us memory. I had to tell a story. I responded to those discoveries of absence, to that invisibility, to that silence, by knowing I had to make up a story. *Our* story."

There are other perceptive articles on the West — Nelson Wiseman's "The Pattern of Prairie Politics" and Martin Robin's "British Columbia: The Company Province" — but as if in answer to Kroetsch's comments and Francis's account of the images by which the West knows itself, the remaining region, the North, is represented by a poem.

The discussion concludes, appropriately, with F.R. Scott's eloquent and impressive poem "Laurentian Shield," in which the North, "inarticulate, arctic," takes shape gradually as language, and the promise of children.

Where the World Began

MARGARET LAURENCE

I wrote this article in 1971, when I was beginning my novel, The Diviners. *I see now that I used it as one more means of working out a theme that appears in the novel, that is, the question of where one belongs and why, and the meaning to oneself of the ancestors, both the long-ago ones and those in remembered history. Until I re-read these articles, I didn't realize I had written so much on this theme before I ever dealt with it fictionally. I didn't realize, either, how compulsively I'd written about the river, the same river that appears in the novel.*

A strange place it was, that place where the world began. A place of incredible happenings, splendours and revelations, despairs like multitudinous pits of isolated hells. A place of shadow-spookiness, inhabited by the unknowable dead. A place of jubilation and of mourning, horrible and beautiful.

It was, in fact, a small prairie town.

Because that settlement and that land were my first and for many years my only real knowledge of this planet, in some profound way they remain my world, my way of viewing. My eyes were formed there. Towns like ours, set in a sea of land, have been described thousands of times as dull, bleak, flat, uninteresting. I have had it said to me that the railway trip across Canada is spectacular, except for the prairies, when it would be desirable to go to sleep for several days, until the ordeal is over. I am always unable to argue this point effectively. All I can say is — well, you really have to live there to know that country. The town of my childhood could be called bizarre, agonizingly repressive or cruel at times, and the land in which it grew could be called harsh in the violence of its seasonal changes. But never merely flat or uninteresting. Never dull.

In winter, we used to hitch rides on the back of the milk sleigh, our moccasins squeaking and slithering on the hard rutted snow of the roads, our hands in ice-bubbled mitts hanging onto the box edge of the sleigh for dear life, while Bert grinned at us through his great frosted moustache and shouted the horse into speed, daring us to stay put. Those mornings, rising, there would be the perpetual fascination of the frost feathers on windows, the ferns and flowers and eerie faces traced there during the night by unseen

---

Margaret Laurence, "Where the World Began," in Margaret Laurence (ed.), *Heart of a Stranger* (Toronto: McClelland and Stewart Limited, 1976), pp. 213–19. Used by permission of The Canadian Publishers, McClelland and Stewart Limited, Toronto.

artists of the wind. Evenings, coming back from skating, the sky would be black but not dark, for you could see a cold glitter of stars from one side of the earth's rim to the other. And then the sometime astonishment when you saw the Northern Lights flaring across the sky, like the scrawled signature of God. After a blizzard, when the snowploughs hadn't yet got through, school would be closed for the day, the assumption being that the town's young could not possibly flounder through five feet of snow in the pursuit of education. We would then gaily don snowshoes and flounder for miles out into the white dazzling deserts, in pursuit of a different kind of knowing. If you came back too close to night, through the woods at the foot of the town hill, the thin black branches of poplar and chokecherry now meringued with frost, sometimes you heard coyotes. Or maybe the banshee wolf-voices were really only inside your head.

Summers were scorching, and when no rain came and the wheat became bleached and dried before it headed, the faces of farmers and townsfolk would not smile much, and you took for granted, because it never seemed to have been any different, the frequent knocking at the back door and the young men standing there, mumbling or thrusting defiantly their requests for a drink of water and a sandwich if you could spare it. They were riding the freights, and you never knew where they had come from, or where they might end up, if anywhere. The Drought and Depression were like evil deities which had been there always. You understood and did not understand.

Yet the outside world had its continuing marvels. The poplar bluffs and the small river were filled and surrounded with a zillion different grasses, stones, and weed flowers. The meadowlarks sang undaunted from the twanging telephone wires along the gravel highway. Once we found an old flat-bottomed scow, and launched her, poling along the shallow brown waters, mending her with wodges of hastily chewed Spearmint, grounding her among the tangles of yellow marsh marigolds that grew succulently along the banks of the shrunken river, while the sun made our skins smell dusty-warm.

My best friend lived in an apartment above some stores on Main Street (its real name was Mountain Avenue, goodness knows why), an elegant apartment with royal-blue velvet curtains. The back roof, scarcely sloping at all, was corrugated tin, of a furnace-like warmth on a July afternoon, and we would sit there drinking lemonade and looking across the back lane at the Fire Hall. Sometimes our vigil would be rewarded. Oh joy! Somebody's house burning down! We had an almost-perfect callousness in some ways. Then the wooden tower's bronze bell would clonk and toll like a thousand speeded funerals in a time of plague, and in a few minutes the team of giant black horses would cannon forth, pulling the fire wagon like some scarlet chariot of the Goths, while the firemen clung with one hand, adjusting their helmets as they went.

The oddities of the place were endless. An elderly lady used to serve, as her afternoon tea offering to other ladies, soda biscuits spread with peanut butter and topped with a whole marshmallow. Some considered this slightly eccentric, when compared with chopped egg sandwiches, and admittedly talked about her behind her back, but no one ever refused these delicacies or indicated to her that they thought she had slipped a cog. Another lady dyed her hair a bright and cheery orange, by strangers often mistaken at twenty paces for a feather hat. My own beloved stepmother wore a silver fox neckpiece, a whole pelt, *with the embalmed (?) head still on*. My Ontario Irish grandfather said, "sparrow grass," a more interesting term than asparagus. The town dump was known as "the nuisance grounds," a phrase fraught with weird connotations, as though the effluvia of our lives was beneath contempt but at the same time was subtly threatening to the determined and sometimes hysterical propriety of our ways.

Some oddities were, as idiom had it, "funny ha ha"; others were "funny peculiar." Some were not so very funny at all. An old man lived, deranged, in a shack in the valley. Perhaps he wasn't even all that old, but to us he seemed a wild Methuselah figure, shambling among the underbrush and the tall couchgrass, muttering indecipherable curses or blessings, a prophet who had forgotten his prophesies. Everyone in town knew him, but no one knew him. He lived among us as though only occasionally and momentarily visible. The kids called him Andy Gump, and feared him. Some sought to prove their bravery by tormenting him. They were the mediaeval bear baiters, and he the lumbering bewildered bear, half blind, only rarely turning to snarl. Everything is to be found in a town like mine. Belsen, writ small but with the same ink.

All of us cast stones in one shape or another. In grade school, among the vulnerable and violet girls we were, the feared and despised were those few older girls from what was charmingly termed "the wrong side of the tracks." Tough in talk and tougher in muscle, they were said to be whores already. And may have been, that being about the only profession readily available to them.

The dead lived in that place, too. Not only the grandparents who had, in local parlance, "passed on" and who gloomed, bearded or bonneted, from the sepia photographs in old albums, but also the uncles, forever eighteen or nineteen, whose names were carved on the granite family stones in the cemetery, but whose bones lay in France. My own young mother lay in that graveyard, beside other dead of our kin, and when I was ten, my father, too, only forty, left the living town for the dead dwelling on the hill.

When I was eighteen, I couldn't wait to get out of that town, away from the prairies. I did not know then that I would carry the land and town all my life within my skull, that they would form the mainspring and source of the writing I was to do, wherever and however far away I might live.

This was my territory in the time of my youth, and in a sense my life since then has been an attempt to look at it, to come to terms with it. Stultifying to the mind it certainly could be, and sometimes was, but not to the imagination. It was many things, but it was never dull.

The same, I now see, could be said for Canada in general. Why on earth did generations of Canadians pretend to believe this country dull? We knew perfectly well it wasn't. Yet for so long we did not proclaim what we knew. If our upsurge of so-called nationalism seems odd or irrelevant to outsiders, and even to some of our own people (*what's all the fuss about?*), they might try to understand that for many years we valued ourselves insufficiently, living as we did under the huge shadows of those two dominating figures, Uncle Sam and Britannia. We have only just begun to value ourselves, our land, our abilities. We have only just begun to recognize our legends and to give shape to our myths.

There are, God knows, enough aspects to deplore about this country. When I see the killing of our lakes and rivers with industrial wastes, I feel rage and despair. When I see our industries and natural resources increasingly taken over by America, I feel an overwhelming discouragement, especially as I cannot simply say "damn Yankees." It should never be forgotten that it is we ourselves who have sold such a large amount of our birthright for a mess of plastic Progress. When I saw the War Measures Act being invoked in 1970, I lost forever the vestigial remains of the naive wish-belief that repression could not happen here, or would not. And yet, of course, I had known all along in the deepest and often hidden caves of the heart that anything can happen anywhere, for the seeds of both man's freedom and his captivity are found everywhere, even in the microcosm of a prairie town. But in raging against our injustices, our stupidities, I do so as *family*, as I did, and still do in writing, about those aspects of my town which I hated and which are always in some ways aspects of myself.

The land still draws me more than other lands. I have lived in Africa and in England, but splendid as both can be, they do not have the power to move me in the same way as, for example, that part of southern Ontario where I spent four months last summer in a cedar cabin beside a river. "Scratch a Canadian, and you find a phony pioneer," I used to say to myself in warning. But all the same it is true, I think, that we are not yet totally alienated from physical earth, and let us only pray we do not become so. I once thought that my lifelong fear and mistrust of cities made me a kind of old-fashioned freak; now I see it differently.

The cabin has a long window across its front western wall, and sitting at the oak table there in the mornings, I used to look out at the river and at the tall trees beyond, green-gold in the early light. The river was bronze; the sun caught it strangely, reflecting upon its surface the near-shore sand ripples underneath. Suddenly, the crescenting of a fish, gone before the eye could clearly give image to it. The old man next door said these leaping fish were carp. Himself, he preferred muskie, for he was a real fisherman and the muskie gave him a fight. The wind most often blew from the south, and the river flowed toward the south, so when the water was wind-riffled, and the current was strong, the river seemed to be flowing both ways. I liked this, and interpreted it as an omen, a natural symbol.

A few years ago, when I was back in Winnipeg, I gave a talk at my old college. It was open to the public, and afterward a very old man came up to me and asked me if my maiden name had been Wemyss. I said yes, thinking he might have known my father or my grandfather. But no. "When I was a young lad," he said, "I once worked for your great-grandfather, Robert Wemyss, when he had the sheep ranch at Raeburn." I think that was a moment when I realized all over again something of great importance to me. My long-ago families came from Scotland and Ireland, but in a sense that no longer mattered so much. My true roots were here.

I am not very patriotic, in the usual meaning of that word. I cannot say "My country right or wrong" in any political, social or literary context. But one thing is inalterable; for better or worse, for life.

This is where my world began. A world which includes the ancestors — both my own and other people's ancestors who become mine. A world which formed me, and continues to do so, even while I fought it in some of its aspects, and continue to do so. A world which gave me my own lifework to do, because it was here that I learned the sight of my own particular eyes.

1
SENSIBILITIES

On the Concept of Region in Canadian History and Literature

WILLIAM WESTFALL

The regional interpretation begins with a direct challenge to the older national schools. It has alleged that national history has been so preoccupied with national unity and national identity that it has become ahistorical in character. National history has focused upon a vision of Canada that bears only a superficial relation to the empirical data of the historical record. Professor Careless has framed this criticism with a characteristic balance and generosity.

> The nation-building approach to Canadian history neglects and obscures while it explains and illuminates, and may tell us less about the Canada that now is than the Canada that should have been — but has not come to pass.

Canadian historians, he goes on to suggest, should set their sights on "Somewhat Narrow Horizons" — a phrase that plays on the grandiose and nationalist titles that often characterize presidential addresses to the Canadian Historical Association. Professor Careless would follow his own advice and turn from national themes to the study of pluralism and limited identities in Canada.

In the field of Canadian literature Professor Northrop Frye has made the same critique of nationalist interpretations. In the 1940s Frye in fact assumed a nationalist position in the debate between internationalism and localism. "Culture," he wrote in 1943, "seems to flourish best in national units which implies that the empire is too big and the province too small for major literature.... The Province or region is usually a vestigial curiosity to be written up by some nostalgic tourist." More recently, Frye has redrawn quite dramatically his evaluation of the significance of the region in the creative process. In the introduction to *The Bush Garden* Frye has made an important distinction between unity and identity: the former is national in scope and tied to a sense of political allegiance, the latter is regional and rooted in works of the imagination. In Canada there is a political sense of nationality but no national identity, and in words that strike the same note that was sounded by Professor Careless (and Professor Cook) Frye has argued that:

> the question of Canadian identity, so far as it affects the creative imagination is not a "Canadian" question at all, but a regional question.

Canada is balanced on a tension between a political feeling of unity and a

---

William Westfall, "On the Concept of Region in Canadian History and Literature," *Journal of Canadian Studies* (Summer 1980), pp. 3–15. Reprinted by permission.

host of regional identities, a tension that Frye willingly accepts in view of what he sees as the alternatives: an homogenizing nationalism or political and cultural separatism.

The next step in the development of the concept of region in these disciplines has proven to be much more difficult. To challenge the nationalist orientation and proclaim the historical and cultural importance of regions and regional identities was fairly straightforward; to try to reconstruct Canadian history and literature along regional lines has presented a considerably more complex task. The problems were (and remain) primarily ones of definition and integration: what is a region, and how do regions relate to one another and to the nation-state of which they are a part?

The term "region" can be frustratingly imprecise, and for the most part disciplines tend to back away from analyzing the assumptions that they invest in the concept, preferring to take the regional structure of Canada as a given. Nonetheless, one can discern two general ways in which history and literature have at least implicitly defined the concept of region. They have relied upon two long-standing themes in Canadian scholarship: the impact of the physical environment and the metropolitan-hinterland relationship. It is important to point out that the new regionalism has yet to develop a clear and explicit concept of region, and for this reason both the environmental and the metropolitan-hinterland approach suffer some serious weaknesses.

The environmental approach to regions and regional cultures has a long history in Canadian studies. According to this approach regions are characterized by a similarity of physical features and climate, and regions are separated from other regions by distinct geographical formations. Consequently the laws of nature have divided Canada into Atlantic, Central, Prairie, and Pacific regions. The very names we apply to regions — "Atlantic" and "prairie" — underline the strength and popularity of associating a region with a dominant physical feature. A strong element of cultural environmentalism has accompanied this way of approaching regions. It maintains that physical features and climate not only define the shape of regions, but also explain their character. A common environment gives rise to common political, social, and cultural characteristics.

Such environmental assumptions have coloured literary criticism especially. "All discussions of literature produced in the Canadian west," writes Henry Kreisel, "must of necessity begin with the impact of the landscape upon the mind." E.A. McCourt has made almost the same point. "If [regional literature] does not illustrate the influence of a limited and peculiar environment, it is not true regional literature." Regional cultures in Canada, such as the prairie west, spring like Sarah Binks' poetry, from the land itself — the flat alkaline soil of Saskatchewan giving birth to a flat alkaline verse.

The same environmental factors also underlie the way this approach has defined the regional structure of Canada as a whole. The rigidity of Canada's physical features and the relative constancy of her climate mean that the regional structure of Canada is also rigid and constant. Similarly these factors explain the apparent weakness of the Canadian nation-state. Land and climate have created and nurtured strong regions and acted as a barrier against national unity. Consequently, we have strong regional identities within a relatively weak nation-state.

At times a cultural value judgment has followed. Not only are strong regions with strong regional identities empirical facts, they are also positive features of Canadian life. They distinguish us from other societies; they make us tolerant of cultural differences; and they restrain the tendency of a nationalistic central government to impose on everyone a single set of "national values." In one case this type of anti-nationalistic analysis has prompted one critic to plea for the radical regionalization of Canada, with political power devolving down to the level of the neighbourhood and the city block.

Regrettably the environmental/landforms approach to regions and regional cultures has not provided a satisfactory foundation for reconstructing Canada in regional terms. A number of geographers, it is interesting to note, have outlined some of the problems with this approach and their criticisms serve as a point of departure for exploring alternate ways of approaching regions and regional cultures.

The concept of region is, of course, an important tool in geography and there is an extensive literature on the use and abuse of the concept. In general, geographers employ the term region in two ways. The first uses region in the way most non-geographers understand the term: to connote an area that exhibits a similarity of features. This sameness draws the region together and separates it from those areas that do not share this quality. Regions that are characterized by such a similarity are called "formal" regions. The second way uses the term to group together the elements that are functionally related within a system. Here similarity is not an issue: diverse elements can form a region if they are integrated within a set of functional relationships. These are called "functional" regions. A wheat field is a formal region, a farm is a functional region. A series of wheat belts would constitute a formal region that would cut across a number of functional regions, while a farm that included a wheat field, pasture, wood lot and so on would constitute a single functional region that would cut across a number of formal regions.

Returning then to the environmental/landforms approach to regions it is clear that this approach is based upon the most elemental type of formal region: a region is defined according to a similarity of topographical features and climate. Geographers have found, however, that this level of formal region does not lead one very far. Topographical similarity, for example, does not produce a similar social and cultural composition. J. Wreford Watson, after comparing adjacent parts of the Canadian and American west — areas with similar climates and landforms — admonished his readers to beware of the specious geographical argument that a common environment gives rise to a uniform reaction, and produces its corresponding geographical region. It does not.

Cultural and political factors have reorganized the landscape so that the "unnatural" international border is in fact a very real boundary.

John Warkentin has carried the critique to the point that he questions the ability of landforms to serve as a useful foundation for building even the most simple of formal regions. In his studies of early penetrations into the Canadian west, he demonstrates how the boundaries and character of what seem to be for topographical reasons a very fixed region can change quite dramatically in relation to a number of non-environmental factors, such as perception, use, and the level of technology. The prairies to an American from the midwest was a northern extension of the great American desert; but the same area assumed a considerably different character for a plains Indian, a fur trader, or, one might add, a Mennonite skilled in dry-land farming with a railroad waiting to carry his grain to market.

These insights lead one to question the assumption that regions are somehow in the land itself. There are no "natural" regions. Rather the land is divided into formal regions only as abstract criteria are applied to it. A similarity of topographical features is one set of criteria, and these criteria lead to a certain regional configuration. But these criteria do not produce the only set of formal regions, let alone the most useful one. By applying other criteria it is possible to produce different, and more analytical, types of formal regions. One can draw regions based upon class, ethnicity, voting patterns, ideologies (and so on). While each of these might occupy a particular space, the topography of this space has little bearing on the character of the region.

By using criteria to create formal regions one can also develop a way of explaining the regional character of a larger area. Here one takes an area as given and proceeds to examine the many types of formal regions that exist in the area. The prairie provinces, for example, include grain-growing regions, ethnic regions, political regions (and so on). The "regional" character of this area then is not produced by the impact of a relatively common environment; rather, it grows out of the pattern that emerges when all the different formal regions within the area are drawn together.

The concept of formal regions also leads one to re-examine the question of the regional nature of Canada from a different perspective. The traditional environmental approach, because it relied on a series of relatively constant topographical and climatic factors, tended to regard history as simply geography in motion. Nature gave Canada strong regions and a weak nation-state and history had little choice but to follow the lines that geography had laid down for her guidance. When one approaches the question through formal regions, however, one finds a considerably different regional configuration.

One is drawn to go beyond the way abstract criteria map out regions to examine the historical character of the criteria themselves, especially the way certain types of criteria indicate the character of the power relationships within the nation-state. If, for example, one were to reflect upon three criteria that one associates with the prairie west — the production of cereal grains, ethnic diversity, and a tradition of political protest — one might easily conclude that these criteria amply attest to the power of external forces to shape the regional character of this area. The pattern of regions within the west might well impart a strong sense of coherence and identity to the area, but the same pattern might also demonstrate the power and willingness of the nation-state to use transportation, immigration and economic policies to organize the west according to its own ambitions.

A similar picture of the regional structure of Canada emerges when one turns from formal regions to functional regions. This type of region — which includes urban regions and provincial regions — is shaped by the linkages that grow out of a series of political, social, economic, and administrative functions. Unlike formal regions which exhibit a consistency of features (in relation to specific criteria), functional regions tend to integrate a wide variety of elements and often cut across the boundaries of formal regions. One example can illustrate these qualities effectively. The urban and economic regions of Toronto and Vancouver extend far beyond the city limits of these metropolitan centres. They include the transportation and financial systems based on these centres and consequently they encompass mines, forests, and farms that are dependent upon these systems. One part of the grain-growing region of the west (a formal region) is part of the Toronto region (a functional region) while another is part of the Vancouver region.

Presented in this way one can readily see that the concept of functional regions fits easily into the metropolitan-hinterland approach to Canadian history that one associates with the staple theory of economic and social development. Here Canada is organized into a series of regions that link together strong metropolitan centres of capital and hinterlands of staple exploitation.

This way of approaching regions has a substantial following, especially in the writing of the history of the Canadian west, and the sub-theme in the story of the exploitation of the western hinterland by an eastern metropolis are familiar to all — monopoly clauses, freight rates, tariffs, and Dominion jurisdiction over natural resources. It is also important to note how recent scholarship on the relationship between Atlantic Canada and the Canadian nation-state also emphasizes the power of the central government to integrate outlying areas into an economic region. Here is an area that initially benefited from national economic policies but then found itself losing out industrially as the nation-state rationalized its economic structure in the early twentieth century. Indeed, the policies supported by one hinterland (a unified freight rate structure) contributed to the deindustrialization of another hinterland. The general thrust of this type of functional analysis seems clear. For both west and east strong national policies have created a series of regions that have drawn wealth and power to certain metropolitan centres.

The metropolitan-hinterland tradition provides a useful approach to understanding the regions of Canada, but the approach can also be easily abused. A more precise understanding of the character of functional regions (the type of regions on which this approach implicitly relies) might well avoid some of the ways in which this approach can obscure rather than illuminate the study of regions in Canada. In the first place there is a tendency for one metropolitan-hinterland representation of Canada — the one with Ontario's head buried in the trough — to become as rigid an orthodoxy as the old environmental/landforms structure of regions. The shape of functional regions changes as the relationship of the elements within them changes. There can be no immutable structures here. The old west of railroads, immigration and the wheat economy is considerably different from the new west of potash and oil; and one cannot transpose the regional relations that characterize the former onto the latter.

Secondly, a clearer understanding of the character of functional regions might avoid the tendency to shift back and forth from functional to formal regions within the metropolitan-hinterland framework. For example, the term "prairie region" generally connotes a formal region and this type of region can be used analytically in a number of ways. The term "prairie region," however is singularly misleading where one is trying to analyze the metropolitan-hinterland relationships between Toronto and the west. It implies that there are two regions here, when there is in fact only one. It is possible to talk of hinterland and heartland relations within this region, but the west cannot be a hinterland unless it is a part of this integrated functional system.

Distinguishing between formal and functional regions also makes the concept of region a more analytical tool in Canadian history. The distinction, for example, helps to analyze some contemporary regional issues and to clarify some of the proposals that have been put forward to solve the "crisis" of regionalism in Canada. The issue of separatism and Quebec is a case in point. Here there are (at least) two types of regions involved. Quebec is a functional region based on the extent of the administrative and legal functions of a provincial government. It encompasses any number of formal regions. French Canada, however, is a formal region based on the criteria of ethnicity and culture. The two types of regions are by no means coterminous and confrontations obviously occur when one tries to fit the one into the other. It is also interesting to note that the rhetoric of separatism seems to be invariably caught up in formal regions — a nation based on linguistic and cultural similarity — while the rhetoric of federalism relies more heavily on functional regions — what will be the place of Quebec within a series of national and international social and economic systems?

One proposal that has been put forward to deal with Quebec and other regional problems would provincialize key political and economic decisions in the hope that local power can deal with regional issues. Again this proposal ignores the way functional regions cut across formal ones. If one follows the functional approach properly, the provincialization of power turns out to be a highly questionable proposition. In the first instance it is by no means clear that the type of region represented by a province is best equipped to deal with contemporary social and economic problems. A recent study by the Economic Council of Canada, for example, discusses these problems in relation to urban labour markets. These fall within provincial jurisdictions, but "paradoxically, perhaps provinces do not appear to be the best candidates to serve as economic regions." In functional terms either the city or the nation-state could make a stronger claim for increased power. Secondly, the proposal to provincialize power breaks down functional economic regions by placing the region under any number of competing (and now more powerful) administrative jurisdictions. The result might well be to institutionalize even further the present levels of economic disparity within economic regions. Certainly the possibility of using national power to reorder the entire system of economic regions would become even more remote.

To summarize the discussion of the concept of region in Canadian history to this point: Canadian scholars have relied on two historiographical traditions when they have tried to analyze the regional character of Canada. One stresses the environment (especially landforms and climate) and represents an elementary, and not especially useful, type of formal region. The other draws on the metropolitan-hinterland thesis and represents an unacknowledged type of functional region. While each of these approaches have provided a foundation for a considerable amount of work, they have also led to a degree of confusion, especially when they come to the question of the relationship of regions within the Canadian nation-state. The distinction between formal and functional regions, however, provides one way through some of this confusion and helps the concept of region to become a more analytical construction in Canadian history.

In Canadian literary criticism one can find the same preoccupation with the role of the environment in the creation of regions, and the same attempt to employ an approach that stresses the tensions within a regional system. The former provides another example of the abuses of simple formalism while the latter is in some respects the literary counterpart to the metropolitan-hinterland approach to regions in Canadian history.

At the same time it is important to emphasize that literature approaches the regional issue with a different set of questions. Critics, as one would expect, have been more concerned with cultural issues than social ones, more concerned with regional identities than the political and economic development of regions. They have also had to address the question of the nature of regional literature on an abstract level: what features distinguish this type of literature from other types of literature? (In history such questions are not asked.) These differences have also affected the way the concept of region has developed in this discipline.

The initial attempt to explain regional literature emphasized how the impact of a particular physical environment imparts a distinctive character to the writing of an area. This approach, as we have seen, has a large following, and it has produced a fairly specific interpretation of the nature of regional literature and the character of the regional writer. The content of regional literature is perforce local and the form of regional literature is realistic: regional literature uses local materials to describe accurately a local environment. In addition, the overwhelming power of the local environment has made the regional writer into a rather passive figure in that his role as a writer is to reflect the character of a local culture that is already in existence.

On an empirical level this conception of regional literature has proved to be very limiting. A number of self-avowedly regional writers do not restrict themselves to the materials of a single local environment and a number are also highly experimental in their use of form. On a more theoretical level this approach has encountered the same type of difficulties that historians faced when they tried to reduce all the characteristics of a region to the physical landscape. In assuming that all aspects of the literary process can be derived from the environment, these literary critics have also assumed that the form that a writer gives to his words can be explained environmentally. The categories of literature, however, like the lines on a map, are abstractions; they are applied by man to give order and meaning to his artistic representation. They do not originate in the land itself. This theoretical consideration brings into the concept of literary regions questions of form, mythology, and identity.

It also introduces a different approach to regional literature and regional cultures. This new approach has identified regional writing through a major literary and cultural tension, and represents in a literary context a variation on the metropolitan-hinterland approach to regions. Like the metropolitan-hinterland approach in Canadian history, this approach avoids many of the problems that stem from the reductionist assumptions of physical environmentalism. At the same time, however, this new approach also lacks precision, especially in the way it applies the tension to the material it is trying to analyze.

The key figures here are Dick Harrison, Eli and Ann Mandel, and W.H. New. They have analyzed regional writing by examining the relationship between content and form. On the one hand, there is a body of experience that provides the material for literature (events, stories, places, and people); on the other, there is a range of traditional forms that writers use to relate and explain that experience. The former is indigenous to an area and represents, one would assume, the sum of all the distinctive features (an environment *broadly* defined) of this place; the latter however is imported. The traditional forms of literature are a part of a literary system that tries to encompass all writing; but these forms tell a story that is not authentic for this particular place. Regional literature then is characterized by the tension between content and form — by the tension of trying to pour local experience into imported literary genres. Regional writers express, and in some way try to resolve, this tension.

Consequently, regional literature has two basic concerns: to focus upon a distinctive experience (whether real or mythical) and to experiment with ways of relating that experience. The first is personal and often autobiographical, and the second is literary in the sense of exploring the relationship between local literary material and the world of literary forms and conventions.

This approach to regions changes the role of the writer in shaping the character of a region in a cultural sense. Writers no longer simply reflect the region they describe; now they help to create the region itself. Art and identity are linked closely together. Regional writers take the cultural material of a place and transform it into a mythology that the people of the region can identify as their own. Without this mythology the cultural region would not exist. The historical, economic, and social criteria might be in place, but the region achieves an identity only when it is identified in art. "In a sense," Robert Kroetsch explains, "we haven't got an identity until somebody tells our story. The fiction makes us real." Prairie writers, Dick Harrison maintains, name an "unnamed country."

W.L. Morton, one of the few dissenting voices in the nationalist era, described the relationship between the historian and his region in much the same way. Morton challenged the Laurentian interpretation of Canadian history because it subordinated the history of the west to the history of the east. Laurentianism did not ignore the west — that was not the problem — but it treated the west as a distant stage for an eastern drama. It tried to squeeze the indigenous western experience into a paradigm that could not do justice to that experience. Carl Berger has summarized this regional tension in Morton's work very succinctly. He argues that Morton devoted much of his career to explaining the history of the west in its own terms: he tried to resolve the "discrepancies that had existed in his mind between the locality he knew and the 'unreal' world he had assimilated from a different literary culture." His book, *Manitoba: A History*, grew out of this tension and it is arguably the finest example of regional historical scholarship in Canada.

There are many positive qualities to this interpretation of regional literature and regional cultures. It replaces the single factor rigidity of environmentalism with a dynamic approach that emphasizes a dialectical tension between experience and form. In regional literature localism confronts a world of literary forms and the resulting tension produces a new type of literature that in turn helps to create the cultural region itself. The region becomes what it beheld in art. The approach has a pleasing symmetry and provides a way of integrating sociological, literary, and cultural factors within the regional concept. At the same time, however, some of the implications of this approach have not been developed as fully as they deserve.

The tension between experience and form is not restricted to what one normally treats as regional literature. Even a cursory review of Canadian literature and art reveals that this tension runs right through Canadian culture. One can trace this tension and the search for an authentic art form back to some of the earliest works of Canadian writers and artists. Susanna Moodie certainly confronted this problem, and the contrast in Paul Kane's work between the immediacy of his sketches and the salon qualities of his finished pictures reveals the same type of tension. Two men as different as Lawren Harris and Harold Innis shared the desire to reject foreign metaphors in order to find a style that would do justice to the unique qualities of the material they were trying to represent. It is perhaps the power of this theme that has led W.H. New to analyze Canadian literature as a whole in terms of the same type of distinction. "The east" represents the known, the ordered, and the empirical, while "the west" represents the unknown, the unstructured, and the imaginative. Canadian writing is marked by the tensions of joining these two polarities, of giving form to the unformed, of extending the domination of rationality, of "articulating west."

The recurrence of this tension might lead one to question the effectiveness of this approach to regional literature and culture. If the tension that informs prairie writing is present in almost all Canadian literature, then prairie writing would seem to lose those qualities that separate it from other types of literature. Or, one might conclude that all writing is regional — an alternative that tends to elevate the entire regional exercise to the highest of metaphysical plains. The recurrence of the tension, however, indicates the complexity of regions and regionalism at the cultural level, and rather than providing a cause for rejecting this approach, it points to the need to study some of the sociological and cultural factors that might explain why the tension recurs so frequently. The criticism of a poet and writer in Toronto — a metropolitan centre where such a tension seems singularly out of place — provides a starting point for such an analysis.

Dennis Lee has expressed the same type of frustration that Mandel and Harrison associate with prairie writers. In a fascinating piece of autobiography and criticism Lee has argued that he was driven into silence because the words that had been given to him could not capture the rhythms of his own experience. It is Lee's explanation of this silence that is most instructive. He believes that technology, materialism, and progress (for Lee the process of Americanization) have destroyed the balance between experience and language. These developments have separated the indigenous rhythm of place, what Lee terms "cadence," from the words the artist can use to give form to this rhythm. In short, a complex social and cultural process has fractured the equilibrium between content and form and the resulting disjunction has created a new cultural region — what Lee identifies as "colonial space."

Lee's account, for all of its personal and speculative qualities, adds at least two important considerations to the concept of literary and cultural regions. By suggesting that the tension between experience and the ways of relating that experience is tied to a specific historical process, Lee underscores both the need to understand the sociological dimension of cultural regions and the need to study the way cultural regions can expand and contract in relation to changes in this sociological context. Historical, social, and cultural forces can create and destroy regions over time.

In short, cultural regions are not static. In the same way that one had to challenge the static environmental representation of regions, so one must also question using terms like "prairie culture" or "Atlantic culture" as if these cultures were ongoing and unchanging phenomena. Cultural regions, in fact, might be more bound by time than by space. The new cultural regionalism of the west might be quite different from the old regionalism of the west; similarly the present cultural question for the west (and for Quebec) might not be the lack of an identity and the lack of a story but the need to reject the old identities and the old stories that they once so readily accepted. The tension between experience and language then might indicate the present boundaries of a cultural region, and the work of Moodie, Kane, and Harris can give us a representation of the cultural regions as they were at that time. It is in this sense that regional art can be called a boundary or borderline art.

Complexity and change must be recognized in any analytical approach to regions in Canadian studies. A map of the cultural regions of Canada in itself would be very complex, and the map would be even more complex when one placed on top of it the maps that outlined the present configuration of the social, economic, political, and administrative regions of Canada. The result would be a far cry from the old environmental/landform representation. It would be multi-faceted and continually changing as new social and cultural forces altered regional boundaries. It would also go a considerable way towards integrating the various levels of regional analysis in Canadian studies. Most importantly, such a composite representation would bring together sociological and artistic elements (history and literature) and provide a sophisticated and analytical representation of the regional character of Canada.

Canadian Regions and Regionalisms: National Enrichment or National Disintegration?

WILLIAM C. WONDERS

No observer of contemporary Canada could fail to have become sensitized to the fundamental importance of regions and regionalisms in the country's national life. Currently this stress is most obvious in the political and economic scenes, as evidenced by the Canadian attempt to sever the last formal constitutional link with the United Kingdom and the efforts to reduce, if not to eliminate, the regional economic disparities emphasized by the present depressed state of world conditions.

Geography and history have combined to endow Canada with strong regional identities. Whether such a variety makes for an interesting, rich and confident nation or for a divisive, inherently weak one, may be debated. Given the enormous area of Canada, almost ten million square kilometres, it was and is inevitable that regions and regionalisms should occur. Most of the regions are larger than most European nations. Our enormity of distance has provided us with that luxury of space so often denied to other nations. It also constitutes a difficult and expensive obstacle with which we must deal.

In any federal state debate and compromise are inevitable. The recent and current political discussions in Canada are viewed by some as a natural and even healthy exchange, but others see them as dangerous confrontations risking the survival of the nation. Attempts to delineate the true nature of Canada and Canadians have thwarted most who have undertaken that monumental task. The contradictions seem to have been so numerous that Canadians themselves often end up agreeing only on their common negative characteristics: "not British, not French, not American."

Writing in the early years of Quebec's "Quiet Revolution," Andrew Clark acknowledged the difficulty of attempting to define the personality of Canada: "Even if the long list of fairly uniform attributes might seem to give sharp definition to the adjective 'Canadian' the stubborn facts of the country's diversity, particularly in its geographical aspects, blur it again, until the image of Canada's personality often becomes a vague and formless thing in the eyes of the rest of the world." Over the intervening decade-and-a-half, old and

---

Abridged from William C. Wonders, "Canadian Regions and Regionalisms: National Enrichment or National Disintegration?" *Canadian Issues*, Vol. V (1983). Reprinted by permission of the author and The Association for Canadian Studies. A selection of the maps from the original article have been included here.

new regional pressures have increased to an unprecedented degree. Quebec now has a government with the avowed ultimate goal of political separation from the rest of Canada and there are some in Western Canada who advocate a similar course. Despite such dangers another Canadian historical geographer and former graduate student of Clark remains confident. Taking his phrase from Elisée Reclus' pessimistic late nineteenth century assessment of Canada's survival prospects, Cole Harris has voiced his optimism for the political future of the nation, concluding that within Reclus' "fantastic frontier," "the country will carry on in all its manifold variety." It is the aim of this paper to review some of the bases and implications of the regions and regionalisms in Canada which underly that manifold variety....

THE ENVIRONMENTAL FRAMEWORK
The starting point for all regionalizations of Canada is the physical skeleton provided by the natural environment. Man modifies it according to his perceived needs and within the limits of his technological abilities, yet he can not ignore it nor totally change it except at enormous cost and even then to limited local extent. Amongst the major elements of the natural environment are physiography, climate, natural vegetation and soils.

Physiography
The most fundamental fact of Canadian regions and regionalisms is the geological and physiographic pattern of the nation (Figure 1). It has endowed the country or more correctly, certain regions of the country, with a rich diversity of minerals and fuels and provided the base for a world-class agricultural industry. It also has fragmented the country harshly into a series of compartmentalized habitation regions separated by hundreds of miles of inhospitable terrain.

"Physiographically and geologically Canada is composed of two great parts: a core of old, massive, Precambrian crystalline rocks forming the Shield, and a surrounding crescent of younger, mainly stratified, rocks forming the Borderlands.... Physiographically the Shield and Borderlands are divided into regions or provinces each comprising many smaller units though the topographic differences of these are much more observable in the Borderlands, as Bostock notes.

The central Shield separates the Borderlands into two sectors of vastly different size — west and east — each of which include two very dissimilar regions — one mountainous and the other plains. The Cordilleran Region in the far west, with its complicated mosaic of ice-capped mountains, high plateaus, and deeply trenched valleys constitutes a major physiographic barrier region, despite its abundant mineral endowment and spectacular beauty. The Interior Plains Region continues northward into the rather more complex regions of the Arctic Islands. Its level to rolling terrain includes Canada's

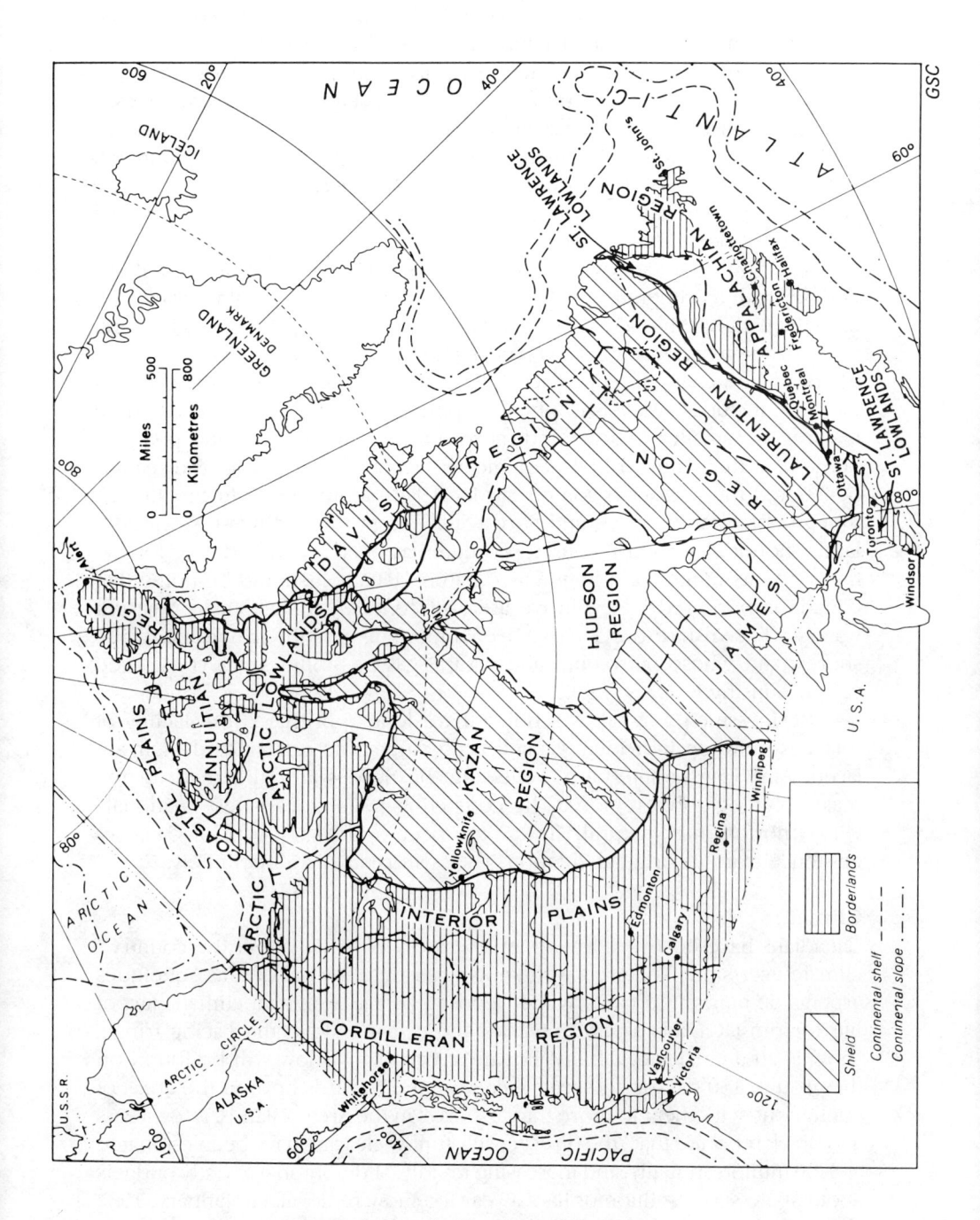

Figure 1 Canada: Physiographic regions

major commercial grain and livestock areas in the south and contains the bulk of the nation's coal, petroleum, and natural gas resources.

The Canadian Shield Region's rocky, ice-scoured surface with its innumerable lakes and bogs continues to divide Canada into "East" and "West." Largely because of its unsuitability to agriculture and resultant contiguous settlement it has been traditionally seen as a barrier to Canadian development, but as Robinson has pointed out, our perception of it has changed as its other economic resources (minerals, hydro-electric power, forests, recreational assets) have been appreciated.

The St. Lawrence Lowlands Region of southern Ontario and southern Quebec with its generally level surface at low elevation sometimes is considered the national "heartland." It includes an important and varied agricultural region, the most densely settled part of Canada, and its major urban concentrations. On the east, the Appalachian Region, like the Cordilleran Region on the west, includes a variety of physiographic units. In the east however these features are smaller in scale and more subdued in elevation and prospect because of their much older geologic age. As on the west coast the sea has penetrated the region to complicate local land and water patterns further, though not on the same grand fjord scale, except for northwest Newfoundland. The rather varied resource potential has been hampered save for the fishery by its limited and fragmented nature. Finally it should be noted that Canada is bordered by extensive areas of continental shelf in its adjacent waters, whose fish resources have been important on both Atlantic and Pacific shores, and whose petroleum and natural gas possibilities are considered very promising.

Businessmen as well as scholars have long appreciated the facility of linkages between individual Canadian physiographic regions and their adjacent American counterparts, reflecting the north-south alignment of the major physiographic regions. The competing pulls of east-west "national" versus north-south "natural" flows have been at the very core of Canada's existence from its original creation. They will remain so indefinitely.

Climate

Canadians have been living with an inferiority complex about the country's climate ever since Voltaire's well-known caustic dismissal of it as "quelques arpents de neige." Certainly winter tends to be the dominant climatic fact of life for most Canadians, and save for those living along the Pacific fringe, snow is an annual inevitability. For most Canadians snow will be found on the ground 150 days in the year, increasing northwards beyond the areas of contiguous settlement to more than 270 days in the Arctic Islands. A few years ago Brack reported that "the direct costs of snow clearing have been estimated at $200 million annually, and increasing rapidly." Edmonton currently budgets about six to seven million dollars a year for snow removal. (In January, 1982 it already had spent more than three-and-a-half million dollars for this purpose!)" Against such costs Brack pointed out the health and income benefits of winter recreational activities — skiers' annual expenditures having been estimated at $287 million in 1970-71 — and suggested that Canadians change their general mentality from battling snow to learning to "ride" with it. Crowe, for example, has been working on a regional winter climatic classification for recreation and tourism in Canada.

Hare and Thomas suggest that seven arbitrary climatic regions may be identified within Canada (Figure 2). Pacific Canada, west of the crest line of the Coast Range and Cascade Mountains is characterized by "year-round moderate temperatures, high rainfall, and the lack of hard winters." To the east, Cordilleran Canada includes a variety of continental climates with increasingly arid conditions in the south, at least. Eastward from the Rocky Mountains, forming a triangular area in the southern Prairie Provinces, the Prairie Region experiences a classic continental climate: very cold winters, short warm summers, and light precipitation. The Great Lakes-St. Lawrence Region is also basically a continental climate, but is modified by its more southern location and by the Great Lakes. It is characterized by marked daily variability of weather, by reliable moderate precipitation, by long, much warmer summers, and by winters of increasing cold from southwest to northeast. The Atlantic Canada Region has essentially a continental climate, lying as it does on the "lee side" of the country with greater temperature fluctuations daily and seasonally than in a true maritime climate. The cold water of the offshore Labrador Current cools the outer coasts of Newfoundland and Nova Scotia, while the Gulf of St. Lawrence retards the advent both of summer and of winter along adjacent coasts. Precipitation is abundant and reliable.

In contrast to the relatively compact climate regions of southern Canada, in the North "the Arctic and Boreal climates form zones (rather than well-defined regions) that sweep across the entire country.... Physically [they are] harshly cold; mean annual temperatures are usually near or below freezing and the winters are frigid." The Boreal Region experiences the most continental climatic conditions in Canada, though the severity of winter cold is counterbalanced by warm summer temperatures particularly in the western areas, reflecting Pacific airstreams there in summer and fall. The Arctic Region on the other hand, is under the influence of the cold Arctic airstreams from the Arctic Ocean or Greenland the year round. Summer temperatures remain cool except in sheltered locales in the interior of the larger islands or the Barren Lands west of Hudson Bay. Precipitation is generally light, particularly in the Arctic Archipelago....

THE CULTURAL FRAMEWORK
The strong regional divisions in Canada established by environmental or "natural" conditions have been reinforced by man and his various cultural manifestations. Without in any way subscribing to the long discredited tenets of environmental determinism, many of Canada's cultural patterns are closely

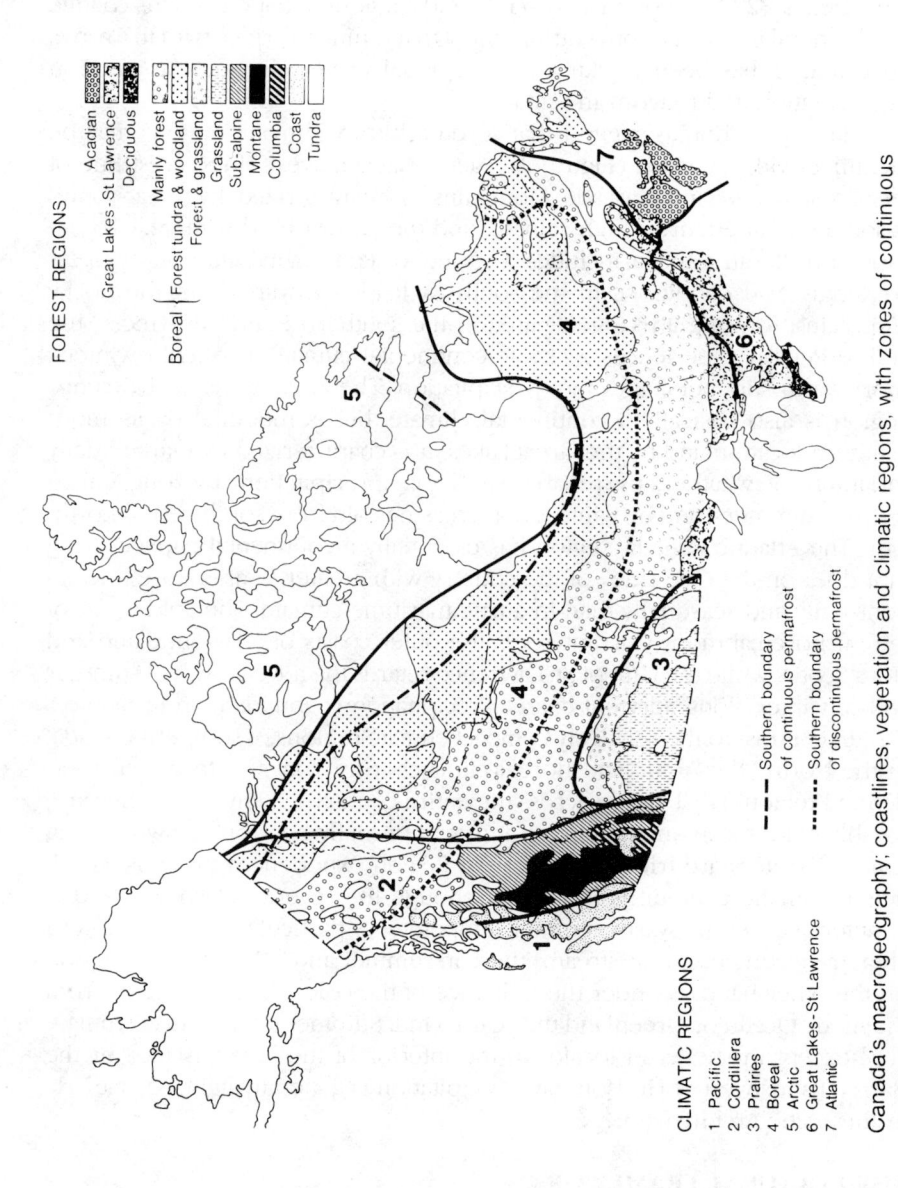

Figure 2 Canada's macrogeography; coastlines, vegetation and climatic regions, with zones of continuous and discontinuous permafrost.

related to the environmental framework which has been sketched. Any number of cultural factors could be examined, but only four are considered briefly here.

Aboriginal Peoples

Long before European man arrived in Canada the aboriginal peoples were in occupation of the area. Though total numbers have been estimated at only about 220,000, "it is important to remember that almost every part of the country was claimed by one or other of the numerous tribes of Indians, and that the Europeans who came to colonize it were usurpers in the eyes of the aborigines, except so far as they received rights to their land from the aborigines themselves." In view of the current debate on "aboriginal rights" in Canada, Jenness' reminder of a half century ago is still most appropriate.

From the anthropological perspective, the aboriginal tribes could be grouped into seven major geographic regions. Though specific tribes had distinctive individual features, there were remarkable similarities shared by the inhabitants of each region. The seven regions set out by Jenness and continuing in use are: the migratory tribes of the eastern woodlands; the agricultural tribes of the eastern woodlands (in southern Ontario and the upper St. Lawrence valley); the plains' tribes (of the interior grasslands); the tribes of the Pacific coast; the tribes of the Cordillera; the tribes of the Mackenzie and Yukon river basins; and the Eskimo (or Inuit as they now prefer to be called, north of treeline).

Thus from earliest times there have been strong regional identities for man in Canada. The traditional antagonism between Indians and Inuit is well known. Even within the Indian population, the intense and long-maintained warfare between forest-dwelling Cree and grassland-dwelling Blackfoot reminds us that regionalism is nothing new in Canada.

Although to-day's native peoples form a small minority amongst the nation's total population of more than over 24 million, their regional distribution pattern is significant. While most live in southern Canada, they are proportionately much more numerous in the northern parts of the country. This has resulted in distinctive ethnic and social conditions in that region. With the increasing sophistication of Canada's native peoples it also has resulted in demands which must be recognized for a much larger voice in northern political and economic decisions.

Population Distribution

Canada's population in no way matches its enormous area, though much of it remains "empty" for very good reasons. Nevertheless, Weir stressed that its relative growth over the century since it came into existence had kept pace with that of the exuberant United States to the south, increasing 5.7 times from its original 3.5 million to more than 20 million by 1967. Over that century "Canada has managed not only to survive, but also to distribute its citizens effectively from east to west, if not from north to south." This has been achieved at considerable cost, however, and the contrasting populations on either side of the international border result in continuing strains on the Canadian population, from higher costs of manufactured goods to near-total immersion in American mass communications culture.

The geographer's familiar population dot and isopleth maps do show the transcontinental extension of population that has occurred across Canada, though some might challenge how "effectively" this is so across the Shield and Cordillera (Figure 3). The fact still remains that 90 per cent of Canadians live within 480 km (300 mi.) of the American border. "Settled Canada" in the main still is a shoestring country strung across its southern border, except in Southern Ontario and in the southern Prairie Provinces where it widens out somewhat. One of our most important regionalisms is this twofold division into "settled" and "unsettled" Canada, about which more will be said later.

Although the proportion of Canadians living in the four original provinces declined from more than 90 per cent in 1867 to 70 per cent in 1967, the population remains heavily concentrated in Central Canada. To-day, 27 per cent of Canadians live in Quebec and 36 per cent in Ontario, largely in the southern parts of those provinces. Translated into political power on the basis of parliamentary seats, it often leaves Western and Atlantic Canada as regions of secondary significance on the national political scene.

The Rural-Urban Mix
Despite the popular image of the average Canadian as a rugged northern outdoorsman, the fact of the matter is very different. Along with the increase in total numbers of population and the westward diffusion, there has been a movement from rural areas into cities. In 1871, 80 per cent of Canadians were rural dwellers and as recently as 1931 these still made up more than half the national population. By 1976 however, 75.5 per cent of the total population were living in urban communities. In addition, more and more Canadians were living in larger urban centres. Between 1961 and 1971, the 22 metropolitan areas in Canada increased their population 11 per cent compared with only 4 per cent for the rest of Canada, and 55 per cent of the total Canadian population was living in those metropolitan areas. The true outdoorsman has become an endangered species!

One of the most dramatic illustrations of both the regional population distribution pattern and the current large numbers of city dwellers as compared with rural residents, was the "Isodemographic Map of Canada" developed by Skoda and Robertson (Figure 4). In this map the usual relationship was reversed — population density was uniform while the land scale varied with the resultant distortion of geographic space and physical features. It has proved particularly useful in stressing the urban geographic "facts of life" to the Canadian public.

Canadian Regions and Regionalisms / 247

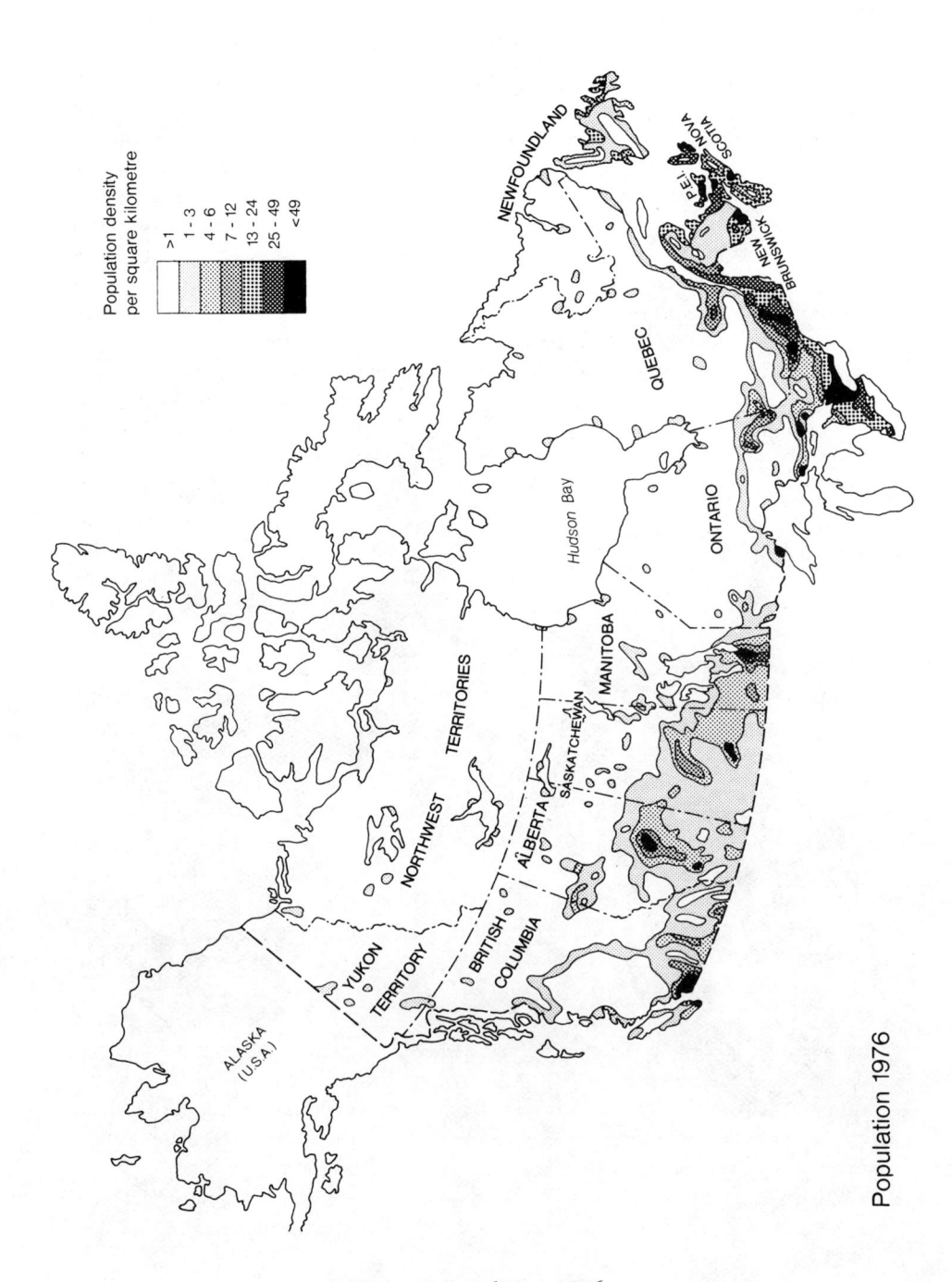

Figure 3 Population 1976

248 / Sensibilities

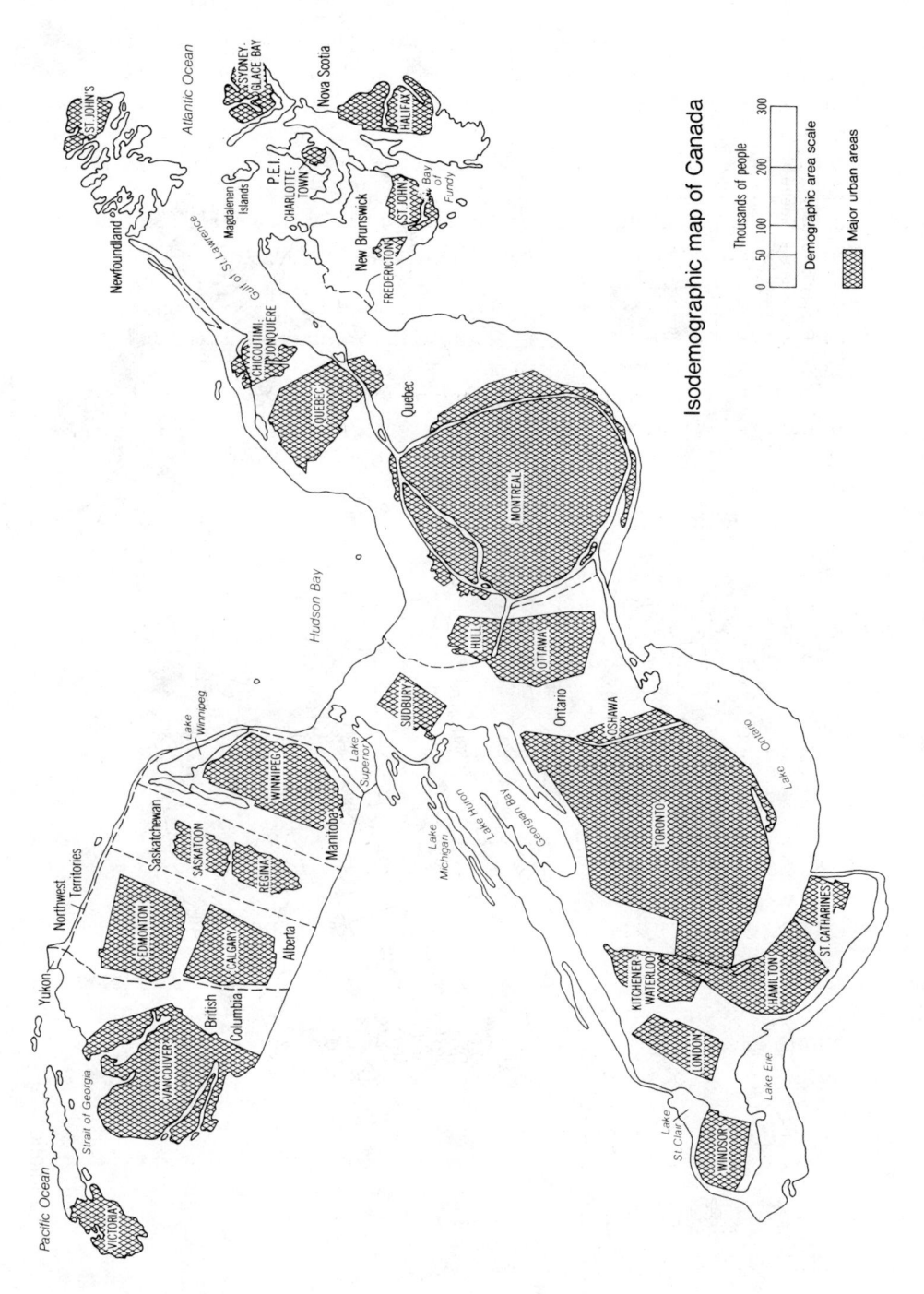

Figure 4 Isodemographic map of Canada

The increasingly urban nature of Canada has attracted the attention of geographers along with scholars from other disciplines. The results have varied, from overviews on the national scale such as that of the Simmons', to Yeates' "Main Street" study of the most highly urbanized region in the nation, to Kerr's examination of the national metropolitan dominance of Canada's two largest cities, both located within that region. The recent, particularly rapid growth of Western Canadian cities has been featured in several special "city issues" in the "Western Geographical Series" of the University of Victoria, and in the "B.C. Geographical Series" of Tantalus Research Ltd., Vancouver. Smith and Johnson have studied the vital corridor linking Canada's two most rapidly growing cities, Calgary and Edmonton — a potential second "Main Street" for Western Canada.

This relatively recent and accelerating shift from a rural to an urban way of life has been accompanied by great social strains as well as by creature comforts. Crime, violence, noise and pollution, breakdown of family relationships, etc., partially reflect the newness of the urban environment and the inapplicability of older rural social guidelines. A generation ago most urban dwellers had relatives still living "in the country" with whom they often exchanged visits. Those ties have become progressively weaker and frequently have disappeared entirely. The city dweller now feels more at ease with his counterpart hundreds and even thousands of miles away than he does with the rural dweller in his immediate geographic region.

Ethnicity
Ethnicity is a widely used word in culture, but the principal criterion involved may vary from language to religion to race, etc. In Canada it is most often associated with language, in the first instance at least.

During the past two decades ethnicity has come to be an even more powerful force in the culture and politics of Canada. "Folk festivals" and "heritage days" have erupted all over the country, from French-Canadian "sugaring-off" parties, to Scottish-Canadian "highland games," to German-Canadian Oktoberfests, to Ukrainian-Canadian dance festivals. They reflect the ethnic mosaic that is Canada.

At the time of the 1971 Census, 44.6 per cent of Canada's population were of British origin, 28.7 per cent were French, and the remaining 26.7 per cent were from other language origins. From the creation of Canada, English and French languages have reflected the fundamental duality of the state. The third element of the "ethnic mix," belonging to neither, has been of growing importance in recent decades. In most cases this third element has opted for English as its working language in its adopted country.

The historical determination of the French ethnic community to survive in the increasingly English-speaking nation, continent and world, is well known. In the early 1960s it took on new vigour and dimension in the so-called "Quiet Revolution." Lee has ascribed this to the impact of three major social processes in Quebec: industrialization, urbanization, and political modernization....

The federal government, whose present governing party draws massive support from that same French ethnic community, has been striving to defuse the situation by widening the opportunities for the use of the French language on a national scale in the areas where it has jurisdiction. In 1969, following the Report of the Royal Commission on Bilingualism and Biculturalism, the Official Languages Bill stipulated that both English and French are official languages of Canada with equality of status and rights of use "in all the institutions of the Parliament and Government of Canada."

Delineation of the English/French linguistic regions was basic to the operation of the Bill. The resultant map (Figure 5) portrays four types of regions: English language zones; French language zones (both such zones being designated where 90 per cent or more of the total population of the census division used one or the other language); bilingual zones (where the minority population constituted 10 per cent of the total population); and language island zones (enclaves of an official-language population situated within one of the unilingual language zones).

The geographic pattern shows the strong French language core within the St. Lawrence Lowlands, with extensions into the southern and northern margins and an outlier beyond, in the Abitibi clay belt. The bilingual zones make up a series of disjointed regions between this core and the English language zone which constitutes most of the rest of Canada. These bilingual zones occur in the southernmost part of Quebec (Eastern Townships, Montreal and vicinity, and the Lower Ottawa Valley) including areas where Anglophones were the original rural settlers, and easternmost Southern Ontario and parts of north-eastern Ontario into which French farmers, miners and forest workers have moved. "To the east in Gaspé and New Brunswick the zone embraced the small English language communities clustered along the shore of Chaleur Bay and the Acadian settlements of northern and eastern New Brunswick." French language islands occur in each of the other Atlantic Provinces, in southern Ontario, and across the Prairie Provinces. Though Cartwright did not include them in his studies, he acknowledged the presence of small English language islands in Saguenay and Nouveau-Québec within Quebec.

Despite their identification, bilingual districts still have not been designated legally as is provided for under the Official Languages Act of Canada. At provincial level there has been mixed reaction toward the federal government's goal of greater mutual accommodation of the two dominant language groups. Most provinces have accepted such goals with varying degrees of enthusiasm — New Brunswick has now become officially bilingual, but Ontario still has not gone that far. At the same time the present Quebec government has dismissed as irrelevant increased accommodation of French-speaking Canadians beyond its borders. In 1977 it proclaimed its own Official Language Charter, requiring exclusive use of French in most situations within the province, resulting in what one Montreal columnist has described as a "five-year dialogue of the deaf" between the two language groups in the province.

Paralleling the rising pressures of French ethnic identity has been the flowering of the non-British, non-French community in Canada. It has been present since the formation of the nation but has become much more evident recently. With or without the general support of many Canadians who still hold to the former policy of not radically altering the ethnic composition of Canada by immigration, the federal government since 1967 has attempted a non-discriminatory and universal policy in this field. Acting on other recommendations of the Royal Commission on Bilingualism and Biculturalism, the government has substituted Multiculturalism for Biculturalism, with a ministry created in 1972 to implement multiculturalism policy. Support is offered for programmes "aimed at retaining, developing and sharing these cultures on a larger scale and [those] which encourage mutual appreciation and understanding among all Canadians."

Traditionally, Germans have constituted the third largest ethnic group in Canada, though the large postwar immigration of Italians now challenges that position. Across Canada, German ethnic regions of varying size can be noted, with varying times of arrival. Earliest were the two hundred families in the mid-eighteenth century who created the new settlement of Lunenburg in Nova Scotia and endowed it with the name of their old country home. Though ultimately they formed the nucleus of "some 16,000 of German origin and speech [they were] without recruits for over a century and were largely assimilated" into the Anglophone community. Thus to-day, while more than 40,000 people in Nova Scotia are of German ethnic descent, only 1,500 have German language as the original "mother tongue" of their early home life.

The strong German ethnic community of southwestern Ontario centred on Kitchener (Berlin)-Waterloo is well known. The earliest arrivals were Mennonites of German and Swiss descent arriving between 1800-1825 from Pennsylvania, while continuing later influences came both from the home country directly and also from the U.S.A., including both religious and secular elements. The third region of significant German ethnicity is the southern Prairie Provinces where the general wave of settlement near the turn of the century included German groups with others and resulted in the heterogeneous ethnic mosaic of to-day. Both religious communal and secular individual settlement has been involved. Much of the recent notable German immigration since the Second World War has been drawn to urban centres in Canada. Apart from the Kitchener metropolitan area, the urban German ethnic community is especially important in the cities of Western Canada. In Edmonton for example, German immigrants play a major role in the construction industry and have created a distinctive ethnic neighbourhood in the southeastern part of the city.

252 / Sensibilities

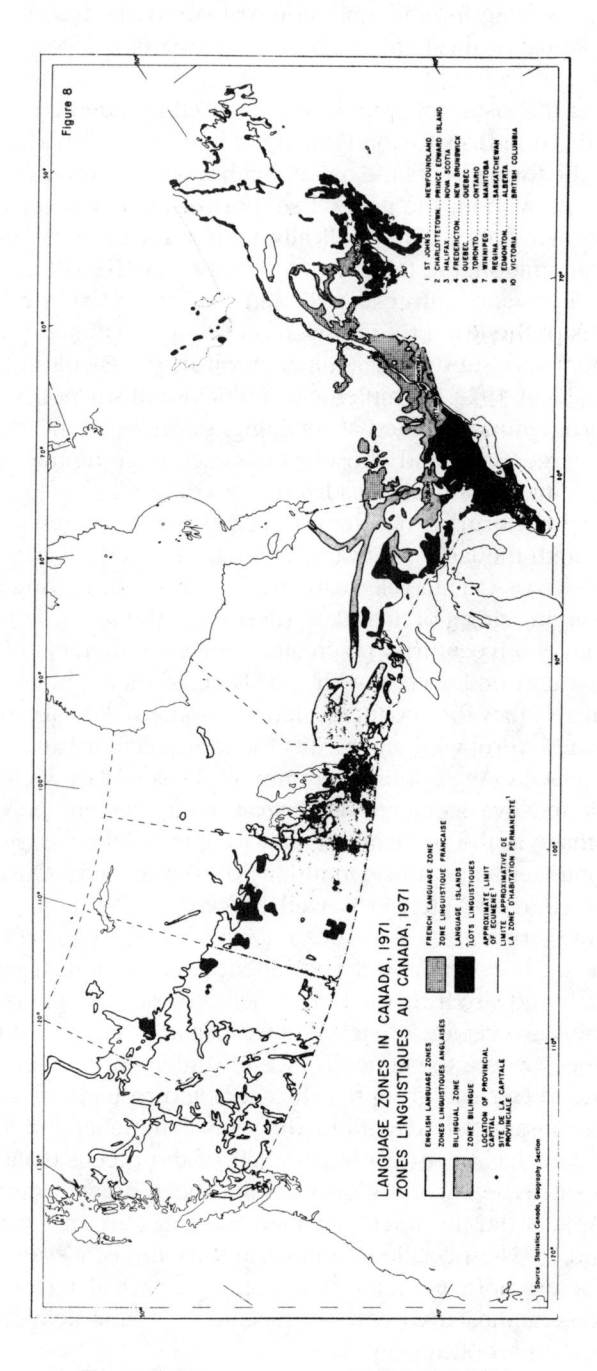

Figure 5 Language zones in Canada, 1971

GEOGRAPHIC REGIONS AND REGIONALISMS

Out of such factors and others, geographers have delineated regions at a variety of scales, though as noted previously I am here concerned only with those on a national level. Amongst those who have explored the theme most fully are Nicholson and Sametz, Robinson, Watson, and Merrill. Many others also have put forward their own particular schema. The geographic regions thus identified may or may not conform with those of others, so that there still is no single regionalization of Canada recognized by all geographers. What follows is an arbitrary selection of representative systems.

Continental Regions

In the eyes of some, the close linkages, both environmental and cultural, between Canada and the United States, justify the outlining of geographic regions that cut across the international boundary, rather than being confined solely to one nation or the other. The regions set out by White, Foscue and McKnight are representative of this viewpoint. As they see it "Canada and the United States have a common heritage and have been moving toward similar goals. These factors, along with geographical continuity and the binational influence of mass media, have produced both commonality of culture and mutual interdependence... [which parallel] the fact that the geographical 'grain' of Anglo-American often trends north-south rather than east-west." At the same time they do acknowledge that there are "clear-cut distinctions between the two countries."

Under White, Foscue and McKnight's system, Canada is divided into eight geographic regions, which can be seen to reflect many of the primary environmental regions outlined earlier (Figure 6). All but one of these regions trended across into the adjacent United States. The sole exception is "French Canada," which unlike the others is defined primarily on the basis of "dominant French-Canadian culture."

Others believe that despite the close ties between the two nations, the differences require separate treatment. A quarter of a century ago the Royal Commission on Canada's Economic Prospects stated: "Canada and the United States live in a kind of symbiosis — two organisms separate and distinct, each with its own ends and laws; but highly interdependent, indissolubly sharing the same continental environment and, in spite of a great disproportion in wealth and power, each necessary to the other." There are "bands that run north and south that loop the two economies together. But there are also highly important bands that run transversely across the continent dividing the two economies." Watson noted this in introducing his article on Canadian regions and treated Canada as separate from the United States in his North American text which later appeared as a separate book. Some other geographers dealing with North America have followed the same approach.

... Wreford Watson sets out five major geographical regions of Canada: the Atlantic Region, Central Settled Canada, The Southern Prairies, Southern

254 / Sensibilities

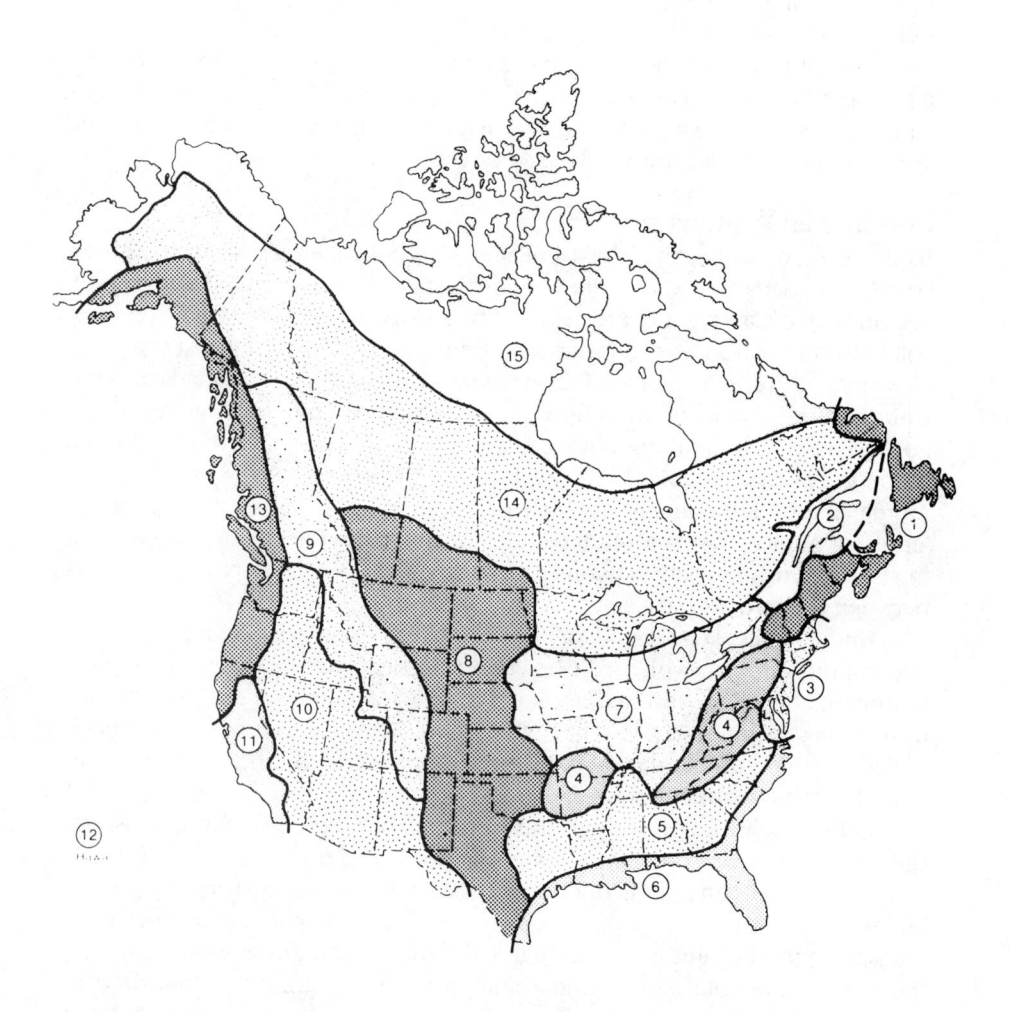

1. Northeastern Anglo-American
2. French Canada
3. Megalopolis
4. The Appalachains and the Ozarks
5. The Inland South
6. The Southeastern Coast
7. The Anglo-American Heartland
8. The Great Plains
9. The Rocky Mountains
10. The Intermontane Basins and Plateaus
11. The California Region
12. The Hawaiian Islands
13. The North Pacific Coast
14. The Boreal Forest
15. The Tundra

Figure 6 Anglo-America: Geographical regions

Canadian Regions and Regionalisms / 255

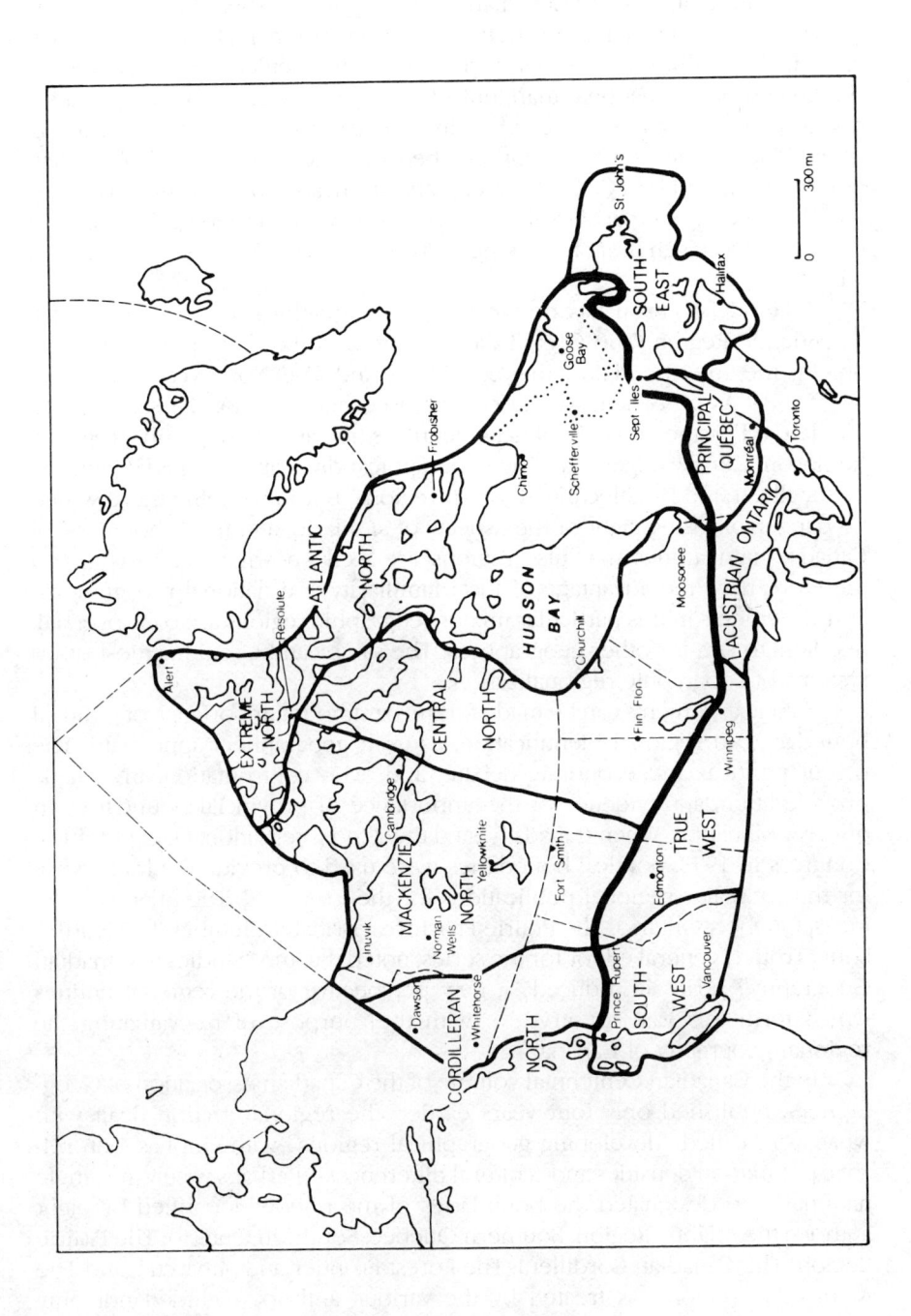

Figure 7 Canada: Major regions

British Columbia, and The Canadian North (Figure 7). These have been characterized by a considerable variety of both environmental and cultural features including historical experience. The Central Settled Canada region, as designated on the national map, unfortunately is at variance with his subsequent treatment of the region wherein he excludes all of northern Ontario. Interestingly, Watson sees strong ties between the two dominant Canadian ethnic communities in Central Settled Canada: "In spite of their initial rivalries and the differences that remain, both groups have an understanding of each other that has given them a working unity and thus given unity to the section where they live."

J. Lewis Robinson has designated six geographical regions in Canada: the Atlantic Region; The Great Lakes-St. Lawrence Lowlands; The Canadian Shield; the Interior Plains; the Cordillera; and The Northwest Territories (Figure 8). As he conceded, the criteria used here are not the same: some are defined on the basis of political identity; some are physiographic regions. Robinson acknowledges that "the geographical diversity of Canada could be better illustrated by selecting 10 or 20 regions, but in so doing there would be danger of losing sight of the aspects of similarity and the 'wholeness' of Canada," and argues that his "regions are well known to Canadians and therefore have the advantage of local familiarity and national recognition." Some elements in this particular mix of geographic regions are controversial, needless to say, for other geographers. The same can be said for most other systems of geographic regionalization.

Strong arguments can be made for the paramount importance of political boundaries in regional identification, as even geographers appreciate. The recent political and economic debate, and even confrontation, in Canada provide abundant evidence of the importance of provincial boundaries in our federal nation. When Canada hosted the 22nd International Geographical Congress in 1972, political boundaries were used to provide the framework for the six major regional publications for the Congress (The Atlantic Provinces, Quebec, Ontario, The Prairie Provinces, British Columbia, The North). Louis Trotier, general editor for the series, noted that the "Studies in Canadian Geography" series introduced "a new perspective of the regional entities which form this vast country ... [with the] purpose of re-evaluating the regional geography of Canada."

In the Canadian Centennial volume of the Canadian Association of Geographers, published only four years earlier, the regional section dealt with what were called "developing geographical regions" with emphasis on relative population densities and "cultural differences." Perhaps wisely, no single national map designated the boundaries of the regions identified by eight authors: the Atlantic Region; Southern Quebec; Southern Ontario; The Prairie Region; The Canadian Cordillera; The Forest Frontier and Subarctic; and The Arctic. The regions, as treated by the various authors, included not only

Canadian Regions and Regionalisms / 257

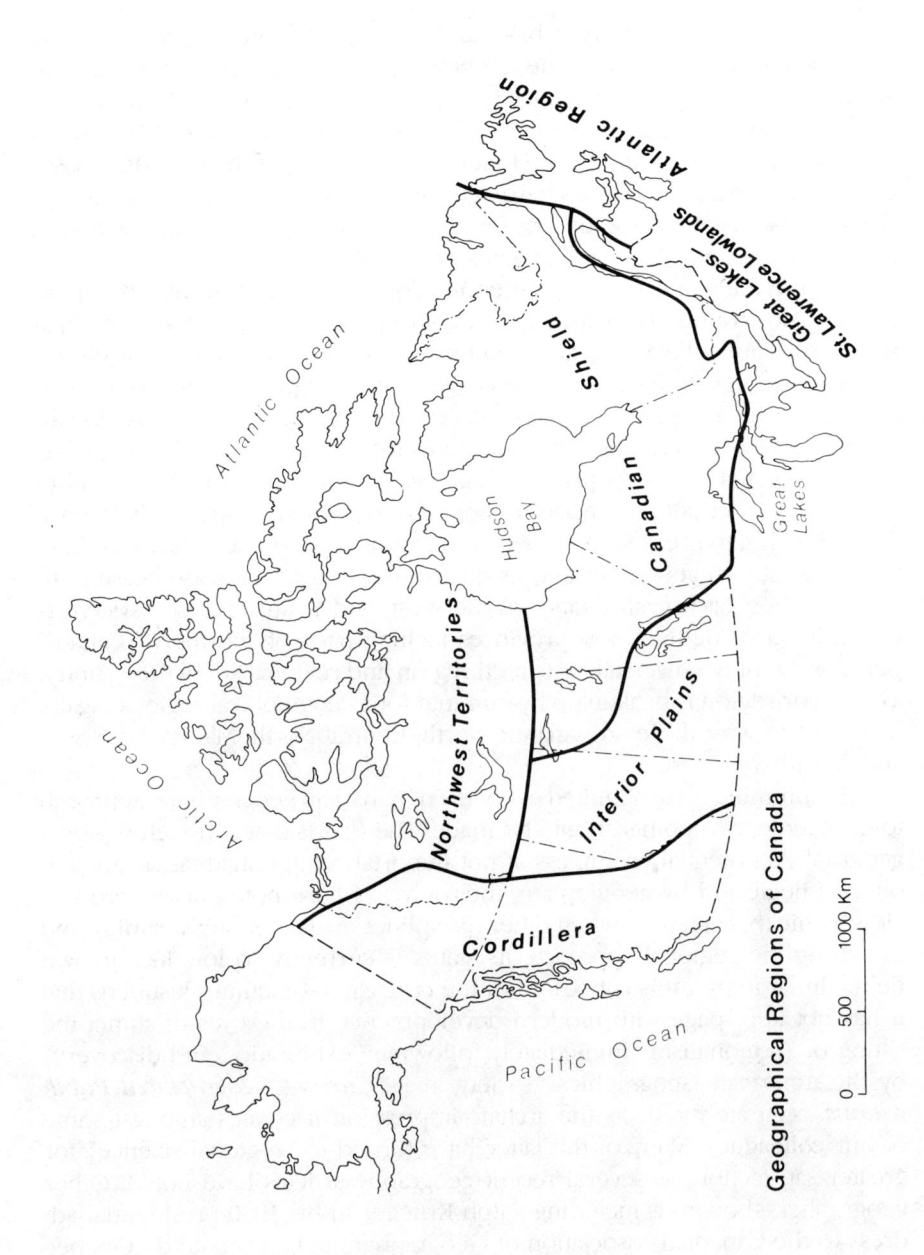

Figure 8 Geographical regions of Canada

political considerations, but others as well, and in some instances even overlapped.

Some mention, however brief and incomplete, must be made of the work of Canadian Francophone geographers in regionalization. Given the strong traditions along those lines in France, it is only natural that they were carried also to Canada. One of the earliest was Raoul Blanchard, who shared with Griffith Taylor the title of Honourary President of the Canadian Association of Geographers. Blanchard set out three major "natural regions" in Quebec (La région laurentienne, i.e. the St. Lawrence Lowlands, La région appalachienne, and Le Bouclier Canadien) with 11 sub-regions in all. This formed the initial framework for Benôit Brouillette, which he later modified slightly. Most of our French-Canadian colleagues, such as Jean-Vianney Frenette and Paul Villeneuve, have continued to focus almost exclusively on regionalization within the province of Quebec. A notable exception has been Louis-Edmond Hamelin, who also has contributed an important regionalization framework for the Canadian and circumpolar North. Hamelin has divided Canada into two primary regions, southern and northern, within which he has set out five and four geographical regions respectively (Figure 9). . . . Seeking to break with "provincial terminology" Hamelin has identified the five southern geographical regions, from east to west as: Southeast; Principal Quebec. Lacustrian Ontario; True West; and Southwest. The system is useful in stressing that most provinces include parts of "northern" Canada, perhaps the only universally accepted region and regionalism in the country. This major region is broken up by him into four geographical regions. Again, from east to west these are: Atlantic North; Central North; Mackenzie North; and Cordilleran North.

In summing up this limited overview of Canadian geographers' approach to the theme, two points should be made. The first is that although regional geography's potential usefulness, if not importance, to Canada is so great, it often is neglected by geographers themselves. I have noted elsewhere that "it is ironic that at a time when other disciplines are increasingly valuing and practising the regional approach, its status is currently so low in our own field." In large part this is because of the criticism (sometimes justified) that it has not kept pace with modern developments. In the eyes of some, the listing of "regionalism" immediately following "exploration and discovery" by the American Geographical Society in its *Current Geographical Publications*, accurately reflects the archaic impression it creates amongst some of our colleagues. Many of the latter have turned to "regional science" for greater satisfaction, as several recent geography articles have noted. Other geographers, however, including Ralph Krueger in his 1980 presidential address to the Canadian Association of Geographers at l'université du Québec à Montréal, stress the value of regional geography and urge a revival of this traditional skill.

Second, the very considerable diversity of geographers' Canadian regions has been indicated. Michael Ray, for example, probed the nature of Canadian regionalism as it is reflected in the social and economic disparities between the major regions of Canada — "one of the most characteristic features of Canadian geography in the present century." To this end he focussed primarily on disparities in income and economic opportunity, in the extent of foreign ownership and in cultural differences, as they vary geographically across the country. In some ways there are as many systems of regionalization as there are geographers. Each weighs the relative importance and selection of the many elements, environmental and cultural, that go into the identity of a geographic region. This in part underlies the vastness and complexity of Canada. It *is* a complicated nation and one hopes geographers bring out not only this fact, but also suggest some comprehensible and meaningful perspectives for its appreciation. One thing should be clear from this overview is that Canada can not be assessed correctly in its present sensitive political and economic situation, as simply two geographic regions: Quebec and "the rest." The reality is much more complex.

CONCLUSION

Regions and regionalism are themes by no means confined to Canada. A variation of these, for example, occupied scholars from the Norden countries recently, gathered to mark the 500th anniversary of Uppsala University: *Regional identitet och förändring i den regionala samverkans samhälle* (Regional Identity and Change in the Regional Co-operative Community). In Canada, however, because of its nature, these themes have been, are, and always will be of vital importance. Similarly, they are not the prerogative of the geographer, regardless of how central they are to his or her discipline. Regions and regionalisms are a geographic fact of life which is reflected in most fields, and quite properly involves a diversity of scholars. The Summer 1980 issue of the *Journal of Canadian Studies*, for example, was given over to the theme of "Regionalism" with more than half-a-dozen different disciplines represented amongst the contributors. Though I have neither the qualifications nor the time to speak for these other disciplines, their input to this common theme is essential and appreciated.

Until recently Canadian historians have tended to understate regionalism. Perhaps this reflected a certain moral imperative since the 1930s, at least, to seek to hold the country together with emphasis on "nation-building," and which has only begun to disintegrate within the past 15 years or so. Such scholars as Ramsay Cook and Maurice Careless have been particularly influential in the new awareness of regionalism, and the subject formed the topic of the Centennial Seminars of the Canadian Historical Association. In Careless' words, "the experience of regionalism remains prominent and distinctive in Canadian history — and time has tended less to erode it than to develop it." David Bercuson has gone so far as to argue that "the sacrifices called for in

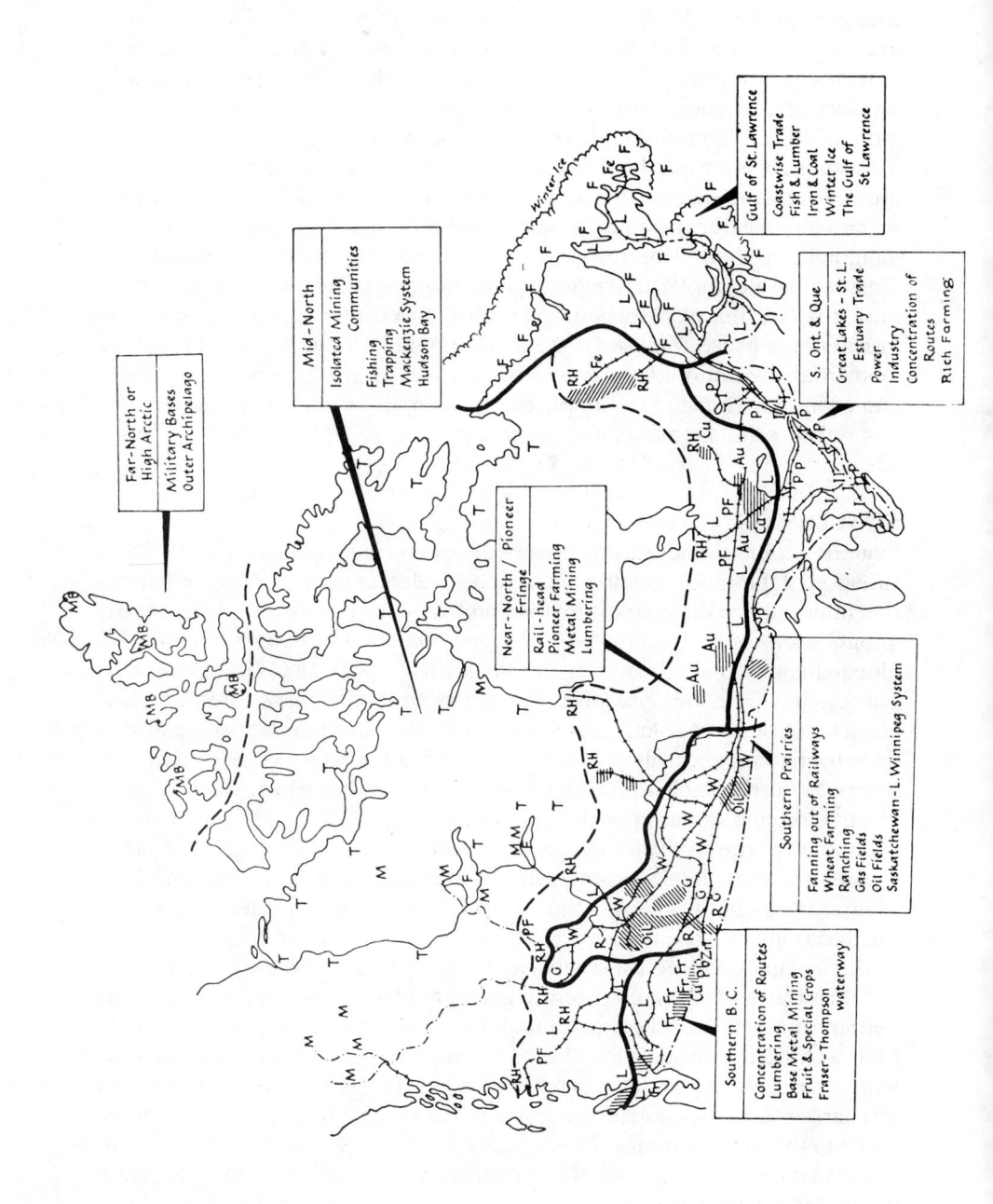

Figure 9 Canada: Major regions

the name of 'national unity' have taken a heavy toll in the hinterland regions and no real national unity can be attained until national priorities have been rearranged ... [though] federalism and regionalism are not incompatible."

Other disciplines are just as aware of the vital significance of regionalism in Canada. The economic implications were noted by the Royal Commission on Canada's Economic Prospects in 1957, and by the Economic Council of Canada in 1977. It has been a strongly held view of the federal government that one of its primary responsibilities is to minimize such regional economic disparities through its equalization grants to the provinces and through the operations of the federal Department of Regional Economic Expansion. That the regions do not feel that this has been achieved to their satisfaction, perhaps underlies the recent re-emergence of the "Theory of the Great Cow" which originally appeared in the 1930s — Western Canada providing the basic resources, Central Canada enjoying the bulk of the benefits, and Atlantic Canada experiencing the hazards of the "wrong end" of the animal!

From a literary perspective, Eli Mandel has concluded that "accounts of the character and development of Canadian writing are marked by the struggle to avoid talking about national identity or local politics as much as by the desire to find distinctive national characteristics." Wreford Watson, however, noted regional modes of thought to be strongly reflected in Canadian literature. Henry Kreisel has stressed a strong regional identity in the literature of "Prairie Canada," with such common elements as distance and isolation, though one of the current practitioners of the art in Western Canada, Rudy Wiebe, has stated: "I'm not sure such a term as regional has any meaning in a country as big and as varied as Canada is. That qualification may mean something to a critic but it certainly doesn't mean much to a working writer."

In the political field, Canadian regionalism traditionally and much more urgently in the past two decades has been dominated by Quebec. More recently, as the costly responsibilities of the provinces have escalated, there has been increasing dissatisfaction on their part towards the central government and even in the federally-administered territories, political pressures have built up to unprecedented degrees. While all provinces have been unhappy, the sentiment is especially noticeable in Western Canada.

The West sees itself as having been treated from the beginning as a mere raw material-producing colonial appendage of Central Canada, citing the long-delayed turnover of their resources to the western provinces, the biased railway freight rates, and other complaints. In recent years, with the growing national value of its resources, especially fuels, its booming regional economy, and growing population, it has come to expect a greater political role federally, but considers it has been thwarted in that, since the real political power has remained in the more populous Central Canada. The resentment has been reflected in the exploration of a possible political unification of the three Prairie Provinces to achieve a more influential role, and even in the appearance of a measure of western political separatism. The place of British

Columbia, in such an extreme potential situation, is uncertain — while usually included in "Western Canada," its strong natural ties to the Pacific Rim result in the designation by some of "B.C." as "Beyond Canada."

Some observers see Canada only functioning efficiently in the face of major external or universal threats, such as military, economic, etc. In the absence of such threats we tend to "come apart at the seams," but somehow to date have managed to survive. Garth Stevenson has stated: "Closely associated and mutually reinforcing, regionalism and continentalism have always threatened the survival of the Canadian state." Assessing the relative strengths of the centrifugal forces of regionalism and the centripetal tendencies of nationalism, Gordon Merrill has concluded: "Unfortunately the [centripetal] forces are not strong." In a television interview recently, the last Minister of Regional Economic Expansion commented that for every Canadian "his region is his universe." . . .

2
QUEBEC

Speak White

MICHÈLE LALONDE

Speak white
it is so lovely to listen to you
speaking of Paradise Lost
or the anonymous, graceful profile trembling in the sonnets of Shakespeare

We are a rude and stammering people
but we are not deaf to the genius of a language
speak with the accent of Milton and Byron and Shelley and Keats
speak white
and please excuse us if in return
we've only our rough ancestral songs
and the chagrin of Nelligan

speak white
speak of places, this and that
speak to us of the Magna Carta
of the Lincoln Monument
of the cloudy charm of the Thames
or blossom-time on the Potomac
speak to us of your traditions
We are a people who are none too bright
but we are quick to sense
the great significance of crumpets
or the Boston Tea Party

But when you really speak white
when you get down to brass tacks
to speak of Better Homes and Gardens
and the high standard of living
and the Great Society
a little louder then speak white

raise your foremen's voices
we are a little hard of hearing
we live too close to the machines
and only hear our heavy breathing over the tools
speak white and loud
so we can hear you clearly
from Saint Henri to Santo Domingo
yes, what a marvellous language
for hiring and firing
for giving the orders
for fixing the hour to be worked to death
and that pause that refreshes
and bucks up the dollar

Speak white
tell us that God is a great big shot
and that we're paid to trust him
speak white
speak to us of production, profits and percentages
speak white
it's a rich language
for buying
but for selling oneself
but for selling one's soul
but for selling oneself

Ah
speak white
big deal
but for telling about
the eternity of a day on strike
for telling the whole
life-story of a nation of caretakers
for coming back home in the evening
at the hour when the sun's gone bust in the alleys
for telling you yes the sun does set yes
every day of our lives to the east of your empires
Nothing's as good as a language of oaths
our mode of expression none too clean
dirtied with oil and with axle grease

Speak white
feel at home with your words
we are a bitter people
but we'd never reproach a soul
for having a monopoly
on how to improve one's speech

In the sweet tongue of Shakespeare
with the accent of Longfellow
speak a French purely and atrociously white
as in Viet Nam, in the Congo
speak impeccable German
a yellow star between your teeth
speak Russian speak of the right to rule speak of repression
speak white
it's a universal language
we were born to understand it
with its tear-gas phrases
with its billy-club words

Speak white
tell us again about freedom and democracy
We know that liberty is a Black word
as misery is Black
as blood is muddied with the dust of Algiers or of Little Rock

Speak white
from Westminster to Washington take turns
speak white as on Wall Street
white as in Watts
Be civilized
and understand our conventional answer
when you ask us politely
how do you do
and we mean to reply
we're doing all right
we're doing fine
we
are not alone

We know now
that we are not alone.

Translated by D. G. Jones

The Development of Ideologies in Quebec

MARCEL RIOUX

HISTORIC OUTLINE

In order to understand the recent evolution of ideologies in Quebec, it is necessary to establish where this period fits in the historical context. What ideas did the Quebecois, that is, the Francophone majority, have of themselves and their society? What goals did they, as a group, have and what means did they advocate for attaining them? The interpretation of ideologies proposed here will take two centuries of history into account and will, therefore, necessarily be schematic.

When can we begin to speak of an ideology for the Quebecois? Usually, as soon as a group has proved itself to be a distinct group and a strong enough "we" has been formed to oppose other "we's," individuals appear who define the situation and who clearly explain this collective consciousness. Under the French regime, it seems that the other group, which Canadiens were beginning to oppose, was still too close to them for the birth of an ideology. Canadiens had a feeling of nonidentity toward French metropolitans, but this feeling was not yet used as an explicit concept.

Conquered in 1760, ruined by the war, deprived of their elites, the Quebec peasants spent their first forty years under English domination just surviving and a new elite slowly emerged from their ranks which assumed the function of defining the Quebec community and representing it politically. This new Francophone bourgeoisie, made up of people from the liberal professions, was to oppose the mercantile class which, in turn, was to represent the Anglophone minority. This social class made up of the liberal professions took it upon itself to define the Quebec nation; this brings us to our first ideology. Fernand Ouellet wrote that, with the appearance of a national consciousness at the heart of the bourgeoisie, its political vocation was greatly strengthened. From that time on, it no longer defended its class interests or proposed abstract values as far as the people were concerned; it represented the nation and its essential attributes. In 1810, Craig wrote:

Marcel Rioux, "The Development of Ideologies in Quebec," originally appeared in French under the title "Sur l'évolution des idéologies au Québec," *Revue de l'Institut de Sociologie*, No. 1 (1968). This translation was prepared by Gerald L. Gold for *Communities and Culture in French Canada* (Toronto: Holt, Rinehart and Winston of Canada Limited, 1973), pp. 260-279. This version, without footnotes, reprinted by permission of Marcel Rioux, Gerald L. Gold, and Marc-Adelard Tremblay.

> In truth, it seems to be their desire to be considered as forming a separate nation. The *Canadien* nation is their constant expression....

What is the relationship between this bourgeoisie and the people? Fernand Dumont gives the following explanation:

> The fact that this bourgeoisie was, at first, accepted by the people as their natural spokesman is clear, and can be explained, we feel, quite easily. As sons of the people, its members kept the essential attitudes of the peasantry from which they came.

From the turn of the century to the 1830s, this new bourgeoisie got on well with the clergy; both groups had approximately the same views about Canadiens. But soon a division occurred in the Legislative Assembly: "with Papineau, the dream of an autonomous French-Canadian Republic began to take form." The period known as the romantic period in French Canada was to finish badly: the Insurrection in 1837-38 was soon checked. The Church was seen more and more frequently by many of the bourgeoisie elite as an ally of the colonizers. When the Church, with Monseigneur Lartigue as spokesman, condemned the Insurrection, it realized that its directives were not well received in the Montreal region. Monseigneur Lartigue's intervention aroused anger which was expressed through popular demonstrations and violently anticlerical articles in patriotic newspapers. In Montreal, where 1200 *patriotes* paraded in front of the Saint-Jacques Cathedral during Vespers, it was said that the pastoral letter would hasten the "revolution," and in Chambly, three men left the church while the letter was being read. They formed a group to welcome Monseigneur Bourget and the clergy after Mass with cries of "Down with the movement!" and "Vive Papineau!" Elsewhere, priests were treated to the singing of the *Marseillaise* and the *Libera*. In 1834, Papineau had already chastised the Church:

> This Act [Quebec Act, 1774] retained all the rights, privileges and power of the clergy (although these advantages are better preserved through the confidence, religious persuasion, and conviction of the people), because it was fast losing its temporal authority with them as far as determining their ideas and opinions was concerned. The clergy eagerly welcomed this Act, took up the government's cause, and, ignoring that of the people, found it good because it was advantageous.

Thus it can be seen that the first ideology of Quebec was formulated by a secular elite who defined Quebec as a nation. Independence was the aim of this nation. In an epilogue to the results of the Insurrection, Etienne Parent, a journalist, wrote in 1839:

> There were people, and we were among them, who thought that with the backing and the favour of England, the French Canadians could flatter themselves for having retained and spread their nationality in such a way as to form an independent nation afterwards....

As Fernand Dumont writes:

> The Insurrection marks the failure in a sort of spasm of agony of this first attempt to define the situation and the future of the French-Canadian nation.

THE RISE OF THE IDEOLOGY OF CONSERVATION

The secular bourgeoisie which dominated the Assembly from 1820-1840 acted like a national bourgeoisie and took upon itself the task of defining the Quebec community and its future. It did not cause a great stir among the people who were afraid of the liberalism, anticlericalism, and anti-British ideas of the *patriotes*. On the whole, the clergy remained faithful to the British Crown. Derbyshire, who was an envoy from Durham, "also reported the noteworthy observation of the Abbé Ducharme, *curé* of Saint-Thérèse":

> 'It was the educated men, the doctors, notaries, and lawyers, who were at the head of the rebellion and were the great seducers of the people, and he seemed to derive from it an argument against educating the lower orders.'

That is why, once the Rebellion had been suppressed and its leaders had fled, the clergy could regain its control over the people, with the aid of the British powers. The British, with Governor Durham as their spokesman, became aware of the prevailing situation in Quebec.

Durham stated that he had come to Canada thinking he would find a conflict between the people and the executive, but instead he had found

> ...two nations warring in the bosom of a single state: I found a struggle not of principles, but of races. The national feud forces itself on the very senses, irresistibly and palpably, as the origin or essence of every dispute which divides the community; we discover that dissensions, which appear to have another origin, are but forms of this constant and all pervading quarrel; and that every contest is one of French and English in the outset, or becomes so ere it has run its course.

Durham's solution was simple; he proposed the assimilation of Lower Canada, which was largely Francophone, with Upper Canada, which was mainly Anglophone.

> I entertain no doubt of the national character which must be given to Lower Canada; it must be that of the British Empire; that of the majority of British America; that of the great race which must, in the lapse of no long period of time, be predominant over the whole North American Continent. Without effecting the change so rapidly or roughly as to shock the feelings and trample on the welfare of the existing generation, it must henceforth be the first and steady purpose of the British Government to establish an English population, with English laws and language, in this Province, and to trust its government to none but a decidedly English Legislature.

Durham added:

> I should indeed be surprised if the more reflecting part of the French Canadians entertain at present any hope of continuing to preserve their nationality. Much as they struggle against it, it is obvious that the process of assimilation to English habits is already commencing. The English language is gaining ground, as the language of the rich and of the employers of labour naturally will.

It is hard to be more explicit.

The Durham Report and the Act of Union which followed the Insurrection, mark a very important turning point in the history of Quebec. It was not until the late 1950s, more than a hundred years later, that there appeared an equally important period, from an ideological point of view. We cannot overemphasize this period. Quebec's professional bourgeoisie was descended from the peasantry and had defended the traditional form of culture which had developed in Quebec since the Conquest. Was this, however, through choice or necessity? Being the ruling class of a people who were dominated politically, economically, and socially, the liberal bourgeoisie was obliged to defend what existed, and what existed was a people that the Conquest had relegated to agriculture. There is nothing to indicate that the Quebecois chose to defend the traditional form of economy they practised. It was the dialectic of the situation which gave it momentum. These people that the liberal bourgeoisie wanted to lead to independence, "with the support and favour of England," were, for the time being, poor illiterate farmers. By opposing the dominators and the Anglophone mercantile class which represents it, the national bourgeoisie defended a way of life imposed on it since the Conquest and the failure of the Insurrection. There is nothing to lead us to believe that it was this way of life that they had defended. Above all, the liberal bourgeoisie was defending the right of the Quebec people to live as a total society. Papineau and his followers were insisting on the liberty of a majority group, which had been conquered militarily, economically, and politically by a minority.

However, everything changed after the 1840s. Despair beset even the most committed Quebecois. It was no longer a question of leading the people to independence, but of fighting against assimilation and Anglicization. With backing from Durham, the clergy became the main spokesman for the Quebec people; they no longer proclaimed an ideology of independence, but one of conservation. From the point of view of the ideology held in the first few decades of the nineteenth century, the new ideology they were expounding marks a tragic contraction. Sensing quite well that they were to become a minority, the Quebecois no longer sought to become an independent society, but strove to preserve their culture. The Quebec group was no longer a nation that had one day to obtain its independence, but an ethnic group with a particular culture (religion, language, customs); this culture would have to be preserved as a sacred heritage. Durham accused the Quebecois of having no history or literature; they had to prove to him that they had a past and that it was great — to such an extent that the period to be glorified by those who defined the situation was to become the past. The English soon realized that it was necessary to divide the Quebecois, both along the St. Lawrence, and later in Acadia, in order to establish a viable state that the English could control at will. Lord Elgin knew this well when he wrote:

> I believe that the problem of how to govern Canada would be solved if the French would split into a Liberal and a Conservative Party and join the Upper Canadian parties bearing the corresponding names. The great difficulty hitherto has been that a Conservative Government has meant Government of Upper Canadians which is intolerable to the French — and a Radical Government a Government of the French which is no less hateful to the British. The national element would be merged in the political if the split to which I refer was accomplished.

Dumont writes:

> Politics will become a ground on which politicians will periodically defend their nationality; but it will only be one area among others for formulating nationalist ideologies.

The arrival of responsible government enabled the elite in the liberal professions to find employment and to acquire a certain vertical mobility in administration and business. George-Etienne Cartier, a businessman and politician, is one of the first examples of a type of Quebecois who was to profit from the new regime. He took part in the 1837 Insurrection, but as Wade writes:

> he took no part in the second rising, having perhaps been led by his lifelong Sulpician friends to see that the clergy was right in condemning opposition to the constituted authorities, a view which he later recognized as "the only one that offered some chance of salvation for the French Canadians."

With the backing of this same clergy, he and his party were to win all the elections in Quebec until the end of the century. Conservatism was triumphant. Some young people from the cities went to settle in the country, in the heart of traditional society. Gérin-Lajoie's novel, *Jean Rivard*, well explains this glorification of the earth. In 1849, the author wrote in his diary:

> I have returned to my project of going to live in the country as soon as possible. Oh, if only I were a farmer! He does not become rich by beggaring others, as lawyers, doctors, and merchants sometimes do. He draws his wealth from the earth: his is the state most natural to man. Farmers form the least egotistical and most virtuous class of the population. But this class has need of educated men who can serve its interests. The educated farmer has all the leisure necessary to do good; he can serve as guide to his neighbors, counsel the ignorant, sustain the weak, and defend him against the rapacity of the speculator. The enlightened and virtuous farmer is to my mind the best type of man.

Several novels from this period were constructed around the theme of fidelity to agriculture and ancestral values. These romantic works, as well as historical studies, were to propagate the ideology of conservation that the petite-bourgeoisie and the Church were systematically building up. The historian Michel Brunet wrote:

> From then on, the Canadian Church enjoyed a freedom it had not possessed since 1760. Without being fully aware of it, it benefitted from the establishment of ministerial responsibility and a new climate of religious tolerance among the Protestant elite in Great Britain and English Canada. From 1840 to 1965, the Canadian episcopacy directed a Catholic counter-reform. This was necessary. Free thought had made considerable progress among the lay ruling classes and the population in general had become accustomed to neglecting its religious duties. The clergy led a vigilant fight against the last representatives of liberal thought. Some of the Institut canadien and all of the anticlericals who remained faithful to the revolutionary romanticism of the decade of 1830 continued to voice their opposition but they no longer influenced the bulk of the population.

The Church profited from the liberty that the English were according them as a reward for their loyalist attitude during the Insurrection, and strove to get the people under their influence again. This thoroughly succeeded. From that time on, the Church fulfilled for the nation the role that it had filled for many minority groups: that of compensation. The minority should not be saddened by its existing situation because the rewards would come much later. If the Quebecois were to realize themselves fully, to become what they really are, it was out of the question to imitate the material successes of the English. It mattered little that they were conquered and poor, because they had a providential mission to accomplish in North America: to evangelize and civilize the continent. National history, particularly in the person of Garneau, helped the Church greatly to build the new ideology of conservation. Nourished by Voltaire and de Raynal, Garneau advocated prudence and fidelity to traditions. He wrote:

> For us, part of our strength comes from our traditions; let us not separate ourselves from these as we change them gradually. We find good examples to follow in the history of our own mother country. Without laying claim to a similar destiny, our wisdom and our strong unity will greatly ease the difficulties of our situation and will arouse the interest of nations and make our cause appear more sacred to them.

The "Catholic reaction," in the words of Father Léon Pouliot, s.j., took several years to sweep away all that remained of anticlericalism in Quebec. The greatest battle that the clergy had to wage was against the Institut canadien, several members of which were free thinkers. August Viatte describes this struggle as follows:

> A final battle remained to be waged. Quebec is evolving. Montreal is becoming inflexible. The Institut canadien is firing red cannon balls and Mgr. Bourget

wishes to stop them. Starting in 1857, a priest destroyed 1500 "indexed" volumes at the Rolland Library, among which were the complete works of Lamartine, including *Jocelyn* and *Chute d'un ange*. In 1858, the Bishop also required the Institut to commit its manuscripts to flames.

Arthur Buies fought a final battle with his *Lanterne*.

> In vain, he peddled his own journal. The depots refused him and the last number appeared in 1869. At this time, Garneau died and Crémazie was in flight; an era was ending; the spring rains that follow so prolonged a drought will disturb the fertility of the soil and will bring about a change in the climate.

Buies resisted until 1869; the "Catholic reaction" had by then had many years to do its work and for the bulk of the population to have been taken into the hands of the Church.

It seems best to follow Dumont's interpretation that the predominance the Church acquired was achieved with the consent of

> leaders, even nonbelievers, who could not help but recognize that religion was an essential factor in social solidarity and a fundamental element in the differentiation of the French-Canadian nation from that of the English.

The federation of the territories of British North America and the British North America Act, which should have been the constitutional document that consecrated this federation, was bound to accentuate what was embryonic in the Durham Report and in the Act of Union. In 1840, the Act which united English Upper Canada and French Lower Canada was supposed to have the result, in the spirit of Durham and the English lawmakers, of rapidly Anglicizing Lower Canada. It had done nothing. But with Confederation, that is, with the union of all British territories in North America (Upper Canada, Lower Canada, New Brunswick, Nova Scotia, and Prince Edward Island), the assimilation process appeared to be unavoidable. As a minority in this new political formation, the Quebecois again strengthened their ideology of defence and conservation. Although the Quebecois remained the majority in Lower Canada, they were no longer the majority in Canada as a whole. Even inside Quebec, where they represented nearly 75 percent of the population of nearly a million inhabitants, their economic and social position no longer corresponded to their numerical importance. The large cities, such as Montreal and Quebec, had just acquired a Francophone majority. But the English dominated commerce, industry, and finance. Thus even within Quebec, English and Canadiens were opposed to each other on all points: the Canadiens, rural and poor, were Catholics and French in their linguistic tradition; the English, urban and better off economically, were Protestants.

Although the period of Confederation marked a great economic boom in Canada, there was also a profound economic malaise in Quebec which was shown by a massive emigration to the United States. The Canadian economy was being displaced toward southern Ontario and the Quebecois were seeking work in New England. To counter this emigration, the clerical elite and the petite-bourgeoisie began a vast movement of colonization and a return to the land. Quebec followed in detail its ideology of conservation which forced it to remain within its borders:

> relatively sheltered from Anglo-Saxon influences, it (Lower Canada) is entirely taken up with the preservation of its personality which it wishes to keep immutable by time and space, in a sealed vase.

An increasingly accentuated rift developed with France. In 1871, the year of the Commune, Mgr. Raymond wrote:

> The capital of France, centre of these uprisings and of this filth, does not seem to me as more than a soiled land, like that of Babylon or Sodom, and as such calling for the vengeance of heaven.

Gradually the theory of the two Frances was built up. Thomas Chapais gave it most explicit formulation:

> There are now two Frances, radical France and conservative France, the infidel France and Catholic France, the France that blasphemes and the France that prays. Our France is this second one.

This distancing from France was not compensated for by any rapprochement with the English in Canada.

In the decade of 1880, the Riel affair again seemed to harden the relations between Quebec and Canada. When Laurier, a Quebecois, became Prime Minister of Canada from 1896 to 1911, it seemed to mark a truce in the struggle between the two groups: he was elected as much by Quebec as by Canada.

During Laurier's term of office, the Quebec economy experienced an accelerated growth. Although the movement toward industrialization was mostly directed from the outside and activated in Quebec by the Anglophone element, it is possible to date the first decades of this century as those of radical transformation which the traditional lifestyle of the Quebecois had to go through. And it was from the perspective of the problem of the worker that Quebec first faced the consequences of its massive industrialization. There, as elsewhere, the ideology of conservation played a strong role. To prevent the Quebecois from joining international unions, the clergy strongly encouraged the founding of Catholic unions that would protect them from the religious neutrality of the Americans.

In 1911, when Laurier left the government after fifteen years in power, Quebec had changed extensively. In 1871 Quebec was 77 percent rural, but forty years later, it was half urban. Because of its industrial and commercial development, Montreal had attracted many rural people who increased the ranks of labourers and salaried workers. The Anglophone minority continued to hold the wealth and the industrial and financial power. Already, at that time, the Quebecois writer Errol Bouchette earnestly advised his compatriots to invest in industry rather than land; for him, the future of Quebec was in industry rather than agriculture. Bouchette stated with bitterness that a Francophone population of 1,293,000 inhabitants sent only 722 students to university, whereas the English in Quebec sent 1358 for a population of 196,000. Only twenty-seven Francophone students were prepared for scientific careers, whereas there were 250 such students among the Anglophones in Quebec.

Viatte wrote:

> About 1890, one would believe that Canadien literature (Quebecois) was going to die. Conformism becomes conservatism and any type of new wave is censured. The critics deplored in vain "this quasi-inability to produce which results from language difficulties, the absence of graduate schools, the scarcity of books, the general indifference to any question that is a bit enlightened, political chicanery to the death, and from the progressive invasion of the American spirit."

A few years later, in the first decade of the twentieth century, the Literary School of Montreal aroused great hopes. But it was necessary to wait forty more years before the movement really had any momentum.

The encounter between Francophones and Anglophones that was evident during the Boer War in 1899, when the Quebecois refused to participate in an imperialist struggle, continued during the Great War of 1914-18. The question of the Ontario separate schools again aggravated the conflict between Quebec and the rest of Canada. In the Legislative Assembly in Quebec, a deputy minister presented a bill aimed at the withdrawal of Quebec from Confederation; the debates lasted for many days. In the end, the deputy withdrew his bill, the Prime Minister of Quebec, Lomer Gouin, declared himself against withdrawal from Confederation, invoking the fate of the Francophone minorities in Canada and the impossibility for Quebec alone to ensure her economic survival. It was during this period that Henri Bourassa, the grandson of Louis-Joseph Papineau, the leader of the 1837 Insurrection, became the champion of a type of pan-Canadian nationalism. Bourassa pleaded for an international policy that was Canadian and no longer British. Toward 1917, facing the facts as he saw them from the turn of events — conscription for overseas service, persecutions of the Francophone minorities in Ontario — he turned to the study of religious problems and published a book, *Le Pape, arbitre de la paix*, and arranged a big conference on "Language, Guardian of the Faith." His influence on generations of Quebecois was profound and explains certain positions of traditional nationalists who today still gravitate around *Le Devoir* and *Action Nationale*.

During the early post-War years, Quebec continued to industrialize at an accelerated pace. The United States increasingly expanded its economic and cultural hold on Quebec. In 1921, the Francophone population of Canada reached its lowest level ever — 27.9 percent. For the first time in history the urban population of Quebec, 56.01 percent, was greater than the rural population. Montreal had 618,506 inhabitants of whom 63.9 percent were Francophones. Many important industrial centres were developing: Three Rivers, Hull, Shawinigan, Grand'Mère, Chicoutimi, La Tuque. The national resources of Quebec continued to be exploited by foreigners. The lack of capital and technicians further accentuated the domination of the country. In the 1930s, a separatist movement arose which was directly descended from the traditional nationalist movement. The War came to put an end to this movement. Not that the conflict between Francophones and Anglophones was mitigated; as in 1899 and in 1914-18, the majority of the Francophone population of Quebec opposed sending troops overseas. The movement of industrialization and urbanization that was produced by the Second World War was bound to lay the ground for lively days ahead.

A CHARACTERIZATION OF QUEBECOIS IDEOLOGIES 1945-1965

We shall use the definition of a global ideology that was developed in the first part of these remarks to describe and characterize the ideologies of Quebec during the last two decades. In summary, a global ideology is a plan for living which is proposed to a society by one of its subgroups and which aims at expressing the total consciousness of the society and sharing its definition of the situation with the whole of the society. In a complex society, the conflict of ideologies expresses above all the conflict of subgroups which are competing for the majority's acceptance of their theory of society and, ultimately, to govern that society.

The Ideology of Conservation

When the Second World War broke out in 1939, the dominant ideology in Quebec was the ideology of conservation that had begun to develop in the second half of the nineteenth century. The majority of those in Quebec who had taken it upon themselves to define the nation and who had directed collective action had rallied to this ideology. For about one hundred years, the ideology of conservation had been dominant, and the clergy and many of the liberal professions had been its champions. This does not imply that this was the only definition of Quebec that had existed during this century, but other definitions did not gain the favour of the public and did not guide the behaviour of the majority of Quebecois. The clergy and the liberal professions were at leisure to disseminate their ideology since they controlled, for all practical purposes, most of the information media, houses of learning, books, and textbooks. It is also necessary to add that the Quebecois also live in another political entity, that of Canada as a whole; they could and can, if necessary, forget the fact that they are Quebecois and participate in the ideology of Canada. The Quebecois can physically or otherwise escape their nationality and live as though they were Canadians or North Americans. Ideological conflicts cannot be produced for this precise reason. In addition, during all this time national education remained in the hands of the clergy, which was thus able to propagate and impose its own definition of the Quebecois group. How does one characterize this ideology? It defined the Quebecois group as the bearer of a culture, that is, as a group with an edifying history which became a minority in the nineteenth century and whose task it is to preserve this heritage it had received from its ancestors and which it must transmit intact to its descendants. This heritage is essentially composed of the Catholic religion, the French language, and an indeterminate number of traditions and customs. The privileged time of this ideology has passed. At the time when it was worked out, the Quebecois were becoming a minority and risking assimilation. It was to be expected that this ideology therefore idealized the traits of Quebec society in the second half of the nineteenth century when it was effectively Catholic, French speaking, agricultural, and traditional. Threatened with assimilation, this type of society and its principal characteristics were not supposed to change. Thus, it had to be rationalized and justified. This culture was not only that of the Quebecois, but the best culture that had ever existed. This ideology took hold over the years; from the end of the nineteenth century, it was transmitted almost intact to the beginning of the Second World War.

The Laval University sociologist Gérald Fortin has analysed the contents of *l'Action française*, later called *l'Action Nationale*, one of the principal reviews that transmitted this ideology over the course of years. His analysis extends from its appearance in 1917 until 1953 and brings out the principal themes of this ideology of conservation. It phrases the merits of the French language, the Catholic religion, the spiritual culture, the national history, rural life, and the family; it warns of the dangers of English imperialism, industrialization, urbanization, and the means of mass communication; it preaches about buying Quebecois and respect for the two cultures and the Francophone minorities. In the last decade, 1945-53, an interest in economic and social questions is growing and the question of the worker appears in the review. Fortin writes:

> If the ends and the means of the ideology are considered, it may be seen that the goals have not changed; they have been more strongly confirmed as new interpretations of the situation have been worked out.

The Ideology of Contestation and Recoupment

After the Second World War, the ideology of conservation was seriously disputed by another strata of the population: union leaders, intellectuals, journalists, artists, students, and some members of the liberal professions. It is obvious that this form of contestation had its historical antecedents; it can, in many respects, be linked to the liberal tradition. This certainly does not question the fact that Quebec possessed a culture that is different from that of the rest of Canada, the principal elements of which must be preserved but, according to this ideology, the culture must be brought up-to-date. The ideological movement which arose during the Second World War was above all a movement of reaction against the old ideology of conservation. That is, its negative aspect, which opposed the old, was the most nebulous and almost always remained implicit.

It can be said that the ideology and old power structure in Quebec were becoming anachronistic in face of the demographic, economic, and social changes that Quebec went through between 1939 and 1945. Its irrationality was obvious. If, for convenience, we consider the decade between 1939 and 1950, it is noticeable, according to the study by Faucher and Lamontagne, that the labour force in Quebec doubled:

> This increase, in absolute terms, is equal to the growth witnessed during the whole century ending in 1939.... During the period under review, the rate of industrialization in Quebec has been higher than that of Canada as a whole. Since 1939, in volume terms, output of manufacturing industries rose by 92 percent in Quebec and by 88 percent in Canada, while new investment in manufacturing increased by 181 percent in this province and by only 154 percent in the whole country.

Nathan Keyfitz, in his book, shows the movement of the population of Quebec from agriculture to industry:

> During the war and post-war years, the population in agriculture in the province of Quebec dropped from 252,000 to 188,000, a decline of 64,000. This decline more than counterbalanced the steady rise that had been shown from 1901, and hence the surprising result that, although the province of Quebec is almost three times as great in population in 1951 as it was in 1901, it contains fewer men in agriculture. The increase in non-agricultural industry is shown in every one of the thirteen main occupational groups, except fishing and trapping which, like farming, declined sharply. The rise from 79,000 to 237,000 in manufacturing occupations is especially conspicuous.

Thus it appears that Quebec has undergone more important changes on a larger scale during the decade of 1939-49 than in any other decade of its history, except those of the Conquest and the Insurrection. The ideology of conservation which had survived all the other waves of industrialization and urbanization could not successfully resist the last. It must be added that this ideology, which had been dominant for so many years, had largely become inoperative on the level of everyday life. It continued to guide the general policies of the nation, but it no longer directed the behaviour of the more dynamic Quebecois who kept to themselves or withdrew into small groups which worked within other frames of reference. The patriotic societies continued to defend French-Canadian culture (our religion, our language, and our traditions) while the majority of individuals shared a number of core images concerning their nation; others were ideologically integrated into other North American societies, particularly into Canada.

The dispute of this ideology began in the post-War years. Clearly the sociologists and economists in the Faculty of Social Science at Laval University formed the most coherent centre for dispute at the end of the 1940s and during the 1950s. This group adopted reviews, *Cité Libre* is the most obvious example, and movements such as the Canadian Institute for Public Affairs (L'Institut Canadien des Affaires Publiques), which brought together intellectuals, professors, union leaders, journalists, and liberal politicians. Drawing their inspiration from the analyses of economists and sociologists from the Quebecois milieu and from their knowledge of other Western democracies, these movements and individuals undertook the systematic criticism of the ideology of conservation as well as of Quebecois culture.

Some writers have said that the 1950s was a decade when social problems were dealt with, that is, when the problems of the workers were recognized. These so-called social themes were even introduced into the pages of *Action Nationale*, which, as we have seen, had long been one of the most representative spokesmen of the ideology of conservation. Already by 1949, the reverberations that were provoked by the asbestos strike had brought about a realization that Quebec was no longer a traditional society living principally from agriculture, but a society in which the majority of citizens were salaried workers; a few years later, it was said that Quebec society was experiencing a slow proletarianization.

It is quite evident that in criticizing the ideology of conservation and Quebec culture in general, opponents had to criticize not only ideas, values, behaviour, and institutions, but also those groups and individuals who, according to them, were responsible for the global orientations that were influencing the direction Quebec was taking. Quite clearly this was a way of getting at the clergy who had always been responsible for national education in Quebec. Open discussions on education, religion, and the traditional interpretation of our history date from these years. There was bound to be criticism of Quebec Catholicism and those who had narrowed, particularized, and "Quebecisized" its content. This fact is well expressed by Maurice Tremblay:

> Through this attitude of fierce defence against Protestant influences and French modernism, the Church has no doubt succeeded in keeping French-Canadian culture entirely Catholic; unfortunately, it must be recognized that this has been, to a great extent, at the expense of a narrow sterile dogmatism and an authoritarianism rooted in conservatism. On the whole, this French-Canadian Catholicism thus appears to us to be a canned Catholicism, at the rear guard of the radical changes the world is demanding of Christianity. We have here an example of this narrow and unproductive ultra-montanism that the Church has made its right arm in a general policy of conservation and defence of French-Canadian Christianity.

This Church has always sided with the traditional society for which it has been largely responsible, and has wished to preserve itself in the North

American world which is repudiating and overtaking it in every respect. Tremblay further says:

> In effect, in a general manner the Church in French Canada tends to run against the increasing industrialization and urbanization, to maintain the structures and lifestyles of a rural civilization that it can dominate and guide in its own ideal of a religious and Christian life for which it has an obvious nostalgia.

The other power that was strongly attacked by this group who were trying to define the situation throughout this period, is the political power that was embedded in Quebec from 1936 until 1960 through the Union Nationale and its leader Maurice Duplessis. Relying on the population, this party put into practice the ideology of conservation that had been perpetuated in Quebec for many decades.

Acting completely pragmatically and distrusting intellectuals and ideologues, Duplessis implemented the most conservative policies in the name of autonomy and of coarse peasant good sense. In the best vein of traditional conservatism, he carried out a form of personal politics in which everyone knew each other and the prince granted his largesse to the good (those who voted for him) and left the wicked to sink (counties and regions which had shown some opposition). This manner of administering Quebec was an anachronistic as the ideology which inspired it. It included many characteristics of pre-industrial society which tallied exactly with those of the ideology of conservation that had been developed expressly to ensure the preservation of the traditional society which Quebec had been in the middle of the nineteenth century.

The liberal opposition which was made up of partisans of the Liberal Party — and other opponents — took fifteen years to defeat these two powers, political and ideological, which were grafted together and worked shoulder to shoulder to rally a majority of electors. The traditionalists leaned on the two fundamental characteristics of the Quebec situation: the fact that the Quebecois have their own identity that clearly distinguishes them from other North American groups, and a second conviction which is a corollary of the first, the fact that they have remained a people whose culture is still traditional while living in a society that is largely industrialized and urbanized. In conclusion, the ideological opposition prior to 1960 wished to fill the gap that had formed between Quebec culture (ideas, values, symbols, attitudes, motivations) and Quebec society (technology, economy, urbanization, industrialization). This gap between culture and society in Quebec produced a global gap between Quebec and other North American countries. It can be said that those who opposed the regime (ideology and power) in Quebec during the period 1945-60, not only supported an ideology of contestation but also an ideology of recoupment.

In criticizing the delay experienced by Quebec in almost every aspect of human activity, the opponents have above all criticized the elites whom they held responsible for such a state of affairs. What did the new ideologists want for Quebec? What type of society did they want Quebec to become? It is necessary here, from the perspective of the analysis of ideologies, to make certain distinctions. It seems that the critical and negative part of this phase has been the most encouraged, the most systematic, and by far the most varied; this is easily explained. The ideology of conservation and the political powers had idealized Quebec culture to such an extent that it became an urgent necessity for opponents to deflate the balloons that had been blown up over decades. According to those in power, Quebec had the best educational system, the purest religion, the language closest to that of the Louis-fourteenth era, and the most humanist traditions. On top of that was grafted a messianism which wished to make the rest of the world participate in these cultural treasures. According to the opinion that has been attributed to Duplessis, the Quebecois had become improved Frenchmen. It is not surprising that the first task of the post-War opponents was to criticize what Quebec had become and to compare the miserable reality to the fantasmagorias of the elites.

The opponents agreed relatively well over what they opposed, but they were not united in a similar manner over the positive objectives that they laid down for the society which they wished to construct. Furthermore, it seems that when mobilized by combat, they submitted to the rule of force and most of them did not question themselves about the positive aspect of their ideology. Opposition to the regime had brought together many individuals and groups who came from very different backgrounds: Catholic and progressive syndicalists, Catholic action leaders, Catholic and progressive intellectuals, members of the Liberal parties of Quebec and of Canada, and students from various disciplines. It would not be exaggerated to say that because of the history of Quebec and its political and intellectual climate, the only other model of society which the protestors could recognize as comparable was that of other North American societies. The majority of them wanted Quebec to become a liberal democracy, like Washington or Ottawa. Some of them had been influenced by European currents of thought, particularly French, for example, the review *Esprit*, but, for the majority it was the Ottawa model that consciously or unconsciously prevailed. During this period, a number of professors and students from the Faculty of Social Science at Laval University openly sided with Ottawa. The most typical example is that of Maurice Lamontagne who was to rally to Ottawa after 1954. Three of the principal leaders of the post-War opposition movement, Marchand, Pelletier, and Trudeau were to join Lamontagne several years later. Others such as Sauvé and Pepin also entered the Canadian government. Although many opposed the Ottawa regime during the 1950s, it is clear, after the fact, that their preferences unconsciously lay here and that the positive aspect of their ideology was largely drawn from the model of the liberal democracy. We have tried to find articles from this period which expressed the positive aspect of the ideology of contestation. They are very rare. One of the few that we have found is that of Lamontagne to which we will return later.

From the point of view of the global ideologism of Quebec, that which we have taken here, we have laid out three principal ideologies: the ideology of conservation which was dominant for a century and which largely remained intact at the end of the War; the ideology of recoupment toward which most of the opposition of the 1950s would turn; the third, the ideology of development and participation, does not appear to have crystallized until the end of the 1950s. In Hegelian terms, a period of affirmation can be seen in the first ideology, in the second, the negation of the first, and, in the third, the negation of the negation.

The Ideology of Development and Participation
If we examine carefully the issues of *Cité Libre*, an organ of opinion which led the most systematic and coherent fight against the ideology of conservation, it will be seen that this was really a review of contestation against Duplessis, the clergy, the educational system, and many other subjects, but it never developed the positive aspect of its ideology in a systematic manner. At the outset, in 1950 and until the beginning of 1960, it fought against the ideology of conservation; beginning with the 1960s, it began to run up against the third ideology; it was only in 1964 that Pierre Elliott Trudeau wrote what seemed to be the most positive statement that the review ever published: "Pour une politique fonctionnelle." We would like now to characterize this third ideology which *Cité Libre* set itself against in the 1960s.

The ideology of recoupment largely contributed to the discrediting of traditional power elites and the ideology of conservation; essentially, it has directed its criticisms against the Quebecois themselves as a group; that is, it has been concerned with internal criticism. If one could schematize the thoughts of the principal spokesmen of this ideology, they do not seem to cast doubt on the fundamental postulate of the ideology of conservation, that Quebec forms a culture, that is, an ethnic group which possesses certain characteristics of language, religion, and traditions that distinguish it from other ethnic groups in Canada or the North American continent. If Quebec is behind compared to other ethnic groups, it is because of its elites which have misled it into the paths of conservatism, nationalism, chauvinism, and messianism. They now want this ethnic group to acquire a more open culture and ideology and integrate itself into Canadian society: according to Lamontagne, it is a question of a clear integration into Confederation. We thus see that this ideology of recoupment retains, for the most part, the essence of the ideology of conservation in that Quebec possesses a distinct culture and that it must accommodate itself to being implicated with Canada. The essential difference between conservation and recovery lies in the type of culture that Quebec should have. The first ideology is directed toward the past; the second is resolutely turned toward the present; it demands that Quebec culture be brought up-to-date and that it be reflected in the rest of Canada.

The third ideology also retains certain elements of the ideology of conservation in that it recognizes that Quebec possesses a different culture from other North American groups. Together with the ideology of recoupment, it recognizes that the elites of the past have perverted this heritage, that this culture and the ideology of conservation have become anachronistic, and that Quebec must move smoothly into the twentieth century. It recognizes that the lag between the social structure of Quebec and its culture must be filled. But the resemblance with the other ideologies ends there. It reaches back across the years to rejoin the first ideology of Quebec, before Confederation and even before Union. Quebec is not only a culture, that is, an ethnic group which possesses certain differences of language, religion, and traditions, but is a society that must be self-determined and gain its own independence. Now, because this ideology is set in the second half of the twentieth century and because Quebec has become an industrial society, it must, as any other industrial society, control its economy and polity. For the holders of this ideology, there can, therefore, be no question that Quebec should integrate itself with other societies such as Canada.

How do we explain the birth and development of this ideology? It could be suggested with some justification that it is written into the line of our traditional ideologies. But that is not the complete answer. The adherents of the two ideologies do not come from the same strata of society. The traditional nationalists or the liberals of the ideology of recoupment do not seem to have become, for the most part, partisans of the third and most recent ideology. Other groups in the population who have become active since 1960, workers, members of co-operatives, white-collar workers, teachers, civil servants, and students are the most active contributors to the development and diffusion of this ideology. It is true that there are several strata of the population who were already beginning to make their presence felt in the ideology of recoupment, but other strata have become more important and others, such as the newly unionized, are tending to subscribe, often implicitly, to this new definition of Quebec society.

In a phenomenon as diffuse as the birth of a new ideology, it is difficult to follow all the stages precisely. The criticism to which Quebec society has been submitted since the end of the last War has not happened without heartrending anguish and profound disequilibrium in a population which traditionally "was in quiet possession of the truth." The most firmly established truths, the most diffused myths, were attacked by more and more individuals and subgroups. Finally, in 1960, what has rapidly become known as the Quiet Revolution began and the time came to change the ideological climate of Quebec in a global manner. From the point of view that we are taking here, that is, of an ideology concerned with the theory that groups advance of their own accord, it is certain that one of the first effects of 1960 and the reforms that followed was to reaffirm the image that many Quebecois held of themselves and their society. One did not willingly boast about being a Quebecois during the dark years. To dethrone Duplessis, it was necessary to attack and to denounce all those teachers, politicians, and professional elites who were responsible for the fact that Quebec was the only feudal state "north of the Rio Grande." The day that more and more Quebecois realized that they could collectively escape from their rut, was the day that they acquired a taste for change and began to redefine themselves, set new goals for themselves, and seek the means to reach them. The ideology of recoupment, which wished to bring Quebec onto an equal footing with the rest of North America, served as a generator of many new policies and reforms. Now, in the same way as in the sixties it was a problem for the people of Quebec to progress to another stage of thinking and development, so the means available to do this and the direction that this reform should take could not be the same as those which had been used many decades ago by the Anglo-Saxon democracies of North America — the societies to which Quebec was catching up.

There had previously been independentist movements during the Duplessis regime. Although the new generation of independentists admitted almost all the critics who had been opposed to the state of Quebec society, they went further than the *Cité Libre* criticism and asked whether many of the problems of Quebec did not come from the fact that it had always been a dominated society; this explained the narrowing of their culture, their economic inferiority, and their morbid fear of losing their identity. They were thus exposing themselves to external criticism. And because on a worldwide scale there was increasing talk of decolonization and of national liberation, these terms quickly came to be used and new goals were set for the collective action of the Quebecois. From the beginning, however, these new movements split into two major factions: those who, like the Alliance Laurentienne, on the whole accepted the definition of the Quebecois group that the ideology of conservation had established; and those who, like Raoul Roy's *Revue Socialiste*, began to give another definition of the Quebec nation. The first more traditional group placed itself in the line of ideological choices that Quebec had known for decades; the second group was to define the ideology of development and participation which will now be discussed in greater detail.

On account of the homogeneity of the Quebecois and their culture (setting aside the Anglophone minority), the political options of Quebec since Confederation and the frame of reference of all political parties has always oscillated between certain more or less rightist tendencies. However, a considerable consensus has always existed between liberals and conservatives on the principal political options. It is still striking today to note that the differences between the partisans of the Union Nationale and of the Liberal Party are quite minimal. The *Journal des Débats* of the Quebec Legislative Assembly gives the impression of a group whose ideas are interchangeable, who share the same values, and whose members are as thick as thieves. Often the only difference that separates them is the width of the corridor between the party in power and the opposition. Their differences are in tendencies rather than in doctrine. It is only recently that a more important cleavage has appeared between the left and the right. This phenomenon is so new in Quebec that at first it was said that these terms had no place in the political vocabulary of the nation since they did not correspond to any reality. Referring only to the members of the Assembly, it is quite evident that these terms do not mean very much. But with the third ideology which has appeared in the past few years, the terms right and left are beginning to refer to an increasingly clearly marked reality. Certainly, on the one hand, the Quebecois have not reinvented socialism, Marxism, self-management, state planning, or participatory democracy, but, on the other hand, it is also evident that the logic of the present situation has motivated them to take inspiration from these ideas to resolve problems that are demanding their attention in a very real way. It seems certain that it is above all the ideas of decolonization and national liberation that have awakened echoes among those who were troubled over the destiny and future of their nation. The phenomena of decolonization and of national liberation, which could be found in many nations of the world during the fifties, brought with them ideas of the good life and the good society, of the role of the economy, and of social classes which were the same as those in the nineteenth century when the bourgeois classes of most Western nations undertook their national revolutions. Thus all these ideas finally reached a small part of Quebec youth who became aware that they could be applied to their own situation. But in explaining the development of ideologies in Quebec the influence of an international convergence must not be exaggerated; it is rather a case of a primarily local aid to phenomena that are the outcome of several decades of history. It must not be forgotten that the three ideologies are superimposed on each other and that they possess characteristics creating a chain of which the links are closely interrelated. The radical falling out of the third ideology is to a large extent developing away from a common understanding about Quebec society.

What precisely is this third ideology? It could be said that the three Quebecois ideologies are not mutually distinguishable and that there is no question, as some could believe, of a seesaw game between political parties. Let us first say that the distinguishing characteristic of the ideology of conservation is to consider the Quebecois group as a cultural minority within Canada; this group is largely centred in Quebec but has offshoots in other provinces. All these groups constitute the bearers of the French-Canadian culture (religion, language, and traditions) that must be preserved and transmitted as intact as possible over the generations. The ideology of recoupment also considers the French Canadians as a minority group spread across the country who must modernize their culture throughout that nation; this is a modern version of the ideology of conservation. There is here a difference between conservatives and liberals: the first want more autonomy for Quebec to ensure the conservation of its culture; the second want Quebec to become more integrated into Canada in order to profit from the advantages of the modern state while still preserving and enriching its culture and allowing it to spread across Canada.

The third ideology seems to be the most radical and from the beginning it was more strongly differentiated from the first two than these are differentiated from each other. It breaks from the other two by defining the Quebecois Francophone group not only as a culture but as a modern industrial society which has been dominated economically and politically by the rest of Canada; it ceases to speak of French Canadians and speaks of Quebecois. For most of the people holding this ideology the minorities outside Quebec participate in French-Canadian culture but not in Quebec society. Of primary importance is that the Quebec nation be saved and liberated. This ideology is in accord with the ideology of recoupment in its fight against the ideology of conservation and in thinking that Quebecois culture must be modernized but not necessarily taking North American societies as models. In effect, the greatest mutation that this ideology represents in comparison with the others is that it develops a different idea of man and society in general, and of Quebecois man in his society in particular. It is here that we return to the Quiet Revolution and the international context in which it came into being.

Not only did the ideology of recoupment borrow its model of a good society from Canadian society, but it can also be said that the ideology of conservation was largely inspired by the same source. These two ideologies, one of which was dominant for many years and the other, long in a minority position, established itself after the Second World War, have both developed a kind of symbiosis with the dominant culture. It can be said that they borrowed from it their dominant ideas on the subject life in society; that is, according to these ideologies, of a more or less developed capitalism which, however, fitted well with the philosophy of American society. The ideology of conservation has preserved or acquired some concepts derived from certain social encyclicals and from certain rightist dictatorships (Spain, Portugal) but, at its base, the model remained that of the so-called liberal democracies. In the 1950s nothing could predict that the upsetting of the Duplessis regime would result in this third ideology. Observers predicted that the ideology of recoupment, shared by the members of the Liberal Party, would become predominant and would take over from the ideology of conservation. But it happened otherwise.

But the independentist movements which had begun to arise again at the end of the fifties did much to attract attention to the idea of domination of one society by another. Still for many it was the question of political independence that was to facilitate the cultural expansion of Quebec. But the logic of the Quiet Revolution as carried out by the liberals must not be underestimated. Not only did their slogan of *Maîtres chez nous* contribute to the reinvigoration of Quebec and the Quebecois in their own eyes, but it also contributed to the launching of reform in the two major problem areas of Quebec both on the national level and on the economic level. It has also helped to link these two objectives which have tended to exclude each other: the national objectives remaining the prerogative of the right and the socio-economic objectives being traditionally those of the left. The task of catching up was initiated through a modern civil service, extensive reforms in education, nationalization of electricity, the S.G.F., conseil d'orientation économique, régime de rentes, caisse de dépôt et de placement, and the B.A.E.Q. The Liberals, through their dynamism, succeeded in interesting large sections of the population in their reforms (educators, civil servants, students, and underdeveloped regions), and kindling among them the desire to participate in this Quiet Revolution.

From an ideological point of view, challenging society and its myth quickly made the Quebecois aware that far from having built their society in its final form in the nineteenth century, it still remained to be built. Part of the population quickly came to see Quebec as a developing nation which not only removed them from their past conservatism but also differentiated them from other North American societies. This is another characteristic that brought them closer to colonized countries on the road to liberation and development. However, as opposed to countries that had developed in the nineteenth century and in the first decades of the twentieth century, the nations of today which are in the first phases of industrialization, or, like Quebec, are behind in relation to highly industrialized countries, have many models of development at their disposal. Even the concept of development no longer has the exclusive economic meaning that it acquired at the time of the triumph of capitalism. Not able or not desiring to entrust the problem of developing society to industrial entrepreneurs or financiers, the nations which are today on the path to development or who consider themselves to have already achieved it, must count on the state and on their whole population in order to reach their objectives.

In Quebec there are many intellectuals, youth, members of unions and co-operatives, and social activists who have realized that for the Quebecois to attain their desire of becoming *maitre chez eux*, there must be planned socio-economic development and the establishment of a participatory democracy. The underdevelopment of Quebec, the relative homogeneity of the population, the exacerbation of national opinion, and the shallow roots of liberal democracy in Quebec have all encouraged the diffusion throughout the population of ideas of development and of participation. The powerful Quebec labour movement and the entry of new strata of the population into the unions give this ideology of development and participation great potential.

Must it be added that these ideologies are presently being disputed? Nothing definite has been achieved and there does not seem to be any way of predicting which of the three ideologies will become dominant in the near future. This should soon develop into a struggle between the two most recent ideologies, that of recoupment and that of participation.

Has the Quiet Revolution Finally Ended?

Ramsay Cook

The year-end assessments of public life in Quebec were more unenthusiastic, even pessimistic, than any in more than two decades. "La plus longue session de l'histoire n'a pu que sonner la fin des illusions," the parliamentary correspondent of *Le Devoir* captioned his article. While much of the problem was blamed on the Lévesque government, some commentators thought that the malaise went much deeper. Playing his accustomed role of prophet, this time of doom, Pierre Vallières wrote perceptively: "Once their institutions, the social framework of their value system had been deconfessionalized then nationalized by the technocratic post-Duplessis petite bourgeoisie, [Quebeckers] put all their hopes in the State, its nationalism and its leaders. Alas, these latter were invested with neither a mission nor divine charisma." There lies the crux of the matter: having replaced the Church by the State as the center of their hopes and their value system, having rejected a religion-centered nationalism for a secular nationalism, Quebeckers have now found that salvation is no nearer. Quebeckers even show signs of losing faith — for a second time.

If Vallières seems a tendentious witness his views find some confirmation in a recent meeting of some fifteen hundred teachers of French language, Quebec literature and culture. Their topic was "Langue et Société au Québec." Their discussions were characterized by pessimism or realism, rather than by the nationalist visions and rhapsodies about cultural flowering. "The great debates on nationalism and the constitution no longer attracted them," a reporter observed. "There were many more participants in the workshops on poetry, the novel and standards, than on the constitution or Francophonie." There can be no doubt that a remarkable change has taken place in the tenor of debate in Quebec.

Nearly twenty years ago the late George Ferguson, editor of the *Montreal Star*, decided that events were moving so rapidly in his province that something should be done to provide English Canadians with reliable estimates of the direction Quebec was taking. Being a journalist, Ferguson naturally gathered other journalists from across Canada to hear some frank, off-the-record comments by eight prominent Quebeckers. Looking back on that "Seminar on French Canada," whose deliberations were recorded, I was struck by several things.

Ramsay Cook, "Has the Quiet Revolution Finally Ended?" *Queen's Quarterly* (Summer 1983), pp. 330–42. Reprinted by permission of the author.

One was how right Ferguson had been in his belief that English Canadian journalists needed help. The superficiality, and even prejudices, expressed by many of the country's senior journalists, commentators and editors was quite astonishing. But they must certainly have benefitted from Ferguson's shrewd choice of speakers, each one of whom was moving from the margin to the center of the discussion of the future of Quebec, and Canada. They included André Laurendeau, then editor of *Le Devoir* and soon to be co-chairman of the Royal Commission on Bilingualism and Biculturalism; Gerard Pelletier, then editor of *La Presse*, subsequently one of Lester Pearson's "Three Wise Men"; Arthur Tremblay, an academic soon to be Deputy Minister of Education in Quebec; Guy Rocher, a sociologist who played an important role in educational and cultural matters in both the Lesage and Lévesque governments; Marcel Faribault, president of the Trust General du Canada and later Robert Stanfield's failed French lieutenant. Finally there was René Lévesque, then Jean Lesage's Minister of Natural Resources, restless, volatile and already a skilled public performer.

Reading the speeches the Quebeckers delivered it is hard not to be impressed by their patience, their firmness and their essential moderation. Perhaps only Faribault, the big businessman and Lévesque, the politician, proposed anything that verged on the radical. Faribault advocated some quite substantial shifts in constitutional power from Ottawa to Quebec. Lévesque was more interested in the uses of that power, specifically for the promotion of Francophone participation in Quebec's economy, a goal which would require increased state intervention.

But whether moderate or radical, each speech was informed by a palpable sense of optimism about Quebec's future and the equally strong conviction that as Quebec changed, Canada would have to change, too. Lévesque, fresh from his triumph in the debate over the nationalization of hydro and therefore the architect of the "maitre chez nous" slogan, provided the best illustration. As always he was engaging, disorganized and rambling. But his point was clear enough:

> Another thing very true in the circumstances and very significant. . . . is the parallel that should be established between the developments in education and the hopes raised by progress, albeit dishevelled at this time — the progress in education and economic problems in the one hand, and on the other the need of accelerated development on three bases — there are others — but these three seem to me essential: increased employment through secondary industry, the development, the transfusion if you will, of new blood into the far off and underdeveloped areas; the French Canadian ownership of the economy. All of this because there is currently occurring under our very eyes an avalanche which will keep on increasing in the sense of progress.

Repeatedly Lévesque emphasized the point that it was not so much a matter of the government leading the people into a bright future as it was of the government being pushed by a nation on the march toward a progressive new society. And he was equally emphatic about the power behind this march of progress and the danger of resisting it. To achieve the goals he believed were essential Lévesque maintained that

> nationalism cannot be avoided nor can the use of the collective strength of the nation be avoided. The question is to use it as much as possible, because no one is ever sure of controlling it, no one can actually control this force. The job is to try to point toward a logical, rational, tolerant way, in a way that will accept the existence of other men. But the other men, the neighbours around us, men of a different cultural group, should not purposely and negatively excite this nationalism. The best way to excite this nationalism is to oppose and systematically block it.

In a general fashion, and perhaps unintentionally, these passages come very close to defining one of the central goals of the Quiet Revolution. That revolution was to transform Quebec materially and intellectually into a modern, dynamic, secular society. The purpose of that transformation was not merely to provide individual Quebeckers with more satisfactory lives. It was something more: it was to strengthen the collective foundations of French Canadian culture, or as Lévesque preferred, "French Canadian Nation," and later the "Quebec Nation." (It is worth noting that Lévesque has always identified the Quebec nation with the Francophone majority.) In that 1963 speech, Lévesque made it clear that while he expected his goals could be achieved within Confederation — revised version — the prospect of a separate Quebec nation — if nationalism was blocked — held no terrors for him. What he had in mind was using the state to rebuild the nation, the Quebec nation. While that objective — making state and nation coincide in Quebec — may not have been fully accepted or even understood by all of Lévesque's colleagues in the Lesage government, that nevertheless was one of the principal thrusts of the Quiet Revolution. Of course the Quiet Revolution had many other aims, aims which during the Lesage years from 1960-66 often seemed primary. These included educational reform, the building of a provincial welfare state, planned economic development, revision of labor laws, and reform of the electoral system. All of these projects were tackled and some of them very successfully. While the transformation has been far from smooth and is more complete in some areas than others, Quebec has become a society where secular rather than religious values govern the lives of its people and set the standards of public life.

But equally important for some Quebeckers was the goal which to them seemed the pre-condition of full success in all other policies: the building of the Quebec national state. That goal seems as far from achievement as ever and I would like to suggest some reasons why that is so.

By 1967 Lévesque, once so optimistic about the progressive flow of events, concluded that the Liberal bus he had boarded in 1960 was running out of gas. The provincial Liberal party which, at his insistence, had separated itself from its federal counterpart, now refused to take the next step and adopt a constitutional policy that would have demanded almost complete statehood for Quebec. Moreover the federal Liberal party, reinforced by the recruitment of Marchand, Pelletier and Trudeau, was determined to halt, if possible, the step-by-step identification of the French Canadian nation with the Quebec state. Lévesque concluded that a new vehicle — one specifically committed to the establishment of a Quebec national state — was required. And so dissident Liberals and various brands of separatists came together to found the *Parti Québecois*.

For Lévesque, and those who supported him, including many who were still undecided on the independence question, the purpose of the PQ was to revive the reformist impulse of the Lesage years, to launch once more the Quiet Revolution, and bring it to completion. A mere eight years and three elections brought the PQ from the political wilderness to political power, a tribute to Lévesque's political skills and the respectability of the team he recruited. But it is as well a comment on the political ineffectiveness of Robert Bourassa's Liberals and the instability of an electorate in a province filled with social turbulence.

On 15 November 1976 Lévesque seemed on the verge of achieving his cherished aim: making the nation and the state conform in what he had called a "logical, rational, tolerant way." But Lévesque and his ministers knew that getting over the last hurdle would be rough and demanding. Or to put the same point more directly, they knew that the majority of Quebeckers, even a large majority, were either firmly opposed to independence or at least still unconvinced of its merits. The PQ had been elected on a promise of good government leaving the sovereignty-association question to a referendum. No doubt the new government was aware from the beginning that success in governing well might prove a double bind. On the one hand it would prove that a PQ government was honest and competent, capable of governing without disruption. In short, that its credentials to govern a sovereign state were in order. But "good government" might also prove that sovereignty was unnecessary. That perhaps was the lesson of the PQ's most controversial and important piece of legislation — Bill 101, the Charter of the French Language. The passage of that Bill, early in the PQ government's first term, meant that Quebec could become virtually unilingual. If that was so, was there any point in pressing for sovereignty? Since the PQ program admitted that Quebec needed Canada in an economic sense, Bill 101 seemed to demonstrate that Quebec already had cultural sovereignty. What would political sovereignty add?

Moreover, since Bill 101 was designed as a socio-economic as much as a cultural measure, its success may have had another negative effect on the drive for sovereignty. By making French the principal language of business in Quebec those middle class Francophones who had always been the backbone of the independence movement discovered that their social mobility was greatly improved. As English-speaking professionals and business people left the province — or refused to move in because of the restrictive provisions of Bill 101 (and the high tax rates) — more jobs opened up for Francophones. While head offices left Quebec in fairly large numbers, the regional offices which remained became almost totally French in their operations. For the upwardly mobile the potential disruption of separation had less and less appeal, especially since it appeared to offer so few additional tangible benefits. The federal government's refusal to challenge Bill 101, as the Anglophone minority in Quebec kept demanding, prevented the PQ from using the language question as a weapon in the fight for sovereignty.

When the date of the much postponed referendum finally arrived in the spring of 1980, the Lévesque government had established a record of solid, honest government. But it had not proven that radical constitutional changes were necessary. Moreover, in making sovereignty an issue over which political parties warred, Lévesque turned the national question into a partisan issue. (He tried to avoid this by defining the referendum as a contest between two "non-political" committees, but no one was fooled by that strategem.) Lévesque had hoped that the issue would be non-partisan so that he could attract at least a substantial majority of Francophones to his banner. But that proved impossible, especially since the PQ leaders were unable to prove that they alone had the interests of Quebec at heart. Trudeau and Ryan made certain of that.

But what the referendum campaign also revealed was that since the 1960s Quebec politics had become increasingly complex. While Lévesque had spoken in 1963 of nationalism as a force which could galvanize all Quebeckers into rebuilding the nation, the situation had become something different. While nationalists like Lévesque saw Quebec mainly in terms of French and English, the reality was far more complicated. At the heart of the new nationalism — indeed about all that made it new — was a bureaucratic middle class: public servants, parapublic employees, school teachers, CEGEPS teachers, university professors, and members of the cultural elite for whom state subsidies, salaries and cultural promotion in general was a direct benefit. To this core the PQ had worked hard — and fairly successfully — to add the support of organized labor. While the bureaucratic middle class might see both material and psychological benefits in sovereignty, working people had little interest in psychological pay-offs and were at least uneasy about the possible economic consequences of sovereignty. Nevertheless it was from that coalition that Lévesque received his quite respectable forty percent of the referendum vote in May 1980. And those who had deserted him on the referendum returned somewhat unexpectedly to the fold to give Lévesque an election triumph in 1981.

But the election of 1981 completed the transformation begun in 1976, and pushed along with the referendum: a transformation which changed the PQ from a nationalist movement into a nationalist political party. And it transformed Lévesque from *un chef* into *un boss*, or we might say, from a nationalist leader into an ordinary politician. In the process the project of making state and nation coincide in Quebec has received a serious setback. The PQ's strategy fell into disarray, its constituency, including some of its most ardent militants, grew confused and angry. And there are reasons.

First, in the battle over the constitution the Lévesque government lost so completely as to be truly astonishing. It lost because the strategy it followed was poorly devised by the Clausewitz of Quebec strategy, Claude Morin, who subsequently was sacrificed. But Lévesque executed the strategy very ineptly. The strategy had only one goal: the paralysis of the process of constitutional change in order to prevent the federal government from fulfilling the promise of constitutional renewal which the Prime Minister and several provincial premiers had made during the referendum campaign. To reach that goal a common front of provinces had to be formed and kept together. In order to form that common front the Lévesque government had to accept a proposal for amending the Constitution which made Quebec a province just like the others — Quebec having no veto. That contrasted with the federal proposal under which Quebec and any other province, or group of provinces, with twenty-five percent of the population would have a veto over constitutional change. That strategy worked for several months with Lévesque and Morin gambling heavily on the willingness of their English Canadian allies to stay out in the cold forever. But in the end Lévesque himself destroyed the common front. The day, in front of national television, that he unthinkingly jumped to accept a challenge by Prime Minister Trudeau that the constitutional issue be put to a referendum, he deserted his allies. The common front broken — the other premiers did not want a referendum, but more important Lévesque and Morin had taken this new position without consulting their allies. This left the other provinces free to act on the realization that Lévesque had never wanted constitutional agreement at all. They therefore moved to work out a compromise position which was acceptable to the federal government and every provincial government except Quebec, a compromise that left Quebec without the veto it would have had under the original federal proposal.

Lévesque returned home empty-handed, but uttering such powerful rhetoric about betrayal that he excited his own troops far more than he had planned. Early in 1982, after his militants had decided that sovereignty without association was the only answer, Lévesque had to put his resignation on the line in a party referendum which he won at the cost of considerable disaffection among his followers. Even worse, perhaps, was the evidence that most Quebeckers believed that he was wrong to reject the new Constitution. Then came the next defeat: in the appeal to the courts to restore Quebec's so-called veto, the Quebec government's position was unanimously rejected in the Quebec and federal courts. Left without a veto or a constitutional strategy, Lévesque was in the embarrassing position of being unable to blame anyone but himself for Quebec's position. In a public letter, dated 25 November 1981,

Prime Minister Trudeau had reminded the Quebec premier of an uncomfortable truth: "Between the year 1971 and November 5, 1981 every government that I have presided over has favoured an amending formula which would have assured a veto to Quebec." The lost referendum of 1980, the misguided constitutional strategy of 1981 and the court decisions of 1982, left the Lévesque government's constitutional position in tatters. And worse, it has left Quebec in a weaker position in the Canadian federal system than at any time since 1960. Immobilized by its own defeats the Lévesque government, in the judgment of one of its former advisors, Daniel Latouche, "stands the risk of joining the government of Adélard Godbout in the unenviable category of the only two governments which have done nothing to advance the cause of autonomy for the Quebec political system."

Officially, of course, the Lévesque government has a new strategy: namely, to make independence, with or without association, the principal issue in the next provincial election. Lévesque, as cautious a revolutionary as the world has ever seen — at least since Louis-Joseph Papineau — is known to be uneasy with that strategy, but it is the price he had to pay to get his party back in line after his defeat at the constitutional conference. His unease is doubtless at least partly explained by his recognition that the strategy has not won much support outside of the ranks of his militants. Perhaps typical of the new mood of scepticism about current PQ strategy is the comment of Lise Bissonnette, editor-in-chief of *Le Devoir* and a supporter of an affirmative vote in the 1980 referendum. On 22 December she wrote that it was no time to be playing Russian roulette with Quebec's future; that the decision of May 1980 had to be accepted. "The only real question for now is the search for a way of giving back to Quebec its political weight by reorganizing its internal coherence, undermined by the aftermath of 1980 and more recently by major social conflicts. That requires exactly the opposite of the impatience which agitates the Parti Québecois, and which seems to win over the premier tempted to try a last chance referendum before passing the reins to a successor. Quebec does not change as easily as the seasons."

Bissonnette's reference to recent "major social conflicts" is an appropriate introduction to a second illustration of the way that the PQ has been transformed from a nationalist movement into a mere political party in the eyes of its clientele. One of the PQ government's successes after 1976 was in restoring social peace to the province. Even the business community, innately suspicious of the PQ, admitted this achievement. It had been labor turbulence, more than anything else, that defeated the Bourassa government in 1976 and Lévesque had capitalized on that very successfully. But the price Lévesque paid for maintaining peace, a price he doubtless hoped would produce an appreciative affirmative vote in the 1980 referendum, took the form of substantial wage increases in the public and parapublic services. The recent recession, the growing government deficit and its declining credit rating, has made it impossible for the Quebec government both to remain solvent and to pay the salary bill. Consequently, for many months the government attempted to re-open collective agreements to negotiate wage reductions. When those negotiations ended in failure the government pushed through legislation unilaterally altering thousands of collective agreements. These changes — *décrets* as they are called — included not only three-month wage reductions of up to twenty percent in some cases, but also involved much else: hours and conditions of work and employment status. In the case of teachers, for example, salaries have been reduced, course loads, class sizes and teaching hours increased. Positions once classified as permanent have now become impermanent again. The full impact of the thousands of pages of *décrets* are still not clear. What is clear is that Quebec has moved into a period of labor relations at least as unsettled as at any time in the past.

Whatever economic justification the government had for its action — and if justified it was partly because of earlier generosity by the same government — the political cost is potentially very high. The 325,000 employees directly affected by this decision include the core of the PQ support in the past: people who expected to benefit directly either from the PQ's nationalism or its apparent commitment to social democracy. Moreover the roughshod fashion with which the government has trampled on legal collective bargaining agreements and, during the debate, attempted to make unions the scapegoats for Quebec's economic ills, will certainly damage the bridges which the PQ painfully constructed to the labor unions generally. Here is how one activist who had worked for the Party since its foundation described her reaction to recent developments:

> The authoritarian tendency has always been present in the Parti Québecois. Until last year it was possible to counterbalance it by the more progressive forces. The defeat of the idea of independence in the referendum, in the constitutional negotiations and in the courts, and the economic crisis have acted to reveal the force of this tendency. Those among us who have dreamed of the birth of an independent and democratic Quebec state can no longer support the Parti Québecois. We have said many times: not just any sort of independence.

That same view was put in a more extreme — and graphic — fashion, at the founding convention of a new political party late in 1982. It is a socialist party whose future is probably no more promising than the several other parties of that sort that have appeared and disappeared since 1960. Yet it attracted many of the kind of people — trade unionists, students, feminists, and assorted radicals — who since the late sixties have been on the PQ side, somewhat uneasily. They cheered loudly when their leader, Marcel Pepin, the former president of the Confederation of National Trade Unions, told them that the great hopes of November 1976 had been dashed, every battle lost, the economy in a shambles. "The Quebec nation?" he declared, "A project always brought forward too late. The PQ has buried independence. It has buried sovereignty-association. It has buried hope. But it has disinterred one thing: the statue of Duplessis. In the field of cultural policy, that is unquestionably its most spectacular achievement. The only monument built in six years of power. It disinterred the statue first. Then the ideas. Finally, the actions. It has invented nothing, but only drafted a new chapter in our history, a chapter entitled neo-duplessisme."

Actors, like poets, are less given to rhetoric. Jean Duceppe, one of Quebec's best known and accomplished actors, star of *Mon Oncle Antoine*, PQ activist and one-time candidate, gave this short summary of his views. "We have been diddled by the PQ."

The fact that such voices of disenchantment have risen from the normal areas of PQ support make them especially significant, though they are still only straws in the wind. But the wind is strong and cold. On 9 December 1982, a public opinion poll reported that eighty percent of Quebeckers believed that things were going badly in their province. Only eighteen percent expressed confidence in their political leaders. Two weeks later, on the sixth anniversary of the PQ's first election victory *La Presse* reported a poll showing that fifty-one percent of voters favored the Liberals — a party without a leader — while only forty-five percent supported the Parti Québecois. By March 1983 the Government's own poll reported that support had fallen to twenty-four percent; an independent survey put the figure at nineteen percent.

The PQ constituency is disintegrating and the issue of national independence is receding into the background. The optimism that marked the beginning years of the Quiet Revolution has dissipated, replaced by what one sixties radical calls "Le Québec Morose." Why has the mood changed, and more important why has the project of making state and nation coincide gone off the rails? There are many reasons.

One obvious fact is that since 1968 the federal government has effectively, and to a considerable degree successfully, challenged the claims of the Quebec government that it alone represented the aspirations of French Canadians. Whatever its other failings, the Trudeau government has demonstrated to Quebeckers that French Canadians can make a powerful impact on policy-making at the federal level. The outcome of the longest political poker game in our history is not yet settled. But those Quebeckers who have played the federal hand these last fifteen years have made sure that not all of the high cards have been dealt to the separatists.

Whatever cards the PQ held, and they included some good ones, they were not played very well. That party's strategy, rational as it may have appeared, was perhaps self-defeating. *Étapisme* — the policy of sidestep-by-sidestep — took too long, and the sovereignty issue became mired in more prosaic though not less important issues. Once in office, as recent events have emphasized, the PQ had to take the blows and bruises that every government experiences in difficult times. But the bruises were more disfiguring, because the PQ had promised so much.

But there is also the possibility that the stakes in the poker game changed. This is only an hypothesis, but it is worth examination. Twenty years ago Raymond and Albert Breton, a sociologist and an economist, made a somewhat cursory examination of nationalism in Canada and especially in Quebec since 1918. For the French Canadians they concluded that the most important stimulus to nationalism was neither dislike of English Canadians nor dissatisfaction about Canada's constitutional arrangements — though it often expressed itself in those terms. Instead, they argued, nationalism in Quebec was rooted in the rigidities of a social structure which, at some times more than others, inhibited social mobility. The removal of those rigidities allowed French Canadians to move more easily up the ladder of social success in business, the public service and politics. With the decline of social tensions, nationalism also moderated.

Here perhaps lies a large part of the explanation for what Dominique Clift has called *Le Déclin du nationalisme au Québec (The Crisis of Quebec Nationalism)*. As the result of changes in the law — the Official Languages Act at the federal level, Bill 101 at the Quebec level — and changes in attitude, French Canadians have, over the past fifteen years achieved a more equitable share of powerful positions in both government and business in Quebec and, to a lesser degree, in the country at large. As legitimate personal ambitions were fulfilled, national grievances attenuated. Nationalism declined.

In this altered atmosphere the René Lévesque who spoke so confidently about the expanding role of the Quebec state in 1963 has had to adopt a new rhetoric. The rhetoric of retrenchment characterized the Inaugural Speech with which he opened the National Assembly in March 1983. Though he reaffirmed his belief in the cause of Quebec independence, the main burden of his message was the need to re-evaluate the role of a state which had become "heavy," badly in need of a "slimming cure." His promises included the abolition of ministeries and government agencies, decentralization, and tax reductions. The spirit, if somewhat less than the letter, of Reaganomics. Catching the mood of these scaled-down ambitions, one commentator drew a remarkable parallel with contemporary France, whose Gaullism in the past had inspired the Quebec independence movement. "Speaking in Paris the same day [as Lévesque's Inaugural Speech] President Mitterrand traced the precise and brutal limits of French sovereignty, as old and proud as it is. France in Europe, France in the Atlantic bloc, is certainly not totally tied down, but the lines are such that cutting them would be suicidal. The tool of sovereignty, at the present time, does not create a magic margin, even if it allows literary devices. The truth in Paris is the truth in Quebec." Obviously the time seemed one for epitaphs more than for new beginnings.

So far as the Quiet Revolution encapsulated the project of making Quebec the national state of French Canadians, it appears on the verge of complete failure. It is failing because it has proved unnecessary. This is not to argue that nationalism in Quebec is a thing of the past, or even that the Parti Québecois will soon dry up and blow away. Neither is true. But what does appear to have happened is that insofar as the Quiet Revolution met the individual needs of French-speaking Canadians for a more equitable distribution of the wealth and power of Canada, it also undermined the claim that national sovereignty was the only genuine road to equity and security. In that sense, then, the Quiet Revolution was both a failure and a success.

3
THE MARITIMES

Author's Note from *Each Man's Son*

HUGH MACLENNAN

Continents are much alike, and a man can no more love a continent than he can love a hundred million people. But all the islands of the world are different. They are small enough to be known, they are vulnerable, and men come to feel about them as they do about women.

Many men have loved the island of Cape Breton and a few may have hated her. Ericson was probably the first to see her. Cabot landed on her, and after Cabot came the French. She seemed harsh and frigid to the first-comers, but the moment the French saw her their imaginations were touched and they called her the Royal Isle. After a while they built on her eastern rim the master fortress of Louisburg to dominate Nova Scotia and guard the St. Lawrence.

When the wars began, the English and the New Englanders came up to Cape Breton and for a time she was as famous as Gibraltar. Louisburg fell, the French were driven out, the English and Americans went home and for a third of a century the island was vacant again.

Then across the ocean in the Highlands of Scotland a desperate and poetic people heard of her. They were a race of hunters, shepherds and warriors who had discovered too late that their own courage and pride had led them to catastrophe, since it had enabled them to resist the Saxon civilization so long they had come to the end of the eighteenth century knowing nothing of the foreman, the boss, the politician, the policeman, the merchant or the buyer-and-seller of other men's work. When the English set out to destroy the clans of Scotland, the most independent of the Highlanders left their homes with the pipes playing laments on the decks of their ships. They crossed the ocean and the pipes played again when they waded ashore on the rocky coast of Cape Breton Island.

There they rooted themselves, big men from the red-haired parts of the Scottish main and dark-haired smaller men from the Hebrides, women from the mainland with strong bones and Hebridean women with delicate skins, accepting eyes and a musical sadness in their speech. For a long time nothing but Gaelic was spoken in the island until they gradually learned English from the handful of New England Loyalists who came to Nova Scotia after the American Revolution.

Hugh MacLennan, "Author's Note," *Each Man's Son* (Toronto: Macmillan of Canada, 1951), pp. vii-ix. Reprinted by permission of Macmillan of Canada, A Division of Canada Publishing Corporation. Also used by permission of Russell & Volkening, Inc. as agents for the author. Copyright © 1951 by Hugh MacLennan.

Author's Note from *Each Man's Son*

To Cape Breton the Highlanders brought more than the quixotic gallantry and softness of manner belonging to a Homeric people. They also brought with them an ancient curse, intensified by John Calvin and branded upon their souls by John Knox and his successors — the belief that man has inherited from Adam a nature so sinful there is no hope for him and that, furthermore, he lives and dies under the wrath of an arbitrary God who will forgive only a handful of His elect on the Day of Judgment.

As no normal human being can exist in constant awareness that he is sinful and doomed through no fault of his own, the Highlanders behaved outwardly as other men do who have softened the curse or forgotten its existence. But in Cape Breton they were lonely. They were no part of the great outer world. So the curse remained alive with them, like a somber beast growling behind an unlocked door. It was felt even when they were least conscious of it. To escape its cold breath some turned to drink and others to the pursuit of knowledge. Still others, as the Puritans of New England had done earlier, left their homes, and in doing so found wider opportunities in the United States or in the empty provinces of western Canada.

But if the curse of God rested on the Highlanders' souls, the beauty of God cherished the island where they lived. Inland were high hills and a loch running in from the sea that looked like a sleeve of gold in the afternoon sun. There were trout and salmon streams lined by sweet-smelling alder, water meadows and valleys graced by elms as stately as those in the shires of southern England. The coast was rugged with gray granite or red sandstone cliffs, splendid with promontories, fog-bound in the spring when the drift ice came down from Newfoundland and Labrador, tranquil in summer, and in the autumns thunderous with evidences of the power of the Lord.

So for several generations the Highlanders remained here untouched, long enough for them to transfer to Cape Breton the same passionate loyalty their ancestors had felt for the hills of home. It was long enough for them to love the island as a man loves a woman, unreasonably, for her faults no less than for her virtues. But they were still a fighting race with poetry in their hearts and a curse upon their souls. Each man's son was driven by the daemon of his own hope and imagination — by his energy or by his fear — to unknown destinations. For those who stayed behind, the beast continued to growl behind the unlocked door.

Daniel Ainslie was one of those who stayed. In the year 1913 he considered himself a freethinker, a man who was proud because he had neither run away nor sought a new belief in himself through hard liquor. But he did not know — how many of us can understand such a thing — that every day of his life was haunted by a sense of sin, a legacy of the ancient curse.

Even when he tried to find strength by denying God's existence, he lived as though the hound of heaven were snapping at his heels. Even when he displayed his knowledge and intelligence as a priest displays his beads, he felt guilty because he knew so little and was not intelligent enough.

In one way or another he was forced to discover, as most of us do, that a man can ignore almost anything in his life except the daemon which has made him what he is and the other daemon which gives him hope of becoming more than any man can ever be.

An Atlantic Region Political Culture: A Chimera

J. MURRAY BECK

In September 1977 Premier Alexander Campbell of Prince Edward Island told Atlantic Canada that it had not even yet made the decision to develop as a region. "We are four separate, competitive, jealous and parochial provinces. We fight each other for industrial development. We fight each other for subsidiaries and we bicker about energy and transportation. And too often, the lines of battle are drawn on purely political grounds or selfish local considerations." Turning more specifically to attitudes, the premier pointed out that the Atlantic provinces "do not have a regional identity; we do not have regional bonds... Our only common rallying points are poverty and a regional inferiority complex, self-destructive negative attitudes, and too often a belief that everything from away is better or that Ottawa has all the answers, all the power and all the money." Premier Campbell's basic conclusions were much like those of S.T. Wood of the Toronto *Globe* who, 66 years earlier, had argued that the "familiar entity, the Maritime Provinces, is entirely a western [he meant an Ontario] creation and has no existence down by the sea." A trip to these provinces had convinced him that their separate institutions, set and hardened by time, yielded only slowly to "the great transformations of life, [and] cannot be fitted to new and artificial decisions."

Between 1911 and 1977 all sorts and conditions of men, residents and non-residents, social scientists and non-academics, have accepted the existence of a Maritime (or Atlantic) region as a fact of life. For some academics the recognition of such a region fits nicely into their scheme of things. If, in conducting a national survey, they are forced to limit the size of their sample to stay within their budget, they may find it necessary to group the Atlantic provinces in order to secure statistically meaningful results; or, if they are compiling statistics relating to the geographical divisions of Canada, their work may be simplified if they need to provide only four or five rows or columns per table rather than ten. Obviously, however, an Atlantic region ought not to be a contrivance based on convenience or budgetary considerations. Recently I have attempted to show that, unless the criteria of a region are to be taken simply as geographical propinquity, likeness in historical and

---

J. Murray Beck, "An Atlantic Region Political Culture: A Chimera," in Bercuson and Buckner (eds.), *Eastern and Western Perspectives* (Toronto: University of Toronto Press, 1981), pp. 147–68. Copyright © 1981 University of Toronto Press. Reprinted by permission of the author and the publisher.

population background, and similarity of economic problems, the Maritime provinces — and, for the same reasons, the Atlantic provinces — do not constitute a region in any meaningful way. Certainly they do not meet the requirements of the political scientist that the adjacent parts of a region should not only differ in character from other entities in the political organism but also be capable of being treated as though they were a political actor; nor those of the sociologist who sees a region "as part of a national domain ... sufficiently unified to have a consciousness of its customs and ideals and thus [possessing] a sense of identity distinct from the rest of the country"; nor those of the planner who defines a region in terms of a set of problems and then estimates the degree of regionalism by the capacity to respond jointly to them. This paper will examine the attitudes towards politics that characterize each of the four Atlantic provinces — their political culture if you will — as a preliminary to understanding the failure to produce a regional political culture and the characteristics of a genuine region. It will start by looking at the internal political attitudes of Nova Scotians and use them as a point of departure for comparison with those of the residents of the other Atlantic provinces.

By general agreement, Nova Scotia is characterized by attitudes fostering conservatism and the maintenance of the status quo. Some social scientists couple these attitudes with a reverence for the value of British institutions and a fondness for an ordered hierarchical society, and attribute them to the United Empire Loyalist cultural fragment. My own view is that the influence of the Loyalists has been exaggerated, in Nova Scotia at least, and that once they established themselves their attitudes towards politics did not differ all that much from those of the pre-Loyalists. I am equally skeptical about viewing the struggle for responsible government in Nova Scotia as rooted in the rivalry between the non-Loyalist immigrants' "desire for greater social equality and the hierarchical aspect inherent in the Loyalist tradition." For the purpose of this essay, however, it is sufficient to accept Professor Rawlyk's view that the political culture probably congealed in the 1840s or 1850s, and that the prevailing attitudes tended to persist because of a largely stagnant population having little in-migration to influence it.

In Nova Scotia, as in the other Atlantic provinces, this resistance to change has militated strongly against the erosion of the tradition that anything goes in politics. Thus the Civil Service Act of 1935 was simply a front under which the government of the day continued to make appointments on the basis of patronage while boasting of its purity, and the merit system for permanent civil servants only became firmly established after World War II. To this day, government purchases and the use of trucks in highway construction remain subject to the old practices. As in the other provinces east of the Ottawa River, the bribery of voters, which at one time allegedly dragged "many of our leading citizens down to the level of gangsters," continues, although generally on a reduced scale. Though it is probably not very harmful to the body politic for "little old ladies" who always vote the same way to expect chocolates or perfume from their favourite poll worker, the unabashed resort to the buying of votes in important contests has thrown the entire electoral process into disrepute....

The conservatism inherent in the political institutions also manifests itself in the phenomenon that the province's first political parties, which appeared in a nascent state as early as 1836, are still the only ones capable of winning a general election. A third party had its greatest success in the provincial election of 1920 when, through a combination of distinctly unusual circumstances, the Progressives — a combination of the United Farmers of Nova Scotia and the Independent Labour party — elected eleven members to the Conservatives' three. Normally, however, Viscount Bryce's description of American political parties might well be applied to the Liberals and Conservatives of Nova Scotia: "[they] now continue to exist, because they have existed. The mill has been constructed and its machinery goes on turning, even when there is no grist to grind." Until at least World War II whole families of Nova Scotians maintained "with a sort of proud tradition an unbroken history as partisans for generations ... Political issues may have changed, leaders may have changed and the party may have gone utterly wrong in the interval, it matters not. The old party traditions have gone on and its adherents have remained serenely blind." Because the circumstances surrounding confederation established the Liberals as the majority party, the strong adherence to party ties enabled them to establish a stranglehold over the province which has only recently been weakened. One rather remarkable outcome is that, until the defeat of Gerald Regan in 1978, no party leader since confederation who had once won an election subsequently lost one. Nonetheless, Nova Scotians usually had the feeling of participating in genuinely competitive politics since the Conservatives normally polled about 40 per cent of the popular vote even though the vagaries of the electoral system gave them few seats.

Since 1945 the traditional adherence to party has weakened somewhat and the winds of political change have blown more freely, partly because of greater urbanization, larger movements of people within the province, and increased in-migration. The altered circumstances permitted Robert Stanfield to lead the Conservatives to their first victory since confederation under non-crisis conditions in 1956, and later to establish a personal dominance over the province. Any shift in the traditional vote seems to have gone mainly to the Conservatives. The New Democratic Party (NDP) continues to be largely hived in the industrial part of Cape Breton County where special factors in the decades around the turn of the century — industrialization, a substantial influx of population, and politically oriented trade-union leadership — made it unique in Nova Scotia and have permitted the Co-operative Commonwealth Federation (CCF) and the NDP to have the only electoral successes they have ever enjoyed in the Maritime provinces....

... The NDP still labours under the handicap of having an explicit philosophy — and democratic socialist at that — in a province whose politics is basically pragmatic. Both old-line parties emphasize that paternal legislation is not the remedy for economic and political ills and that a government ought simply to create conditions under which the citizenry can work out its own destiny. This is the closest that either comes to having a philosophy, but "it is at least flexible enough to permit a government to meet the needs and desires of a small community which is not characterized by a sharp conflict of interests."

Recently, in my study for the Nova Scotia Royal Commission on Education, Public Services, and Provincial-Municipal Relations, I suggested that "there now appears to be a somewhat greater resilience in the political culture than might be expected" and that "rational proposals, presented in a form that is intelligible to the ordinary Nova Scotian — far-reaching though they may be — have a much greater chance of acceptance today than at any previous period in provincial history." But the commission's report started out by laying rough hands on the municipal units, many of them going far back into the last century, and it has apparently been discarded as a political albatross. Robert Stanfield, who read the Nova Scotian psyche as well as anyone, followed two maxims in making changes: first, to bring them about piecemeal so that each step was digested in turn and, secondly, to ensure that new or increased taxation was directly connected in the public mind to a new service of which it approved. The first permitted massive changes in temperance legislation; the second allowed hospital insurance to be adopted with scarcely a flurry on the political scene.

New Brunswick, which is somewhat less industrialized than Nova Scotia, exhibits even more the characteristics of a non-urbanized, rural society in which conservatism and traditionalism are dominant. The abolition of patronage has not proceeded as far as in Nova Scotia, and politicians conduct themselves on the principle that elections are not won by prayers. More than in most jurisdictions, but much as in Nova Scotia, the defeat of a government is usually a vote against the party in office. Thus, in the last change of government in October 1970, which brought Richard Hatfield and the Conservatives to power, New Brunswickers were voting for neither a charismatic leader nor an attractive program. They were just using their undeniable prerogative to vote not for but against something. For these reasons, Professor P.J. Fitzpatrick of the University of New Brunswick has described the province's politics as "parochial, stagnant, and anachronistic." The nature and working of the party system account for much of this dismal conclusion. Though the Liberals and Conservatives do not have distinct, coherent philosophies and both are treated with cynicism between elections, the conservatism of New Brunswickers works against their recognizing a practical alternative. . . .

While hereditary voting has decreased somewhat, though probably not to the same extent as in Nova Scotia, ethnic voting has increased. In a real sense there are two New Brunswicks based on ethnic lines and almost meriting the description "two solitudes." To the south of a line drawn from Grand Falls in the northwest to Sackville in the southeast the generally more affluent and better educated Anglo-Saxons predominate, while to the north francophones constitute a strong majority. Although once passive politically, the Acadians have recently become much more assertive. Before 1900 they tended to vote Conservative, but in this century the majority have followed the Québécois into the Liberal camp. In contrast, English-speaking voters, who had previously preferred the Liberals, moved to the Conservatives, although less markedly so....

... Seemingly many New Brunswickers are obliged to follow ethnic rather than political imperatives in their voting, but the phenomenon is not as simple as it once was now that more and more francophone voters realize, and the politicians know they realize, that they can use their king-making power to redress their inferior position in the New Brunswick scheme of things.

In Prince Edward Island the common features of the Atlantic political culture or cultures tend to be exaggerated because of the smallness of the community. An all-pervasive conservatism permitted a unique, but altogether outdated, franchise and representation system to survive until 1963, and its vestiges still remain. The act that in 1893 abolished the Legislative Council let each of the province's fifteen districts elect a councillor on a property qualification and an assemblyman on an unrestricted franchise, both to sit in the same assembly. Because non-residents could vote in any district in which they held the requisite property, all sorts of anomalies and irregularities developed and some islanders spent election day moving from district to district, seeking to cast votes. Even when the assembly eliminated the property franchise in 1963, it let each district elect an assemblyman and a councillor, and hence permitted retention of the convention that specific assembly or council seats were the preserve of one religious group. As Marlene Clark has suggested, "the only way to end this convention would be to terminate the practice of pairing candidates on separate ballots."

No less marked is the island's traditionalism in its hereditary political loyalties. According to Professor Frank MacKinnon, to some islanders "being a Liberal or a Conservative [attained] almost religious significance," and anyone outside the fold became "a political heathen." Most observers agree, too, that the erosion of traditional voting on the island has not proceeded as far as in the neighbouring provinces. Its voters have always been satisfied with their pragmatic old-line parties and have shown even less inclination to support third parties than those of Nova Scotia and New Brunswick....

Not surprisingly, the politics of a small, poor, and dependent province is in some respects a "politics of acquisition." Thus island voters make sure, sometimes by anticipation, that their provincial government is of the same complexion as the federal, the best guarantee, they think, of their remaining the fortunate beneficiary of Ottawa. Similarly party adherents expect that, within the limits of practicality, a provincial government of their own party will allocate limited resources to its own and their advantage. Much as in Nova Scotia and New Brunswick, voters call upon party workers to "grease their palms" or "quench their thirst." ...

Highly revealing of Prince Edward Islanders' attitudes towards political action has been the experience with the P.E.I Development Plan. Despite extensive public relations activities it proved highly difficult to "plug" islanders into the policy process. Liberal adherents among the grass roots grudgingly accepted the plan, but perceived it only in vague, general terms as having something to do with economic and social improvement; Conservative supporters tended to regard it as another threat to the island way of life. Apparently few in either party had a genuine desire to "participate in meaningful political activity of any kind, let alone in an activity as esoteric, vague and uncertain as development planning."

Because of the paucity of survey data and the failure, in some cases, to provide a breakdown by province, the general attitude of Maritimers towards the political system may best be summarized collectively. Several studies have demonstrated that adults and adolescents in all three provinces are less convinced than other Canadians that their governments can be trusted, or that the voters can influence them, to do the right thing. Coupled with these harsh attitudes towards the political system is an equally unfavourable view of politicians. One study showed that 45 per cent of New Brunswickers believed that "quite a few" in government were crooked and that Nova Scotians were not far behind in professing the same opinion. But in equating the mentality of Maritimers who are "patient and willing to wait for spoils ... from political jobbery and favouritism" with that of wreckers who profit from ship disasters by seizing their cargoes, Professor Bellamy perhaps goes too far. Also to be treated with caution are the limited data which suggest that the political knowledgeability of Nova Scotians and New Brunswickers is exceeded only by that of Newfoundlanders. The surveys, it should be emphasized, made no attempt to measure sophistication in political knowledge, but concerned themselves mainly with the identification of specific politicians in which, for at least two reasons, residents of the Atlantic provinces might be expected to do well. Not only is the profile of politicians high in small, largely rural communities, but in political systems where patronage is extensive, "the politician probably becomes better known than in a society where universalistic, bureaucratically administered programs are of primary significance in the operations of the state." Quite congruent with their ability to identify politicians although completely out of keeping with their high level of cynicism and their low level of trust and efficacy, Maritimers have a greater involvement than Canadians as a whole, as expressed for instance in voter turnout. Perhaps, as Professor Bellamy suggests, electoral and voting participation is simply "a ritual or social activity" which Maritimers carry on with little reference to the affairs of state, or, put in another way, "a kind of game that has been continued from generation to generation, not for any great good that is expected from it, but for personal amusement and entertainment."

Newfoundland's past makes it politically distinctive in more than a few respects. Except for a relatively small number of Scottish merchants who settled in St John's, the bulk of Newfoundland's population came in the late eighteenth and early nineteenth centuries from Ireland and the English West Country. While out-migration was pronounced in later years, Newfoundland was to receive no other large influx of settlers, and by 1857 90 per cent of the population was native born. To a large extent the cultural background of the Irish and English shaped their responses to the new environment and to each other: "for the Irish brought with them a national heritage of poverty, Roman Catholicism, and hatred of their English oppressors; while the English brought with them from the west country a heritage of puritanical Protestantism, social deference, and semi-feudal economic relationships." In these differences lay the seeds of social conflict in the new environment.

The Irish (and hence Catholics) constituted a great majority in St John's and the east and the Protestants elsewhere, but the populations of the outports tended to belong exclusively, or almost so, to one religious faith. This phenomenon tended to facilitate the accommodation of sectarian differences, worked out — as became the practice in Newfoundland politics — by élite consensus. One outcome was a system of education that was, and continues to be, church controlled, in which Roman Catholic, Anglican, United Church, and Salvation Army schools, supported by per capita government grants, are the primary units. Even today a Catholic teacher who marries an Anglican risks dismissal. As late as 1955 the electoral map was drawn so as to ensure that Catholics, Anglicans, and non-Conformists were likely to elect the same number of assemblymen. "In Newfoundland affairs, most issues still carry some degree of religious overtone, and secularism comes slowly."

Yet, on the whole, class interests have overshadowed sectarian interests. Until recently dwellers in the outports existed in a feudalistic type of relationship in which they sold their fish to merchants, mostly based in St John's, receiving credit in return but little in the way of money. Because it symbolized the harsh realities of the "truck" system, Water Street, the centre of the merchants' operations in St John's, was regarded with utter distaste. Indeed, according to Professor Noel, much of Newfoundland's history "may be viewed as a struggle between those who sought to preserve the existing economic system by maintaining and exploiting existing social cleavages and those who sought to bring about social and economic changes by persuading the majority of the people of the paramountcy of their common class interests."

Momentous changes have occurred in outport living during the past three decades. Federal social service payments introduced a steady influx of cash, large trawlers replaced the smaller fishing boats, and governments undertook programs to eliminate or consolidate the smaller outports and to introduce a greater measure of industrialization, hoping, in Joseph Smallwood's words, to drag Newfoundland "kicking and screaming into the twentieth century." As a result, the forces of urbanism and industrialism have been eroding the traditional, subsistence, outport economy, and the political culture has been moving towards that of those parts of Canada with a similar economic structure. Accordingly, Professors Neary and Noel have pictured Newfoundlanders as being "in a half-way house between two economies and two styles — the traditional and the modern." Some observers like Harold Horwood and Farley Mowat have lamented the abandonment of the serenity and the country values of the outports for "the fantasies of the factories and the offices of Upper Canada." But when they described the typical outport as "a haven of contentment in a world of confusion, strivings, nervous prostrations and jungle warfare," Fred Rowe had a simple reply: "balderdash."

Largely because of social and economic factors, Newfoundlanders were not in a position until recently to develop "a very deep understanding of or attachment to democratic values." The province has had its populist, reformist politicians — Edward Morris, William Coaker, and Joseph Smallwood — but forces of conservatism inherent in the economic and demographic characteristics of the society have tended to undermine the basis of their popular support. The quiet acceptance of commission, non-elective government between 1934 and 1946 illustrated the fact that "there was much in their history that had conditioned Newfoundlanders, especially those who lived in the tradition-bound outports, to expect authority to flow from above." The Smallwood domination of the province is equally illustrative; indeed, it has been suggested that "his standing with the electorate was such that one might well look to the third world rather than the other Canadian provinces for a suitable standard of comparison." Contributing to his success were his public-speaking techniques which, although they may have appeared vulgar and simple-minded to some sophisticated residents of St John's, were extraordinarily effective in the outports, partly because they were highly entertaining, and partly because they resorted to the re-echoing of a few simple facts and ideas.

No less significant was his role as distributor of the federal largesse which in a real sense transformed Newfoundland life even as it consolidated his hold on office. Under him federal politics became an adjunct of provincial politics, and he the chief federal as well as provincial leader. . . . Party organization and party meetings, except at election time, had no place in the Smallwood scheme of things; he did not need them and they did not conform to his approach to politics. . . .

But despite the increasing modernization of its institutions, Newfoundland is simply moving from a pre-industrial society to one more closely resembling those of the Maritime provinces, and like theirs, its political culture is basically conservative. The Liberal party quickly established itself after

1949, while the Conservatives, as anti-confederates, were initially hived in the Avalon peninsula which had stoutly resisted union with Canada. Once they developed support elsewhere, however, the political battles became joined between them and the Liberals, and other parties came to be regarded as intruders. The absence of radicalism in Newfoundland politics may seem all the more surprising since its per capita income is the lowest in Canada and its unemployment rate invariably the highest. But, as Professor McCorquodale points out, "in the context of the Newfoundland political culture there is no place for a mass party with a progressive philosophy; to many outport voters, at least until recent years, it was almost presumptuous to question what the 'big fellows' were doing." Yet although Newfoundlanders are reluctant to try a new brand of politician, survey material indicates that 50 per cent of them think their government is extremely wasteful and 42 per cent regard politicians as basically crooked. Perhaps even more than in the Maritimes, electoral corruption and patronage still abound, although recently the civil service commission has made considerable headway in introducing the merit principle in permanent appointments. In allocating government resources, however, there is still "a tendency to spend in accordance with the self-interested needs of the politically successful."

Other aspects of Newfoundland's political culture distinguish it from the remaining provinces. The most British of all Canadians, Newfoundlanders have great respect for British institutions and symbols, and at the time of the flag debate Premier Smallwood declared that no matter what the Canadian parliament did the Union Jack would remain the provincial flag. Before 1949 a well-developed Newfoundland nationalism existed, based partly on folk-heroes and epic events in its history, but the increasing integration of the province into the Canadian community has apparently weakened the place of this form of nationalism in the political culture and relegated it largely to the area of traditional ballads and folklore. Yet the Quebec example and Ottawa's failure to cope with the province's economic distress may have rekindled it in 1977.

Perhaps more than that of any other province, Newfoundland's political culture is also characterized by "the persistence of attitudes supporting factionalism," which Professor Bellamy attributes partly to the Irish fragment in the political culture and partly to the struggle to obtain the "limited good" in a society where resources are scarce. Most unique of all is the preservation over many years of self-images which are, in fact, myths. One relating to "rural fundamentalism" is illustrated by Joseph Smallwood's references to "the great yeomanry, the great peasantry, the great farming class, the great countryside class, the great outport class ... socially and politically the soundest people of any country." A second pictures Newfoundland as a potential source of vast wealth, indeed, another El Dorado, and was a key to the electoral success of Edward Morris, Richard Squires, and Joseph Smallwood. "For each, the means of unlocking the land's wealth has been to give it to outside capitalists, often along with generous guarantees and government absorption of risks," but always with limited success at best.

Some political scientists have considered the patterns of values, beliefs, and attitudes towards government and politics in Nova Scotia, New Brunswick, and Prince Edward Island as sufficiently alike to constitute a Maritime province political culture, but have chosen to treat Newfoundland's political culture as something quite distinctive. It is at least arguable, however, that the political values, beliefs, and attitudes of the four provinces are similar enough to posit a regional political culture; and it may be most arguable of all that there exist four provincial political cultures marked by many common values, beliefs, and attitudes.

None would deny that Newfoundland, in its exodus from pre-industrial society, has moved steadily in the past three decades towards the type of society characteristic of the Maritime provinces. Clearly, in their pro-British attitudes, the conservatism and rejection of radical politics, their toleration — if not approval — of patronage and electoral corruption, their cynical attitudes towards politicians and the political process, their ability to identify politicians and their high turnout at elections, and their apparent lack of desire to participate meaningfully in political life above the municipal level, Newfoundlanders bear a striking resemblance to Maritimers. In their general satisfaction with out-and-out pragmatic parties, they are also like Maritimers and, according to the general thrust of this article, the phenomenon in all four provinces is natural in conservative political cultures that have long congealed. Recently, Douglas McCready and Conrad Winn have shown that, much as the departments in the south of France, the economically disadvantaged peripheral areas of Canada, unlike the affluent peripheral areas, find it difficult to spawn parties of the left, but even they admit that, at best, this provides only a partial explanation of the lack of success of third parties in Atlantic Canada. In their attitudes towards the federal authority Maritimers and Newfoundlanders differ only in degree. While a cynic might say that both Maritimers and Newfoundlanders look upon Ottawa as an inexhaustible milch cow upon which to make unrelenting demands, they would reply with one voice that it is of the very essence of federalism that a federal government should take action to reduce disparities in provincial per capita incomes and to ensure that all the provincial entities may provide much the same level of social, educational, and developmental services. Without minimizing the emotional tie of patriotism, the major glue binding the Atlantic provinces to the Canadian federation is that of utility, although there is something of a difference between the old and the new. In the Maritimes, which have long recognized that they have hitched themselves permanently to the Canadian federation, alienation no longer proceeds to the point of a serious threat of separation. But this glue has not hardened nearly as much in Newfoundland, even though it is the greatest financial beneficiary of the federation, and during the economic difficulties of 1977 its premier talked of drawing up a comprehensive balance sheet to discover if the losses of confederation had not exceeded its gains.

Yet, simply because residents of the Atlantic provinces share common values, beliefs, and attitudes, it by no means follows that there is a common Atlantic or even Maritime province consciousness, or that Atlantic province residents see themselves as having a sense of identity distinct from that of the rest of the country. As far back as 1911, S.T. Wood wrote: "One meets plenty of Nova Scotians, New Brunswickers and Islanders, and may meet some who make no claim beyond Antigonish or the Annapolis Valley. But no one ever claims to be a man of the Maritime Provinces." Later studies offer no clear-cut evidence that these attitudes have changed markedly....

The story of interprovincial activity is equally negative in suggesting a regional consciousness. Painting a bleak picture of Maritime prospects, the Deutsch commission in *The report on Maritime union* (1970) found that the most serious threats facing the three provinces were continued slow economic growth and a continued inferior level of participation in the economic and political life of Canada. Putting it bluntly, the *Report* told Maritimers they were confronted with starkly contrasting alternatives: either to maintain "local attachments, local diversities, local autonomies, small scale relationships, and the existing structure and pace of life," or to achieve "a more rapid rate of economic development in order to raise average living standards and to provide more adequate employment and career opportunities." If they decided to give a higher priority to the second alternative, they had no choice but to "establish immediately a method of co-operation which would envisage the attainment of full political union as a definite goal." At first sight Professor Deutsch and his associates appear to have had good grounds for their basic recommendation since an opinion poll they had commissioned showed that 64 per cent of Maritimers favoured political union. But they were much more optimistic than they ought to have been for a variety of reasons. The survey provided no inkling of the intensity of the respondents' feelings towards political union. Indeed, posed as the question was, it might have been seen as eliciting support for virtue against evil and, most significant of all, it asked for the respondents' opinion almost in a vacuum. Would, for example, the respondents have given the same reply if they had realized that the capital of the new province might not even be within their original province? Perhaps it was inevitable that the Deutsch commission should go astray since its leading members were an outsider who did not fully appreciate grass-roots attitudes in the Maritimes and a technocrat with an exaggerated view of the goodness of his finely laid plans. In any case Premier Gerald Regan of Nova Scotia, an excellent interpreter of public attitudes, could say after four years that Maritime union was "as dead as a door nail... Integration, yes... unification, no."

Perhaps Maritimers display their co-operative attitudes to better advantages in less grandiose matters. A specialist in this area, Professor Richard H. Leach of Duke University, has shown that over time "a spate of Maritime or Atlantic regional bodies and programs were developed, until by 1969, virtually every field of provincial activity was involved in one or more Maritime interprovincial relationships." In confirmation, the Institute of Public Affairs of Dalhousie University identified 181 active organizations in which senior governmental officials and private citizens throughout the Maritimes influence and are influenced by co-operative activity, and Guy Henson, its director at that time, suggested that this "whole complex of voluntary provincial activity... constitutes an identifiable, distinctive, and apparently unique regional life of the Maritime or Atlantic Provinces."

Nonetheless, Professor Leach himself warns that evidence of this kind reveals little of the attitudes prevailing at the grass-roots level; indeed, he believes that the concept of Maritime interprovincial co-operation is grasped only by governmental administrators, not by the people or their assemblymen. In his view neither the provincial parties nor pressure groups have "yet fully accommodated themselves to a co-operative pattern and still frequently work at cross-purposes with similar units across provincial boundary lines." He even plays down the kind of co-operation that occurs among the top civil servants because it often takes place through annual conferences held at resort centres where the social side predominates, and because the agenda of the conferences are so full they tend to become "more reporting sessions than occasions for the discussion and evolution of co-operative relationships." Most telling of all is his conclusion that these activities have been primarily incremental in their practical effects, "concerned... with small adjustments and minor accommodations and seldom with the potential of a really bold and original intergovernmental action."

If further evidence were needed of the lack of a will to co-operate meaningfully, it is provided by the Council of Maritime Premiers, intended by the Deutsch commission to play a major role in planning for political union, but relegated instead to promoting the integration of services. Since its establishment in 1971, it has produced a complicated maze of committees, agreements, codes, policies, and "even that ultimate 20th century mark of institutionalization — its own logo!" Its misfortune, as I have written elsewhere, is that it has been unable to develop a backbone. Undoubtedly the council has had some successes, but they have been qualified and limited — as the provincial premiers themselves admitted as early as 1972 — because integration is difficult in fields where there are "important vested interests in existing machinery and in established ways of doing things"; consequently success has occurred only in matters that have "not seriously challenged the political process in each province." Thus, even though the common centre for police training associated with Holland College in Charlottetown has been handicapped because of the failure of the Halifax police force — the largest in the area — to co-operate, the Nova Scotia government has apparently put no pressure on the Halifax civic authorities to alter their stance. Premier Regan was unable to say nay to the influential agricultural interests in his province which opposed the establishment of a common veterinary college in Prince Edward Island and wanted it in Nova Scotia, even though the Maritimes might lose it as a result. Most divisive of all was Nova Scotia's intervention in October 1977 in a hearing of the National Energy Board on an application to build a liquefied natural gas terminal using Algerian gas at Lorneville near Saint John. When Nova Scotia argued that the Strait of Canso area was a more suitable location for the plant, Premier Hatfield lamented that "this kind of intervention revives the policy of cut throat competition when co-operation among provinces . . . is essential."

If the Maritimes have only a limited will to co-operate, the inclusion of Newfoundland lowers it further. From the beginning that province turned thumbs down on any suggestions that the Council of Maritime Premiers should be a council of Atlantic provinces. Although the four governments may unite to press Ottawa to deal more effectively with financial and economic disparity, it is not uncommon for them to speak with discordant voices. Thus Newfoundland, believing it had a better legal case, refused to make common ground with the Maritimes on offshore mineral rights, while New Brunswick remained aloof from Nova Scotia and Prince Edward Island on energy questions because their problems were substantially different.

Outsiders who are surprised at the Atlantic provinces' unwillingness to accept major changes to improve their position in the Canadian federation fail to appreciate that for over two centuries the people of these provinces have developed such an attachment to their own political entity, its capital, and its institutions that they look with suspicion, even hostility, upon attempts to tamper with them. Though it took no little time for the provincial capitals to establish their hegemony over the scattered out-settlements, once it was established the provinces' residents turned to their provincial governments as the source of benefits, in the beginning for expenditures on roads and bridges, later for a growing multitude of other services. More and more they rated their premier by his competence in safeguarding their interests. Hence arises the difficulty of his making concessions to his fellow premiers even if it is simply a question of arranging "trade-offs," and the more political he is the less he is likely to engage in genuine co-operation. The outcome is inevitable: to New Brunswickers and their premier, for example, Halifax, Charlottetown, and St John's were almost as much foreign capitals as are London and Washington.

The traditionalism and conservatism of the four provinces reinforce their reluctance to establish strong attachments broader than the provincial; so do the rural values which are highly significant throughout the area. Because the Atlantic provinces generally have not undergone modernization, there is little of the cultural homogeneity which is marked by the appearance of those patterns of belief and behaviour common to all industrial societies; still prevalent in all four provinces is the fragmented particularism that is characteristic of non-industrialized societies. Because distinct provincial identities and loyalties constitute so important a feature of the political culture, I think it is highly misleading to talk and think in terms of a Maritime or Atlantic provincial culture. It is much more meaningful to recognize the existence of four provincial political cultures having many values, attitudes, and beliefs in common.

4
ONTARIO

To the Avon River Above Stratford, Canada

JAMES REANEY

What did the Indians call you?
For you do not flow
With English accents.
I hardly know
What I should call you
   Because before
I drank coffee or tea
   I drank you
   With my cupped hands
And you did not taste English to me
   And you do not sound
   Like Avon
   Or swans & bards
But rather like the sad wild fowl
   In prints drawn
   By Audubon
And like dear bad poets
   Who wrote
   Early in Canada
And never were of note.
You are the first river
   I crossed
And like the first whirlwind
   The first rainbow
   First snow, first
   Falling star I saw,
You, for other rivers are my law.
   These other rivers:
   The Red & the Thames
   Are never so sweet
To skate upon, swim in
   Or for baptism of sin.
   Silver and light
The sentence of your voice,
   With a soprano
Continuous cry you shall
   Always flow
   Through my heart.

To the Avon River Above Stratford, Canada

The rain and the snow of my mind
Shall supply the spring of that river
   Forever.
Though not your name
Your coat of arms I know
   And motto:
A shield of reeds and cresses
   Sedges, crayfishes
The hermaphroditic leech
Minnows, muskrats and farmers' geese
And printed above this shield
One of my earliest wishes
"To flow like you."

Is There an Ontario Identity?

ROBERT DRUMMOND

It has become a truism of Canadian studies that Ontario's identity is clearer to those who live outside its borders than it is to its own residents. In western Canada, it is Ontario that people regularly have in mind when they speak of "the East" in tones of grievance over the financial and political dominance of that region. (Westerners generally express alienation not from the country as a whole but from Ottawa and Toronto.) In the Atlantic provinces, Ontario is often given the pre-Confederation name of Upper Canada — a title bestowed with some irony, suggesting that the people of the province consider themselves not only up-river but up-scale. When they consider their fellow citizens in the Maritimes, it is implied, they look not only down the St. Lawrence but down their noses as well. However, in 1968, when historian A.R.M. Lower addressed the question "Ontario — does it exist?" his answer was a resounding no. He argued that Ontario's capacity for a unique identity was impaired both by diversity within the province and by the erosion of any early distinctiveness through the forces of urban and industrial growth.[1]

Peter Oliver, a historian specializing in the study of Ontario, has found little in the literature or geography of the province to provide its inhabitants with a sense of place. He concurs with geographer John Warkentin's observation that Ontario lacks overwhelming natural features that could "grip the imagination and serve as points of orientation or as a means of identification, for the people who live there."[2] From the perspective of his own discipline, Oliver asks whether Ontario's identity remains to be discovered (or perhaps forged?) from a closer examination of the province's history.

Canadians who have been subject to seemingly interminable discussions of national identity may be forgiven if they doubt the wisdom of extending those discussions to cover *sub-national* areas. However, it is an important question in the comparative study of societies whether the people living in any definable geographic area or political jurisdiction comprise an integrated society; and social identity may be an important element of that integration.

Identity has been described as a "detailed structure of self-attitudes," and it has been observed that such attitudes may contain references to one's nation or province.[3] Such references in a definition of self presumably reflect a recognition of similarity with one's co-residents (and difference with outsiders) sufficient to define a significant boundary for one's national or provincial group. Of course such characteristics may be differentially visible

---

Robert Drummond, "Is There an Ontario Identity?" was specially commissioned for this book.

within and without the group, and the significance of the boundary may differ accordingly. Allan Kornberg and Marianne Stewart, in an analysis of data from the 1979 National Election Study, hypothesized that Canadians "would be as likely to include their province as their country in their concepts of self." However, when respondents were given three sentences to answer the question "Who am I?" only 10 percent cited their province.[4]

Certainly it would be inappropriate to conclude that Ontario lacked an identity because few of its residents mentioned the province in a very short definition of themselves. That there was any mention of Ontario at all in such circumstances might even be taken as heartening evidence of provincial identity, albeit somewhere below the surface of most people's consciousness. Although it provides no conclusive resolution of this question, some further evidence of the place Ontario holds in the minds of its residents can be gleaned from Jon Pammett's analysis of the 1974 National Election Study.[5] Pammett found that nearly a third of Ontario respondents did not think of Canada as being divided into regions at all; conversely, almost 19 percent did think in regional terms *and* identified Ontario as the region in which they lived. Fourteen percent cited a region *within* Ontario, either specific (4 percent, mainly Toronto) or general (10 percent, mainly Northern or Southern Ontario). Sixteen percent saw themselves as living in a region larger than Ontario (3 percent, the East; 13 percent, Central Canada). A reasonably large group (11 percent) gave non-geographic responses, mainly related to economic or linguistic factors.

From these data, one might reasonably conclude Ontario's geographic boundary does not define a social group that is significant for the bulk of the province's citizens. If one believes that an Ontario identity exists, one must argue that it has not been uncovered by the measures mentioned. Perhaps it is the inability to imagine better measures that has driven most concerned scholars to examine characteristics of the province from which the missing sense of identity might eventually emerge.

Ironically, the impediments to an Ontario identity are like forces pulling in opposite directions. The province is characterized by great internal diversity in geography, economy, ethnicity, and religion. At the same time, its residents are mostly concentrated in urban areas in the southern half of the province and exposed through an integrated communications network to the secular, technocratic culture that is common to all of northeastern North America. Ontario may lack identity because of differences between Sudbury nickel miners and Toronto office workers, or because of similarities among residents of Toronto, Montreal, New York, and Cleveland.

In 1981, Ontario's population was approximately 8.6 million (less than the population of New York City) and was spread over an area more than twice the size of France. Nonetheless, Ontario's population density is more than twice the average for the country as a whole (even including the Territories) and is exceeded only by the three most southerly Atlantic provinces.

With over 80 percent of her population in urban areas, Ontario is the country's most urbanized province. The extreme concentration of Ontario's population may be indicated by the fact that over 60 percent live in ten census metropolitan areas, and over 46 percent live in the Toronto-centred conurbation that forms the so-called "Golden Horseshoe" from Oshawa to Niagara Falls, around the western end of Lake Ontario.[6] Still the vast area of the province makes some communities very isolated. The Sudbury and Thunder Bay census metropolitan areas — each with population over 120,000 — are nearly 900 kilometres apart by road, and the latter is farther from the provincial capital in Toronto than Chicago is from Atlanta.

In 1981, over 77 percent of Ontario residents spoke English as their first language, but the less than 6 percent who spoke French as their first language constituted, in absolute numbers, the largest provincial contingent of Francophones outside Quebec. Over 70 percent of the population are adherents of the Roman Catholic, Anglican, or United Churches, but I have been told that almost fifty religious denominations are represented in the school population of one Toronto suburb.[7]

Manufacturing employs over 20 percent of the Ontario labour force, with over 60 percent employed in various service industries, including trade, public administration, finance, and real estate. As in much of the northeastern United States, employment in manufacturing has been declining (at an average annual rate of 4.9 percent between 1981 and 1983) while employment in services has been increasing (at an average annual rate of 2.7 percent in the same period).[8] Nonetheless, when two Japanese automobile makers (Honda and Toyota) recently announced plans to open Canadian plants, they chose to locate them in Ontario.

On many socio-economic dimensions, the differences within Ontario are at least as great as those between Ontario and neighbouring regions. As well, comparisons with Canadian averages are often futile, because Ontario's population is so large that its characteristics contribute heavily to the definition of those national averages. If Ontario is not easily identifiable as a unique and homogeneous geographic or socio-economic region, its identity may depend on its distinctiveness as a historical and political jurisdiction. In short, the search for an Ontario identity may be resolved into the search for a distinctive Ontario political culture.

If the study of political culture has exercised Canadian scholars less in the early 1980s than it did in the middle 1970s, it may be because they have been frustrated in seeking a satisfactory definition of this slippery concept. However, while the culture of politics has been approached from a number of different directions, we need not merely be confounded by conceptual diversity, but rather, we should be encouraged by the opportunity for convergent validation.

Most treatments of political culture are concerned (explicitly or implicitly) with matters of the mind, but none entirely ignores the institutions and processes in which ideas are formed and expressed. Indeed some approaches insist on exploring the almost tangible material base they presume underlies the more impalpable ideal concept. By the same token, individual ideas are aggregated by all students of the subject, since culture implies a *sharing* of orientations, but some scholars concentrate on the historical development of these ideas from a holistic and macroscopic perspective, while others mainly treat contemporary orientations as revealed in individual survey responses. I believe it does not do excessive violence to the literature in this area to array these approaches along two separate continua: the ideal/material and the microscopic/macroscopic. A third dimension, historical/contemporary, may reasonably inform more specific categorization. If each of these analyses were applied to Ontario, and if the results converged to produce a consistent picture of the province's political culture, we would have come a long way toward the definition of the Ontario identity.

The most macroscopic and historical approach to the Canadian political culture is found in the work of Louis Hartz and his colleagues, notably in *The Founding of New Societies*.[9] Hartz's theory, first elaborated in his book *The Liberal Tradition in America*,[10] treats North American societies as fragments of the European experience. The dominance of liberalism in the United States is explained, at least in part, by the absence of a conservative challenge such as would be found in the European context. Kenneth McRae and Gad Horowitz, who applied and extended Hartz's theory using Canadian material,[11] asserted the presence of a touch of Toryism in the Canadian political tradition. Horowitz relied to some extent on this "Tory touch" to explain the greater success of socialism in Canada than in the United States. The dialectic between liberalism and conservatism could arise in the Canadian case, producing socialism, where it was rendered impossible in the American case by the absence of a conservative tradition. There is more to Horowitz's explanation than that, of course, since the rooting and flowering of a socialist movement required not only that the soil be receptive, but that there be regular nutrients supplied from respected sources outside the country. Immigration from the mother country provided familiar nutrients in Canada, while European immigration to the United States was always perceived as alien. The work of Hartz, Horowitz, and McRae engendered a debate over the character and significance of various migrations into Canada in terms of the contribution they made to the development of a unique Canadian political tradition. The influence of the United Empire Loyalists received particular emphasis, with scholars disagreeing over the extent to which these migrants embodied a conservative strain amid the dominant liberalism of the continent.

While all the scholars pursuing this line of inquiry admitted the necessity of exploring the material circumstances behind the ideological struggles they described, this school of analysis must still be placed closer to the idealist end of the continuum.[12] For these observers, "tradition" that forms the basis of political culture is very much a matter of values and beliefs, and people, institutions, and processes are rendered significant by their embodiment and elaboration of this tradition.

What is important for the question of Ontario identity, however, is the relative lack of attention paid in these works to the differences in political tradition that can arise *within* a country. Apart from the differences between English and French Canada, readers of these theorists could be forgiven for believing that a homogeneous political tradition characterized most of the nation. In the United States, Daniel Elazar has explored regional differences in the distribution of subcultures — contending elements of the American political tradition. He isolated three strains — traditionalistic, moralistic, and individualistic — and linked their distribution to patterns of migration and historical experience. He further asserted their importance in helping determine the policy preferences of American state governments.[13] I know of no comparable work in the Canadian milieu that could assist us in defining an Ontario political tradition, although some attention is paid to the general problem by David Bell and Lorne Tepperman in *The Roots of Disunity*.[14]

Similarly, political sociologist Seymour Lipset has addressed the problem of political culture from a historical perspective, concentrating on the formative events that have shaped the values of the community.[15] His work included some attention to the contemporary society as well as the past, and he moved a little closer to the material end of the continuum. While his ostensible concern was societal values, he measured those values, on the whole, by applying Talcott Parsons's pattern variables to the institutions of the society he was studying. In this respect, his work may be said to be more microscopic in its attention to values and more materialist in its measurement than the work of Hartz and his colleagues. The debate his work has engendered concerns the accuracy with which institutions are "coded" according to the pattern variables[16] and the likelihood that particular events have actually contributed to the formation of those institutions and values.

As with the Hartzian school, there is little attention to the regional variation within the country. Thus it would be difficult to conclude from his analysis that Ontario, for example, was distinct from other provinces in the structure of its institutions and the values they implied.

Two other approaches are somewhat more promising with regard to provincial differentiation. John Wilson has addressed provincial political cultures from a materialist perspective, arguing that political culture is best understood as political development, derived from economic development and indicated by the nature of the provinces' party systems.[17] Richard Simeon and David Elkins have explored provincial differences in orientations to political objects as expressed in mass surveys, following the lead of Gabriel Almond and Sidney Verba.[18] Unlike Almond and Verba, however, they are not content to identify culture with the orientations observed, but rather they seek to explain variance in those orientations by means of socio-economic predictors. The interprovincial value difference that cannot be explained by differences in the distribution of socio-economic characteristics — the residual variation — represents what they call political culture.

Wilson (materialist, macroscopic, and historical) or Simeon and Elkins (idealist, microscopic, and contemporary) may thus be able to provide some insights — convergent or discriminant — into the nature of Ontario political culture, and hence into Ontario's identity.

John Wilson neatly summarized his treatment of political culture as follows:

> If it is possible to argue . . . through an examination of the kind of development which has taken place in the party system, that different political communities are at different stages of political development, it is open to us to advance the hypothesis . . . that they also have different political cultures.[19]

This hypothesis was pursued in the context of a premise that every independent political system, such as a province, would have at least one political culture, "even if in many cases the similarities are so great as to make any distinction between them irrelevant."[20] Wilson's approach is not narrowly and rigidly materialist, since he admits that evidence of different cultures in the provinces would require a national survey "designed to probe attitudes and orientations at the most fundamental level."[21] Nevertheless he is not content to consider attitudes and actions without reference to their roots in material circumstances:

> Both [political behaviour and political culture] are consequences of a more important underlying factor. I take that factor to be the state of economic development which the society in question has reached, and in particular the dominant economic and social relationships of the time.[22]

Wilson suggested a number of possible measures of the political development he associated with stages of economic development, but, for purposes of illustration, he selected the party system as his principal indicator because of the range of political activities it included. Following a reasonably detailed examination of party system types found in other Western democracies, Wilson assessed the level of development implicit in the observable Canadian provincial party systems. His most important conclusion, for purposes of this analysis, is that Ontario's three-party system is a "transitional" one. It stands between the traditional two-party system, in which party divisions are on other than economic grounds and both parties represent the interests of fractions of the dominant class, and one of the modern two-party systems, in which the interests of the wage-earning class have either replaced one of the traditional parties or been accommodated within one of those parties. Accordingly, Ontario's level of political development is said to be transitional, and its political culture is hypothesized to be, in Almond and Verba's terms, mixed subject-participant, but somewhat more participant than subject.

Wilson dashed any hope one might have that such findings could permit us to define a unique Ontario identity, when he observed that Manitoba and

British Columbia could also be called "transitional" according to this schema, and that Quebec demonstrated the basis for a similarly mixed culture, with perhaps an edge of "subject" over "participant."[23] Since Wilson's analysis was published in 1974, the party systems in Manitoba and British Columbia may have become more clearly two-party ones. The same may be true of Quebec, although it is perhaps a little early to tell what may become of the Parti Québécois following the retirement of its leader, René Lévesque, and its electoral defeat in 1985.[24] For the moment, Ontario may be the only real three-party system left among the provinces, but one may reasonably ask if that is enough on which to base a unique provincial identity.

Even if Ontario's party system is unique, it clearly is not genuinely homogeneous. By a fairly liberal definition of three-party competition, fewer than half the constituencies in the present legislature can be said to be three-party contests. These seats are concentrated, with few exceptions, in the urban or suburban areas of the province (as Wilson might have predicted), but other urban seats do not fit this pattern.[25] Almost a third of the current seats display two-party competition between the Liberals and Conservatives of a kind that Wilson might have identified as traditional, characteristic of a pre-industrial society. However not all of these seats are located in the rural areas of the province where such pre-industrial characteristics might be expected to be found. Further analysis of party competition in Ontario might well improve our understanding of subcultural differences, but an Ontario identity does not seem to lie in this quarter.

Can a more clear-cut description of provincial identity be found in the sort of analysis pursued by Simeon and Elkins? In their book, *Small Worlds*, these authors employed a variety of measures to elucidate interprovincial differences but laid heavy emphasis on survey findings about policy preferences and about the elements of political culture identified by Almond and Verba — political efficacy, participation, and trust in government.

Simeon and Elkins found that "provincial populations were becoming more similar to each other in their policy preferences and expectations of government," with convergence being most noticeable in respect of economic and social policy. Where divergence appeared, it was mainly in regard to French-English relations or to various symbols of nationhood.[26] From an examination of some thirty years of Gallup polls, they concluded that regional opinion was converging "on most important public policy issues" and that Ontario residents did not appear to be sharply distinctive in any policy domain.[27] When this author and F.J. Fletcher made a similar analysis of Gallup polls between 1960 and 1978, we found that convergence on social issues was not matched on economic questions; however, the economic differences were, as might be expected, with respondents expressing opinions in line with the economic interests or conditions of their provinces. Ontario did not appear distinctive in that analysis when compared to provinces of similar wealth or similar economic demands.[28]

The survey data explored by Simeon and Elkins revealed a complex mix of identities in the minds of many respondents, although there was "considerable evidence for a relative growth in orientation to provincial governments and a decline in attachments to the centre."[29] However, Jon Pammett, using similar data, found some Ontario distinctiveness in this area. Over half of the Ontario respondents in the 1974 Election Study felt "closer to" the federal than the provincial government; over half found the federal level "most important"; and over half paid more attention to federal politics. In each case, these proportions were the highest of any provincial group.[30]

The centrepiece of Simeon and Elkins's, analysis was their examination of participation and associated feelings of trust and personal efficacy across the provinces, in general and controlling for other socio-economic predictors. With respect to participation and involvement, they found little difference across the country. In all regions, about the same proportion of respondents were active and interested in politics. Perhaps a little higher level of activity was indicated in the Atlantic region, where voter turnouts have traditionally been very high. More significant regional differences appeared in the measurement of political efficacy and trust in government, and the differences persisted with the introduction of control variables.[31]

Simeon and Elkins characterized their respondents according to their trust and efficacy as falling into four categories: supporters (high trust, high efficacy); critics (low trust, high efficacy); deferentials (high trust, low efficacy); and disaffected (low trust, low efficacy). They found that "British Columbia, Manitoba, Ontario, and English Quebec are what might be called citizen societies."[32] In all of these groups, the authors found relatively high levels of trust and efficacy.

> Only in Ontario, British Columbia and Manitoba do supporters outnumber the disaffected. In addition, in these latter provinces a substantial proportion of those who distrust the government are confident of their ability to do something about it: they are much more likely to be critics than to be disaffected. This is not to say these provinces have perfectly homogeneous populations.... Each type is found in each province; it is the proportions which differ.[33]

Again, as with John Wilson's analysis, Ontario appears in the company of Manitoba, British Columbia, and (possibly, or partially) Quebec. Clearly, there is something similar being tapped by these different approaches. If it *is* political culture, then the approaches appear to provide convergent validation for a shared culture involving three, and possibly four, provincial groups. In that case, Ontario's identity will need something more to distinguish it from the identities of other provinces.

It may be that the similarity of culture between Ontario, Manitoba, and British Columbia is testament to the success of efforts to enhance Canadian national unity, at least in those communities most easily exposed to such efforts. Messages of this sort may radiate out from the national capital in

Ottawa and/or the metropolitan corridor of economics and culture that runs from Toronto to Montreal. They may be resented or resisted in the other provinces, but they will be impossible to ignore where populations are concentrated and where those concentrations are themselves metropoles for their regional hinterlands, like Winnipeg or the lower mainland of British Columbia. These provinces may share as well the ethnic and economic diversity that results from widespread immigration and trade, and that diversity may breed different attitudes to politics than may be found in more homogenous settings. Of course, such speculation obviously requires much more investigation before it can be accepted with confidence.

But what of Ontario's identity? The province may partake in a political culture that transcends provincial boundaries, born perhaps from the particular salience in these few provinces of the struggle between urban and rural interests and nourished by successive waves of immigrants and the diversity of commerce. But where can one look for the events or forces that might give the province of Ontario some uniqueness? Is it enough to say that Ontario is the only province with a three-party system and the one with the highest level of positive orientation to the national level of government? If the country is becoming more homogeneous, even these slim differences may disappear in time. However, if regional differentiation persists, it will do so because the provinces have different interests in the federal system and different experiences in the modern history of Canadian society.

If distinct identities did not emerge from the interests and experiences of the past, they may yet do so from the interests and experiences of the future. Ontario may share a culture of politics with two or three other provinces, but the details of its political life have been unique, and in those details may be found the basis for a unique identity. Of course, if the province's residents are to be cognizant of that identity, they will have to become familiar with those details. They might do well to begin with interests.

First, Ontario remains the premier manufacturing province in the Canadian economy. Traditionally it has been the locus of the most high growth, high technology industries and the principal beneficiary of trade in manufactured goods. In a country that has often accepted resource exploitation as the main engine of economic growth, Ontario continues to swim against the tide, for good or ill. Indeed, a major tension in the internal politics of the province has often been between its urban, industrial centre and its own resource sector, located mainly in the north.

Second, Ontario is a consumer, not a producer, of the main fossil fuels, and in an age when energy policy has been central to the politics of the country, Ontario has often stood apart from some of its western *and* Atlantic cousins. Ontario has not been alone in this stance, but this fact undoubtedly contributed to its identity.

Third, Ontario is crucial to the national system of income redistribution. From the periphery, it must often appear that Ontario has benefited most from the economics of Confederation, but it is worth remembering that when it appeared in 1982 that Ontario might be eligible to receive equalization payments, that observation was taken as prima facie evidence that a new formula was required to calculate the grants.

Fourth, Ontario remains the dominant source of power in national politics. With the largest number of seats in the Commons and necessarily prominent representation in any federal cabinet, Ontario influences the national agenda even beyond what might be expected by reason of its wealth.

Finally, Ontario (and more particularly Toronto) predominates in the creation and transmission of arts and popular culture, at least in the English language. Of course, in a country that has explicitly aimed to decentralize its artistic production and is at the same time assailed overwhelmingly by the arts and culture of its neighbour to the south, this observation will not remain unchallenged. Still the homogenization of culture so often bemoaned in other regions of the country is probably a result (at least in part) of the filtering of cultural images through the lenses of Ontario's artists, journalists, academics, and critics before they are transmitted back to the hinterland by the Toronto-centred media. Even if the observation is false, it is probably an element of the Ontario identity that is so often believed to be true within the province.

If these are Ontario's interests, what have been the (particularly political) experiences that might also help to shape a unique sense of provincial identity? The question may be further subdivided: what have been the enduring divisions of Ontario society that have created political issues at various stages of its history; and what have been the most salient themes of Ontario politics in the modern era, for example, the period since the Second World War?

One of the longest-standing cleavages in Ontario political life has been the division between Roman Catholics and others over the operation of the separate school system. The division began as one between Catholics and Protestants even before Confederation and has become more diversified on the non-Catholic side as the society has become both more religiously differentiated and more secular. Since the Roman Catholic separate schools were granted rights at Confederation at least equal to those they possessed prior to that date, there has been a recurring controversy about the adequacy of funding for those schools. While the question was overlaid with considerations of language around the turn of the century, it has become much more clearly religious in later years. It was featured in the politics of the 1930s, when Mitchell Hepburn's plans to improve the balance of provincial funding for public and separate schools were abandoned after his Liberals lost a by-election that allegedly turned on the issue. It surfaced again in 1981, when the two opposition parties promised an extension of funding to the upper grades of high school, and the governing Conservatives refused to agree. And it formed the main unstated issue of the 1985 election, when all three parties agreed to extend full provincial funding to all grades, but opposition surfaced in other areas of the community, including some teacher groups who feared declining enrolment in the public system as a result of the change.

In recent years, the open religious bitterness of the nineteenth century seems to have been abandoned in favour of arguments about the preservation of public education and the fairness of tax support for a variety of religious schools. These arguments may hide anti-Catholic sentiment in some quarters, but they may as easily be taken as genuine secular and/or equity responses to the existing system. Religious school controversies are not unique to Ontario, but the persistence and peculiar character of the debate may be unusual.

The cleavage between an industrial wage-earning class and the owners of capital is certainly not unique to Ontario, but it has persisted in the province without becoming as polarized as it is sometimes said to be in other places, notably British Columbia, or as muted as it has become in the United States through the co-optation of labour by a major brokerage party. In Canada, Ontario was a pioneer in labour relations and the regulation of working conditions (e.g., workers' compensation), but the province remains, in the eyes of trade unionists, less "progressive" than some other provinces in protecting the right to organize and bargain collectively. In particular, the governments and labour boards of the province have been reluctant to shift the balance in favour of unions by ensuring the rights to a first contract or restricting the rights of employers to hire strikebreakers.

In addition, Ontario has been the locus of some important struggles between fractions of the owning class, notably resource exploitation firms (mining and forestry), manufacturing concerns, and those involved in finance, trade, and real estate development.

A third continuing basis for political conflict has centred on issues of public morality. Ontario's "bluestocking" image in the rest of the country is probably undeserved and may result mostly from its proximity to the allegedly less puritan Quebec. Still, it is true that issues of temperance and censorship have regularly recurred in Ontario political life. Although Ontario was one of the last provinces to adopt prohibition in 1916, the Liberal party of that era consumed a great deal of its energy debating questions of liquor abuse and regulation. The short-lived United Farmers administration of Premier E.C. Drury prosecuted the liquor traffic so vigorously that it may have hastened the end both of prohibition and its own tenure. Mitchell Hepburn, certainly no teetotaler, combined the "wets" and "drys" in support of his party by attacking the liquor licensing process as a "toll-gate of graft." When George Drew's Conservative government introduced liquor lounges into the province, the premier was defeated in his own riding by a CCF candidate who was a prominent temperance crusader. It may indicate something of the change that has taken place in Ontario politics that the Liberals are believed to have gained more votes than they lost by promising (in the 1985 election campaign) to permit the sale of beer and wine in corner grocery stores. That the matter was an election issue at all suggests that liquor remains a surprisingly important matter on the province's political agenda. In addition, Ontario remains one of the few provinces whose film classification board still occasionally orders scenes to be cut from films before they may be shown legally in the province.

If religion, class, and morality have been the enduring themes of Ontario politics throughout its history, what have been the salient elements of political life in Ontario in the four decades since the Second World War?

It is probably surprising to many observers outside Canada that the most urbanized, industrialized, populous province in the country could have been governed for a period of forty-two years by one party, let alone a party of conservative stripe. The dominance of the Progressive Conservative Party was of course not as complete as their control of the legislature would suggest. In no election between 1943 and 1985 did the Conservatives receive a majority of the votes cast, but the opposition remained so divided prior to the latter year that the PCs regularly formed majority governments (nine out of thirteen times) with pluralities of the popular vote. The success of the party has been attributed to many things, including leadership and traditional voter loyalty, but any party with that sort of longevity has clearly mastered the art of brokerage politics. The party succeeded at least in part because they could always appear to balance the interests of rural and urban dwellers, capital and labour, Protestants, Catholics, and others. As early as the Whitney and Hearst administrations after the turn of the century, the Conservatives managed to lead in cautious adjustment to a transforming society. The reluctant acceptance of the welfare state in the post-World War II era, the extension of French-language services without declaring French an official language, even the turnaround on separate school funding, appeared to many voters as appropriately cautious without being unduly intransigent. Of course, the relative prosperity of the province in the post-war era undoubtedly helped the incumbent governments, but it is interesting to note that they lost power in an election in which their new leader was widely identified as more conservative (and rural) than the two previous leaders had been.

If politics in postwar Ontario has been marked by the stability of its governing party, it has also been characterized, perhaps paradoxically, by elements of enormous change. Like other provincial governments, Ontario's has grown geometrically in size, expenditure, and intervention in the economic and social life of the province. That this growth should have taken place under a Conservative aegis is perhaps surprising, but in Ontario the laissez-faire liberalism of modern Canadian Conservatives has been tempered, however, reluctantly, by a Tory concern for the broader community. Admittedly, the growth of expenditure in some areas came as a result of federally initiated joint programs (like Medicare, hospital insurance, and the Canada Assistance Plan). In other areas, however, the growth came as a response to demand within the province and a sense of public responsibility for such matters as education, transportation, and urban development. Ontario was not unique in this respect, but the rhetoric of Conservative governments in this province may have been a little less individualist than it was in other regions.

Perhaps the greatest changes in the social life of the province have not come as a result of government action, but because of the diverse immigration of the last twenty-five years. Around 20 percent of Ontario's population are not native-born Canadians, and it is no longer the case (as it was in the 1950s) that the only "foreign" accents heard in Toronto streets are those of the British Isles. Together with the postwar baby boom, whose impact on mores, culture, and government services has yet to be fully appreciated, this injection of new influences to the Ontario milieu makes the discerning of a stable Ontario identity even more difficult. In time, of course, these social changes may help shape a new identity. Will it be any easier to discover, or, perhaps as a sign of maturity, will we cease to care?

NOTES

1. A.R.M. Lower, "Ontario — Does It Exist?" *Ontario History*, 60 (1968).
2. John Warkentin, "Southern Ontario: A View from the West," *Canadian Geographer*, 10 (1966) quoted in Peter Oliver, *Public and Private Persons* (Toronto: Clarke, Irwin, 1975), 5.
3. Allan Kornberg and Marianne Stewart, "National Identification and Political Support." In Allan Kornberg and Harold D. Clarke eds., *Political Support in Canada: The Crisis Years* (Durham, N.C.; Duke University Press, 1983), 75.
4. Ibid., 78, 85.
5. Jon Pammett, "Public Orientations to Regions and Provinces." In D.J. Bellamy et al., eds., *The Provincial Political Systems* (Toronto: Methuen, 1976), 86-99.
6. Statistics Canada, *Canada Year Book 1985*, Department of Supply and Services, 1985.
7. Ibid.
8. Statistics Canada, *Canada, The Provinces and the Territories: A Statistical Profile*, Department of Supply and Services, 1983, Table 3.2.
9. Louis Hartz et al., *The Founding of New Societies* (New York: Harcourt Brace, 1964).
10. Louis Hartz, *The Liberal Tradition in America* (New York: Harcourt Brace, 1953).
11. K.D. McRae, "The Structure of Canadian History," in Hartz et al., *The*

Founding of New Societies; K.D. McRae, "Louis Hartz's Concept of the Fragment Society and Its Application to Canada," *Etudes Canadiennes*, 5 (1978), 17-30; Gad Horowitz, "Conservatism, Liberalism and Socialism in Canada," *Canadian Journal of Economics and Political Science*, 32 (1966), 143-171.
12. But see David Bell and Lorne Tepperman, *The Roots of Disunity* (Toronto: McClelland and Stewart, 1979), 11-71 (especially 38-39, n. 57).
13. Daniel Elazar, "The States and the Political Setting." In Ira Sharkansky, ed., *Policy Analysis in Political Science*, (Chicago: Markham Publishing, 1970), 171-183, originally published in D. Elazar, *American Federalism: A View from the States* (New York: Crowell, 1966).
14. Bell and Tepperman, *Roots of Disunity*, 145-209.
15. S.M. Lipset, *The First New Nation* (New York: Basic Books, 1963) and *Revolution and Counter-Revolution* (New York: Anchor Books, 1970).
16. See for example, Tom Truman, "A Critique of Seymour M. Lipset's Article, 'Value Differences, Absolute or Relative: The English Speaking Democracies'" *Canadian Journal of Political Science*, 4 (1971), 497-525.
17. John Wilson, "The Canadian Political Cultures: Towards a Redefinition of the Nature of the Canadian Political System," *Canadian Journal of Political Science*, 7 (1974), 438-483 and "On the Dangers of Bickering in a Federal State," in Kornberg and Clarke, *Political Support in Canada*, 171-222.
18. Richard Simeon and David J. Elkins, "Regional Political Cultures in Canada," *Canadian Journal of Political Science*, 7 (1974), 397-437 and *Small Worlds: Provinces and Parties in Canadian Political Life* (Toronto: Methuen, 1980); Gabriel Almond and Sidney Verba, *The Civic Culture* (Boston: Little Brown, 1965).
19. Wilson, "Canadian Political Cultures," 455.
20. Ibid., 440.
21. Ibid., 446.
22. Ibid.
23. Ibid, 474, Table IV and n. 50.
24. Saskatchewan poses problems for Wilson on other grounds, since it remains a two-party system, but the Liberal Party, which opposed the CCF/NDP for over forty years, seems to have been replaced by the Progressive Conservatives who currently form the government of that province.
25. See R.J. Drummond, "Voting Behaviour: Dancing in the Dark on a Moving Floor." In Donald C. MacDonald, ed., *The Government and Politics of Ontario*, 3rd edition (Toronto: Nelson, 1985), 219-237.
26. Simeon and Elkins, *Small Worlds*, 274.
27. Ibid., 99-100.
28. F.J. Fletcher and R.J. Drummond, *Candian Attitude Trends, 1960-1978* (Montreal: Institute for Research on Public Policy, 1979), 75.
29. Simeon and Elkins, *Small Worlds*, 274.

30. Pammett, "Public Orientations," 95, Table 3.
31. Simeon and Elkins, *Small Worlds*, 68.
32. Ibid., 51.
33. Ibid.

5
THE WEST

On Being an Alberta Writer

ROBERT KROETSCH

How do you make love in a new country? I used that question as a refrain in a paper I read two years ago, at a conference held in Banff under the general title, "Crossing Frontiers"... These conferences, these visits, these occasions of talk connect in our lives (connect our lives, even); we begin to weave our own significance.... How do you make love in a new country? Obviously, I believed that I had an answer. But, alas, no one asked.

One way to make love is by writing. Indeed, without writing, I sometimes suspect, there would be no such thing as love. Surely without the lyric poems of Sappho, the sonnets of the Renaissance — without the pastoral dialogue (of which I still hear traces in prairie fiction) or the long history of theatre, our concept of love would be much diminished. Perhaps the sub-question is, then: How do you write in a new country?

I'll attempt an answer. Perhaps a tangential answer, an evasive answer. Perhaps even a fictitious answer. But an answer that is as honest as I can make it, since memory is a disguise as well as a recollection.

I remember how I first began to be skeptical of the writing that I read.

I was a child — I don't know how old (I was born in 1927, if that helps you to locate these matters) — my parents took me to Spring Lake, to a picnic. Spring Lake is a small round lake, surrounded by willows and poplars; it was the centre of the community that my mother grew up in — in the parklands south-east of Edmonton, a few miles from the valley of the Battle River. I was playing in a large, shallow depression in the ground, a depression that somehow wasn't natural. My father came by, looking for me. I asked about the place where I was playing. He said, casually, that it was a buffalo wallow.

It's where buffalo rolled and scratched, he said. He could tell me a little more — the lake never went dry, he explained, the buffalo came here to drink.

What buffalo? I asked. Or wondered, if I didn't ask. I don't remember now. When? From where?... Even at that young age I was secure in the illusion that the land my parents and grandparents homesteaded had had no prior occupants, animal or human. Ours was the ultimate tabula rasa. We were the truly innocent.

Abridged from Robert Kroetsch, "On Being an Alberta Writer," *Open Letter*, Fifth Series, No. 5-6 (Summer/Fall 1983). Copyright © 1983 by Robert Kroetsch. Reprinted by permission of the author.

There was an older boy a mile from our farm who, as we kids liked to put it, knew everything. He was so smart a lot of people thought he'd become a priest. I remember that he could recite the names and dates of kings and prime ministers from whomever was thought to be first to the latest. I asked him about buffalo wallows. He'd never even heard of buffalo wallows. But more: he made considerable show of not caring that he hadn't heard. He was educated.

My sense of the gap between me and history was growing. History as I knew it did not account for the world I lived in. Present here in this landscape, I was taking my first lesson in the idea of absence.

There was, half a mile south from our farm, a ring of stones in the prairie grass. My dad and the hired men, strangely, plowed around it. One day, again when I was a child, I ran away from home; instead of going to a neighbor's house, where I could play, I went to that ring of stones ... and again I began to wonder. I went back home and asked my mother about those stones. She had, then, never heard of a tipi ring; she said the stones were magical. I suspect now that her notion of magical went back two or three generations to the forests of southern Germany, surviving that long transcription through Wisconsin and Minnesota to the District and then the Province of Alberta. The connection between the name and the named — the importance and the failure of that connection — is one of my obsessions.

I was that day on my way to embracing the model of archaeology, against that of history. The authorized history, the given definition of history, was betraying us on those prairies. A few years after I sat in that tipi ring and cried and then began to notice and then began to wonder, a gang of dam-builders from a Battle River site came by and picked up the stones, and my father broke the sod. If history betrayed us, we too betrayed it. I remember my father one night at supper, saying out of nowhere, he'd made a mistake, letting those men pick up those stones. For reasons he couldn't understand, he felt guilty. Where I had learned the idea of absence, I was beginning to learn the idea of trace. There is always something left behind. That is the essential paradox. Even abandonment gives us memory.

I had to tell a story. I responded to those discoveries of absence, to that invisibility, to that silence, by knowing I had to make up a story. *Our* story.

How do you write in a new country?

Our inherited literature, the literature of our European past and of eastern North America, is emphatically the literature of a people who have *not* lived on prairies. We had, and still have, difficulty finding names for the elements and characteristics of this landscape. The human reponse to this landscape is so new and ill-defined and complex that our writers come back, uneasily but compulsively, to landscape writing. Like the homesteaders before us, we are compelled to adjust and invent, to remember and forget. We feel a profound ambiguity about the past — about both its contained stories and its modes of perception.

There are, first and always, the questions of form and language. For reasons which are not very clear, the prairies developed a tradition of fiction before developing a tradition of poetry. This seems to be contradictory to the cultural experience of most societies. I suspect it has to do with the nature of the experience — in one word, often harsh (that's two words). And there was available, to record that harshness, the realistic mode of fiction.

But even as I say this I ask: Might it not be possible that we now look back on the experience as having been a harsh one because the realistic (or even naturalistic) mode of fiction pictured it so? What if the prairies had been settled — as much of the United States was in the 19th century — at a time when the Gothic model was easily available to the novelists?

The effect of perceptual models on what we see is now the concern of social and literary critics (thanks to such books as Dick Harrison's *Unnamed Country*). I was living outside of Alberta (and outside of Canada) while writing most of my fiction and poetry. Perhaps for that reason I was constantly aware that we both, and at once, record and invent these new places called Alberta and Saskatchewan. That pattern of contraries, all the possibilities implied in *record* and *invent*, for me finds its focus in the model suggested by the phrase: a local pride.

The phrase is from William Carlos Williams — indeed those three words are the opening of his great poem *Paterson*, about Paterson, New Jersey: *a local pride*.

The feeling must come from an awareness of the authenticity of our own lives. People who feel invisible try to borrow visibility from those who are visible. To understand others is surely difficult. But to understand ourselves becomes impossible if we do not see images of ourselves in the mirror — be that mirror theatre or literature or historical writing. A local pride does not exclude the rest of the world, or other experiences; rather, it makes them possible. It creates an organizing centre. Or as Williams put it, more radically: the acquiring of a local pride enables us to create our own culture — "by lifting an environment to expression."

How do we lift an environment to expression? How do you write in a new country?

The great sub-text of prairie literature is our oral tradition. In the face of books, magazines, films and TV programs that are so often someone else, we talk to each other by, literally, talking.

The visit is the great prairie cultural event. People go visiting or they go to other events in order to visit. This accounts for the predominance of the beer parlor and the church in prairie fiction. Beyond this, we see fictional characters going to stampedes and country dances and summer resorts — those places where we talk ourselves into existence.

Oral history is not likely to go back more than two generations — to parents and grandparents. Beyond that little remains — with huge consequences for our sense of history. Within that time-framework exists an enormous prospect of fiction-making. Individuals in a lifetime become characters. Events become story, become folklore, edge towards the condition of myth. Many of our best novels — the novels of Margaret Laurence and Rudy Wiebe especially — assert the primacy of the act of speech over the act of writing. The poetry of Andy Suknaski acknowledges a huge and continuing debt to the oral tradition. The sophisticated sound poetry of Stephen Scobie and Doug Barbour, in Edmonton, suggests that print is merely the kind of notation for speech, as a musical score is for music.

A local pride leads us to a concern with myths of origin. Obviously, on the prairies, there has been an enormous interest in ethnic roots — that version of the myth of origin. But now, in our growing urban centres, there is a new kind of myth emerging. Again, for writers like Laurence or Wiebe, there is available to our imaginations a new set of ancestors: the native or Metis people, Big Bear, Riel, the fictional Tonnerre family of *The Diviners*, Dumont. And I would suggest that along with this comes the urban dream that our roots are just over the horizon, in the small towns and the rural communities of the prairies. This dream of origins is already evident in Laurence's work. It is already evident in a larger Canadian context — surely it is no accident that the classics of modern Canadian writing are set in rural areas: Sheila Watson's *The Double Hook* with its setting in the Cariboo Country, Ross's Saskatchewan, Ernest Buckler's Nova Scotia in his novel, *The Mountain and the Valley*. The oral tradition, become a literary tradition, points us back to our own landscape, our recent ancestors, and the characteristic expressions and modes of our own speech.

It is a kind of archaeology that makes *this place*, with all its implications, available to us for literary purposes. We have not yet grasped the whole story; we have hints and guesses that slowly persuade us towards the recognition of larger patterns. Archaeology allows the fragmentary nature of the story, against the coerced unity of traditional history. Archaeology allows for discontinuity. It allows for layering. It allows for imaginative speculation.

I am aware that it is the great French historian, Michel Foucault, who has formalized our understanding of the appropriateness of the archaeological method. But the prairie writer understands that appropriateness in terms of the particulars of place: newspaper files, place names, shoe boxes full of old photographs, tall tales, diaries, journals, tipi rings, weather reports, business ledgers, voting records — even the wrong-headed histories written by eastern historians become, rather than narratives of the past, archaeological deposits.

For me, one of those deposits turned out to be an old seed catalogue. I found a 1917 catalogue in the Glenbow archives in 1975. I translated that seed catalogue into a poem called "Seed Catalogue." The archaeological discovery, if I might call it that, brought together for me the oral tradition and the myth of origins. . . .

Changing Images of the West*

R. Douglas Francis

At times one has the impression that the historians of western Canada have assumed that the best way to understand the evolution of their region is to compile study upon study of the most intricate and minute historical detail. Yet the history of the West is more than a total of its parts. There is an aspect of its history which transcends the decisions of politicians, the intricate workings of the economy, and the daily activities of its people; it exists in the mind. The history of the West has often been governed as much by what people imagined the region to be as the "reality" itself. This paper will explore the changing images of the West by examining the secondary literature on the subject — to look at studies which attempt to explain the image in a particular time period — in an effort to discover what research has been done and what still remains to be done.

Historical geographers of western Canada have argued that prior to 1850 the North West was viewed as an area unsuitable for agricultural production and settlement. The image was first projected in Henry Kelsey's poetic report to the Hudson's Bay Company which resulted from his 1690-1692 expedition into the interior of western Canada. The report included such terms as "desert" and "barren ground" to describe the grassland region. John Warkentin notes that this negative image also prevailed in later fur trading accounts. Another historical geographer, D.W. Moodie, demonstrates the difficulty faced by such opponents of the Hudson's Bay Company as Arthur Dobbs, a spokesman for British commercial interests, in refuting this negative image prior to 1850, even with the use of accurate scientific information. As Wreford Watson points out, the terms "barren" and "desert" were equated with the lack of trees in the minds of Englishmen and eastern Canadians.

> In Canada the matter did not end with semantics. People came actually to believe that where trees did not grow the soil could not produce. There was a mental equation that ran: bareness equals barrenness equals infertility equals uselessness for agriculture. Kelsey's report came out in a mental context which led to the illusion of a western wasteland.

An equally unpopular view of the British North West existed in the United States. Warkentin notes that as early as 1820 the American explorer, Stephen

---

*The term "West" refers to the North West in the fur trading era and the Prairie provinces in the post-confederation era.
R. Douglas Francis, "Changing Images of the West," *Journal of Canadian Studies* (Fall, 1982), pp. 5-19. Reprinted by permission.

Long, mapped the existence of a "Great Desert" north and east of the American Rocky Mountains which, it was believed (although not scientifically proven), existed from Mexico northwards into the Canadian West. That image prevailed well into the 1850s and influenced John Palliser's perception of the area. Thus the Canadian West was viewed in negative terms from both a northern and a southern perspective with a resulting loss of interest in the agricultural potential of the region and an acceptance of the Hudson's Bay Company's undisputed control.

In the 1850s there was a marked change to a more positive image of the West. Douglas Owram's extensive study, *The Promise of Eden: The Canadian Expansionist Movement and the Idea of the West, 1856-1900*, documents this changing perspective. He leaves no doubt that a few visionary and aggressive individuals in a mid-nineteenth century Canadian expansionist group helped to mould a new and positive image of the West in the mind of the British and Canadian public which in turn contributed greatly to Canada's decision to acquire the North West.

Owram attributes the rising interest in the North West in the early 1850s to changing economic conditions. The prosperity following the Reciprocity Treaty of 1854 and the optimism of the railroad age made it feasible for the first time for Canadians to consider acquiring an economic hinterland of their own. The idea interested businessmen in Canada West, and they provided the financial backing necessary for such an enterprise to succeed. The expansionists also appealed to the agricultural interests of the United Canadas by warning them of the rapidly declining good agricultural land within their own boundaries and thus the need to look to the North West for further growth. Adding weight to the economic arguments of the expansionists were moral ones. The North West was seen as "the basis of power for the whole British Empire." Thus even before Canadians had had an opportunity to assess the potential of the land in the North West in order to judge its intrinsic value for agricultural settlement, there existed in the mind of powerful eastern commercial, political and expansionist interests an image of the North West. They saw it as a great agricultural hinterland which one day would make the united colonies of British North America a great and powerful nation and indeed the vital link in a greater British Empire. As a result, when the Hudson's Bay Company's charter came up for renewal in 1859, tremendous pressure was put on the Company to relinquish its hold on the North West and to sell it to Canada for settlement purposes.

Owram's study can be supplemented by other available materials on the period. L.H. Thomas has compiled a useful collection of primary sources on "the Mid-Century Debate on the Future of the North West" which includes helpful introductions and a good balance of excerpts from scientific reports, political speeches and newspaper editorials. F.H. Underhill's early article on the Clear Grit Movement is also useful because of its liberal quotations from George Brown's *Globe* concerning western expansion. The geographer G.S.

Dunbar has shown the importance of Loren Blodgett, the noted American climatologist. Using the concept of isotherms as conceptualized by the European climatologist, Alexander von Humboldt, Blodgett compared the Canadian North West to similar regions in northern Europe for agricultural possibilities and concluded: "Climate is indisputably the decisive condition, and when we find the isothermal of 60° for the summer rising on the interior American plains to the 61st parallel, or fully as high as its average position for Europe, it is impossible to doubt the existence of favourable climates over vast areas now unoccupied."

An important development in the mid-fifties was the sponsoring of two scientific expeditions to Rupert's Land: John Palliser's British expedition, and Henry Youle Hind's Canadian expedition, both of which resulted in extensive and comprehensive reports. Two articles by John Warkentin already mentioned offer good insights into the images of the West in the two expeditionary reports. In addition, Irene Spry's valuable introduction to *The Papers of the Palliser Expedition, 1857-1860* discusses the background to the expedition and the image of the West which emerged from it. W.L. Morton's recent biography of Henry Youle Hind partially fills a large gap in our knowledge of this man who so greatly influenced the perception of the West in British North America in the mid-nineteenth century. Morton devotes two chapters to discussing Hind's expeditions to the West in 1857 and 1858. While the chapters are more narrative than analytical, Morton does judge Hind's importance in popularizing the positive image of the West as a region with an extensive "fertile belt" — as a phrase which unlocked the North West. "Fertile belt" was the positive side of Palliser's negative image of the "desert" region conjured up by the term "Palliser's triangle." Morton notes:

> The *Narrative* is first rate of its kind as a perceptive description of lands which, if known for over half a century, were to most people only vaguely known. Particularly was this true of the Canadian prairies. The fur traders had kept to the northern forests and explorers such as Franklin and Richardson had followed the routes of the fur trade. Hind had first presented, with the vividness which was his peculiar gift, the wide spaces and deep valleys of the grass and aspen country of the west. The *Narrative* was like a ship bursting into unknown seas. As such it remains at once a source of much and various detail and a brilliant description of the plains on the eve of settlement.

Owram's *The Promise of Eden* gives the impression that the expansionists of the 1850s were working in a vacuum, without the support of other groups — politicians, businessmen, artists and literary writers. In fact, their sudden success owed a great deal to the romantic image of the West as depicted in the artistic works of Paul Kane, the literary writings of John Ballantyne, and the propaganda of Captain William Francis Butler. Romanticism in the mid-nineteenth century was a strong force which inspired individuals and nations to open up new vistas of exploration. J. Russell Harper argues that Paul Kane had a tremendous impact in arousing interest in the West and its native people through his romantic image of the land and his depiction of the "noble savage." Harper notes:

> He painted the grass of the wildest regions trimmed like an English green sward. Trading boats descending the Saskatchewan River have the dignity of Roman galleys, and buffalo hunts are like wonderful tableaux on some gigantic stage.... The stiffly posed warrior chieftains have a noble bearing. His personal romantic nature... was consistent with the spirit of the age.

Kane was not the only artist to paint or sketch the region. Lesser known artists were making their contribution such as Peter Rindisbacher, George Brodie, George Frost, R.B. Nevitt and William C. Hind. These artists, notes Lorne Render in a chapter on "The Expeditionary Artists" in *The Mountain and the Sky*, were usually amateurs with some training who painted for practical purposes — often as members of a scientific expedition so as to provide visual information for official reports or illustrations for scientific journals. Thus their paintings need to be judged not only on their aesthetic merits but also on their historical importance. As historical documents they reveal less a West actually seen than the romantic image of the West in the painter's eye before he actually saw the West. Ronald Rees notes that their early prairie scenes "were viewed through a filter of Victorian optimism with the result that most of the drawings and paintings presented an unforbidding, even cheerful image of the West." J. Russell Harper draws the same conclusion in his biographical sketch of W.G.R. Hind: — "While William portrayed the factual elements of Indian life, he also must have had some feeling for the exotic and unknown... life, a feeling which was rooted in a romantic strain that was an integral facet of the Victorian age." These romantic scenes greatly influenced subsequent perceptions of the West with the result that the "real" West for many people was the image perceived through the eye of the artist. Rees concludes: "As the first pictorial interpretations of the West they were instrumental in helping to establish images of the region in eastern North America and Europe."

The romantic literature of the period had the same popular impact. Dick Harrison devotes part of a chapter in *Unnamed Country* to discussing the difficulty early travellers and settlers had in seeing the West on its own terms. Their eastern bias dictated what they wanted to or would see, and that bias was a mixture of romanticism and realism. It was a pastoral ideal moulded by perceptions of the West popular in Europe, the United States and eastern Canada. Harrison describes writers like R.M. Ballantyne and J.C. Collins as giving "the prairie a distinctly Walter Scott or Fenimore Cooper cast." Ballantyne's image of the West as the home of great adventure coloured his own self-image, and he spent the latter days of his life in Scotland "lecturing about his experiences in Rupert's Land, striding purposefully across the stage, black-bearded and handsome, and dressed in the colourful coat and leggings of a North American trapper."

This new positive image of the Prairie West in the 1850s contributed to the decision of the Canadian government to purchase Rupert's Land in 1869 and to incorporate it into the Dominion. What image was in the mind of the Fathers of Confederation when they thought of the West? Unfortunately little work has been done on the subject, but in the late 1960s and early seventies a lively debate developed on the West and Confederation which centred on the image of the nation as reflected in the issue of language rights in the Manitoba Act of 1870 and the North West Territories Act of 1875. Stated simply, the question was whether the Fathers of Confederation envisioned the West (and ultimately the nation) as unilingual and unicultural, or bilingual and bicultural. Donald Creighton, in "John A. Macdonald, Confederation and the Canadian West," argued that the Fathers of Confederation, particularly the nation's first prime minister, did not favour a bilingual West but were forced into recognizing the two languages in the Manitoba Act by a dictatorial Louis Riel. Macdonald's image was of a West which was a reflection in language and culture of Ontario, very much in line with expansionist views as outlined by Owram. Ralph Heintzman rejoined with a persuasive argument that the Fathers had a "spirit" of co-operation and goodwill at the time of Confederation which extended to the view of the North West's constitutional structure. A third article on the subject, by David Hall, attacks Heintzman and endorses Creighton's position.

Less controversial was the image in the minds of individual English-speaking Canadian politicians, and in the collective mind of Ontarians, of the West as a colony of central Canada. W.L. Morton, the dean of western Canadian history, first presented this argument in his ground-breaking article "Clio in Canada: The Interpretation of Canadian History," and extended it in "The Bias of Prairie Politics" and in his excellent study, *Manitoba: A History*. J.E. Rea speculated further on the implications for western attitudes. Using Louis Hartz's model of fragmented cultures, Rea argued that the West (particularly Manitoba) was a fragment of the dominant culture of Ontario. The early migrants implanted their Ontario culture on the West so successfully that Manitoba adopted a more Ontario perspective than the original province itself. The image was "rural Ontario West." L.H. Thomas and Donald Swainson agree with Rea on the dominant image of a colonial west. Two other historians, Greg Thomas and Ian Clarke, claim that the human landscape of the early fur traders with their palisaded forts, and the first British-Ontario farmers with their tree-walled homesteads was an attempt to recreate the West in the image of the eastern landscape from which they had come; it belied the reality of the existing landscape.

The Canadian artists of the late nineteenth century reflected this central Canadian vision. In his recent study, *Our Own Country, Canada*, Denis Reid contends that the artists of the period 1850 to 1900 were driven as much by "a sense of advancement and self-improvement" as by visions of national grandeur, but that the two concepts — the ideal and the reality — became indistinguishable. Their artistic renditions of the Canadian drive to the West were depicted in "romantic and naturalistic images of the noble adversary, the strong and resistant land itself." Reid makes the link more explicit:

> In the mid-eighties this romantic involvement with the land found concrete manifestation in the ribbon of steel that sought to physically bind the nation together. The promotors of the CPR understood the force of images, and they encouraged the associations artists made between their road and the picturesque wonders it opened. If they saw themselves as nation-builders, they were also eager to be seen as enriching the cultural life of the nation.... The remarkable success of the CPR programme in promoting interest in artistic views of the Rockies and the West Coast represents the first significant instance of a widespread acceptance in Canada of the myth of the land as the basis of a national art.

No individual is more identified with the CPR and the optimistic vision of the West than John Macoun. He played an important role in projecting an image of the North West as "the greatest agricultural region of the world." In a study of John Macoun's writings on the West, W.A. Waiser argues that the botanist's optimistic image was simply a reflection of the prevailing view of his time. In the United States, for example, "the Great American desert became known as the Great American Plains — what was termed as 'an imaginative conquest.' Men's illusions about a new environment were more important than the real geography of the land itself." In Canada, the West was linked to the national potential of the new Dominion. Macoun provided the bond in his exaggerated vision of the entire region — even the southern grasslands — as having agricultural potential. In *Manitoba and the Great North-West*, Macoun wrote:

> Want, either present or future is not to be feared, and man living in a healthy and soul invigorating atmosphere will attain his highest development, and a nation will yet rise on these great plains that will have no superior on the American continent.

It was Macoun's optimistic image of the southern grasslands that helped persuade the Canadian Pacific Railway Company to build its line via the southern route rather than follow the North Saskatchewan River valley.

Two articles offer some insight into the romantic images in the literature of the late nineteenth century. The first, Irene Spry's "Early Visitors to the Canadian Prairies," introduces a multiplicity of writings of early visitors to the West and the images they portrayed. The second, Patrick Dunae's " 'Making Good': The Canadian West in British Boy's Literature, 1880-1914," explains the romantic vision of the West which inspired "the immigration of youthful and ambitious British males to western Canada in late-Victorian and Edwardian times," and thus goes a long way to explaining the large number of young, single British settlers in western Canada at the turn of the century. Dunae notes that:

> western Canada was a popular setting for much of this literature. The region offered a hardy climate plus an impressive landscape and, with a little embellishment, boys' writers could readily introduce hostile natives and a population of struggling white pioneers.

Of related interest is an article by the western Canadian historian, L.H. Thomas, which examines the increasing interest in the West after 1885 by a growing number of middle-class British visitors who for the first time could afford the journey west thanks to cheaper and more efficient transportation.

This positive image contrasts strikingly with the negative one in the mind of Quebecers. Arthur Silver offers evidence that French Canadians were discouraged from going West because Quebec politicians, newspaper editors and parish priests convinced them that "western settlement was the sole concern of Ontario." These formulators of public opinion established three major images of the Canadian West: that the land was infertile and "agricultural failure was almost certain"; that it was unsafe for a French Canadian to live outside the province of Quebec for "in the rest of the dominion his national identity would be endangered"; and that Manitoba could never be considered "part of their country." This Quebec image of the West — more mythologized than factual — had tremendous implications for the cultural tradition of the West.

Robert Painchaud has added a new dimension by looking at the image of the West in the minds of those French-Canadian priests who were already in the West. He argues that despite a concerted effort by these priests to persuade Quebecers to come West, they failed because the Quebec priests and politicians saw the West as a weakening influence, with its separate school problems and multicultural immigration, on a strong French-Canadian identity. Better for French Canadians to remain in a strong Quebec.

What still remains somewhat of a mystery is the way in which this central Canadian image of the West in the minds of the early western settlers was transformed during the late nineteenth century into a western Canadian consciousness. Indeed, many of the Ontario expansionists later became the strongest exponents of western regionalism and led the struggle of the West to liberate itself from alleged eastern oppression. Owram devotes a chapter to the question, and attributes the shift in loyalty to the economic depression of the 1880s and the resulting tarnished image of this land of opportunity. As Gerald Friesen has shown, "the myth of the West" which lay at the base of its regional consciousness in the late nineteenth century was rooted in

> an emphasis upon the new society which would be created in an "empty" land. Environmentalism, pastoral and agrarian myths, physiocratic beliefs, and elements now associated with the "frontier" thesis — democracy, egalitarianism,

individualism, co-operation, virility, opportunity, innovation — were aspects of the new society in popular estimation.

Friesen, however, does not explain how these images became part of western consciousness nor how they affected the way westerners saw themselves.

Paul Rutherford argues that "the western press was the chief exponent of western regionalism" in the late nineteenth century and that the press instilled into the minds of its readers a strong regional image based on the myth of the superiority of the West:

> The myth presumed that the west was destined to become the granary of the world, the last and richest frontier of European expansion.... [The press] argued that the "new Canada" would be a better society, free from the mistakes of other lands. By "better" they meant more simple, more individualistic.

It was an image based upon a suspicion of eastern interests and a feeling that the West was a region with its own ideals which, paradoxically the press argued, were still "Canadian." Hence Rutherford concludes that "western regionalism seemed based upon two opposed concepts, regional alienation and 'Canadianism.'"

The positive image of the West in the formative period of western development in part stimulated the large-scale surge of American, British and European immigration at the turn of the century. There is no definitive study of the various images of the Canadian West presented in the extensive immigration propaganda distributed by the Canadian government, the Canadian Pacific Railway Company, and private land companies. Klaus Peter Stich has made a beginning from the literary perspective by analyzing five samples of propaganda literature *qua* literature. He denies that such literature was simply "distortions and lies" but was, rather, one genre of popular *fiction* — "realistic-cum-romantic" — which, like all literature, helped to shape "western Canada's cultural image at home and abroad." It was an optimistic vision of "Canada's Century."

An offshoot of this immigration propaganda was boosterism — a deliberate attempt by urban leaders to present an inflated image of their home town in hopes of an eventual self-fulfilling prophecy. Urban historians are only beginning to examine this side of urban growth, but Alan Artibise speculates that boosterism was as important a factor in urbanization on the Prairies as were natural physical factors. He notes:

> explanations of prairie urban development cannot be carried on entirely in terms of the usual factors of site and situation.... The physical and economic environments are inert and unimportant until human effort is applied to them. Urban centres and regions do not grow in the organic sense of the word; they are rather, the product of thousands of individual and group decisions. These decisions, in turn, are a product of a particular cultural milieu and reflect the biases and knowledge of the actors.

Boosterism was particularly strong in the West because of the underdeveloped prairies, the lack of natural physical advantages, and the uniform topography. In such an environment, the mental component — the positive image in the minds of a city's elite and citizenry — was often the deciding factor in urban success or failure.

Ethnic historians have often neglected the role of imagery in evaluating the conditions that caused immigrants to leave their native land and to react as they did in Canada. There are two notable exceptions. In his study of Dutch immigration to Canada in the years 1892-1940, Herman Ganzevoort devotes a chapter to the role of the emigration agent "who depended on myth rather than fact to recruit. And it was all too obvious that myth and not reality was the great drawing card for potential emigrants." A further chapter discusses the images of the West projected by emigration societies and in governmental propaganda. Anthony Rasporich's study of western Canadian utopian settlements examines the vision which inspired a significant number of ethnic, religious and social groups in the pre-1914 era. He concludes:

> The ideals of social co-operation and of work as a creative act of self-fulfillment, and the concept of the garden city were all essential components of these strains of late-century liberal-imperial thought which shaped the Anglo-Canadian mentality of the early Northwest before the First World War.

This idealism, he implies, was a strong force behind the agrarian protest which followed the war. When the initial idealistic utopias were inevitably unfulfilled in the harsh economic and physical realities of western Canada, these individuals simply substituted their earlier more naive image with one more closely rooted in the economic and political realities of the time. Yet it can be argued that the agrarian ideology of the twenties was no less idealistic in its fundamental perception. The western farmer premised his fight against the East, big business and urban encroachment on the image that "God Made the Country, Man Made the Town" — that farmers were God's Chosen People, and that the family farm was the ideal social unit. Unfortunately, the ideology of agrarian reform has received less attention than the politics and economics of western protest.

Utopianism was only part of a much broader image of the West as "the new and ideal society," so popular in the first two decades of the twentieth century. This vision sustained the farmers' protest movement; it also inspired the Social Gospel Movement — which drew much of its leadership and support from, and had its most significant impact in, the West. As the newest region of settlement, the West held out higher hopes than the older and more established areas. This image of a "new society" was reflected in the early western Canadian literature. Whether one is discussing the tremendous popularity of Ralph Connor, R.J.C. Stead, Nellie McClung, Emily Murphy (Janey Canuck) or lesser literary figures, there is a sameness in their romantic image of the Canadian West as "the garden of the world." As Dick Harrison notes in *Unnamed Country*:

> Like Eden, their West had no past, only a present beginning when the settlers arrive, and a better future. This was, of course, a time of boom and optimism and, for the writers at least, a time of agrarian ideals.... There is no doubt that at this stage the literary imagination was out of touch with certain hard realities of the plains, though no more so than the practical minds that planned the agricultural expansion in the West.

Gerald Friesen, a cultural historian, indicates that this image was transformed into "reality" by associating the pastoral ideal directly with the physical locale of western Canada in the minds of both western writers and politicians.

> Whether described as a former garden or an untouched land, the west was to be the home of a new society; the pastoral ideal was thus moved from literature into history, from form into reality, and became both a place and a mode of belief.... The "West," which in post-confederation Canada had a precise geographical location, had become an idyllic region.

This early group of western literary figures described their region in terms of its contrast to the East. They imagined the West to be "young, not old; free, not restrained by convention; egalitarian, not caste-bound; virile, not feeble; close to nature, not urban. It offered a new start, not enslavement by history." The explanation for the contrast was environmental; the land itself moulded an individual's character. One of Ralph Connors' characters explained: "How wonderful the power of this country of yours to transform men." The ideal West lay in the future, a Golden Age, when the "good guys" moulded by their western environment would prevail over the "bad guys" who came West contaminated by their eastern environment.

This image was reinforced in the historiography of the West in the period up to and including the 1920s. Doug Owram examines the historiography of western Canada up to 1900 and concludes that there emerged during this period an interpretation of history which emphasized the uniqueness and strength of western Canada in contrast to the region to the East. Owram concludes:

> Resentful of their treatment at the hands of the East and Ottawa, westerners had rejected the eastern interpretation of their place within the nation and had looked to the land around them for a new definition of their role. In so doing they developed all the necessary prerequisites for a strong sense of regional identity. ... The West was no longer merely an adjunct of the East or an annexed land; it was, westerners felt, something more than "a new Upper Canada," and something better.

The frontier school of thought which was borrowed from F.J. Turner's thesis in American historiography and which became popular in Canadian historical writing in the 1920s, reinforced the image of the West as superior to the East. The West was seen as the home of democracy, the inspiration for reform, and the seed-bed of individualism, radicalism and freedom, in contrast to the more privileged conservative and reactionary East. As J.M.S. Careless concluded: "Canadian environmentalists frequently displayed the compelling mood of the frontier school, with its moral implications of a struggle between sound native democratic forces [in the West] and elements that cling to privilege, exploitation, and empty Old-World forms [in the East]."

The emphasis on environment affected the image of the West in Canadian literature as well. In the 1920s, a new "realistic" image emerged (in contrast to the earlier romantic literature) with the publication of three notable prairie novels — Martha Ostenso's *Wild Geese* (1925), Robert Stead's *Grain* (1926), and Phillip Grove's *Settlers of the Marsh* (1925). All three depicted a hostile and alien prairie environment. The strong emphasis on environmental influences on the characters in these and other prairie novels has led some literary critics, notably E.A. McCourt, Henry Kreisel, and Laurence Ricou, to conclude that the image of the West must be sought through an understanding of the impact of environment on perception. Kreisel writes: "All discussion of the literature produced in the Canadian west must of necessity begin with the impact of the landscape upon the mind." Similarly, Laurence Ricou concludes that prairie fiction illustrates "both the prevalence of the myth of the land in Canadian writing and the regional qualities which derive from the encounter with a specific distinctive landscape."

Western Canadian artists in the 1920s — L.L. Fitzgerald, W.J. Phillips, Illingworth Kerr and Robert Hurley — also looked to the landscape to create a new regional consciousness. They were doing for the West what the Group of Seven was doing for Canada in general: namely, discovering images of the land which could become symbols of identity. One of the best known was Robert Hurley, an English painter who came to Saskatchewan in 1923. He broke with the romantic tradition in western Canadian art by shifting the iconography from streams and wooded valleys — uncharacteristic prairie landscape scenes — to flat prairie, railways, telephone posts, grain elevators and an expansive sky — images that he stereotyped as representing the essence of the prairie. Ronald Rees describes Hurley's technique: "By suppressing detail and by using hard, clean outlines and bold, exaggerated colours, Hurley was able to convey a sense of the simplicity and emptiness of the landscape and evoke the clarity and harshness of the prairie light." Hurley inaugurated a new era in western Canadian art by shifting the artistic image of the West from a promised land to a harsh environment, and hence forcing the artist to seek its meaning in abstraction or symbolism.

The onslaught of the Great Depression erased the remaining vestiges of the West as a promised land. As the hardest hit region, the West came to symbolize all the worst aspects of the Depression. They very phrase "The Dirty Thirties" conveyed the new image and conjured up awesome pictures of defeat, long lines of unemployed; boxcars covered by men "riding the rods"; the boredom of relief camps; windfall apples and surplus cod; whirling plagues of dust and grasshoppers; the interminable bitter heat of the unrelenting prairie sun.

A useful study for a cultural historian would be to examine the image of the West in the popular literature of the decade. One would expect to find a similar view to the negative one in the classic novel of the prairie West in the 1930s — Sinclair Ross's *As For Me and My House,* "the most severe of the Depression novels." According to Dick Harrison:

> we see the complete progress of the prairie from beneficient to indifferent to hostile environment. What is new is a strain of desert imagery, with its inevitable suggestion of spiritual sterility extending to characters like Philip and Mrs. Bentley.

Not surprisingly, the Great Depression witnessed a new environmentalist approach to Canadian history which was as harsh in its image of the West as that depicted in the literature of the time. The Laurentian thesis argued that the metropolitan centres of central Canada formed a commercial, political and cultural empire that dominated and exploited the hinterlands, like the West, which came under its influence. Thus the West ceased to be seen as the creative centre of the nation which had constantly thrown up new ideas and democratic movements (as in the frontier thesis) and was depicted instead as a region subordinate to the East and one essentially conservative and even reactionary in its ethos. Careless summarized the idea this way:

> The Laurentian School ... looked not from the forest-born frontiers for its perspective of Canadian history but from developing eastern centres of commerce and industry. Indeed, it primarily studied the effects of the East on the West, and largely regarded business men and conservative urban political elements as agents of national expansion who might well be more far-sighted in their outlook than were their agrarian opponents.

Out of the West there arose in the post-World War II era a voice of protest. The western Canadian historian, W.L. Morton, accepted the validity of the Laurentian interpretation for an understanding of Canadian history but objected to the negative image of western Canada it implied. This image, he believed, could only lead to an inferiority complex among western Canadians which would ultimately be more pervasive in influencing the history of western Canada than the impact of the environment itself, a case of mind over matter. Truth is how an individual perceives it, which in the case of a western Canadian would be that of a second-class citizen of Canada.

Morton set out to dispel this negative image by attempting to create a new self-image in the minds of westerners through an appreciation of their history. He would have agreed wholeheartedly with his colleague, A.R.M. Lower, who argued that history is myth and the historian a myth-maker. Morton described *Manitoba: A History* as "a history that informs and shapes our minds." The history — and therefore the image — of the West that Morton created was one which saw the region as attempting to be like, not different from, the rest of Canada. He argued in fact that the West has been germane to the Canadian experience and that its history could be seen as a miniature replica of the nation itself.

Yet Morton's image of the West had its own limitations. J.E. Rea has observed in an appropriately entitled article, "Images of the West," that Morton could not get beyond his own image — moulded by his personal experience of growing up in a British family on a prairie homestead — of the West as an essentially rural, agricultural and British society; his vision could not incorporate the European immigrants and the urban West. Morton reveals the roots of his agrarian image in "Seeing an Unliterary Landscape," an article characterized by imagery. It can also be argued that, by emphasizing the constant struggle of western Canada for equality with and recognition by the rest of the nation, Morton has reinforced the subordinate position of the West while ironically trying to dispel it. In "The Bias of Prairie Politics," for example, he argued that "the subordinate status given the West in Confederation was the initial bias that set in train the development of prairie politics towards an increasing differentiation from the Canadian standard." To Morton this initial bias explained all of western Canadian history, from the struggle for political equality in Confederation in the period 1870 to 1905, to the rise of agrarian revolt in the years 1905-1925, to the utopian period from 1925 to the present.

What Morton did for the historiography of western Canada current literary critics, such as Eli Mandel, Dick Harrison and W.H. New, have done for its literature. They have challenged the "environmentalist approach" with its belief that literature is a product of the landscape. In "Images of Prairie Man," Mandel characteristically reverses the earlier association of environment and mind, to argue that the landscape is itself nothing more than the image which exists in the mind of the beholder. Thus writers are also "conscious mythmakers" who do not simply reflect the region itself but help to create it. Robert Kroetsch expresses the idea this way: "In a sense we haven't got an identity until somebody tells our story. The fiction makes us real." Social mythologies — the myths of history — create the mind-set which in turn superimposes a form of reality on the particular place being mythologized. With respect to the prairies, Mandel expresses it thus: "What isn't clear is whether the prairies themselves are a form that imposes itself on the resistant self or whether it goes the other way around: we possess these stories, not even our own, and try to put their shapes on a world which resists fiercely." A study of regional literature becomes a search for identity — a search characteristic of Morton's search by means of history for his identity — his image of the West as his homeland, his cultural roots.

A similar internalizing of the landscape has occurred among Canadian geographers, resulting in a new interpretation of regionalism which in turn has affected their image of the West. Some current geographers have argued that there are no "natural" regions in Canada based upon formal physical features. Instead regions should be defined according to the perceptions and use that man makes of his particular physical environment at any given time, which in turn changes over time. As Wreford Watson explained the concept:

> physical geography should be brought into regional geography, as something which, when perceived by man and translated into certain images based on the aims and powers people have at their time, then becomes a cogent, meaningful reality: but always a reality in terms of man's perception. The real "reality" is the image in the mind, rather than the pattern on the ground.

Thus man's changing images of the land become the primary concern of geographers.

This new approach has led geographers to argue that a region must be understood according to man's perception of its *function*, i.e. its relation to other regions or to the nation as a whole, rather than its *form*, i.e. its natural environment. Hence J. Howard Richards has seen the uniqueness of the Prairie region not in its physical form but in its functional role as the economic hinterland of wheat production for external metropolitan centres — a view very much in keeping with the metropolitan-hinterland concept of Canadian history. The image he depicted was an isolated region — isolated not only nor primarily by vast spaces and sparse population but by an attitude — a perception — which has kept the West distinct from the urban and industrial growth of the rest of the nation. The physical and political isolation of the West has been, in Richard's view, further "reinforced by a sense of psychological separateness and difference which modern communications have not removed." It is this perceptual isolation in particular that

> has helped to create a special identity, and common acceptance of this has induced a conceptual frame in which popular characterizations such as "bread basket" and "colonial economy" are frequent, and vague ideas exist of second class economic status *vis-à-vis* the rest of Canada.

Wreford Watson raised the further question:

> to what extent the Prairie People, having found in wheat a commodity that in a sense defied isolation, entrenched themselves as wheat producers, thereby isolating themselves from the incentive and the opportunity to engage in industry? Perhaps we have blamed the natural environment for what the environment of the mind really caused.

The image of an inferior region in its historical relationship to the nation reinforced a way of life and a perception of the landscape which became a self-fulfilling prophecy. This has led Watson to appeal to his fellow geographers to study "mental images of our environment" — the internal landscape — as the most fruitful means of understanding the geography of a region or the nation. "Somehow the mental images of our environment must be measured by geographers and become part of geographical study because they affect the actual way in which men use their world and make their geographies."

Prairie painters also turned to the internal landscape by means of abstract painting as the best means to capture the image of the West. Patricia Bovey claims that the prairie landscape has been particularly suited to abstract painting because of its common denominators of sky and land. Illingworth Kerr, Saskatchewan's native-born professional painter, was one of the first prairie artists to attempt abstract painting, claiming that "abstract was the answer to Western space with its vast scale, its power of mood, rather than tangible form." Abstraction has done for the western Canadian artist what the search for universals did for its literary writers or what functional regionalism did for historical geographers or historians: freed him from the restrictive search for the image of the West in the physical landscape and enabled him to search within himself. Northrop Frye observed in a different context:

> The effect of stylizing and simplifying is to bring out more clearly not what the artist sees, but what he experiences in his seeing. Abstraction sets the painter free from the particular experiences, and enables him to paint the essence of his pictorial vision.

The "real" landscape is within the mind of the artist, and it changes as each prairie artist paints his own West anew.

The underlying premise in the metropolitan interpretation of Canadian history, in the functional approach to regionalism in Canadian geography and in the mythical concept of Canadian literature, is of a region that has been predominantly an agricultural hinterland in its nature and in its association with the rest of Canada. Yet western Canada has undergone tremendous economic and social changes since World War II which have led to increased urbanization and industrialization. Have these changes resulted in new images of the West? Only recently, in the past two decades, have historians, geographers, political scientists, artists and literary critics addressed themselves to this question.

A number of historical geographers argue that the social changes have had little impact because the prevailing image of the West as an agricultural hinterland has continued to exert a powerful influence on the development of the region long after it ceases to be valid. Despite the increase in urban population and the development of new primary industries based on the new staples of fossil fuels and potash and the resulting increase in tertiary industries, there has been no change in the western image of itself as an economic hinterland. Prairie urban centres still see themselves in relation to metropolitan centres in the East rather than as foci for national centres on their own. Within the West itself, the towns and cities continue to function as "service centres for farms and ranches" long after agriculture and ranching have ceased to be the dominant economic activities of the region. Hence Kaye and Moodie conclude, in "Geographical Perspectives on the Canadian

Plains," that the historical evolution of the West as an agricultural hinterland has given the region a uniformity and a sense of uniqueness even after it has become urbanized and industrialized like the rest of the nation. Past images still dictate present developments. In a study of architecture in small towns of Saskatchewan, the historical geographer, Ronald Rees, reinforces the view. Rural values — thrift, industry, pragmatism and sobriety — still dictate prairie architectural styles:

> The small frame buildings, the unpaved streets, the false fronts, and the general air of seediness and decay give the small towns a look of impermanence which is only slightly offset by the occasional brick building such as a bank, station or municipal office. The larger and sturdier centres are more reassuring. But in these, too, the visitor is conscious of only a partially developed urbanity, for the general aspect is an expression of utilitarian rather than social or aesthetic values.

Kaye and Moodie conclude as well that "the cultural patterns established during the classic period of plains agricultural occupance are still the dominant ones today."

This hypothesis is consistent with recent work by Alan Artibise on the impact of boosterism on current trends in prairie urban development. He argues that the image of tremendous growth of urban centres within the context of an agricultural hinterland role, which was so much a part of the booster mentality in the pre-1914 era, continued to exert a powerful influence in subsequent periods including the post-1950 era when the West ceased to be a predominantly agricultural region. "By the 1950s prairie cities were in most respects still tied to structures, ideas, and routines of a bygone era, and no amount of simple manoeuvering could alter this legacy in a major way." Thus the image the elites attempted to foster tended to retard rather than to stimulate growth.

These conclusions differ markedly from that of the political scientist Roger Gibbins in his recent study, *Prairie Politics and Society*. He claims that the prevailing image of the West as a rural agricultural hinterland victimized by eastern interests is no longer applicable in the urban industrial West of today. The result is a decline in regional consciousness and a rise in provincial power. Yet Gibbins fails to explain why modernization should lead to an even narrower base of identity than the region itself. One would expect a similarity in economic, social and demographic trends in the West to that of the nation in general to foster a national identity. Westerners should become more like other Canadians in attitude and political behaviour, yet Gibbins concludes otherwise. It would appear that images of injustice, victimization and inequality still prevail as "western" traits in all three provinces of the West (although Gibbins' evidence emphasizes Alberta); they are simply linked to the provinces rather than the region as a whole.

Yet has this not been "traditionally true"? The West has never been a common political region to the same extent that it has been a common economic, cultural or social region. If regions are defined in functional terms, as geographers have argued, then the West can have different boundaries if one is speaking in political terms as opposed to cultural or economic terms. Thus the traditional images continue to exist and to assert the influence they did in the past. This conclusion is reinforced in a recent article, "Political culture in the West." David Smith argues that throughout the history of the Prairie provinces there have been certain ideas which have prevailed, in spite of the changing nature of western Canada, and which have become part of the political culture of the West: a rejection of English-French dualism on the prairies; a distrust of central control, either public (governmental) or private (corporate); and a need to struggle consistently to protect regional resources and to assert regional autonomy against central domination. The image of the West as a victimized region lives on.

Prairie writers have been sensitive to the changing nature of the West. To contemporary writers the old agrarian West is gone, the subject of reflection and reinterpretation. More than this, it has become, according to Dick Harrison, a subject of rediscovery since it is necessary to discover new images of the West in order to free it from the restraints of the older images which no longer fit. This required "re-naming the past," the title of the last chapter of Harrison's *Unnamed Country*, which deals with the views of contemporary western Canadian novelists. In a prairie world out of touch with the images of an agrarian West, the past events can no longer be real but must be symbolic acts. As Harrison writes: "The prairies become less a thing 'out there' which must be shaped physically as well as imaginatively and more a territory within the psyche which must be explored and understood...." Eli Mandel explains it thus:

> it is not place but attitude, state of mind, that defines the western writer — and that state of mind, I want to suggest, has a good deal to do with a tension between place and culture, a doubleness or duplicity, that makes the writer a man not so much in place, as out of place and so one endlessly trying to get back to find his way home, to return, to write himself into existence, writing west.

To be western is a way of perceiving that becomes "real," independent of the physical place itself. Still it is the myths, legends and feelings of the region, evoked by its geography and history, which will decide the imagery that writers use in recapturing their lost home. For the search for home is but an understanding of self which, in turn, is a product of time and place. The search must continue to be pursued within the traditional framework — the altering image — of the region itself. But these entities no longer have a narrow, restrictive role; they are fluid entities which influence each individual differently and hence make the West very much an image within the mind of the beholder. There continues, therefore, to be a healthy and creative tension between "perception" or "imagery," and "reality."

The search for home, for self, the need to define oneself in context of time and place — to discover images of the West — which have concerned contemporary literary writers, have also been the subject of western Canadian art, particularly the paintings of William Kurelek. In a penetrating analysis of Kurelek's paintings, Ramsay Cook notes that the artist's "farm paintings and his religious paintings were the product of the same imagination." It was an imagination moulded by the Prairies — the product of a particular time and place. His paintings are part of "Kurelek's creation of a new past, part of his search for himself, a coming to terms with his own past by recreating it." It was a search within for the images which best captured the West that was so much a part of himself — a journey taken by a number of western Canadian writers, including W.L. Morton. His images of the West have become part of our perception of it, as much a part of the West as the physical landscape itself.

In conclusion, it is evident that the West has changed over time, and that the change has been due as much, if not more, to the altering perceptions or images of the region as to the changing physical environment. The change has been within the mind. The West is, as Richard Allen notes, "a mental construct." And the image has imposed a form on the external entity which has transformed it into the identity given to it at a particular period in history. Each generation searches anew for an image that gives meaning to its perception of the physical locale and historical evolution of the region. Hence the changing images of the West.

The Pattern of Prairie Politics

NELSON WISEMAN

Canadian historians and social scientists have usually thought of the prairies as a more or less homogeneous unit whose politics have been essentially a response, a reaction, to externally imposed conditions: the tariff, the withholding of authority over natural resources by the federal government, discriminatory transportation policies, etc. This approach tells us substantially about east-west Canadian relations. By itself, however, it tells us little about diversity of political traditions *on* the prairies. What is needed is an interpretive analysis which comes to terms with intra-regional differences. Why, until quite recently, has Manitoba politics been so dominated by Liberal and Conservative regimes? Why has Saskatchewan been so receptive to the CCF-NDP? Why did Alberta spawn such a durable and unorthodox farmers' government (the UFA) and then, overnight, become the bastion of an equally unorthodox Social Credit regime?

Answers to these questions do not lie (although some clues do) in an analysis of the east-west relationship. Nor do the answers lie in analyses which focus strictly on party systems or economic conditions. An economic analysis may be used to explain why, in the landmark federal election of 1911, Saskatchewan and Alberta endorsed the Liberals and freer trade, but it will not explain why Manitoba endorsed the Conservatives and protection. An analysis of party systems may be used to explain why, at the provincial level, Saskatchewan and Alberta rejected the two older parties in favour of third parties. It will not explain, however, why those two third parties are at opposite poles of the Canadian political spectrum. Identifying and accounting for the differences among the three prairie provinces, therefore, is essential. But this too is insufficient because striking diversities are to be located not only among but also *within* the provinces. By the 1890s, for example, Manitoba had been remade in the image of western Ontario. Yet in 1919, Winnipeg exhibited a level of class consciousness and class conflict that was decidedly more reminiscent of the European than the North American scheme of things. In Saskatchewan, until 1945, the federal Liberal party was consistently stronger than in any other English Canadian province. But it was this same province that returned North America's first social democratic government, a CCF government whose ideology was rooted in the British Labour party. Inconsistent political patterns seem no less profound in Alberta where governing parties that are defeated at the polls have faded almost immediately.

Nelson Wiseman, "The Pattern of Prairie Politics," *Queen's Quarterly*, Vol. 88, No. 2 (Summer 1981), pp. 298–315. Reprinted by permission of the author.

The analysis employed here utilizes the concepts of ideology and ethnicity. Elements of Canadian toryism, liberalism, and socialism have been present in varying positions in each province. Political representatives of these ideological tendencies on the prairies include men as diverse as Rodmond Roblin, John Diefenbaker, Charles Dunning, J. W. Dafoe, J. S. Woodsworth, Tommy Douglas, Henry Wise Wood, and William Aberhart, none of whom were born on the prairies. Because the prairie provinces and their societies were moulded in the late nineteenth and early twentieth centuries this is not surprising. Ideas and ideologies first appeared on the prairies as importations.

It is very unlikely that a Rodmond Roblin or a Tommy Douglas, preaching what they did, could have become premiers of Alberta. William Aberhart would not likely have succeeded in Manitoba or Saskatchewan. Politicians are reflectors of their society, their environment, their times. They may be examined in terms which transcend quirks of personality. Their ideas and actions may be seen as reflections of the popular and ideological-cultural basis of their support.

The key to prairie politics is in the unravelling of the dynamic relationship between ideological-cultural heritage and party. In Manitoba, the imported nineteenth-century Ontario liberal party tradition (with "a tory touch") maintained political hegemony until 1969. In Saskatchewan, the dominant tone of politics has reflected a struggle between Ontario liberal and British socialist influences. In Alberta, Americans' populist-liberal ideas gained widespread currency beginning in the very first decade of that province's existence. In all three provinces minorities of non-Anglo-American origins have, in their voting, helped make and break governments. These minorities, however, have not determined the ideological coloration of any major party.

Prairie political culture is best seen as the product of the interaction of four distinct waves of pioneering settlers. The first wave was a Canadian one. More precisely, it was largely rural Ontarian. This wave was a westward extension of English Canada's dominant charter group. Ontarians were a charter group in each prairie province but their impact was greatest in Manitoba. It seemed both fitting and telling, that one of Manitoba's premiers (Hugh John Macdonald) was the son of Canada's first prime minister. Tory-touched Canadian liberalism was the ideological core of nineteenth-century Ontario and its prairie offshoot.

A second distinct wave in prairie settlement was a new, modern, British group. Coming near the turn of this century, it was largely urban and working class. Transformed and battered by nineteenth-century industrialism, Britain's working class had begun to turn to socialism. Despite the cultural and ideological differences between the Ontario and new-British waves, their social status in the west was roughly equal, both groups being British subjects and Anglo-Saxon pioneers in British North American. The new-British wave had its greatest impact in the cities, most powerfully in the largest prairie city, Winnipeg. In Saskatchewan relatively large numbers of new British (and

European-born) immigrants settled in rural areas and they produced Canada's most successful provincial social democratic party. It seemed both fitting and telling that Saskatchewan's premier in this labour-socialist tradition (Tommy Douglas) was British-born and grew up and was politically socialized in Winnipeg's new British labour-socialist environment.

The third wave in prairie settlement was American. More specifically it was midwest, great plains American. Like the Ontario wave, but unlike the new-British wave, it came out of an agrarian setting with deeply rooted agrarian values and settled, in overwhelming numbers, in rural areas. Because of their values and racial origin American Anglo-Saxons became the only non-Canadian, non-British charter group on the prairies. The dominant ideological strain carried by the American wave was similar but not identical to that carried by the Ontarians. It was, to be sure, liberal, but its liberalism was devoid of toryism. It was a radical "populist" liberalism that stressed the individual rather than the community or the state as a tory or socialist would. This wave's greatest impact was in rural Alberta, the continent's last agricultural frontier. Populist liberalism expressed itself in an unconventional farmers' movement/government known as the United Farmers of Alberta (UFA) and in the long tenure of Social Credit. It seemed both fitting and telling, that this wave's leading representative figure was a veteran Missouri populist (Henry Wise Wood).

The fourth and last wave of prairie settlement consisted of continental Europeans. Because of their numerous national origins, their roots and traditions were the most diverse of the four waves. They were, however, neither a charter group nor did they have a significant ideological impact (the eastern European and Finnish influences in the Communist Party being a minor exception). The non-Anglo-Saxons were "alien" and suspect in the eyes of the other three groups. At times their very presence was attacked and challenged; at best they were tolerated. The ideological and political role of the continental wave became largely one of deference. The continental wave had its greatest urban impact in Winnipeg and its greatest rural impact in Saskatchewan. These areas were also those in which the new-British wave had its greatest impact. The combined voting strength of these two waves was to lead to CCE-NDP victories in Manitoba and Saskatchewan in later years. The Old World ideological attributes of the continentals were dismissed as illegitimate on the prairies. Because of this, continentals deferred to the parties based on the other three groups; but the continentals represented the largest swing factor in voting of the four waves. They helped elect and defeat parties anchored by the other waves; they neither anchored nor led a major party.

The foregoing description of the four distinct waves of prairie settlers is not intended to imply that all Ontarians were tory-touched liberals, that all new Britons were labour-socialists, that all Americans were populist-liberals, and that all continentals deferred ideologically and politically. Furthermore, it should be understood that not all Ontarians voted for the Liberals and Conservatives, not all new Britons voted CCF, and not all Americans voted UFA-Social Credit. The contention here, simply, is that without the new-British impact the CCF would never had attained the stature it did (indeed, it might not have been created at all); similarly, without the American impact the UFA-Social Credit phenomenon in Alberta would not have been anything like what it was; and without the Ontarians, prairie Liberal and Conservative parties would not have gained early hegemony.

The evidence for the interpretation presented here is to be found in prairie historiography, but this evidence is generally disregarded. The notion that Ontario, British, American, and continental European people and influences have helped shape prairie politics is not a new idea. But it might as well be, because it is an idea that has never been developed. There are ten excellent books in a series entitled "Social Credit in Alberta: Its Background and Development." Not one of these books, however, devotes one paragraph to the American impact on Alberta, an impact unparalleled in Canada.

The impact of transplanted ideas was greater in Canada's west than in the United States because the physical impact of immigrants was greater. In 1914, for example, the year of greatest immigration to the U.S. in the decade, one immigrant arrived for eighty in the population. In Canada, in contrast, one immigrant arrived for every eighteen in the population in 1913. The bulk of them, whether from Britain, continental Europe or the United States, went west.

Initially, Ontarian settlement prevailed on the prairies. Ontarians occupied the best agricultural lands and secured homesteads along the new Canadian Pacific Railway. Their power was most profound in Manitoba which, having entered Confederation in 1870, offered the first and most accessible frontier for westward migration. The Ontarians were soon followed by waves of Britons, Americans and continentals. The British came from the most urbanized industrial society in the world, but one that offered no rise in real wages between 1895 and 1913. More than a century of slowly developing working-class consciousness was represented by this new-British group. The American settlers, in contrast, came largely from the rural midwest. The Jeffersonian physiocratic notion that the soil was the sole source of wealth guided their policies. Their interest in the Canadian frontier was fueled by Canadian government propaganda which employed the agrarian ideal, the Horatio Alger tradition and the log cabin stereotype, all prominent features of American liberal mythology. The continental immigrants were largely from eastern and central Europe, where land tenancy systems were in some cases only a half-century removed from feudalism. Of these three groups the Americans were the most likely and the British the least likely to homestead. Many Britons and continentals were to find their way into the new and growing prairie cities: Winnipeg, Regina, Calgary and Edmonton.

In addition to differences in immigrant distribution among the provinces there were differences within each province. Although there were equal numbers of Americans and Britons in Alberta, for example, in the 1920s Americans outnumbered Britons in all fifteen of Alberta's rural census divisions, by a ratio of about two to one. In a province where the rural MLAs prevailed this meant an extraordinary American political influence. In twelve of the fifteen rural census divisions in Alberta Americans also outnumbered continental-born settlers. All three exceptions were in the northeast — that part of the province that provided the strongest rural opposition that both the American-influenced United Farmers of Alberta and Social Credit encountered.

In Saskatchewan, in the 1920s, Britons only slightly outnumbered Americans. The relative rural homogeneity of Saskatchewan, however, produced a dramatically different equation than in Alberta: the overwhelming majority of Britons settled in rural areas. Paradoxically, Saskatchewan had fewer Britons than either Alberta or Manitoba, but the Britons it did have penetrated rural Saskatchewan in a way that the Britons in neighboring provinces did not. Furthermore, in Alberta the majority of American settlers were Anglo-Saxons; in Saskatchewan Anglo-Saxons were in a minority among Americans. This was important because a condition for political success was an Anglo-Saxon background. The largest number of Britons who entered Manitoba and Alberta generally headed for the cities; in Winnipeg population quadrupled between 1901 and 1915.

The four distinct waves of immigrants differed in religion as well as political ideology. Methodists and other social gospellers had their greatest impact in places in Winnipeg where the British-born labourist wave was particularly strong. Catholicism, brought over by many continental Europeans, was strongest in Saskatchewan and contributed to the Liberals' long hold on power there. Anglicans, with roots in both Ontario and Britain, reinforced Conservative tendencies in all three provinces. Many fundamentalists, and they represented an exceptionally high twenty percent of Alberta Protestants, came to that province as American Bible Belt populists.

Ethnic voting studies have not been able to provide a coherent interpretation of prairie politics because studying "ethnic" voting by listing "Anglo-Saxons" as against Germans, Ukrainians, French, etc., fails to appreciate that some "Anglo-Saxons" were from the "Red" Clyde of Glasgow, others from Perth County, Ontario, and still others from the populist state of Kansas. Different types of divisions of course existed within other ethnic groups. Between the 1920s and 1950s the key distinguishing features in Anglo-Saxon voting in Winnipeg were class status and birthplace. For example, in one part of Winnipeg represented almost continuously since 1921 by MPs J.S. Woodsworth and Stanley Knowles, large numbers of British-born, low-income residents voted overwhelmingly CCF. The city's highest income Anglo-Saxon area with relatively fewer British-born, in contrast, voted overwhelmingly Liberal and Conservative. In both areas Canadian-born Anglo-Saxons far outnumbered other Anglo-Saxons. This revealed that second and third generations reflected inherited ideological-cultural traditions which continued to be expressed in party voting.

Although their demographic impact was great, continental immigrants did not play a leading role in early political developments. Rather, they yielded to the politics of the charter groups. Large numbers of them were isolated in rural ethnic colonies; many were in marginal farming areas where federal agents had directed them. In response to their new opportunity, and in their related effort to prove their loyalty to their new country, these minorities voted Liberal in Alberta from 1905 to 1921, and Liberal in Saskatchewan from 1905 to 1944. In Manitoba too the Liberals were the main beneficiaries of this vote although occasionally, as in 1914, proof of loyalty expressed itself in a Conservative vote. Winnipeg was an exception to the rest of the prairies only in that its working-class continentals were sufficiently numerous, concentrated and class-conscious to form a vibrant community party after 1920. The politics of deference, however, did little to raise the status of the European minorities. Racist prejudice against the continentals was widespread.

Ontarian influence seemed dominant in all three provinces until at least 1921. During World War I, for example, all three provincial premiers, their ministers of agriculture, and a majority of MLAs were Ontarians. In Manitoba the grit agrarianism of Ontario expressed itself in the selection of every premier from the 1880s until Ed Schreyer in 1969. Its distinct mark was reflected in the transplantation of the Ontario municipal system and in the School Question. In Saskatchewan this same, essentially Protestant and English grit outlook dominated the Saskatchewan Grain Growers Association (SGGA), the province's federal and provincial Progressives, and the Liberal party. But in Saskatchewan, unlike Ontario and Manitoba, the dominance of this liberal grit tradition was dependent on support from other elements in the population, specifically non-Anglo-Saxons, of which Saskatchewan had English Canada's highest percentage. Moreover, Saskatchewan's version of grit agrarianism was to encounter a powerful ideological competitor in the form of British-style socialism. The votes of the continentals helped elect a prairie version of the British Labour party in 1944.

American populist influences were greater in Saskatchewan, than in Manitoba but they were secondary and not nearly as significant as in Alberta. In Alberta the American-style populist farmers association (the UFA) determined the complexion of successive provincial governments for years. Alberta populism, like American populism, attracted some socialists, but it rejected socialist ideology. CCF socialism, embraced in Saskatchewan, was rejected by Alberta farmers on the peculiarly American grounds that it represented a repudiation of their "rugged individualism."

Manitoba was the province most true to the values of rural Ontario. In the language rights debates it was more Orange than Ontario. Manitoba imported its early American-inspired farm organizations — the Grange and the Patrons of Industry — only after they had become established in Ontario.

Manitoba's Tory farmers rejected any suggestion of possible seccession from Confederation and American annexation in the 1880s.

A good representative of Manitoba's tory-touched liberalism was Rodmond Roblin, premier from 1900 to 1915. His toryism was reflected in the debate over direct legislation, an idea brought to the prairies from the United States. Every political party on the prairies supported the proposal except Roblin's Conservatives in Manitoba. Roblin attacked direct legislation on the basis that it was "A Socialistic and Un-British Plan." This permitted him to appeal to a fundamentally liberal but tory-touched rural Manitoba. According to Sir Rodmond, direct legislation represented a form of "degenerate republicanism," much too strong a phrase to use successfully in Alberta, but not in Manitoba.

T. A. Crerar was a typical Ontarian in rural Manitoba. As a member of the dominant charter group on the prairies, Crerar became a spokesman for the west but remained a product of the east. Between 1919 and 1922 he was offered the premierships of both Ontario and Manitoba. Crerar's liberalism was expressed in his leadership of the Progressive party and in his role as the architect of federal Liberal-Progressive rapprochement. He insisted that his party was not appealing to any specific class in society. Alberta's Henry Wise Wood, in contrast, insisted that it must make a class appeal to farmers by demanding occupational representation or what became known as "group government." Wood's approach was typical of the American left, wholly within the confines of monolithic American liberalism, defining class in liberal (equality of opportunity) rather than socialist (equality of condition) terms. Crerar's liberalism, closer to British liberalism, denied any connection with class politics. Crerar represented the tory-touched rural liberalism of Manitoba; Wood reflected the radical populist liberalism of Alberta.

Although Manitoba Liberal and Conservative governments relied on rural support from continental-born immigrants, few Europeans, of either British or continental origins, were to be found in the higher echelons of either of these parties. Nor were many to be found in the United Farmers of Manitoba (UFM). "Canadian Ukrainians do not have any influence," declared one Ukrainian paper in 1932 the year of the CCF's birth. "We are poor and need political help. Ukrainian farmers and workers depend for their livelihood on the more powerful. This forces us to support a politically influential party. Affiliation with small radical parties brings us Ukrainians only discredit, and ruin." Such deference, however, did little for continental immigrants in the city. In the 1930s none of Winnipeg's banks, trust companies, or insurance firms would knowingly hire a Jew or anyone with a Ukrainian or Polish name. Nor would Anglo-Saxon premiers pick them for their cabinets.

Labour-socialist politics in Manitoba were as much determined by newly arrived Britons and Europeans as agrarian politics were determined by Ontarians. Winnipeg became the home of Canada's first independent Labour party (ILP), and by 1899, twenty-seven separate unions appeared at the May

Day parade. A year later, the editor of Winnipeg's labour newspaper *The Voice* was elected to the House of Commons.

Within a decade the labour-socialist sectarianism of Europe was reproduced in Winnipeg. Two groups working outside of the dominant ILP influence were the Social Democratic party and the Socialist Party of Canada. By 1920-21 the two permanent parties that emerged were the British-led labourist ILP and the continental-based Communist party. Every imprisoned 1919 strike leader, except one, came from Britain to Winnipeg between 1896 and 1912. So too did most of the ILP leadership. The Communists, on the other hand, drew their inspiration from the Russian Revolution and scientific socialism. A small and insignificant British minority, including One Big Unionist and strike leader, R. B. Russell, stayed out of both camps. In Manitoba, as in Britain, labourism won over Marxism and syndicalism. By 1923, when the Ontario ILP was falling apart, the Manitoba ILP could boast that it held more than two dozen municipal and school board seats, the mayorality of Winnipeg and representation in both federal and provincial parliaments. This modern, turn of the century British labourist tradition had its greatest Canadian urban impact in Winnipeg and Vancouver and, thus, the strength of the CCF-NDP in these cities.

Until at least 1945 much of the politics of the large Ukrainian community in North Winnipeg were still tied to the Russian Revolution and its aftermath. Those against the Revolution supported the Liberals. The CCF, for many virulent anti-communists, was a socialist step in a hated communist direction. Those supporting the Revolution embraced the Communist Party. The CCF, for many communist sympathizers, was a naive, liberal, social democratic, reformist gang. Since World War II, however, ethnic assimilation has contributed to strengthening the CCF-NDP position within both the former Liberal and Communist Ukrainian groups. The CP withered because the older continental-born generation died and the party lost its base. The ideology of British labourism, in contrast, in the form of the ILP-CCF, survived and took root. Other socialist traditions among British and continental immigrants either accommodated themselves to this dominant influence on the left or they generally faded as did the SPC and CP.

Liberal, Conservative and Farmer governments dominated provincial politics. Winnipeg counted for little in the government's considerations and center and north Winnipeg, where the British and European-born had settled, counted for less. It was unpenalized neglect because a rurally biased electoral map ensured agrarian dominance. Between 1920 and 1949, for example, Winnipeg had only ten seats in a fifty-five seat legislature. In the 1922 election labor votes equalled those for twenty-seven non-labor MLAs, but Labour won only six seats. In 1945 the CCF received as many votes as the Liberal-Progressives and almost double the Conservative total, but the CCF won only ten seats to the Liberals' twenty-four and the Conservatives' thirteen.

Successive Manitoba governments reflected an alliance of Anglo-Saxons in the southwestern wheat belt and in south Winnipeg. This alliance went under various labels at different times: Liberal, Conservative, United Farmers of Manitoba, Progressive, Liberal-Progressive, Brackenite, Coalition, and even Non-Partisan. What distinguished it from its main ideological opponent was class and heritage, not ethnicity. In 1919 the warring Strike Committee and Citizens Committee had one feature in common: Anglo-Saxon backgrounds. In working-class Winnipeg the European minorities lined up behind the British-born Strike Committee because the Citizens Committee gave them little choice, identifying them as alien radicals. In rural Manitoba these minorities deferred to the established Canadian-born anti-strike forces.

These divisions were reflected in voting patterns. There seemed little basis for farmer-labour cooperation in Manitoba. They shared little in common. Labour issues, such as the eight-hour day, were ridiculed in the countryside, and every rural newspaper in Manitoba condemned the 1919 strike. Labour's attitude to Manitoba's farmers was also suspicion and until 1927, UFM members were ineligible to join the ILP.

Manitoba's farm leaders went the way of Ontario's. Alberta's UFA, Saskatchewan's UFC (SS) and even Ontario's UFO affiliated with the federal CCF in 1932 (although the latter disaffiliated in 1934). The UFM, like its forerunners a half-century before, was true to the values of rural Ontario and remained aloof. In the late 1940s agrarian politics in Manitoba began to shift somewhat with the rise of the Manitoba Farmers Union (MFU). The MFU's membership came largely from more northerly, less prosperous, continental-born, and second generation Canadian farmers. By the 1950s, ethnic interaction over the course of forty years made possible the viability of such an organization. To the MFU leadership the Manitoba Federation of Agriculture, like its UFM predecessor, represented the wealthier, established, Anglo-Saxon Liberal farmers. After John Diefenbaker and provincial Conservative premier Duff Roblin left their respective leadership posts in 1967, the provincial NDP capitalized on gaining informal MFU support in certain rural areas. It was a breakthrough that helped the NDP win enough rural seats to form a government in 1969. For a combination of reasons, including the fact that he was the son-in-law of the first president of the MFU, Ed Schreyer was the only figure in the Manitoba NDP who could attract such support.

Manitoba was ripe for an NDP victory in 1969 in a way that Ontario was not. In Ontario the impact of Anglo-Saxon voters, most of them long established in Canada, was more powerful than in Manitoba. This is another way of pointing out that Ontario is ideologically older than Manitoba in its conservatism, particularly in the rural areas, but in the cities too. There was a significant new British labourist impact in Ontario (e.g. Toronto mayor Jimmie Simpson in the 1930s) but, because of Ontario's relative oldness, it was not as profound as it was further west.

Manitoba had enough of Ontario in it to have sustained the only provincial Conservative party west of Ontario that has never collapsed. But it also had enough of modern Britain and continental Europe to provide CCFer J. S. Woodsworth and provincial Communist leader Bill Kardash with parliamentary seats between the 1920s and 1950s. Manitoba also had enough of the prairies in it to produce national and provincial Progressive parties in the 1920s. Their Ontario-born liberal leadership however, led both of them back to the Liberal party.

As in Manitoba, provincial politics in Saskatchewan initially meant transplanting Ontarian politics. The provincial Liberal government operated at the pleasure of the Saskatchewan Grain Growers Association, the dominant political and economic organization in the province. Both the Liberals and the SGGA were led by the same figures and most of them had Ontario roots. The Progressive debacle in Ottawa, however, and the inability of the SGGA to break with the Liberals fuelled the formation of a rival agrarian organization: the Farmers Union of Canada. It was founded and first led by L. B. McNamee, a former British railway worker and trade unionist. This difference between the SGGA's Ontarian leadership and the Farmers Union British leadership broadly represented the difference between Ontario liberal and British socialist influences. The division became a central feature of Saskatchewan politics.

The success of the Farmers Union led to the formation of the United Farmers of Canada (Saskatchewan Section) and that, in turn, led directly to the Farmer-Labour party, led by British socialists and Canadians sympathetic to socialism. It then took three elections and ten years, from 1934 to 1944, to catapult this party to power under a CCF label. This became possible because enough continental-origin voters transferred their preferences from the Liberals to the CCF.

Liberalism at first seemed unbeatable in Saskatchewan. Although it came later than in Manitoba, the Ontarian impact was the first in Saskatchewan and it was, as in Manitoba, generally Liberal. While the national, Manitoba, and Alberta Liberal parties were rejected in the early 1920s, the Saskatchewan Liberals carried on. All six of Saskatchewan's daily newspapers supported them. A key factor for the Liberals in Saskatchewan was the province's large numbers of Catholics and eastern and central Europeans. In eastern and central European rural districts the provincial Liberals reaped the rewards of the federal government's immigration program.

In Saskatchewan, however, unlike Manitoba and Alberta, there was a significant new-British *rural* presence. Although Saskatchewan attracted fewer Britons than either Manitoba or Alberta, it had almost as many British-born farm operators as the other two provinces combined. This British influence, coming later than the Ontario influx, took a longer time to assert itself. The farmer-labour connection in the Farmer's Union was unique among prairie farm organizations of any significant size. Much of its support came from farmers in continental-based areas, areas that switched from the Liberals to the CCF between 1934 and 1944. The SGGA, like the neighboring UFM and UFA, had largely ignored the non-Anglo-Saxon farmers and had almost no following in areas settled by Europeans. All three organizations were rooted in the oldest and most established areas.

The United Farmers of Canada (Saskatchewan Section), a product of a merger of the growing Farmers Union and the declining SGGA in the mid-1920s, was socialist in a way that no other Canadian farm organization had ever been. That socialism, like Saskatchewan's early made-in-Ontario liberalism, was imported. The two most important permanent officials of the new UFS (SS) were former members of the British Labour party and the Socialist Party of the United States. The UFC (SS)'s socialist, British, labourist, and agrarian heritages could be summed up by isolating two planks in its 1930 platform: "Abolition of the competitive system and substitution of a cooperative system of manufacturing, transportation, and distribution," and "Free trade with the mother country." The UFC (SS) also endorsed a land nationalization scheme, one patterned on the British Labour Party's rural program. The UFC (SS) also forged a political alliance with the Saskatchewan Independent Labour Party. Formed in the late 1920s, the ILP was largely composed of teachers, some unionists and British socialists. It was patterned on the successful Manitoba ILP. When the UFC (SS) and the ILP came together in 1932 they formed the Farmer-Labour party and elected a British-born Fabian, M.J. Coldwell, as their leader.

A contributing factor to the rise of socialism in Saskatchewan was that the cooperative movement was stronger there than any other province. Moreover, Saskatchewan's cooperators were more socialist than their provincial neighbors. The cooperative movement became an integral part of the CCF's constituency in Saskatchewan and all the movement's growth in the province was aided by a provincial government branch headed by a British immigrant experienced in the British cooperative movement. This "British" link reappears often in Saskatchewan history.

The CCF succeeded because it was British-led and ideologically British-based. The CCF's Britishness, its cultural acceptability, made it difficult to attack as alien. Its cultural legitimacy made it politically acceptable. It could therefore become an alternative to the Liberals for Saskatchewan's continental-origin citizens. Even more than in Manitoba, continental-origin citizens represented a large potential swing factor in voting. This helps explain why the CCF-NDP's success in Saskatchewan came twenty-five years before it did in Manitoba and why it was more profound in terms of votes and seats. The large rural British presence, combined with a large rural continental presence relative to Manitoba and Alberta, made it easier for continental-origin citizens in Saskatchewan to attach themselves to the CCF. This was exhibited in 1943 when another barrier to CCF aspirations was lowered: the Catholic Church declared its support for the cooperative movement, expressed concern respecting social welfare, and told its members they were free to vote for any party that was not communist. The CCF victory in 1944, therefore, was no surprise.

The surge in CCF support in 1944 was most dramatic in the previously Liberal, continental-origin areas. Many CCF rural leaders were of non-Anglo-Saxon origins, a dramatic contrast to the overwhelming Anglo-Saxon character of the Liberal and Conservative leaders. The swing among continentals from the Liberals to the CCF was no less pronounced in urban areas. Between 1934 and 1944, for example, support for the CCF rose 218 percent in the most European part of Regina.

American influences in Saskatchewan were secondary to the Ontario and British influences. In contrast to Alberta, however, the Americans in Saskatchewan tended to help the fortunes of British-led anti-liberal organizations such as the Farmers Union and the CCF. In Saskatchewan, unlike Alberta, the majority of Americans were non-Anglo-Saxons. Moreover, fewer of them in Saskatchewan had English as a mother tongue. Among these European-Americans in Saskatchewan were large numbers — larger than in Alberta — of Scandinavians. European and American Scandinavians in Saskatchewan were much more receptive to socialism than Anglo-Saxon Americans — the majority American group in Alberta. Therefore, European-Americans, such as Scandinavians, encountered a powerful, legitimate and culturally acceptable ideological ally in Saskatchewan in the form of the British-influenced CCF. In Alberta, in contrast to Saskatchewan, there were both fewer British farmers and fewer European-Americans. British labor-socialism, moreover, was not a leading ideological force in rural Alberta as it was in Saskatchewan. In Alberta European-Americans represented a minority among Americans in rural areas. Moreover, they had no corresponding powerful rural British labor-socialist strain to attach themselves to. Thus in Alberta, there never arose a socialist agrarian rival to the UFA as there was to the SGGA in the form of the Farmers Union.

The connection between British birth and labor-socialist politics has been demonstrated in Manitoba. It was also reflected, as late as 1942, in Alberta where four of five CCF provincial executive members were British-born, and in British Columbia where nine of the fourteen CCF MLAs were British-born. In Saskatchewan, in slight contrast, there were four Americans yet only three Britons among the eleven-member British-led CCF caucus at this date. Some of the Americans elected as CCF MLAs in 1944 had voted for Socialist Eugene Debs in the United States. In the United States, as the Socialist Party withered, socialist supporters of European origins on the American great plains returned to the established American parties. In Saskatchewan, in contrast, as the socialist-farmer-labor movement grew, American socialist sympathizers of European ancestry, not overwhelmed by American liberalism as they were in the U.S. had alternatives not restricted to the established parties.

In the late 1950s Saskatchewan produced another political phenomenon, John Diefenbaker, who made it possible for the Conservatives to become a national party for the first time since 1935. In the 1940s, Manitoba preferred the Liberals, Saskatchewan the CCF, and Alberta Social Credit. Diefenbaker, unlike other national leaders, was neither Anglo-Saxon nor was he identified with Central Canadian financiers. This made it possible for European-origin farmers to flock, for the first time, to the Conservative banner. Ethnic interaction and the passing of earlier prejudices no longer crippled the Conservatives in Saskatchewan's European-origin areas. At the same time, Diefenbaker's toryism and commitment to agricultural interest made him equally acceptable to rural, Anglo-Saxon, prairie farmers. They recognized him as an established, Ontario-born Canadian not as a European, naturalized one. Diefenbaker's populist image, another side of this phenomenon, helped him in Alberta where agrarian populism, as in the United States, eased its way into agribusiness. The prairies could therefore embrace the federal Conservative party after the 1950s because it was a qualitatively different party under Diefenbaker than it had been under Arthur Meighen, R. B. Bennett, John Bracken, and George Drew.

Seymour Lipset's *Agrarian Socialism* is something of a misnomer in reference to Saskatchewan. The Saskatchewan CCF-NDP consistently fared better in cities than in the countryside. More precisely, it had been a case of British-style socialism succeeding in an unexpected agricultural setting. M. J. Coldwell, Tommy Douglas, Woodrow Lloyd, and Allan Blakeney were never farmers. Nor was British-born and longtime Toronto MP Andrew Brewin who drafted Saskatchewan's "showpiece" labour legislation in the 1940s. Saskatchewan did produce one British-born non-socialist premier: Charles Dunning. But he represented an older part of Canada's British heritage. Dunning succeeded as easily in Prince Edward Island, which he went on to represent as finance minister in Mackenzie King's cabinet. The only part of the Maritimes that would have sent a Tommy Douglas to Ottawa was Cape Breton because it had been subject to the same type of new British influx as Saskatchewan. This connection between British-birth and socialist inclinations was revealed in the 1970s when Douglas represented Nanaimo (British Columbia) as an MP. In the 1920s, Nanaimo was the most British city in Canada, almost half its residents having been born in the British Isles. The British labourist-socialist connection became, paradoxically, most successful in Canada's most agrarian province.

The politics of rural Alberta was as much influenced by the values of the American great plains as the politics of rural Manitoba by the standards of rural Ontario. In Alberta the various cultural waves, from Ontario, Britain, continental Europe, and the United States, came closest to arriving simultaneously. Early Ontario settlers in rural Alberta, as in Saskatchewan, encountered another ideological strain. It was not, however, a socialist challenge as it had been in Saskatchewan. It was, rather, a more militant, more radical, less tory form of petit-bourgeois liberalism, than was the Canadian norm. It was not so much a challenge as a reinforcement, a radicalization, of the natural liberalism of transplanted Ontarians. There seemed little need, as there had been in Saskatchewan, for two rival agrarian organizations or for an ideologically distinct opposition party. The older parties simply re-oriented themselves. The Liberals and Conservatives became competitors vying for support from the American-influenced UFA. An MP remarked in the House of Commons that Alberta, "from the border northward to Edmonton, might be regarded as a typical American state."

American populism pervaded Alberta politics. Many Canadian- and British-born settlers, to be sure, were to be found in the vanguard of the agrarian movement. But Americans and American ideas played an influential role in Alberta that was unparalleled in Canada. An early example of this in the UFA was that both sides in the debate over whether or not to enter electoral politics argued their cases with references to experiences south of the border, one side referring to the sad end of the People's party and the other side pointing to the Non-Partisan League's success in North Dakota.

When Social Credit came to power in 1935 there was no significant shift of ideological allegiance in rural Alberta. UFAers had been nurtured on inflationary monetary theories in the United States and at UFA conventions throughout the 1920s. The overwhelming majority of UFAers found socialism alien and voted for a technocratic, "pragmatic" remedy in Social Credit. It was a response with American (Free Silver, Greenbackism), not Canadian, antecedents.

The American influence in rural Alberta expressed itself in many ways. In sheer numbers, more than one in five Alberta residents at one point was American-born while the national ratio was less than one in twenty-five. Canadian branches of the American Society of Equity, containing large numbers of transplanted Nebraskans and Dakotas, were the core of the UFA when it was formed in 1909, and about one-half of the directors on the UFA's board were American-born, outnumbering both British- and Canadian-born.

American-style populism prevailed in Alberta because a heavily rurally oriented electoral map, like Manitoba's, meant agrarian dominance. The new British labour-socialist impact in Calgary and Edmonton was insufficient to offset American populist-liberal dominance in the rural areas. Although one-third of Calgary was British-born and it served as the site of the founding conventions of both the OBU and the CCF, as well as being the constituency of Labour MP William Irvine, Calgary was in the largely rural province of Alberta and was also subject to an American impact: it became the headquarters of the Society of Equity, the Non-Partisan League, the UFA, prairie evangelism, and Social Credit, all of which had American roots.

Alberta's preoccupation with monetary theories was a result of the American influence. Low agricultural prices in the United States led American farmers to fight for the free coinage of silver and an inflation in the money supply. When J. W. Leedy, the former populist governor of Kansas, and U.S. credit expert George Bevington and many other Americans emigrated to Alberta, they brought along their monetary theories. Throughout the 1920s and 1930s UFA conventions became debating forums for the monetary theorists. The monetary issue was second to none. In Manitoba and Saskatchewan, in contrast, it was rarely debated. When C. H. Douglas's Social Credit theories appeared they had much in common with notions already present in the UFA. The UFA had contributed to this link by distributing Douglas's books throughout the 1920s. Social Credit, therefore, could be regarded as a supplement rather than as an alternative to UFA thinking.

Social Credit was the political heir of the American-influenced monetary reform wing of the UFA. William Aberhart succeeded only because the monetary reformers in the UFA had tilled the soil so well for him. It was the UFA, he continually reminded his audiences, that had introduced Social Credit thinking into Alberta. By 1935 UFA locals throughout the province were clamoring for some form of Social Credit. During the election campaign Social Credit was really not a partisan issue: few dared attack it. It became, rather, an assumption. Even the Liberals promised Social Credit and the Alberta Federation of Labour indicated enthusiasm as well. Aberhart's Social Credit message was consistent with Alberta's populist history. The American monetary reformers had done their work well. Social Credit's sweeping victory in 1935 was therefore no surprise. Had Social Credit not appeared, another party would have arisen preaching much the same gospel.

American analogies are logical in Alberta. There is something to the argument that Aberhart comes closest among Canada's premiers to looking and sounding like a radical, populist, American governor. Many of his supporters referred to him as Alberta's Abraham Lincoln. But no one could compare prairie CCF leaders such as Douglas, Coldwell, Woodsworth, Queen, or even Irvine to American populists. One could identify them with a Norman Thomas but, to be more accurate, one would have to look to a Briton like Ramsay MacDonald, Labour's first prime minister.

An examination of Alberta's voting patterns reveal that they may be related directly to the patterns of settlement and to the ideological-cultural heritages of the settlers. Initial Ontario settlers in the south, particularly those who came before 1896 and settled along the CPR line, voted for the party of the railroad, the federal Conservatives. The early twentieth-century American influx altered this. The American impact was most pronounced in southern and eastern Alberta, an area representing the key to political power in the province just as the southwest represented that key in Manitoba. The southern, American-settled parts of Alberta which were most favourable to prohibition in 1915 became the most favourable to the UFA from 1921 to 1935 and to Social Credit from 1935 to the early 1970s. Those areas in northern Alberta that tended toward the UFA were those whose population most closely resembled the American-anchored south.

Continental-origin and French Canadian voters in northern Alberta represented a Liberal electoral base for the same reasons as in Saskatchewan and Manitoba: the Liberals were the party of immigrants and Catholics. The UFA, in contrast, was overwhelmingly Anglo-Saxon, composed of Canadian-,

American- and a sprinkling of British-born farmers. I argue UFA and Social Credit majorities were produced by the electoral map which ensured that the party that swept the south was the party that won elections. UFA and Social Credit vote totals were never as high in the continental and French Canadian north as in the Ontario and American south. These patterns reflected how much the UFA and Social Credit had in common with each other and how little either had in common with the CCF.

The new British labour-socialist element in Alberta was largely isolated in the urban centres. Consequently, the CCF floundered. The British-anchored provincial CCF never managed to win more than two seats in Alberta. Significantly, both CCF MLAs in the 1950s were from the north and were second generation Ukrainians, as were large numbers of their constituents. These northeastern areas were among the very few where, in the 1920s, continental-born farmers outnumbered American-born ones. The CCF success here confirmed the shift, in a much less dramatic fashion than in Saskatchewan, from the Liberals to the CCF among non-Anglo-Saxons of continental, particularly eastern European, origin. In Saskatchewan, large numbers of rural continentals had swung their votes to support the party of large numbers of rural Britons, the CCF. In Alberta, however, there were both fewer continentals and fewer rural Britons. Thus, the CCF was a relatively minor force in Alberta's rural areas.

Manifestations of the American influence in Alberta abound. One example of a republican liberal tendency was the Alberta government's refusal to appear in 1938 before the Royal Commission on Dominion-Provincial Relations, addressing its comments instead to "the Sovereign People of Canada." Parliamentary government was described as a form of state dictatorship. Another example was the complaint of a Nebraska-born MLA who called the caucus form of government undemocratic and criticized the speech from the throne for making more of the 1937 coronation festivities than of Social Credit. Could such a sentiment respecting the coronation have been expressed at Queen's Park or in any other English Canadian provincial legislature?

In the 1970s prairie politics continued to be tied to prairie history. The hegemony of Ontario-anchored politics in Manitoba had succumbed temporarily to an alliance of an urbanized multi-ethnic working class and poorer non-Anglo-Saxon farmers led by the NDP. This alliance was unlike Saskatchewan's because it had little rural Anglo-Saxon support. In Saskatchewan, the CCF "formula" of 1944 has repeated itself with some consistency. Urbanization and ethnic assimilation in both provinces have generally aided the CCF-NDP, although this pattern may yet reverse itself as intermarriage and acceptance of ethnic leaders in the older parties increases. In Alberta, Social Credit gave way to the Conservatives; both are right-wing liberal parties which have, for half a century, offered politics that are either American in origin or in benefit. In part, Social Credit led to the Conservatives in the evolutionary, not radical, ways that the UFA led to Social Credit. Although the conditions of the 1980s are different from those of the 1930s, Alberta Social Credit may yet disappear, just as the UFA did. The Conservatives have captured the ideological and popular base of Social Credit support just as Social Credit captured the ideological and popular base of UFA support.

British Columbia: The Company Province

Martin Robin

SOCIAL STRUCTURE

The British Columbia party system has evolved from and reflects a unique social environment. Frequently designated a fragment of western Canadian society, British Columbia is as distinct in social structure and party politics as it is in ideology and culture. British Columbians are westerners, but they share little in common with the prairie provinces. They are Canadians, but only half-heartedly attached to their loose and variegated federation. British Columbians cultivate and feed on a sense of uniqueness and they are aided in their narcissistic idolatry by the great Rocky Mountain divide which separates this remarkable land of mountains, forests, and sea from the flattened land mass to the east.

Prairie politics in Canada have been indelibly stamped with the ideology of agrarianism. Industrialism, with its concomitant changes in class structure, is a late-comer to the Canadian prairies, and the western provinces, outside of British Columbia, have been until the Great Depression predominantly rural expanses populated by independent commodity producers. In all three provinces, Manitoba, Saskatchewan, and Alberta, indigent farmers banded together in social and economic organizations to oppose the railways, the urban middlemen, and the eastern financial interests that controlled the institutions and made the decisions that affected their lives as consumers and producers. They organized politically as well to oppose the major national parties traditionally responsive to the eastern financial and industrial interests. . . .

The British Columbia frontier differs from the Prairie frontier. The latter was settled by independent commodity producers who owned the means of production they worked with, produced agricultural commodities for sale to a largely external market, and refrained from employing wage labor except on a small scale. British Columbia society developed as a corporate frontier and the agrarian sector has always played a smaller part in the economy, society and politics of the province than has its equivalent in the Prairies.

The British Columbia economy is peculiarly dependent, directly and indirectly, on the extraction of natural resources, particularly forest and min-

---

Abridged from Martin Robin, "British Columbia: The Company Province," *Canadian Provincial Politics: The Party Systems of the Ten Provinces*, 2nd edition (Toronto: Prentice-Hall Canada Inc., 1978, pp. 28–40). Reprinted by permission of the publisher.

eral. The primary industries, producing goods for export, form the hub of the economy. Auxiliary industries which supply goods to the other industries of the province, and the consumer-oriented industries, are both dependent on the primary industries. The auxiliary industries exist only to service the basic industries, and without the income and employment provided by these two classes, the local consumer-oriented industries would have no market.

The shape of the British Columbia economy has not altered since the turn of the century. The fortunes of different industries have risen and fallen with economic expansion. The relative importance of agriculture and fishing has declined while others such as petroleum and natural gas, has flourished. But the structure of the economy, tied to the foundations of the primary-resource-extractive industries, has remained unaltered. British Columbia has long been a "company" province and the large enterprise, rather than the small family homestead, is the dominant shape on the social landscape. Scattered throughout the province are company towns, single-enterprise communities subsisting on the activities of resource extraction which provide the goods for an economy serviced and administered by the heavily populated area of metropolitan Vancouver.

Along with the rise of an industrial economy based on resource extraction there has grown a labor movement stronger and more articulate than most in Western Canada. Agrarianism has colored the economy and culture of the prairie provinces. The labor movements in all three provinces, with the possible exception of Manitoba, have been relatively weak and wielded little effective political power. In British Columbia, there grew steadily, from the onset of industrialism, a political labor movement intent on checking the powers of the employing class in a company-dominated province. Carried by radical British and American workers, socialism emerged as a viable ideology around the turn of the century, at a time when the movement was weak and ineffective in most other Canadian provinces.

Large-scale production and the structure of employment in the coal and metal mining industries ensured that industrial unionism, with its radical ideology, was well represented within the provincial labor movement. The British workingmen who first led the unions and worked the coal mines of Vancouver Island were not the highly skilled and exclusive artisans who dominated the trade assemblies of Ontario during 1880s. They were men from the north of England who brought to Canada organizational skill and a marked propensity toward independent politics characteristic of the English and Scottish northern mining communities. Equally militant were the many American workers who provided the early constituency of radical unions like the Western Federation of Miners. The frontier labor conditions prevailing in the metal mining areas of the Pacific Northwest shaped the outlook and temperament of many of the miners who settled in the B.C. interior. The employing class's views of property rights were narrowly and rigidly defined. The proliferation of company towns, the struggles of the hardrock miners, the millmen and smeltermen within the bowels of the earth, the rapid proliferation of militant employers' associations and the frontier tradition of violence as a solution to social conflicts, contributed to the creation of a "heritage of conflict" between capitalists and workers.

The legacy of class opposition, forged over decades of struggle, persists today and colors the ideology of contemporary workers. The coastal labor movement is highly politicized. Labor has unabashedly engaged in partisan politics, not simply the Gompersian variety of rewarding friends and punishing enemies, but ideological politics. The question of labor's political action, together with a host of issues arising from working-class participation, form enduring themes of the British Columbia political culture.

British Columbia labor leaders have acted politically, in both pragmatic and ideological ways, because they perceived that the problems the workers faced were insoluble except by state intervention through partisan alignment. Workers organized politically to overcome problems and lessen insecurities which could not be remedied by industrial organization alone. The problems facing coast workers were legion and their political response was correspondingly strong. The perceived insecurities of coast workers stemmed from a variety of causes and circumstances. The province has been subject to waves of immigration — Oriental, central and eastern European, and American — which have created an unstable labor market. For decades, trade unions sought to restrict the influx of Oriental immigrants, who were used by the employing class to break strikes and lower wage rates in mining and other employments.

The insecurity that many workers felt in the face of foreign labor was reinforced by the employment and wage fluctuations of a specialized resource-based economy responsive to and dependent upon the vagaries of external markets. A much larger percentage of the wage income of British Columbians, as compared to Canada as a whole, derives directly from the export of goods and services and is subject to the rise and fall of world prices. Construction, mining, and lumber workers have been particularly vulnerable to seasonal and cyclical unemployment and to high job turnover. Workers quickly understood that the problems of cyclical unemployment could not be solved by union action alone. During depressed periods large groups of unemployed were radicalized and when conditions improved they brought their militant ideology into the organized labor movement. Workers became equally restive during inflationary periods, when real income fell. Socialist and labor parties enjoyed their greatest support during periods of rising prices rather than during periods of recession.

Large sections of British Columbia industry have been prone to conflict and the frontier conditions which obtained in the American Pacific Northwest and Mountain states were equally in evidence across the international boundary. The maritime, mining, longshoring, and lumber industries were plagued by harsh conditions: a high accident rate, geographical and social isolation, a high turnover rate, and unstable family circumstances. The closed nature of many homogeneous single-industry mining communities with no middle-class to mediate industrial conflict, in which class lines were clearly drawn, contributed to the development of an intense working-class consciousness freed from the restraints of traditional conservative institutions like the church, family, and an "enlightened middle class." A significant portion of the west coast labor force has been located in non-urban areas where little contact is maintained with the urban middle classes. Workers in these outlying communities developed an intense group consciousness, a cohesive isolation experienced by miners, loggers, and fishermen who lived and worked on "the periphery of modern society." Many of the employers in these industries tended to be robust newly-risen capitalists intent on extracting as much surplus profit as circumstances would allow. Men like James Dunsmuir, proprietor of a vast industrial empire on Vancouver Island at the turn of the century, were captains of industry untroubled by a conservative ethic of social obligation.

The industrial class struggle in British Columbia has necessarily involved a struggle for political power. The early union of industrial captains and political parties was fruitful and the state was used to create and consolidate company empires which flourished in the frenetic business environment of the mountain province. Many labor leaders quickly realized that what the state granted the state could take away, and they worked to curb business' hold on government by exerting influence within the non-socialist parties through support of "independent" candidates sympathetic to labor's claims. A significant section of the labor movement has, for many decades, by-passed the non-socialist parties and candidates altogether, and channeled the resources of organized labor into support for socialist parties.

In contrast to the labor movement in the coastal province, and to the farmers' movements in the other western provinces, British Columbia agrarians have never paraded a myth of social regeneration and have rarely strayed from the quiet confines of the major non-socialist parties in their search for economic redress. The major struggle in the fractured coastal community, aside from regional disputes of varying intensity, has been the class struggle between worker and capitalist. The British Columbia agrarians have not viewed themselves as an oppressed class and have refrained from importing or creating on their own a social philosophy, or myth of agrarianism, which would articulate their desire for a new golden age of blissful cultivation. Thomas Jefferson, William Jennings Bryan, and Henry Wise Wood have received a cold reception in the sunny orchards of the Okanagan and pretty greenery of Saanich. . . .

Farming in British Columbia has been a relatively successful operation and the ample monetary returns cooled whatever ardor agrarians may have had for social reform. Favorable climatic conditions and cost structures have allowed common B.C. farm commodities like fruit, milk, and vegetables to compete successfully in foreign markets, and the internal market for these commodities has been stable. Tree farming and ranching attracted capitalistically oriented farmers, some of whom began operations with substantial investments. Their native conservative sentiments were reinforced by the discipline of occupations that placed a premium on patience and long-term planning.

British Columbia agriculture is highly varied and the great regional and occupational diversity has retarded the development of common rural culture and group consciousness. Unlike Saskatchewan, where farmers were common residents of a great wheat culture, the perceived particular interest of regional rural groups, wedded to a common employment, superseded any generalized conception of the farmers as a class, with a separate class interest. "Strictly speaking," wrote Louis Aubrey Wood in his pioneering study of Canadian farm movements, "the physical characteristics of British Columbia and the diversity of its farm occupations have been, and still are, the main hindrances to an evolution of class-consciousness among its rural dwellers." . . .

The high standard of living of British Columbia farmers derived not merely from careful cultivation and favorable market conditions. Since the 1920s, the farmers have been accommodated by the major parties and agrarian lobbyists have gained a host of important legislative enactments. . . .

Today the farm communities receive priority treatment from the Social Credit government. The farmers enjoy, in addition to special land purchasing rights, a variety of fiscal concessions (especially under Property and Income Tax laws), special credit facilities, technical and marketing assistance, certain direct subsidies to agricultural products, and a large number of privileges and priorities not available to other industries. Provincial legislation relating to forest, water, game, trespass, motor vehicles and so on, all provide special privileges to farmers.

POLITICAL CULTURE
British Columbia has long been a fractured community. The major divisions in coast society are class and regional. A religious or racial cleavage, such as exists in Canada as a whole between the English and French, or in the province of Quebec between the two groups, has never taken root in the ethnically polyglot coast community. This is not to suggest that ethnic and religious differences do not exist, or fail to motivate people politically. Party support varies among the different ethnic groups and religious and ethnic questions occasionally bubble to the surface as did the Catholic school question during the historic 1952 election. But class, rather than religious or ethnic identification, seems a greater determinant of political preference, and ethnic and religious issues have not been major political questions dividing the political parties. British Columbia's separation from Canada is not a religious or ethnic difference, and group splits within the province revolve more around regional and economic issues than around ethnic or religious questions. Only one of

the two ethnic elements which have divided federal and provincial politics in Canada — the English — is present in any number in British Columbia. The French-Canadians remain a tiny group little different in number and consciousness from other exotic specimens which honeycomb the province.

It is difficult to say which cleavage, class or regional, is more critical in determining the structure of British Columbia politics. Divided as it is into distinct and separate cultural and geographic entities, enjoying different rates of growth and histories, and only slowly brought into greater union through the expansion of the provincial communication system. British Columbia is a society rife with xenophobia, with antagonisms between regions whose residents often rely only on the honeyed words of the party politician or the insular prose of the local press to gain mutual knowledge. The manipulation of regional antagonisms is a prime requisite of any successful coast politician and the Social Credit party have proved themselves experts in this ancient political game. The earliest significant split was between the Island and Mainland and rivalry between the two regions provided ample fuel for politicians in the decades following Confederation. Subsequent population explosions increased the claims of new regions for representation and legislation. British Columbia today displays a high degree of concentration with more than two-thirds of the population crowded into the Lower Mainland region. Although it has made significant inroads into the Lower Mainland region since 1952, an advance which assured its retention of power, the Social Credit party has enjoyed great and consistent support in the rural interior, in the north, and in the metropolitan area of Victoria. The Vancouver area has never been the happiest hunting ground for the governing party.

British Columbia exhibits a high degree of nodality and the conflict between the center and the periphery is a nagging fact all politicians have to take into account. Metro Vancouver, the central place of the economy, exists in a state of symbiotic tension with the hinterland. The city of Vancouver is the administrative center of the provincial economy, the locale of the regional head offices of the leading business firms and financial institutions. Here too are concentrated the major auxiliary service industries and distribution facilities. The port and major overland transportation routes all radiate from the metro area. Whatever its role as a provider of services for the producers of the interior, Vancouver is often seen by the plain folks in non-urban areas as a threatening parasite, rather than a symbiotic partner....

Regional and class divisions have both contributed to the persistence of a tenuous community in British Columbia whose residents share little else than the vague conviction that coast society is somehow different, and better endowed than the rest of the country. Otherwise there are few effective bonds tying estranged groups into greater communion. An important factor guaranteeing the persistence of the tenuous community is the high immigration rate. In 1961 more than half of the local residents were born outside the province. Existing at the periphery of the western frontier, British Columbia has served as a magnet for persons discontented with their lot, personally, economically, and politically. Being a high income region, the province is an obvious attraction for fortune seekers and for ordinary people seeking a modest improvement of their standard of living.

British Columbia provides a safe home for the acquisitive spirit. From the days of Captain Vancouver when the white men came and traded utensils for otter with the Indians, to the 1850s when the province was flooded with "off-scour-rings of the world" in search of gold, up to recent years when rustic buccaneers like Ben Ginter built strange empires in the northern wilderness, the province has provided a haven for fortune seekers, boodle hunters, and promoters with questionable pasts and devious ways. Poets and plunderers have sung hymns of praise to the beauty and fleshly delights of the pacific land and celebrated the opportunity for every man there to become a king. While many perished in the uncertain hunt for the golden calf, and still more languished in a state of proletarian torpor from which they had tried desperately to escape, not a few became rustic capitalists who wielded their new power with the brash abandon of the parvenue. "Hobos in evening clothes," Joseph Martin described a motley gang of businessmen in Rossland, the early Johannesburg of British Columbia.

It is a common view that buccaneer capitalists, striving in a competitive state of nature, prefer that state which governs least. Capitalists have traditionally warned of the danger of state intervention, but the action they have decried is the sort that redistributes opportunities and incomes in favor of the lower classes. Intervention that guarantees further opportunities and greater incomes for the upper classes has never met with much opposition but, on the contrary, has enjoyed considerable favor in Canada as a whole and in British Columbia in particular. Neither God, nor the exceptional financial or industrial talents of particular individuals who claim to be favored by God, created the great bulk of corporate wealth in British Columbia. It arose instead from the monopolistic advantages conferred by governments on favored persons through mineral grants, forest management licences, utility franchises, land grants, public contracts and so on.

The British Columbia government has been the grantor and regulator of the greatest material prizes this economy has to offer and businessmen have striven, in large measure successfully, to influence governments as a prelude to capturing economic resources. From the earliest days of the province, they went about the task of buying governments with the same audacity displayed in purchasing lands or floating companies. Without a friendly government, Oriental labor could not be imported at lower wage rates, unions could not be easily combatted, or timber licences and railway charters gained in ample number. "The people will always accept a railroad," commented one knowing local observer at the turn of the century, "if it is vigorously thrust down their throats." Corporate investment in politics has always yielded ample returns.

The political intervention of corporate business, with the resultant buying and selling of politicians, early debased the level of political morality in coast politics. In British Columbia, there is a curious tension between the inherited British ideal of constitutional and representative government operating through a parliamentary system, and a furious commerce intent on creating its own rules and rendering the political system subservient to its goals; a conflict perceived early by observers like Frances MacNab, who in his *Handbook for Settlers*, attributed the coast's acquisitive spirit to the presence of American speculators. MacNab noted that while British Columbia was part of the empire of Great Britain, the province was similar to parts of the southern United States or California "... inasmuch as there is a sudden enormous increase of wealth in a country whose constitution is scarcely hatched, whose system of administration is half-fledged, and whose laws have to be framed without the light of previous experience." MacNab felt that the experience of older states like Britain could not "offer much assistance in solving the political and economic problems relating to a highly advanced commerce which invariably shows a determination of establishing and creating a code for itself."

The code dictated by the furious commerce, which shaped political institutions in its own image, was not a pretty one, and British Columbia is possessed of a politics as corrupt as any in the country. Since the inception of self-government, scarcely an administration has survived without a serious financial scandal and British Columbians have become so accustomed to scandal during good times that the fate of governments seems unaffected by the financial misdemeanors of its ministers....

British Columbians are tolerant of corruption in prosperous times. During depression periods, however, the masses wax restive. The apprehensions of the working class were aroused early in the province's political history and socialism as a political philosophy and movement became a strong indigenous force at the very onset of industrialism. To the poets and plunderers, British Columbia is a province of promise, but to many who tasted the familiar fruits of exploitation and unemployment, it became a province of disappointment. Two philosophies and value systems exist in opposition within the coast society and are reflected in the party system. An acquisitive individualism, which advertises a dynamic approach to the development of natural resources through private enterprise is opposed by a strong collectivism, engrained in the strong trade union and socialist movements, who maintain that private enterprise tends to exploit resources, human and material, wastefully and immorally. The opposed philosophies are represented in the major political parties: the Social Credit Party, imbued with the religion of growth, and the New Democratic Party, taken with the values of collectivism. The parties, of course, are not nearly as polarized as their ideologues insist. Social Credit, if only for pragmatic electoral reasons, lives comfortably with the welfare state while the NDP searching for the center vote, has admitted, in word and deed, the viability of the mixed economy.

In the elusive search for votes, Social Credit has so far been the more effective competitor. The Socreds have successfully advertised and sold the ideal of stable government in a society divided by regional and class loyalties, where a multitude of parties have flourished in a changeful climate. Stable government, in British Columbia, implies strong executive leadership described by some as a legacy from Britain, where deferential norms in the social system reinforce strong leadership in the political system reflected in the legitimacy of cabinet government. But, in British Columbia, it is more likely due to the effects of an acquisitive frontier culture. Action not deliberation, results and not methods, are important in a society where the British respect for parliamentary form has been undermined by the frontier's thrust to possess and hold no matter what....

Finally, the stable government ideal in British Columbia, where socialism is a bogey as well as a movement, promises a favorable investment climate. Majority, free-enterprise government ensures the expansion of new investment frontiers, and the perpetuation of a legal environment favorable to corporate business. Both public order and the good life depend upon the pacification of the wants of all classes which, the free enterprise elite maintains, can be achieved through the free flow of capital into the province, providing employment and high wages for the workers as well as profits for the employers. The proper function of a stable government is to protect property, facilitate the investment flow through grants of timber and mining rights, ensure a "reasonable" tax structure and restrict and control unions as much as possible.

In the eyes of the governing business elite, socialist politicians and labor leaders have been ardent proponents of instability. Equally obstructive has been the federal government, which has served as a favorite whipping boy of provincial politicians. By doing battle with the federal authorities, the Socreds and their predecessors prey on and activate regional sentiments and deflect internally divisive sentiments on to an external enemy. The community created is an artificial community, a unity that exists only in opposition to the federal government. The community is tenuous because regional sentiments in British Columbia are not, as in Quebec, passionately held. British Columbia has a distinct society, history, and political tradition, and it has a unique ethos. But British Columbians are not ardent anti-federalists and anti-nationalists. Their separatist sentiments are not reinforced by ethnic, religious, or national differences. Quebeckers see themselves as a nation, a conquered nation, and French Canadians are concerned with the preservation of their language and culture. British Columbia is an ethnic hodgepodge with a majority of the contemporary population born outside of the province. When claims are pressed on the federal authorities, they are couched in material rather than cultural or nationalist terms. British Columbia wants "better terms" and a fair deal, rather than an opportunity to develop its cultural personality. Being more regional than cultural, coast separatist sentiments are only mildly held, but they have been prone to effective manipulation by resourceful premiers who, in arduously tilting at federal windmills, pre-empt feelings of regional patriotism and isolate opposition groups as alien apologists of a hostile external authority.

6
THE NORTH

Laurentian Shield

F.R. Scott

Hidden in wonder and snow, or sudden with summer,
This land stares at the sun in a huge silence
Endlessly repeating something we cannot hear.
Inarticulate, arctic,
Not written on by history, empty as paper,
It leans away from the world with songs in its lakes
Older than love, and lost in the miles.

This waiting is wanting.
It will choose its language
When it has chosen its technic,
A tongue to shape the vowels of its productivity.

A language of flesh and of roses.

Now there are pre-words,
Cabin syllables,
Nouns of settlement
Slowly forming, with steel syntax,
The long sentence of its exploitation.

The first cry was the hunter, hungry for fur,
And the digger for gold, nomad, no-man, a particle;
Then the bold commands of monopoly, big with machines,
Carving its kingdoms out of the public wealth;
And now the drone of the plane, scouting the ice,
Fills all the emptiness with neighbourhood
And links our future over the vanished pole.

But a deeper note is sounding, heard in the mines,
The scattered camps and the mills, a language of life,
And what will be written in the full culture of occupation
Will come, presently, tomorrow,
From millions whose hands can turn this rock into children.

Contemporary Native Life: Images and Realities

MICHAEL ASCH

Most Canadians are conversant with the fact that descendants of the aboriginal peoples of this country face a litany of social, psychological, and economic problems unparalleled in any other segment of Canadian society. Indeed, it is mainly the presence of such problems that comes to mind when the majority of Canadians are asked to differentiate Canadian Indians from the general population. Thus, I venture to say that most Canadians would agree with Frideres's notion that despite differences in geography, culture, and legal distinctions, "Native Canadians do share one common feature: across Canada, they lead marginal lives, characterized by poverty and dependence. Indeed, many people argue that Natives are members of a culture of poverty."

There is no doubt but that this image appropriately reflects one reality faced by aboriginal society. But does it tell the whole story? Are, in fact, native society and culture indistinguishable from the Canadian mainstream, except for certain "curious" cultural practices and the extremeness of certain endemic material, social, and psychological pathologies? Is contemporary native society truly just a culture of poverty?

The answer to all these questions, in my view, is "no." In this article I wish to present an image of native peoples that counters that held by most Canadians. I focus not on the very real problems faced by aboriginal peoples, but rather on those cultural features that remain in place and that, even after the long period of contact, still shape these societies in a manner distinct from the Canadian mainstream.

I wish to make it explicit at the outset that the perspective advanced here is not intended to deny that serious problems exist, or to assert that nothing has changed. Nor is this piece written as a *justification* for the acknowledgement of "special" political rights for aboriginal peoples. Rather, my analysis is intended to balance the partial image that now rests in the public mind with a different perspective and through such a process provide a better factual and conceptual framework against which current proposals can be assessed.

Obviously, the best way to accomplish such an objective would be to record the present way of life for as many native societies as exist. However,

---

Abridged from Michael Asch. "Contemporary Native Life: Images and Realities, *'Home and Native Land: Aboriginal Rights and the Canadian Constitution* (Toronto: Methuen Publications, 1984), pp. 13–25. Copyright © 1984 by Methuen Publications. Reprinted by permission of the author and the publisher.

such a task would be well beyond constraints of space and the ability of this writer. A second alternative would be to survey findings made by others; indeed, a number of detailed studies have been published recently upon which one could draw. A third approach would be to focus on one specific situation to illustrate the general theme. I have chosen the latter course, focusing on one case study, that of the Dene of the Northwest Territories, and utilizing information about other groups only to elaborate particular points. I chose the Dene because it is the society with which I am most familiar and because the Dene have developed a proposal for self-government, called Denendeh, that, I believe, is relevant to the discussion on self-determination.

Dene society is quite complex. It exists in various forms and covers a geographical region that extends over 500,000 square miles. Hence, to deal effectively with the Dene situation requires further constraints. Rather than discuss many aspects of Dene life, I shall concentrate on the economy—primarily because I am convinced it is harder to imagine continuity here than in other areas (such as religion, language, and worldview). Furthermore, since the Dene economy varies from one region to another, I shall concentrate on one region—the Slavey (it is the region I know best, and comparative studies indicate that the Slavey economic pattern holds for other regions as well). In addition, because my intent is to illustrate patterning over time, the discussion includes both the contemporary situation and historical antecedents. As a result, detailed coverage of the contemporary economy will be less than might otherwise be expected.

In sum, what follows is a discussion of the economy of the Dene who live in the Slavey region, as their economy has evolved over time. It is intended to illustrate that dynamics existing outside the framework of the Canadian mainstream are still operative in native society.

THE DENE

The Dene (pronounced de-nay in English) is an aboriginal nation whose homeland encompasses an area of over 460,000 square miles in Western Canada's sub-Arctic and Arctic regions. The term Dene itself means "people" in a number of their own languages, and is used extensively today as a term of self-designation by members of the nation. The nation is made up of a large number of regional groupings, some of whom speak different but often mutually understandable languages. Among these groupings are the Hare, Dogrib, Slavey, Kutchin, and Chipeweyan. Collectively, the Dene are known in the anthropological literature as Northern Athapaskan-speaking Indians.

The Slavey grouping inhabit the area stretching from Lake Athabasca (Alberta) to the south, then northward along the Athabasca, Slave, Liard, Hay, and Mackenzie rivers to a point near the Mackenzie Delta. It is bounded in the west by the Rocky Mountains and in the east by the northern extension of great plains, known as the barren grounds. The region is dominated by lakes, rivers, and other waterways cutting through low-lying plains. The forest cover is mainly jack pine, birch, and spruce. Depending on how far north the location is, the land remains frozen and covered with ice and snow for up to seven months each year. Summers, though as short as three months in places, are surprisingly warm, with sunshine for most of the day. The two dominant seasons are separated by brief transition periods known as "freeze-up" (when the land becomes frozen) and "breakup" (when the ice on the rivers, lakes and land melts). The region is rich in fish resources, as well as small game such as beaver, rabbits, marten, and lynx. Moose and woodland caribou are also found extensively. Breakup and freeze-up are times when migratory birds pass through the region in large numbers, and summer provides an intense growing season for a wide variety of berries such as rosehips, strawberries, raspberries, and "saskatoons," as well as other plants.

The economy of the Slavey prior to first contact with Europeans in 1789 was based entirely upon the consumption of locally produced and finished materials. The primary unit of consumption and production was the local band, which consisted of approximately twenty to thirty individuals related by kinship ties. In the winter, these local groups camped along the shores of the larger lakes, where small game and fish—the major dietary staples—were found in most constant supply. In the summer, a number of bands would assemble together for a time at one of the more productive lakeside spots (probably in areas of fish runs). Such an assembly, known as a regional band, consisted of about 150 people. Among the Slavey, the total population in this period is estimated at 1,250 individuals, comprising eight regional bands.

The division of labour within a local band was organized by age and sex. Adult men were responsible primarily for hunting big game and for fishing; women, children, and elderly men for small game and berries. Women's tasks included, among other jobs, the making of clothing out of such materials as moosehide and rabbit skins. The productive technology used to capture game was mainly snaring or trapping; even moose were taken by this means. Given such a technology, it is apparent that the harvesting of resources was a labour-intensive activity that required both individual skill and much cooperation.

Circulation of goods within local bands was accomplished on the basis of reciprocity or mutual sharing. Generally speaking, the evidence indicates that all members participated equally in the good fortune of the hunters, and all suffered equally when their luck turned bad. Although distribution within the group was generally informal, there was some degree of formal recognition given to the individual hunter through the retention of certain parts of the animal for the use of his family. In this way, individual hunting skill was acknowledged, but not at the expense of the well-being of the group as a whole.

In good times, it appeared that there was little circulation of goods between local bands. However, occasionally the local region harvested by one or more of these groups was found wanting. Usually, this did not indicate a general regional scarcity, but rather a shift in distribution of certain game, and this meant that other bands in the Slavey region were likely experiencing some surplus. At such times, the problem for the Slavey became how to create a balance between those bands with a surplus and those with insufficient resources. The answer, given the nature of the technology and the kinship system, as reported by earlier travellers, was not to move the goods to the bands, but rather to move people from areas of scarcity to those of plenty. As a result, the concept of mutual sharing was extended both in principle and in fact to the regional band as a whole.

In the 200 years since first contact, the Dene of the Slavey region have been introduced to much European-based technology, institutions, and values. A few examples will suffice to illustrate the extent of this penetration. Through the fur trade in the nineteenth century the Dene were offered and adopted a wide variety of trade items. Of these, among the most important included flour, tea, tobacco, and sugar, which soon became dietary staples; repeating rifles and steel traps, introduced in the late 1800s, which helped to make hunting and trapping more efficient; and, by the turn of the twentieth century, cloth and clothing of Western manufacture. Missionaries of both the Roman Catholic and Anglican faiths established their first missions in the region in 1858, and within fifty years had converted, at least nominally, all the Slaveys to one of these faiths.

Government, as well, has had a major impact on Slavey life. Although it established a presence in the latter part of the nineteenth century, it was not until after the Second World War that it became a major force. Since 1945, the government has introduced family-allowance and old-age-pension benefits, which, along with welfare, have provided major sources of non-labour-based cash to the Slavey economy. It introduced compulsory education programs and established permanent schools in many settlements in the region; it constructed housing and nursing stations; it introduced such improvements as water delivery and electricity in the communities; and provided much of wage employment for Slaveys in the region. All of these "benefits" have been accepted by the Slavey people.

When one looks at any Slavey community today, the results of these adoptions are clearly visible. People live in towns serviced by water delivery and electricity rather than in the bush, dwell in permanent houses and not in tents, attend Christian churches, send their children to public school, speak fluent English, accept welfare among other cash benefits from government, and often work for wages—sometimes on a full-time basis. It is apparent from such facts that Slavey society in general and the economy in particular have shifted greatly, in certain respects, from its pre-contact form.

The Slavey way of life is no longer identical to that which existed prior to contact. Along with the above changes have come a litany of social, economic, and psychological problems that have become typical of contemporary native societies. Among these are a higher rate of alcoholism than the majority of the Slavey would desire; an economy that generates less cash income than is necessary to fulfill material needs without greater reliance on welfare payments than is characteristic of the national average; and poor-quality houses that often do not have running water or indoor toilet facilities.

From this evidence, then, one could conclude that Slavey society today is characterized by a lifestyle that is distinguishable from the Canadian mainstream, primarily by its societal pathologies. But would such an assessment be completely accurate? The answer, as the discussion below should attest, is no. There are other significant differences.

One of the most clearly observed manifestations of change in the Slavey economy is found in the wholesale adoption of Western technology and goods. One significant example is Slavey reliance on store-bought foods. Observing a Slavey child eating a candy bar or drinking a soft drink, one might be tempted to conclude that the Slavey diet is comparable to that of the average Canadian child—or at least to one who is poor. Yet, although some Slavey families do rely heavily on store-bought foods, generally, bush foods such as those harvested in the pre-contact period (and prepared in the traditional manner) still provide significant nutrition in their diet. One measure of the continued reliance on these foods is provided by government statistics. According to 1968 government figures (a time after people had moved into town), regional country food production (excluding rabbits and fish, which, although dietary staples, were not included in the statistics) exceeded 180 pounds of meat (edible weight) per capita. This meant that Slaveys were able to sustain their meat needs at a level equal to that of the average Canadian without making one purchase from the store.

But research has shown this figure to be low. According to Rushforth, who surveyed country food production in Fort Franklin, members of that community harvested (excluding small game such as rabbit and beaver which are often eaten) over 150,000 pounds of meat (edible weight) or over 400 pounds per capita. One portion of this production was used to fulfill human subsistence requirements and another, mainly fish, the needs of sled dogs. According to his estimates, one-third of the total food requirements for humans and animals was met through country food production: an amount that saved the community approximately $200,000, which otherwise would have been spent to purchase store foods imported from southern Canada. Another study by Ken Bodden shows parallel results for the Slavey community of Fort Resolution on the south shore of Great Slave Lake. His statistics indicate that income from country food and fur production used to fill domestic needs (as opposed to sale) accounted for 35.6 percent of total income in 1975–76 and about 27.5 percent in 1977–78. The report of the Mackenzie Valley Pipeline Inquiry, which examines the socioeconomic and other impacts of a proposed gas pipeline in the region, confirms the general accuracy of the specific findings made by Rushforth and Bodden. According to this report, in the mid-1970s, Dene, in their homeland as a whole, generated approximately 34 percent of their total income through bush-food and fur-collection activities (for domestic consumption). To paraphrase Usher, upon citing statistics concerning Inuit country food production: If these are "poor" people, they are surely the only ones in Canada who regularly go to bed with their bellies full from meat provided from their own larders.

The ability to sustain such a significant level of country food production is based largely on the use of Western technology such as the rifle, the skidoo, and the steel trap. It is therefore ironic that many people consider the adoption of such items as symbolizing the abandonment of native traditions. Often, given the contemporary situation, it is only through the use of this frequently expensive technology that native people are able to pursue their traditional land-based subsistence activities. As Derek Smith pointed out with respect to the native people in the Mackenzie Delta:

> More people are engaged in casual labour and are living in settlements in improved housing. But this does not mean that the land and its resources have become less significant for native people. There is less fishing, since there are fewer dogs to feed, but there is more hunting (and more effective hunting) for meat for human consumption. Our 1965–1967 data on the use of land resources estimated native peoples' reliance on these resources in terms of cash equivalent values. This showed that land activities were very significant. There are other more powerful ways of estimating the relationship of the land. For example, a quick re-examination of our 1965–1967 data shows that *over 75%* of the protein demand of native people was met by land resources. An equally quick calculation based on more recent figures showed that this *scale of reliance on land resources is essentially the same*. (original emphasis)

This statement applies equally to most Dene communities.

There are obvious changes, as well, in the institutional and value structures on which Slavey economic life is organized. One, of singular importance, has taken place in the primary unit of production and consumption. While the people lived in the bush, the local band was the primary unit of production and consumption, even into the mid-twentieth century. But the move into communities since that time has led to the band's rapid demise, nor has the band been replaced by the nuclear family, as might be expected. Rather, the primary unit today is the household: a grouping that typically consists of at least three generations of family members. Furthermore, for many economic activities, this group expands to incorporate kin who normally live in other households, as, for example, is the case when cousins go to the bush to hunt and trap together. Thus, the household appears to be a compromise between the collective orientation associated with the local band form of production and the individualized, self-sufficient nuclear family organization of mainstream Canadian society.

In other respects, the household provides a locus for the continuity of many of the institutions and values associated with the traditional Slavey economy, particularly because of the direct link between the household and participation in activities associated with bush production. Each household tends to remain self-sufficient in country food production, and to accomplish this end is organized so that bush-related activities remain a central pivot for all family members. Typically, Slavey men, regardless of age, and even full-time jobs, regularly harvest big game, fur-bearing animals, and fish, even when this means returning to the sites of traditional bush camps for long periods without their families. Other members of the household maintain their roles in the traditional division of labour, hunting small game, gathering berries, and processing the raw materials harvested by the men. In exploiting bush resources, members of the household, despite the introduction of rifles and snowmobiles that allow the possibility of individual production, still use cooperative and collective forms of labour; for example, when herding caribou or moose toward a particular kill-site. This possibility is extended on a regular basis to multiple households and even to communities through participation in communal hunts. Finally, despite the introduction of freezers, which would allow game to be kept for long periods, surpluses are not hoarded by individual households. Rather, as is traditional, when a household's luck is good, the "fortune" is generally shared with other households in the community on the basis of mutual reciprocity.

In sum, although significant changes have taken place, resulting in obvious problems, it would be wrong to conclude that they indicate the demise of an economic formation that is distinctly Slavey. Rather, to be accurate one must describe contemporary Slavey economy as a mix of innovation and continuity that allows for the maintenance of traditional Slavey institutions and values, as well as bush products. Similarly, I would argue that an analysis of kinship, ideology, or any other factor would provide convincing evidence that, despite long and sustained contact and the adoption of non-traditional lifestyles and values, Slavey society is still distinct from the way of life of non-native Canadians, regardless of their economic background. In short, despite what appears to be obvious evidence, it would be highly inappropriate to reduce Slavey society to a "culture of poverty."

SOME COMPARISONS
Detailed research into the economies of such diverse native societies as the Inuit of Labrador, the Cree, and the Montagnais-Naskapi of James Bay, Quebec, and the Beaver and Shuswap of British Columbia confirm these observations. On the one hand, important new technologies have been adopted, some groups have been employed in wage labour to a significant degree, and there have been cases of serious economic and social problems. But, on the other hand, despite these factors, many contemporary native societies retain strong elements of autonomous cultural systems. As Feit suggests for the James Bay Cree:

> production and sharing of (country) food, and economic interdependence among Cree themselves, remain central to Cree economic and social life. Although

hunting and wage employment provide roughly equal contributions in dollar value to the total economic outputs at a community level, hunting is the more valued activity, it is the more stable activity and it remains most closely and reticulately linked to the local social and cultural structures that are central to Cree life and that the communities clearly desire to maintain.

In sum, despite certain outward appearances, nations such as the ones cited above cannot be characterized as cultures of poverty, nor can it be said that their members are merely assimilated poor people who happen to be of aboriginal ancestry.

The cultures cited thus far do share one important feature in common: they are all associated with the production of bush resources. It is therefore fair to ask if hunting and trapping are essential to the maintenance of viable cultural traditions among contemporary native peoples. One point is clear: it appears to be more certain that aboriginal peoples will retain significant autonomy in their way of life if such activities are practised than if they are not. For example, although the Shuswap Indians of Alkali Lake in the interior of British Columbia live near urban centres and often have full-time jobs, their cultural traditions remain distinct from those of other residents in the region. A key factor that accounts for this phenomenon is hunting.

Obviously, one reason that hunting persists is economic. Alkali Lake people, like many others (native and non-native alike), find game less expensive and more tasty than store-bought meat. However, the main reason is found in the institutions and values associated with success in hunting itself. For instance, the act of hunting provides the context for the culturally appropriate way to transmit values about the land and the Shuswap's place upon it. The food obtained in this way enables young band members to learn production techniques such as preparing meat and dressing hides. Most important, in my view, is that the distribution of country food functions as a rationale to continue the custom of traditional sharing among band members. This institution, which characterizes many contemporary native societies, is, even among the more urbanized Shuswap, crucial in linking band members into a cohesive unit based on traditions and values that are unlike those found in the Canadian mainstream. In short, it is in the reciprocity associated with successful hunting that, along with institutions related to kinship and ideology, one finds evidence of the continuity of an autonomous way of life. Indeed, I would argue that it is the association of institutions such as reciprocity with hunting, rather than the production of country food itself, that is the crucial factor that accounts for autonomy.

Given that this is so, clearly, hunting itself is essential mainly in that it provides the best opportunity for traditional values to be practised within contemporary settings. However, other settings can be used, and I am certain that production of any sort can be used in the same way. The difficulty is that often they are not. Yet, this is not to say that when hunting is lost so are traditional institutions and values.

There are instances, even in cities, where this is not the case. For example, kinship relations and institutionalized reciprocity are used to link individuals who no longer participate in bush activities to traditional lifeways. Often this takes place through sharing between city- and country-dwellers who belong to the same nation and thus can act to link urban native persons to their traditional setting and values. However, reciprocity can also be used to create cultural networks among urban native peoples themselves. Often these exchanges involve sharing Western technical expertise (such as how to repair a car or truck), staging of native events (such as pow-wows), or teaching traditional skills (such as handicraft-making, dancing, or story-telling). When effective, these act to bind individuals together more tightly than is usual among members of the Canadian mainstream, and this network often allows the transmission of cultural information that traditionally took place in different settings. Finally, when reciprocity is bound up with such mechanisms as Native Friendship Centres, which provide foci for larger social networks to develop, the opportunity for the maintenance of distinct cultural systems increases. Thus, despite the possibility of extreme poverty in an economic sense, urban native peoples often have the institutional resources necessary to retain their identity as people who live within, but do not wish to be assimilated into, the Canadian cultural mainstream. As such, it is impossible to state with certainty that even urban native people with no direct links "back to the land" have lost contact with an autonomous past to become transformed into members of a "culture of poverty."

CONCLUSIONS

It is clear that the image Canadians have of aboriginal peoples does not conform well to reality. Why is this so? In my view, the answer lies in the fact that the average Canadian is not confronted with sufficient information to discourage a stereotyped image.

Stereotypes are created out of partial images and tend to dominate perception primarily when there are few facts with which to make judgements. Thus, as Levi-Strauss has illustrated, indigenous societies, perhaps because of the paleness of the European skin colour in comparison to their own, frequently stereotyped the explorers who first contacted them as ghosts, gods, or ancestors. In one celebrated case, Cortes, the Spanish conqueror of Mexico, was mistaken by the Aztecs for Quetzalcoatl, an Aztec culture-hero of light skin colour, recently transformed into a god. A confused Montezuma, then king of the Aztecs, openly welcomed Cortes into the city, which he immediately conquered. Given the consequences of this stereotype, there can be little doubt but that the Aztecs quickly replaced this image of Cortes with one which took into account facts more relevant to their circumstances than his skin colour.

Early European perceptions about aboriginal peoples are also full of stereotypes. For example, early in the history of contact, there was a serious debate among the colonists as to whether the human-like creatures found in the New World were in fact people, for there is no mention of their existence or ancestry in our charter myth—the Bible. It was a stereotype that was overcome only after the Pope declared, in 1512, that the inhabitants of the New World were in fact human.

However, although Papal authority managed to dispel this stereotype, it was quickly replaced by another and then yet another. But what is even more unique than the persistence of stereotyping is the degree of consistency in the manner in which the images are formed. Thus, the gulf between "our humanity" and "their non-humanity" characteristic of the pre-1512 view was replaced in the seventeenth and eighteenth centuries with a distinction between the original inhabitants of the New World, who were construed to live in a "state of nature," and the creators of the image, who were seen to be living in a "state of society." This image, in turn, has been translated in the nineteenth and twentieth centuries into one that contrasts the "primitive" state of native peoples and their society with the "civilization" of Europeans. In short, whatever the terms of the comparison, Canadians, from first contact to the present, have maintained a single stereotyped view of native peoples: they are distinguished by their inferior and undesirable qualities. . . .

. . . The stereotyped image of contemporary native peoples is inaccurate. The fact that these societies exhibit continuities that clearly link their present institutions, values, and other aspects of their lifestyle to a history that reaches back to an aboriginal past establishes firmly that native societies continue to survive, at least in some significant respects, as autonomous entities. In not taking this reality into consideration the conventional perception has produced an image of contemporary native peoples as inaccurate as Montezuma's image of Cortes.

But what is a realistic image? In the first place it is one that acknowledges that aboriginal societies today are more than just cultures of poverty. There is no need to recount the course of colonization to accept that its introduction of new populations, technologies, values, and institutions into previously autonomous lifeways is unparalleled in recorded history. Given the massive scale of this process over the past four centuries, it would be no wonder if, as the conventional image portrays, aboriginal cultural patterns had been completely destroyed. Yet they withstood the impact. One may well ask whether the lifeways of Europeans and their descendants could have survived as well, if at all, under the same historical conditions. In short, given the evidence of continued autonomy, native peoples ought to be perceived not as failures, with undesirable qualities, but rather as successful survivors worthy of admiration. . . .

SELECTED READINGS IN CANADIAN STUDIES

Asch, Michael. *Home and Native Land: Aboriginal Rights and the Canadian Constitution*. Toronto: Methuen, 1984.
Atwood, Margaret. *The Animals in That Country: Poems by Margaret Atwood*. Toronto: Oxford University Press Canada, 1968.
———. *Second Words*. Toronto: Anansi, 1982.
———. *Survival*. Toronto: Anansi, 1972.
Baillargeon, Samuel. *Littérature canadienne-francais*. Rev. ed. Montreal: Fides, 1965.
Ballstadt, Carl. *The Search for English-Canadian Literature*. Toronto: University of Toronto Press, 1975.
Banting, Keith and Richard Simeon, eds. *And No One Cheered: Federalism, Democracy and the Constitution Act*. Toronto: Methuen, 1983.
Bealieu, Victor-Levy. *Manuel de la petite littérature du Québec*. Montreal: L'Aurore, 1974.
Bell, David and Lorne Tepperman. *The Roots of Disunity*. Toronto: McClelland and Stewart, 1979.
Bercuson, David, ed. *Canada and the Burden of Unity*. Toronto: Macmillan, 1977.
——— and Philip Buckner, eds. *Eastern and Western Perspectives*. Toronto: University of Toronto Press, 1981.
Berger, Carl, ed. *Approaches to Canadian History*. Toronto: University of Toronto Press, 1967.
———. *The Writing of Canadian History*. Toronto: Oxford University Press, 1976.
Bessette, Gerard. *Une littérature en ébullition*. Montreal: Editions du Jour, 1968.
Black, Edwin. *Divided Loyalties: Canadian Concepts of Federalism*. Montreal: McGill-Queen's University Press, 1975.
Bowering, George. *The Mask in Place*. Winnipeg: Turnstone Press, 1982.
———. *A Way With Words*. Ottawa: Oberon Press, 1982.
Brazeau, J. Raymond. *An Outline of Contemporary French-Canadian Literature*. Toronto: Forum House, 1972.
Brown, E. K. *On Canadian Poetry*. Rev. ed. Toronto: Ryerson, 1944.
———. *Responses and Evaluations: Essays on Canada*. Edited with an introduction by David Staines. Toronto: McClelland and Stewart, 1977.
Cameron, Donald. *Conversations with Canadian Novelists*. Toronto: Macmillan, 1973.
Clark, S. D. *The Developing Canadian Community*. Toronto: University of Toronto Press, 1968.

Clement, Wallace. *The Canadian Corporate Elite: An Analysis of Economic Power*, Toronto: McClelland and Stewart, 1975.
———. *Class, Power and Property: Essays on Canadian Society*. Toronto: Methuen, 1983.
Collin, W. E. *The White Savannahs*. Toronto: Macmillan, 1936.
Cook, Ramsay. *Canada and the French-Canadian Question*. Toronto: Macmillan, 1966.
———. *Canada, Quebec and the Uses of Nationalism*. Toronto: McClelland and Stewart, 1986.
———, ed. *French-Canadian Nationalism*. Toronto: Macmillan, 1969.
———. *The Maple Leaf Forever*. Toronto: Macmillan, 1971.
Creighton, Donald. *The Empire of the St. Lawrence*. Toronto: Macmillan, 1956.
———. *The Passionate Observer: Selected Writings*. Toronto: McClelland and Stewart, 1980.
———. *Towards the Discovery of Canada*. Toronto: Macmillan, 1972.
Dacks, Gurston. *A Choice of Futures: Politics in the Canadian North*. Toronto: Methuen, 1981.
Davey, Frank. *From There to Here*. Erin, Ontario: Press Porcépic, 1974.
———. *Surviving the Paraphrase*. Winnipeg: Turnstone Press, 1983.
Dewitt, David and John Kirton. *Canada As A Principal Power*. Toronto: John Wiley and Sons, 1983.
Dictionary of Canadian Biography. Toronto: University of Toronto Press, 1966.
Doran, Charles. *Forgotten Partnership: U.S.-Canada Relations Today*. Baltimore: Johns Hopkins University Press, 1983.
Dorsonville, Max. *Caliban Without Prospero: Essay on Quebec and Black Literature*. Erin, Ontario: Press Porcépic, 1974.
Dudek, Louis and Michael Gnarowski. *The Making of Modern Poetry in Canada*. Toronto: Ryerson, 1967.
Duhamel, Roger. *Manuel de littérature canadienne-francais*. Ottawa: Editions de Renouveau Pédagogique, 1967.
Edwards, Murray. *A Stage in Our Past: English-Language Theatre in Eastern Canada from the 1790s to 1914*. Toronto: University of Toronto Press, 1968.
Eggleston, Wilfred. *The Frontier and Canadian Letters*. Toronto: Ryerson, 1957.
Egoff, Shiela. *The Republic of Childhood*. Rev. ed. Toronto: Oxford University Press, 1975.
Farley, T. E. *Exiles and Pioneers*. Ottawa: Borealis Press, 1976.
Forbes, Ernest. *The Maritime Rights Movement, 1919-1927: A Study in Canadian Regionalism*. Montreal: McGill-Queen's University Press, 1979.
Frideres, James. *Native People in Canada: Contemporary Conflicts*. Scarborough, Ontario: Prentice Hall, 1983.
Friesen, Gerald. *The Canadian Prairies: A History*. Toronto: University of Toronto Press, 1984.

Frye, Northrop. *The Bush Garden*. Toronto: Anansi, 1971.
_____. *Divisions On A Ground*. Toronto: Anansi, 1982.
Garnet, Eldon. *Where? The Other Canadian Poetry*. Erin, Ontario: Press Porcépic, 1974.
Gay, Paul. *Notre littérature. Guide littéraire du Canada Francais*. Montreal: Editions H.M.H., 1969.
Gibbins, Roger. *Regionalism: Territorial Politics in Canada and the United States*. Toronto: Butterworths, 1982.
Gibson, Graeme. *Eleven Canadian Novelists*. Toronto: Anansi, 1973.
Glenday, Daniel, Hubert Guindon, and Allan Turowetz, eds. *Modernization and the Canadian State*. Toronto: Macmillan, 1978.
Grandire, Pierre De et al. *Histoire de la littérature francais du Québec*. Montreal: Beauchemin, 1967-1969.
Grant, George. *Lament for A Nation: The Defeat of Canadian Nationalism*. Toronto: McClelland and Stewart, 1965.
_____. *Technology and Empire*. Toronto: Anansi, 1968.
Hardin, Herschel. *A Nation Unaware*. Vancouver: J. J. Douglas Ltd, 1974.
Harris, R. Cole and John Warkentin. *Canada Before Confederation*. Toronto: Oxford University Press, 1974.
Hartz, Louis. *The Founding of New Societies*. New York: Harcourt, Brace and World, 1964.
Innis, Harold. *Essays in Canadian Economic History*. Toronto: University of Toronto Press, 1956.
_____. *The Fur Trade in Canada*. Toronto: University of Toronto Press, 1930.
Jones, Douglas. *Butterfly on Rock. A Study of Themes and Images in Canadian Literature*. Toronto: University of Toronto Press, 1970
Keith, W. J. *Canadian Literature in English*. New York: Longmans, 1985.
Klinck, Carl F., ed. *Literary History of Canada: Canadian Literature in English*. Rev. ed. Toronto: University of Toronto Press, 1976.
Kroetsch, Robert. "Robert Kroetsch: Essays." *Open Letter* (Spring 1983) Fifth Series: No. 4.
_____. "Robert Kroetsch: Reflections." *Open Letter* (Summer-Fall, 1984) Fifth Series: No. 8-9.
Laurence, Margaret. *Heart of a Stranger*. Toronto: McClelland and Stewart, 1976.
Lee, Dennis. *Savage Fields, An Essay on Literature and Cosmology*. Toronto: Anansi, 1977.
LeMoyne, Jean. *Convergences*. Translated by Philip Stratford. Toronto: Ryerson, 1966.
Lower, A. R. M. *Colony to Nation*. Toronto: McClelland and Stewart, 1977.
MacLennan, Hugh. *Each Man's Son*. Toronto: Macmillan of Canada, 1951.
Mandel, Eli. *Another Time*. Erin, Ontario: Press Porcépic, 1977.
_____, ed. *Contexts of Canadian Criticism*. Chicago: University of Chicago Press, 1971.

———, ed. *Five Modern Canadian Poets*. Toronto: Holt Rinehart and Winston, 1970.
Manzer, Ronald. *Public Policies and Political Development in Canada*. Toronto: University of Toronto Press, 1985.
Marcotte, Gilles. *Une littérature qui se fait*. Rev. ed. Montreal: Editions H.M.H., 1968.
Mathews, R. D. *Canadian Literature: Surrender or Revolution*. Toronto: Steel Rail, 1978.
Matthews, John. *Tradition in Exile*. Toronto: University of Toronto Press, 1962.
Matthews, Ralph. *The Creation of Regional Dependency*. Toronto: University of Toronto Press, 1983.
McCall-Newman, Christina. *Grits: An Intimate Portrait of the Liberal Party*. Toronto: Macmillan, 1982.
McCourt, Edward. *The Canadian West in Fiction*. Rev. ed. Toronto: Ryerson, 1970.
McGregor, Gaile. *The Wacousta Syndrome*. Toronto: University of Toronto Press, 1985.
McKillop, A. B., ed. *Contexts of Canada's Past: Selected Essays of W. L. Morton*. Toronto: Macmillan, 1980.
McMullen, Lorraine, ed. *Twentieth Century Essays on Confederation Literature*. Ottawa: The Techumseh Press, 1976.
McRoberts, Kenneth and Dale Posgate. *Quebec: Social Change and Political Crisis*. Toronto: McClelland and Stewart, 1980.
Minister of Supply and Services Canada. *Royal Commission on the Economic Union and Development Prospects for Canada Report*. Ottawa, 1985.
Morton, W. L. *The Canadian Identity*. Toronto: University of Toronto Press, 1972.
———. *Manitoba: A History*. Toronto: University of Toronto Press, 1967.
New, William. *Among Worlds*. Erin, Ontario: Press Porcépic, 1975.
———. *Articulating West*. Toronto: New Press, 1972.
Northey, Margot. *The Haunted Wilderness*. Toronto: University of Toronto Press, 1976.
Owram, Doug. *Promise of Eden*. Toronto: University of Toronto Press, 1980.
Pacey, Desmond. *Creative Writing in Canada: A Short History of English-Canadian Literature*. Rev. ed. Toronto: Ryerson, 1961.
———. *Essays in Canadian Criticism, 1938-1968*. Toronto: Ryerson, 1969.
———. *Ten Canadian Poets*. Toronto: Ryerson, 1958.
Panitch, Leo, ed. *The Canadian State: Political Economy and Political Power*. Toronto: University of Toronto Press, 1977.
Porter, John. *The Vertical Mosaic*. Toronto: University of Toronto Press, 1965.
Quinn, Herbert F. *The Union Nationale: A Study in Quebec Nationalism*. Toronto: University of Toronto Press, 1963.
Rashley, R. E. *Poetry in Canada, The First Three Steps*. Toronto: Ryerson, 1958.
Rawlyk, G. A., ed. *The Atlantic Provinces and the Problems of Confederation*.

St. John's: Breakwater, 1979.
Richards, John and Larry Pratt. *Prairie Capitalism: Power and Influence in the New West*. Toronto: McClelland and Stewart, 1979.
Richardson, Keith. *Poetry and the Colonized Mind*. Oakville, Ontario: Mosaic Press, 1976.
Rioux, Marcel. *Quebec in Question*. Toronto: James Lorimer and Co., 1971.
Russell, Peter, ed. *Nationalism in Canada*. Toronto: McGraw-Hill, 1966.
Scott, F. R. *The Collected Poems of F.R. Scott*. Toronto: McClelland and Stewart, 1981.
Shek, Ben-Zion. *Social Realism in the French-Canadian Novel*. Montreal: Harvest House, 1977.
Silver, A. I. *The French-Canadian Idea of Confederation, 1864-1900*. Toronto: University of Toronto Press, 1982.
Smiley, Donald. *Canada in Question: Federalism in the Eighties*. 3d ed. Toronto: McGraw-Hill Ryerson, 1980.
Smith, A. J. M. *Masks of Fiction*. Toronto: McClelland and Stewart, 1961.
―――. *Masks of Poetry*. Toronto: McClelland and Stewart, 1962.
―――. *On Poetry and Poets*. Toronto: McClelland and Stewart, 1977.
―――. *Toward a View of Canadian Letters*. Vancouver: University of British Columbia Press, 1973.
Staines, David, ed. *The Canadian Imagination*. Cambridge, Mass.: Harvard University Press, 1977.
Steele, Charles, ed. *Taking Stock, The Calgary Conference on the Canadian Novel*. Toronto: E.C.W. Press, 1982.
Stevenson, Garth. *Unfulfilled Union: Canadian Federalism and National Unity*. Toronto: Gage, 1982.
Stratford, Philip, and Michael Thomas. *Voices from Quebec*. Toronto: Van Nostrand Reinhold, 1977.
Sutherland, Ronald. *New Hero: Essays in Comparative Quebec/Canadian Literature*. Toronto: Macmillan, 1977.
―――. *Second Image*, Toronto: New Press, 1971.
Sylvestre, Guy et al. *Canadian Writers/Ecrivains Canadiens*. Toronto: University of Toronto Press, 1966.
Thomas, Clara. *Our Nature, Our Voices*. Toronto: New Press, 1973.
Tougas, Gerard. *Histoire de la littérature canadienne-francaise*. 2d ed. Paris: Presses Universitaires de France, 1964.
Toye, William, ed. *Oxford Companion to Canadian Literature*. Toronto: Oxford University Press, 1983.
Trudeau, Pierre Elliot. *Federalism and the French-Canadians*. Toronto: Macmillan, 1968.
Urbas, Jeanette. *From Thirty Acres to Modern Times*. Toronto: McGraw-Hill, 1976.
Wallace, W. Stewart. *The Macmillan Dictionary of Canadian Biography*. Toronto: Macmillan, 1963.

Warwick, Jack. *The Long Journey*. Toronto: University of Toronto Press, 1968.
Waterston, Elizabeth. *Survey*. Toronto: Methuen, 1973.
Wilson, Edmund. *O Canada: An American's Notes on Canadian Culture*. New York: Farran Strauss, 1964.
Woodcock, George, ed. *The Canadian Novel in the Twentieth Century*. Toronto: McClelland and Stewart, 1975.
―――――, ed. *A Choice of Critics*. Toronto: Oxford, 1966.
―――――, ed. *Colony and Confederation*. Vancouver: University of British Columbia Press, 1974.
―――――. *Odysseus Ever Returning*. Toronto: McClelland and Stewart, 1970.
―――――. ed. *Poets and Critics*. Toronto: Oxford, 1974.

Index of Names

Aberhart, William, 361, 374
Acheson, T.W., 102
Acton, Lord, 49
Adams, John, 191
Ainslie, Daniel, 303
Allen, Grant, 152
Allen, Richard, 359
Almond, Gabriel, 326
Aquin, Hubert, 198–99, 205
Aristotle, 183
Armstrong, Hugh, 111
Artibise, Alan, 349, 357
Atwood, Margaret, 199–201, 215
Augustine, 191

Bacon, Sir Francis, 184
Baker, Russell, 133–34
Ballantyne, John, 344
Banfield, Edward, 70
Barbour, Doug, 341
Bell, David, 326
Bellamy, David, 310–11
Bennett, Arnold, 154
Bennett, W.A.C., 122
Berger, Carl, 236
Bernard, André, 120
Berton, Pierre, 179
Bevington, George, 373
Binks, Sarah, 229
Birney, Earl, 203
Bissonnette, Lise, 295
Blais, Marie-Claire, 203
Blake, W.H., 151
Blakeney, Allan, 372
Blanchard, Raoul, 258
Blodgett, E.D., 202
Blodgett, Loren, 344
Bodden, Kenneth, 393
Bolt, Carol, 176
Borduas, Paul-Emile, 215
Bouchette, Ernest, 274
Bourassa, Henri, 87
Bourassa, Robert, government of, 295
Bourgault, Pierre, 112
Bourget, Ignace, 272
Bovey, Patricia, 356
Brady, James, 71
Brecht, Bertolt, 180
Bremer, Arthur, 136

Breton, Albert, 297
Breton, André, 196
Breton, Raymond, 297
Brodie, George, 345
Brooke, Rupert, 207
Brossard, Nicole, 201–2
Brown, George, 44, 55, 56, 62, 343
Brunet, Michel, 272
Bryce, James, 68, 70, 72
Bryce, Viscount, 307
Brébeuf, Jean de, 174–75
Buckler, Ernest, 166, 341
Buies, Arthur, 273
Bunbar, G.S., 344
Burnet, Jean, 91, 94–95
Burroughs, William S., 194
Burt, A.L., 55
Butler, William Francis, 344

Cabot, John, 39
Callaghan, Morley, 150, 152, 153–54, 156
Calvin, John, 303
Campbell, Alexander, 305
Campbell, William Alfred, 47
Careless, J.M.S., 228, 259–61, 352, 353
Carleton, Guy, 74
Carman, Bliss, 152, 158, 209
Carr, Emily, 47, 208, 209
Carrier, Roch, 166, 179–80
Cartier, George-Etienne, 271
Cartier, Jacques, 23
Chartier the mad bomber, 178
Child, Phillip, 153
Chou En-lai, 133
Churchill, Winston, 131–32, 139
Clark, Andrew, 239, 240
Clark, Marlene, 309
Clark, S.D., 68, 70, 76, 81
Clarke, Ian, 346
Coaker, William, 312
Cohen, Leonard, 197
Coldwell, M.J., 372, 374
Colville, Alex, 215
Connor, Ralph, 350, 351
Conrad, Joseph, 152
Cook, James, 41
Cook, Ramsay, 228, 229, 359
Cooper, James Fenimore, 160
Corry, J.A., 115

406 / Index of Names

Cortes, Hernando, 397
Coulter, John, 175
Crawford, Isabella, 209
Creighton, D.G., 58
Cremazie, Octave, 47
Crerar, T.E., 366
Cullen, Maurice, 209

Dafoe, J.W., 53, 361
Dalhousie, Lord, 75
Dandurand, Raoul, 132
Davies, Robertson, 203
Davies, Thomas, 208
de la Roche, Mazo, 150, 154
Debs, Eugene, 371
Dickens, Charles, 174
Diefenbaker, John, 361, 368, 371-72
Dion, Léon, 122
Dobell, Peter, 144
Dosman, Edgar, 106
Douglas, C.H., 374
Douglas, T.C., 122, 361, 362, 372, 374
Doyle, Sir Arthur Conan, 163
Drew, George, 332
Drummond, William Henry, 198
Drury, E.C., 332
Duceppe, Jean, 297
Ducharme, Abbé, 269
Dumont, Fernand, 268, 269, 271, 273
Dunae, Patrick, 347
Dunning, Charles, 361, 372
Dunsmuir, James, 380
Duplessis, Maurice, 124, 280
Durham, Lord, 43, 269-70, 273

Eayrs, Hugh, 150
Edwards, Jonathan, 160
Elazar, Daniel, 326
Elgin, Lord, 271
Eliot, T.S., 152
Elkins, David, 326, 328-30
Ellice, Edward, 33
Emerson, Ralph Waldo, 149, 160, 191
Engel, Marian, 215
Erikson, Leif, 302

Fathers of Confederation, 45, 208; see also Macdonald, Sir John A.
Faisal, King of Saudi Arabia, 142
Falconer, Sir Robert, 75
Faribault, Marcel, 290
Farrell, James T., 154
Feit, Harvey, 395
Felton, J.R., 154
Ferguson, George, 289
Fitzpatrick, P.J., 308
Fitzgerald, L.L., 352
Fitzgerald, Lemoine, 210

Fletcher, F.J., 328
Fletcher, Phineas, 164
Fortin, Gérald, 277
Franklin, Benjamin, 160
Franklin, Sir John, 41
Frechette, Louis, 47
Freud, Sigmund, 182
Friedrich, Carl, 125
Friesen, Gerald, 348-49, 351
Frost, George, 345
Frye, Northrop, 174, 178, 228-29, 356

Gandhi, Mahatma, 131-32
Ganzevoort, Herman, 350
Garneau, Saint-Denys, 203, 272
Gérin-Lajoie, Paul, 271
Gibson, Graeme, 166
Gibbins, Roger, 357
Ginter, Ben, 383
Godbout, Adélard, 295
Godbout, Jacques, 199, 200, 201, 203
Grant, George, 213-14
Gray, John, 33
Grove, Frederick Phillip, 204
Group of Seven, 203, 208
Gutteridge, Don, 175

Haidasz, Stanley, 93
Haliburton, Thomas Chandler, 149, 211
Hall, David, 346
Hamelin, Louis-Edmond, 258
Hamilton, Alexander, 119
Hardy, Thomas, 210
Harris, Cole, 240
Harris, Lawren, 47, 237
Harrison, Dick, 235, 236, 237, 340, 345, 351, 353, 354, 358
Harper, J. Russell, 344-45
Hartz, Louis, 325, 326
Hatfield, Richard, 308
Hawthorne, Nathaniel, 149, 160
Heavysege, Charles, 47, 149
Hegel, Georg, 184
Heintzman, Ralph, 346
Hémon, Louis, 151
Henry VII, 39
Hepburn, Mitchell, 331, 332
Herzl, Theodor, 134, 135
Hiebert, Pierre, 48
Higham, John, 88
Hind, Henry Youle, 344
Hind, William C., 345
Hitler, Adolph, 90
Hobbes, Thomas, 132
Hodgins, Jack, 203
Holmes, John, 136
Horowitz, Gad, 325
Howe, Joseph, 43, 121

Howells, William Dean, 154
Hurley, Robert, 352

Iberville, Pierre le Moyne, Sieur d', 40
Inge, Dean, 114
Innis, H.A., 58–60, 237
Irvine, William, 373, 374

James, Helen, 163
James, Henry, 152, 191
Jefferson, Thomas, 160
Jeffersonian Democrats, 69, 74
Johnson, William, 41

Kaganovich, Lazar, 140
Kahn, Herman, 134
Kane, Paul, 208, 237, 344–45
Kardash, Bill, 369
Kelsey, Henry, 342
Kennan, George, 141
Kennedy, John F., 134
Kerr, Illingworth, 352
Keyfitz, Nathan, 278
King, Mackenzie, 53, 89, 129, 137–39
King, Martin Luther, 132
Kissinger, Henry, 132
Knowles, Stanley, 364
Knox, John, 303
Kornberg, Alan, 323
Kreisel, Henry, 229, 261, 352
Krieghoff, Cornelius, 47, 208
Kroetsch, Robert, 203, 236
Krueger, Ralph, 258
Kurelek, William, 359

Lacombe, Patrice, 198
Lamontagne, Maurice, 278, 281–82
Lampman, Archibald, 47, 152, 153, 157, 177
Landon, Fred, 56
Langevin, André, 204
Lapointe, Gatien, 196
Lartigue, Msgr., 268
Latouche, Daniel, 295
Laurence, Margaret, 165, 202, 203, 341
Laurendeau, André, 290
Laurier, Sir Wilfrid, 84, 87, 131, 274
Lawrence, D.H., 210
Leach, Richard H., 316
Leacock, Stephen, 48, 150, 160
Lee, Dennis, 179, 237–38
Leedy, J.W., 373
Lemieux, Jean-Paul, 204, 215
Lesage, Jean, 122
    government of, 123, 290, 291
Lévesque, René, 201, 211, 290–92, 294, 295, 328
    government of, 291–96
Levi-Strauss, Claude, 397

Lewis, Wyndham, 207
Lighthall, W.D., 149
Lipsett, S.M., 326, 372
Livesay, Dorothy, 203
Livingston, W.S., 115, 116
Lloyd, Woodrow, 372
Lloyd George, David, 136
Locke, John, 43
Long, Stephen, 343
Lougheed, Peter, government of, 105
Lower, A.R.M., 55–56, 79, 322, 353–54

Macdonald, Hugh John, 361
MacDonald, J.E.H., 208
Macdonald, Sir John A., 63, 121, 175, 346, 361
MacDonald, Ramsay, 374
MacEwen, Gwendolyn, 215
Machiavelli, Niccolo, 183
Mackenzie, William Lyon, 57, 177, 179
MacKinnon, Frank, 309
MacLennan, Hugh, 154–55, 198, 207
MacNab, Frances, 384
Macoun, John, 347
Maillet, Antonine, 197
Mallory, J.R., 125
Mandel, Ann, 235
Mandel, Eli, 235, 237, 354
Manning, E.C., 122
Mansergh, Nicholas, 138
Mao Tse-tung, 133, 211
Marchand, Jean, 281
Marcuse, Herbert, 182, 187, 188, 206
Marlborough, Duke of, 41
Marlatt, Daphne, 203
Marlyn, John, 166
Martin, Chester, 53
Martin, Joseph, 383
Masters, D.C., 60
Mathews, Robin, 178
Maurois, André, 150
MaCarthy, Joseph, 70
McCarthy, Justin, 149
McClintock, Sir Francis Leopold, 41
McClung, Nellie, 350
McCourt, E.A., 229, 352
McCready, Doug, 314
McGill, James, 33
McNamee, L.B., 369
McRae, Ken, 325
Merrill, Gordon, 262
Merton, Robert, 71
Milne, David, 210
Miron, Gaston, 196
Molotov, V.M., 140
Montcalm, Marquis de, 196
Moodie, D.W., 342
Moodie, Susanna, 237
Moore, Mavor, 175

Morin, Claude, 121, 123
Morris, Edward, 312, 313
Morton, A.S., 55
Morton, W.L., 68-69, 75, 236, 344, 346, 353, 359
Moynihan, Daniel P., 94
Murphy, Emily, 350
Musgrave, Susan, 215

Naegele, Kaspar, 68, 72
Nelligan, Emile, 203
Nevitt, R.B., 345
New, W.H., 235, 237, 354
Newlove, John, 215
Nietsche, Friedrich, 183, 184, 193, 194

Oliver, E.H., 55
Oliver, Peter, 322
Ostenso, Martha, 352
Ouellet, Fernand, 267
Owram, Douglas, 343, 344, 351

Pahlavi, Shah of Iran, 142
Painchaud, Robert, 348
Palliser, John, 343, 344
Pammett, Jon, 323
Papineau, Louis-Joseph, 268, 295
Parent, Etienne, 268
Parry, Sir William Edward, 41
Parsons, Talcott, 182, 193, 326
Pavlov, I.P., 182
Pearson, Lester B., 139, 140-41
Pelletier, Gérard, 281
Pepin, Marcel, 296
Peskett, S. John, 135
Phillips, Paul, 103-4
Phillips, W.J., 47, 352
Pierce, Franklin, 191
Plato, 183
Poe, Edgar Allan, 160
Porter, John, 73, 93, 115-16
Pouliot, Father Léon, 272
Pratt, Christopher, 215
Pratt, E.J., 47, 161, 165, 174-75, 179, 209, 210
Pratt, Larry, 104-5
Proxmire, William, 133
Purdy, Al, 203, 205

Qadaffi, Moamar, 136
Quetzalcoatl, 397

Rae, John, 41
Rasporich, Anthony, 350
Ray, Michael, 259
Raymond, Msgr., 274
Rea, J.E., 346, 354
Reaney, James, 163
Reclus, Elisée, 240

Rees, Ronald, 345, 352, 357
Regan, Gerald, 307, 315, 317
Reid, Dennis, 346-47
Reischauer, Edwin O., 134
Richards, J. Howard, 355
Richardson, John, 33
Richler, Mordecai, 197
Ricou, Laurence, 352
Riddell, R.G., 140
Riel, Louis, 175
Rilke, Rainer Maria, 207
Rindisbacher, Peter, 345
Riopelle, Jean-Paul, 208
Roberts, Charles G.D., 149, 162
Roblin, Duff, 368
Roblin, Rodmond, 361, 366
Rocher, Guy, 290
Roosevelt, Franklin D., 137
Ross, Sinclair, 166, 204, 341, 353
Rousseau, Jean-Jacques, 183-84
Rowe, Fred, 312
Roy, Gabrielle, 197, 198
Roy, Raoul, 284
Russell, R.B., 367
Rutherford, Paul, 349

Sacouman, James, 103
Sage, W.N., 55
St-Laurent, Louis, 155
St. Just, 184
Salutin, Rick, 180
Schreyer, Ed, 365
Scobie, Stephen, 341
Scott, F.R., 203
Seton, Ernest Thompson, 162, 163
Shakespeare, William, 174
Silver, Arthur, 348
Simcoe, John Graves, 74
Simeon, Richard, 123, 129, 326, 328-30
Simpson, Jimmie, 368
Skelton, O.D., 53
Skinner, B.F., 182
Slick, Sam, 48, 149, 213
Smallwood, Joseph, 122, 312, 313
Smith, D.A., 35
Smith, David, 358
Smith, Derek, 394
Socrates, 183
Solzhenitsyn, Alexander, 133
Somers, Harry, 175
Spry, Irene, 344, 347
Squires, Richard, 313
Stanfield, Robert, 290, 308
Stead, Robert, 350, 352
Stevenson, Garth, 109
Stewart, Marianne, 323
Stich, Klaus Peter, 349
Strathcona, Lord: see Smith, D.A.

Suknaski, Andy, 341
Sulzberger, C.L., 144
Sutherland, Ronald, 204
Suzor-Coté, A. de F., 209
Swainson, Donald, 346

Taylor, A.J.P., 135
Taylor, Griffith, 258
Tepperman, Lorne, 326
Thackeray, William Makepeace, 158
Thomas, Dylan, 210
Thomas, Greg, 346
Thomas, L.H., 343, 346, 347
Thomson, Tom, 208, 209
Tocqueville, Alexis de, 77
Tremblay, Arthur, 290
Tremblay, Maurice, 279-80
Troeltsch, Ernst, 185
Trollope, Anthony, 153
Trotier, Louis, 256
Trotsky, Leon, 132
Trotter, R.G., 53
Trudeau, Pierre
  and bilingualism, 197, 297
  on Canada's power, 141-42
  on government's worth, 144
  goverment of, on multiculturalism, 93
  joins Liberal party, 281, 292
  motto of, 204
  and Quebec Referendum, 294-95
Turner, Frederick Jackson, 54-55, 57
Tweedsmuir, Lord, 156

Underhill, F.H., 55, 56, 81, 343
Usher, Peter, 394

Vancouver, George, 383
Vallières, Pierre, 289
Verba, Sidney, 326
Viatte, August, 272, 275
Voltaire, 242, 272

Wade, Mason, 271
Waiser, W.A., 347
Wallas, Graham, 26
Warkentin, John, 231, 322, 342
Washington, George, 132
Watson, J. Wreford, 230, 261, 342, 355-56
Watson, Sheila, 341
Watkins, Mel, 105-6
Weaver, Robert, 163
Weber, Max, 182, 184
Weller, Sam, 149
Wharton, Edith, 152-53
Whitman, Walt, 215
Wiebe, Rudy, 203, 341
Wiles, Peter, 144
Williams, William Carlos, 340
Wilson, James, 70
Wilson, John, 326, 327-28, 329
Wilson, Sir Daniel, 155
Winn, Conrad, 314
Wolfe, James, 196
Wood, Henry Wise, 361, 362, 366, 380
Wood, Louis Aubrey, 381
Wood, S.T., 305, 315
Woodsworth, J.S., 361, 364, 369, 374
Wrong, Dennis, 72

Zangwill, Israel, 83

Index of Subjects

Act of Union, 33, 36
Agriculture, 103, 104
Alberta
    and petroleum, 104, 105
    political culture of, 361, 363, 364, 372–75
    population of, 364
    and reciprocity with U.S., 360
American Revolution, 28, 74, 212, 213
Annexation Manifesto, 101
Atlantic Canada, 102–3, 305–6, 310–11, 314–18; *see also* individual provinces; Deutsch Report on Maritime union
Atlantic seaboard colonies, 21–23; *see also* New England

Bank of Montreal, 33
Banks
    Canadian system of, 36, 102
    international, 107, 108
    in 19th century, 33, 34
Beothuk, 215
Bilingualism, 197, 297
Bill 101, 292–93, 298
Boer War, 275
Branch-plant economy, 97, 99–100, 107
Britannic School, 52
British Columbia
    early economy of, 27, 32
    politics of, 125
    political culture of, 329, 381–86
    social structure of, 377–81
British North America Act, 36, 44, 273

Cabinet government, 44, 45, 69
Calgary, 363
Canada
    alliance with U.S., 46, 137–40
    as colony, 21–25
    compared to U.S., 68–81
    ethnicity of, 249–52; *see also* Multiculturalism
    as middle power, 136–44
    population of, 245–49
    see also individual provinces and regions; Class system, Canadian; Culture, Canadian; Economy, Canadian; Geography, Canadian; Government, Canadian; Investment; Native peoples; Political system, Canadian

Canadian National Railway, 36
Canadian Pacific Railway, 35, 103, 104, 207, 347
Canadian (Pre-Cambrian) Shield, 23–24, 29, 32–33, 35
Canal construction, 33
Capitalism, 34–36, 97–99
Class system, Canadian, 109–12
Clear Grits, 55, 57
Colonies, North American, 22–24
Communist party, 367
Constitution, Canadian, 293–95
Co-operative Commonwealth Federation, 332, 360, 361, 363, 364, 366, 367, 370–71, 375–77; *see also* New Democratic Party
Coughlanism, 70
Coureurs de bois, 40
Cree, 395–96
Culture, during colonization, 26
Culture, Canadian
    American influence on, 43, 151, 209, 211, 212
    British influence on, 43, 156, 209, 211, 212
    French influence on, 43, 209
    patterns in, 243–52
    see also Literature, Canadian; Painting, Canadian

Death
    as literary concern, 173, 174–80, 215
    rate during colonization, 26
Democracy, 56, 68–69
Dene, 390–95
Deutsch Report on Maritime union, 118, 121, 315, 316

Economy, Canadian
    American influence on, 21–22, 28, 34, 41, 98–100
    branch plant, 97, 99–100
    British influence on, 34, 97–99
    government and, 35–36
    history of, 27–28, 35–36, 38–40, 101–3; *see also* Forest industry; Fur trade; Wheat
Edmonton, 363
Environmentalist School, 54

Federalism: *see* Politics, Canadian

Forest industry, 33–34, 38
Forsythe, Richardson & Company, 33
French colonization of Canada, 21, 23, 31, 42
French Revolution, 42
Frontier thesis, 37, 51, 54–55, 351
Fur trade, 28–33, 39, 40

Geography, Canadian
　climate, 242–43
　culture, 243–52
　and imagination, 206–7
　physiography, 240–42, 322
　regional, 229, 34, 253–59
Globe, Toronto, 55, 305
Government, Canadian
　borrowing by, 109
　bureaucracy of, 120, 122
　and capitalist class, 108–9
　growth of, 117–20, 333–34
Grand Trunk Railroad, 34, 35
Great Depression, 352–53
Greenland, 38–39
Halifax, 41, 317
History, Canadian: *see* Britannic school; Economics, Canadian, history of; Political Nationhood, School of; Environmentalist School
Hudson's Bay Company, 29, 35, 41, 103, 208, 342

Immigration
　boom in, 83–88
　postwar, 88–92
　to Toronto, 214
Industrial Revolution, 36
Interest groups, 126
International affairs
　Canada in, 136–44
　theory of, 131–36
　U.S. in, 137–40, 144
Investment, 34–36, 97–99, 106, 107

Japan, 85, 134
Jay Treaty, 29
Jeffersonian Democrats, 69, 74
Jesuit Relations, 208

Ku Klux Klan, 70

Liberal party, 292, 312, 332, 360, 361, 362, 365
Literature, Canadian
　colonialism and, 154–58, 209
　economics of, 150–51, 152–54
　English-Canadian, 151–52, 155, 197–98, 199–201, 202–3, 204–5, 209
　French-Canadian, 151, 197–99, 201–3, 204–5, 210, 275
　hero in, 173–80

humour, 48, 149–50
　and nationalism, 210–11
　and nature, 208–9, 215–16
　outlook of, 47, 48
　Puritanism and, 158–59
　regional, 234–38
　and society, 160–61
　and U.S., 151, 206–7
Loyalists, 43, 44, 74

Manitoba
　and bilingualism, 197, 365
　political culture of, 329, 361, 365–69
Manitoba Act, 346
Manufacturing, 102, 103, 106, 324
McCarthyism, 70
Monarchism, 43–45, 68–69
Montreal, 30, 330
Multiculturalism, 92–95, 214

National Policy, 102–3
Nationalism, 210–11, 228–29, 322
Native peoples, 106, 214–15, 245, 345, 389–98
New Brunswick, 308–9, 310
New Democratic Party, 307, 308, 360, 365; *see also* Co-operative Commonwealth Federation
New England, 22, 31, 209, 274
New France: *see* Quebec, colony of
Newfoundland
　early economy of, 27, 39, 214–15
　political culture in, 311–14
North, Canadian
　challenge of, 46–47
　early economy in, 23–25
　staples economy and, 105–6
North West Passage, 41
Northwest Company, 29, 31, 36
Northwest Territories Act, 346
Nova Scotia
　early economy of, 41, 74
　19th-century politics of, 44
　political culture in, 306–8, 309, 310

Official Languages Act, 298
Organization of Petroleum Exporting Countries, 105
Ontario
　early economy of, 32, 106
　economy of, 324, 330–31
　geography of, 322, 323
　government of, 124
　identity of, 322–23, 326–29
　manufacturing in, 103, 106, 324
　political culture in, 324–26, 331–34
　population of, 323–24
　and western-Canadian culture and

expansion, 346, 361, 363, 365, 366, 372

Painting, Canadian
English-Canadian, 203, 204
French-Canadian, 203–4, 209–10, 215
and nature, 47, 208, 214, 215–16
Parti québécois, 114, 292, 295–97, 298–99
Petroleum industry, 104, 105–6
Political Nationhood, School of, 52–54
Political system, Canadian
decentralization in, 128–29
federalism, 115–17, 120–21, 125–26
party system of, 117, 126–27
pragmatism of, 129–30
provincial ascendence, 115–18
provincial interests and, 121–22, 126–27
Prairies: *see* Alberta; Manitoba; Saskatchewan; Western provinces
Pre-Cambrian Shield: *see* Canadian Shield
Prince Edward Island, 305, 309–10
Progressives, 57
Progressive Conservative party, 333–34, 360, 363

Quebec, colony of
conquest of, 21, 28, 197
economy of, 30–35
government of, 31–32
Quebec, province of
bourgeoisie in, 269, 289
conservatism in, 269–77
culture of, 197–98
developmental stage of, 282–88
government's role in, 123–24, 290–91
history of, 267–69
manufacturing in, 103
political culture of, 329
regionalism and, 233
transition in, 277–82, 289–90
Quebec Act, 28, 84
Quebec Referendum, 293–94
Quiet Revolution, 291, 298–99

Railroads, 43, 102, 207; *see also* Canadian Pacific Railway; Grand Trunk Railroad
Reciprocity Treaty, 101, 343
Regina, 363
Regionalism, Canadian
and economic development, 101–6
in art, 159–60, 229–30, 234–38
Restoration, 43
Rupert's Land, 35, 344, 346
Rupert's Land Act, 29

St. Lawrence River system
colonies of, 21–22
importance of, 23–25, 209
Saskatchewan
literature of, 229
political culture of, 360, 361, 369–72
population of, 364, 369
Separatism, 211–12, 292
Social Credit, 362, 363, 374, 375–76, 385
Staples economy: *see* Economy, Canadian, history of; Forest industry; Fur trade; Petroleum industry; Wheat
Suffrage, 69
Sushwap Indians, 396

Technology, 115, 211, 214
Third World politics, 129–30
Toronto, 214, 232, 331

Unions, 100, 125, 277
United Farmers parties, 362, 363, 365, 366, 367, 368, 369, 370, 374
United States
as colonies, 21–22
economy of, 25, 42, 100, 107
expansion of, 24, 36
in international affairs, 137–40, 144
politics in, 68–69
Urbanization, 246–49, 324

Vancouver, 232, 367
Vinland, 38
Voting patterns, 362–63, 364–65

War of 1812, 212
Waterways
canal construction, 33
and imagination, 209
and railroads, 34
westward expansion, 22–24, 40
Western provinces
economy of, 103, 104–5
expansion of, 343–45, 347–51
literature of, 229, 236, 345–46, 351, 358
painting of, 345, 346–48, 359
political culture in, 357–58, 361–62, 375–76; *see also* individual provinces
prairie settlement, 361–63
romance of, 351–52, 353–54
see also individual provinces
Wheat, 35, 102
Winnipeg, 360, 363, 366–69
World War I, 275
World War II, 276

Grateful acknowledgement is made to authors and publishers for permission to reprint the following.

Margaret Atwood, "At the tourist centre in Boston," *The Animals in That Country: Poems by Margaret Atwood* (Toronto: Oxford University Press Canada, 1968), pp. 18-19. Copyright © 1968 by Oxford University Press Canada. Reprinted by permission of the publisher. Also used by permission of Little, Brown and Company in association with the Atlantic Monthly Press.

Leonard Cohen, "The Only Tourist in Havana Turns His Thoughts Homeward," in Eli Mandel (ed.), *Five Modern Canadian Poets* (Toronto: Holt, Rinehart and Winston of Canada, Ltd., 1970), pp. 83-4. Reprinted by permission of the author and McClelland and Stewart, Ltd.

Anne Hébert, "Manor Life," translated by F.R. Scott, *The Collected Poems of F.R. Scott* (Toronto: McClelland and Stewart Limited, 1981). Reprinted by permission of the author.

Dennis Lee, "Elegy 9," *Civil Elegies and Other Poems* (Toronto: House of Anansi Press, 1972), pp. 55-57. Reprinted by permission.

Michèle Lalonde, "Speak White," translated by D.G. Jones, in Philip Stratford and Michael Thomas (eds.), *Voices from Quebec* (Toronto: Van Nostrand Reinhold Ltd., 1977), pp. 4-6. Reprinted by permission of the translator.

James Reaney. "To the Avon River Above Stratford, Canada." *Selected Shorter Poems* (Victoria: Press Porcépic Ltd., 1975). Copyright © 1949, 1972, 1975 by James Reaney. Reprinted by permission of the author and Press Porcépic Ltd.

F.R. Scott. "Laurentian Shield," *The Collected Poems of F.R. Scott* (Toronto: McClelland and Stewart Limited, 1981), p. 58. Used by permission of The Canadian Publishers, McClelland and Stewart Limited, Toronto.